"... psychiatrists telling us what psychiatrists do, what works, what is difficult, where improvements are needed ... And it is not just about mental illness! It asserts that we all have to take care to nurture our emotional well-being ... a timely contribution that will lead to greater understanding and acceptance."

Dr. Margaret Leggatt
President, World Schizophrenia Fellowship

"The users of mental health care services are only able to play their part if they have an understanding of how professionals see things. *Understanding Troubled Minds* furthers this process of understanding by providing an easy-to-read introduction to psychiatry for a general readership. As such we heartily welcome its publication."

Dr. Jorge Alberto Costa e Silva
Director, Division of Mental Health, World Health Organization

"Drs. Bloch and Singh have written an account of mental illness for the layman that is up to date, comprehensive and authoritative. They have written lucidly and with humanity and I recommend their book to anyone who wishes to learn more about mental illness and about the remarkable advances that have been made in the understanding and treatment of these common conditions."

Emeritus Professor Michael Gelder,
Department of Psychiatry, University of Oxford

"The end of the twentieth century is marked by profound changes in the provision of mental health care ... it is of vital importance to develop a common language which patients, family members as well as other carers and members of health and social programmes will understand. This book contributes to the creation of this common language ... It is therefore most welcome."

Professor Norman Sartorius
President, World Psychiatric Association

understanding troubled minds

# understanding troubled minds

## A Guide to Mental Illness and Its Treatment

**Sidney Bloch and Bruce S. Singh**

NEW YORK UNIVERSITY PRESS
Washington Square, New York

First published in the U.S.A. in 1999 by
NEW YORK UNIVERSITY PRESS,
Washington Square, New York, NY 10003

First published 1997
Reprinted 1997, 1998

Typeset in Malaysia by Syarikat Seng Teik Sdn. Bhd. in 11 point Bembo
Printed in Australia by Australian Print Group

Library of Congress Cataloging-in-Publication Data,
Bloch, Sidney.
Understanding troubled minds: a guide to mental illness and
its treatment/Sidney Bloch and Bruce S. Singh.
p. cm
Originally published: Carlton South, Vic.: Melbourne University Press, 1997.
Includes bibliographical references and index.
ISBN 0-8147-9858-6 (cloth: alk. paper).—ISBN 0-8147-9859-4 (paper: alk. paper).
1. Mental illness—Treatment. I. Singh, Bruce. II. Title. [DNLM: 1. Mental Disorders—
therapy. WM 400 B651u 1997a]
RC480.8569 1999
618.89–dc21
DNLM/DLC                99-24160
                    CIP
for Library of Congress

*We dedicate this book to all those people who have been affected by mental illness, and to their families. We admire your courage. May our words be a source of support and hope.*

# Contents

# *Illustrations*

The black and white engravings, all glimpses from the history of psychiatry, are from the Wellcome Centre Medical Photographic Library in London.

Michael Leunig's cartoons were first published in the Melbourne *Age*.

Pictures of the brain are from the Mental Health Research Institute in Melbourne and the Royal Melbourne Hospital Illustration Department.

The paintings are from the Cunningham Dax Collection of Psychiatric Art, University of Melbourne, except for two children's paintings from the collection of Julie Jones.

# Preface

In mid-1994, we emerged from our publisher's office clutching our edited volume *Foundations of Clinical Psychiatry*. We hoped that it would demystify the subject of psychiatry for the medical students for whom it was principally intended. It dawned upon us then, perhaps for the first time seriously, that another readership, the general community, was in need of a clear, readable account of the nature of mental illness and its treatment. The seeds of this book were sown.

When we shared these budding thoughts with our colleagues, they obviously had mixed feelings. They could see the need, and the potential benefits to the community, but were surprised that we were prepared to devote substantial time and effort to such an unconventional pursuit. After all, academics are meant to operate at the 'cutting edge'—occupied with new ideas, busily involved in research and writing up their findings in professional journals. This is indeed what we have done over more than a quarter of a century.

The luke-warm reaction of our colleagues made us all the more aware of why an authoritative book, written by psychiatrists working in the field, with an intimate knowledge of their subject and substantial experience of caring for patients and their families, is rare. By contrast, so-called 'pop psychology' fills endless bookshop shelves. Most of these books are written by non-professionals, or by professionals who have a relatively narrow involvement with mental illness or are riding a hobby-horse. They tend to be selective in portraying their subject, even idiosyncratic. Often they convey the impression that the particular psychiatric condition or conditions can be easily understood and treated.

As we looked along those shelves, we became more and more concerned about how unbalanced many of the books are. And they promised too much—raising readers' expectations, then leaving them vulnerable to disappointment when they discover that mental illness does not respond to recipe-like remedies. Misconceptions about the helpfulness of various interventions, both conventional and alternative, are widely held—as studies at the Australian National University's Psychiatry Research Unit have shown.

We hope that *Understanding Troubled Minds* avoids the pitfall of offering facile solutions for complex problems. By constantly reminding ourselves to avoid our own biases and prejudices, we have sought to give an honest, objective account. In other words, where the message is an optimistic one, we convey that sense; where progress has been slow and treatment is still in an early stage, we do not disguise this reality. Our 'bottom line', however, is always one of providing hope. And, indeed, psychiatry in the twentieth century, especially since the Second World War, has progressed phenomenally, and continues to do so.

There is much to be optimistic about, and much reason for hope for the future. The brooding mental hospital on the hill has shut its doors forever. New treatments—both medications and 'talking therapies'—have flourished in recent decades. The community is coming to accept that people who suffer from mental illness are not 'freaks' but ordinary human beings with maladies, much as we all have physical ailments.

Why have we called our book *Understanding Troubled Minds*? Firstly, the phrase 'troubled minds' reminds us of the blurred boundary between the ordinary experiences of disappointment, sadness, anxiety and bewilderment on the one hand and 'formal' psychiatric disturbance on the other. This will become obvious, particularly in the earlier chapters and in the final one where we talk about promoting good mental health, even in the face of a vulnerability to recurrent psychiatric illness. In other words, the distinction between the mentally well and the mentally ill is not a matter for easy definition, and, by its nature, cannot be.

We struggled to find the right verb to precede 'troubled minds'. The book is intended to provide the reader with a means to 'stand under' the subject. It is not only a matter of objective detachment and intellectual appreciation, although it is certainly true that knowledge is power. Assuming the additional role of participant observer is vital, and sparks an assortment of questions. How does it feel to be mentally ill? How does one deal with feelings of stigma and shame? How do people sort out whether they need professional help? What is it like to trust professionals who seemingly know nothing about one's inner anguish but call upon honesty with them and, more importantly, with oneself?

The notion of understanding attracted us, as it refers to the sensitive concern that one person has for another. The mentally ill have not always

been regarded as deserving of such concern, and have therefore not bene-fited from the altruistic impulses usually available to people in need. We have tried to take readers down this 'sensitivity' path so that they may resonate with the sentiment expressed in the native American proverb, 'To understand me, you must walk a mile in my moccasins'.

Both intellectual and emotional understanding is all the more crucial given the stark facts about how common mental illness now is. The research figures are astonishing. Even when using a tight definition of mental illness and rigorous diagnostic criteria, one in five people will suffer a diagnosable mental illness during their lifetime. In Australia, for example, with its population of 18 million, there are 20 000 new cases of mental ill-ness each year, and 3 million people will suffer a major depressive disorder in their lifetime. Dr Hiroshi Nakajima, the Director-General of the World Health Organization, highlighted in 1996 the immense need for mental health care world-wide by quoting some startling statistics—400 million cases of anxiety disorder, 340 million cases of mood disorder, 45 million cases of schizophrenia, 100 million cases of alcohol abuse—and the list goes on.

In the light of these figures, it is no surprise that only the exceptional family remains unscathed. Furthermore, even when a family seems immune, the truth of the matter has often been concealed, either to themselves or from others.

All the above sobering issues led us to ponder the question of whether to write a book on mental illness for the general reader. But the catalyst that committed us firmly was a series of personal experiences involving friends and acquaintances who were confronting the reality of mental illness in themselves or in their loved ones—an adolescent son with panic attacks and his bewildered parents; a mother with ghastly suicidal impulses; a family's distress at witnessing their mother's inappropriate, disinhibited behaviour; a daughter's descent into overwhelming preoccupation with her weight. All these people were generally competent and confident in their personal and professional lives, but were reduced to a state of bafflement, fear and uncertainty, which in turn led to paralysis of action. *Understanding Troubled Minds* is designed in large measure to meet the needs of these people whom we have known and thousands of others like them who face the mystifying spectre of mental illness, often without preparation or warning.

### How to use this book

*Understanding Troubled Minds* can be used in two main ways: for an overview of modern psychiatry with its many dimensions, and for a sound understanding of a specific mental illness, of particular groups affected (women, children, the elderly), and of the range of available treatments.

The first section of the book, to the end of Chapter 5, introduces a general approach to psychiatry. Chapter 1 sets psychiatry in a historical context, Chapter 2 distinguishes between 'common-sense' and 'psychiatric sense', using the case of Vincent Van Gogh to illustrate psychiatrists' thinking. Chapters 3 and 4 deal with the causes of psychiatric disorders and their classification, and Chapter 5 gives an insight into how psychiatrists work—how they make sense of what people bring to them.

Chapters 6 to 14 lead the reader through the range of psychiatric disorders encountered in practice. The sequence is from those that can be understood from a common-sense perspective, such as reactions to stress through anxiety and mood changes, to psychiatric illnesses less easily comprehensible. Chapters 15 to 19 are concerned with particular groups: children and adolescents, women, the elderly, self-destructive people and those with mental illness who are caught up in the legal system. Chapters 20 to 22 cover the range of treatments available. The book ends with a guide to promoting and maintaining sound mental health—and a discussion of some helpful further reading.

Our firm belief is that understanding troubled minds is not the exclusive domain of the psychiatrist as medical scientist. Artists of every kind, philosophers and the humanities generally all contribute richly, so complementing scientifically based knowledge. A poem by William Blake on infancy, a description of the life cycle by Shakespeare, Edvard Munch's painting *The Scream*, and a view of the human condition from Jean-Paul Sartre can tell us as much about mental illness as the experimental findings of the scientist. We have woven the human dimension into the text through the stories of real people, the sombre testimony of sufferers and their families, and the insight of writers, poets and philosophers. We hope that we have done justice to both the science and the art.

# Acknowledgements

*Understanding Troubled Minds* is based on our edited textbook *Foundations of Clinical Psychiatry*, published in 1994 by Melbourne University Press. We are indebted to our colleagues who contributed to that book and then gave us permission to use their material as a scaffold for the present book. We take great pleasure in expressing our thanks to the following people (whose names are coupled with the chapters they wrote):

Norman James (A historical context), George Szmukler (Making sense of a life), Eng-Seong Tan (Aetiology), George Mendelson (What does psychiatry encompass?), Nicholas Keks (The psychiatric interview and evaluation of the mental state), Jennifer Dakis (Making sense of the psychiatric patient), Graham Burrows and Ruth Vine (Anxiety disorders), Issy Schweitzer (Mood disorders), David Clarke and Graeme Smith (Disorders of somatic function), George Patton (Eating disorders), Richard Ball (Sexual disorders), David Kissane (Sleeping disorders), Jayashri Kulkarni and Sandra Hacker (Personality disorders), Paul Brown and Paul Holman (Substance abuse), Patrick McGorry (Psychotic disorders), David Ames and John Lloyd (Organic disorders), Robert Adler, Bruce Tong, Helen Driscoll and Pia Brous (Child and adolescent psychiatry), Lorraine Dennerstein (Psychiatry of women), Daniel O'Connor and Edmond Chiu (Psychiatry of old age), Paul Mullen (Forensic psychiatry), John Tiller (Suicide and parasuicide), Fiona Judd (Principles of treatment), Helen Herrman (Providing mental health care), David Copolov (The biological therapies) and Edwin Harari (The psychotherapies).

We thank David Ames, Paul Brown, Edmond Chiu, George Halasz, Edwin Harari, Julie Jones and Patrick McGorry for reading parts of the manuscript and providing helpful feedback. We are enormously grateful to Anne Deveson, Michael Gelder, Margaret Leggatt, Norman Sartorius and Jorge Costa e Silva for their comments on the manuscript.

We were exceptionally well served by the staff of the St Vincent's Hospital Medical Library and the Mental Health Library of Victoria, and wish to record our thanks to Sandra Hodgson, Lorraine Bell, Kathleen Ignatius and Jillian Hiscock for their kindness and co-operation whenever we needed their assistance.

We hope *Understanding Troubled Minds* attracts the reader's eye through its pictorial dimension. We thank Michael Leunig most sincerely for permitting us to use ten of his cartoons. Michael is a brilliant observer of human behaviour as is so well demonstrated in the selection in our book. Eric Cunningham Dax has been a model for both of us for many years— a distinguished psychiatrist who has made an enormous contribution to psychiatry in Australia and Britain. Among his many accomplishments is his collection of psychiatric art which can be seen to great advantage in the gallery named after him in Melbourne. We thank Eric very much for giving us permission to reproduce the plates in this book. Julie Jones is a doyenne of child psychiatry in Australia and has always emphasised the relevance of non-verbal expression in her patients. We thank her for granting us permission to use pictures from her collection of child psychiatric art. The staff at the Wellcome Centre Medical Photographic Library in London were extremely hospitable to us when we sought photographs to illustrate the history of psychiatry. Dennis Velakoulis of the Mental Health Research Institute, Melbourne, has a great talent in developing computer graphics of the brain, and we thank him most cordially for helping us in this area.

We thank Belinda Singe, Julie Larke and Rita Costas for their secretarial support, always provided with marvellous enthusiasm and good humour.

John Iremonger was the Director of Melbourne University Press when we first came up with the idea for this book. His eager response and wise guidance spurred us on. At Melbourne University Press, Teresa Pitt, Allison Jones and Diana O'Neil have similarly given us every support and encouragement, and Jean Dunn did a marvellous editing job on our previous volume and an equally good one this time. She has the knack of turning convoluted prose into straightforward English, a distinct advantage when writing on the complicated subject of psychiatry. We are immensely indebted to Jean for the hard work she put into the project and for her warm colleagueship.

Many self-help organisations collaborated with us in looking for the best way of communicating with our intended readership. We are particularly grateful for the efforts of the Post- and Ante-Natal Depression Association and the Anorexia and Bulimia Nervosa Foundation of Victoria.

**Acknowledgements**

This book, with its many illustrations, could not have been produced at such a reasonable price without the generous sponsorship of the following pharmaceutical companies: Eli Lilly, Organon, Pfizer, and Roche. We are especially grateful to Janssen Cilag for their generous donation to cover the cost of marketing. All five companies have made enormous contributions to the welfare of psychiatric patients through the discovery of modern drugs. We not only thank them for their financial sponsorship but also for recognising the importance of promoting community awareness of mental illness and its treatment.

Finally, we thank our long-suffering families for putting up with our decidedly unsociable schedules. Our spouses and children have all appreciated the importance of what we were doing, and gave us every support and encouragement.

# 1  *The Story of Psychiatry*

The word 'psychiatry' comes from the Greek *psych*, meaning '*soul*' (derived in turn from Psyche, the goddess of the soul) and *iatros* meaning 'treatment'. It has been used for a hundred years, but attempts to grapple with the plight of mentally ill people go back to earliest recorded times. Over the millennia, disturbance of the mind has undergone several name changes. Madness became lunacy (derived from the false belief that people are more obviously ill at the time of the full moon) and then insanity (the strict meaning of which is simply 'unwell'). Today we use the clumsy euphemism 'mental (from the Latin *mens*, meaning mind) health problems'.

Madness has always held a peculiar fascination, involving as it does a fear of unfettered passions and of the loss of rational thinking, which is the essence of being human. Indeed, the whole basis of being, the continuity of the self and one's relationships with others, are fractured.

Possibly the earliest account of a disturbed mind is recorded on a fragment of the Ayur Veda, a sacred Hindu text of the fourteenth century BC. A man is described as 'gluttonous, filthy, walks naked, has lost his memory and moves about in an uneasy manner'. In the Bible, the first Book of Samuel notes King David as pretending madness and so gaining safety when he lived among the enemy:

> And he changed his behaviour before them, and feigned himself mad in their hands, and scrabbled on the doors of the gate, and let his spittle fall down upon his beard. Then said Achish unto his servants, Lo, ye see the man is mad: wherefore then have ye brought him to me? Have I need of mad men, that ye have brought this fellow to play the mad man in my presence? shall this fellow come into my house?

We read in the Book of Daniel that:

> . . . there fell a voice from heaven, saying, O king Nebuchadnezzar, to thee it is spoken; The kingdom is departed from thee. And they shall drive thee from

men, and thy dwelling shall be with the beasts of the field: they shall make thee to eat grass as oxen … The same hour was the thing fulfilled upon Nebuchadnezzar: and he was driven from men, and did eat grass as oxen, and his body was wet with the dew of heaven, till his hairs were grown like eagles' feathers, and his nails like birds' claws.

These words, written over two thousand years ago, are a vivid depiction of insanity, with the loss of social graces and personal care and the stigma that we witness among people who are severely mentally ill. Interestingly, even then it was appreciated that the disturbed were not responsible for what they did and did not warrant punishment.

The ancient Greeks also wrote about insanity, Aristotle locating it as a disturbance in the head. The current biologically based explanations for many forms of mental illness have their beginnings in the Greek idea of an imbalance of bodily fluids. This theory was vigorously promoted in the second century AD by the Roman physician, Galen, who thought that an excess of black bile caused depression (the word 'melancholia' translates as 'black bile'), a view which held sway for almost fifteen hundred years.

During the Middle Ages, the monasteries preserved this view, seeing madness as an illness and the afflicted people as free from blame. At the same time, other more malevolent influences believed that possession by devils was the central cause of the troubled mind. Sufferers were taken to recognised healers of the time, usually priests (a practice still prevalent in many non-Western societies).

People who failed to respond to ordinary treatment then, as now, sought out the best specialists. Take, for example, the life of Saint Guthlac, an eighth-century English monk. A young man named Hwaetred became afflicted with an 'evil spirit'. So terrible was his madness that he tore his own limbs and attacked others with his teeth. When men tried to restrain him, he snatched up a double-bladed axe and killed three of them. After four years of this madness, he was taken by his parents to several sacred shrines, but alas with no relief. His despairing parents, wishing more for his death than for his life, eventually heard of a hermit, Guthlac, who lived in the fens north of Cambridge. They took their son, with limbs bound, to the hermit. After three days of prayer and fasting he suffered no further trouble.

Sin was rarely seen as the cause of mental illness. Rather, it was a visitation from without, afflicting even the righteous. A particularly tragic period was the seventeenth century, when religiously inspired persecution of the mentally ill was justified by the clerical hierarchy, who designated

Death by public drowning was once the not uncommon fate of mentally ill women branded as witches (from *The Remarkable Confession and Last Dying Words of Thomas Colley*, London, undated).

them as witches. The church was torn by schism and heresy; its authority and influence were being challenged more determinedly than for a thousand years. This coincided with a time when medicine's claim to exclusive practice of the healing arts, such as they were, distanced itself from its former links with the priesthood. A new consistency and fairness in treatment of deranged people resulted both from the church's emphasis on charity and medicine's emphasis on physiological causes of insanity.

Life just before the Industrial Revolution has been portrayed as one of bucolic tranquillity. The countryside was supposedly scattered with picturesque villages. Their inhabitants, simple country folk, tilled the fields, held colourful markets and festivals and otherwise passed the time in songful merriment and cared for their own and others' temporal needs in cooperative spirit. The reality was far from this. Thomas Hobbes, the social philosopher, described the lives of these folk as 'solitary, poor, nasty, brutish and short'. The insane have been depicted as 'miserable individuals, wandering around in village and in forest, taken from shrine to shrine, sometimes tied up when they became too violent'. They met with the full range of responses to the mad through the ages—from support through benign tolerance to cruel persecution.

The late eighteenth century was important in the history of psychiatry. The insanity of King George III of England focused most strikingly society's ambivalence to the mentally ill (vividly captured in the play and film *The Madness of King George*). In France, Philippe Pinel, among others, released the chains that had fettered the 'lunatic' for centuries, ushering in an unprecedented phase of benevolent institutional care. Few convincing accounts of the form and nature of mental illness appeared before this time.

An early literary description is found in Balzac's novel, *Louis Lambert*, published in 1832. Lambert is a tragic figure, a highly intelligent young man who becomes infatuated with a childhood sweetheart. Upon his marriage he rapidly plunges into the world of lunacy. He is taken to Paris to be seen by the great physician Esquirol (who had been a pupil of Pinel); 'The doctors in Paris considered him incurable and unanimously advised leaving him in the most absolute solitude'. The narrator of the story, a boyhood friend of Louis, notes: 'If he has really fallen victim to that disease, still unobserved in all its developments, which we call madness, I'm inclined to attribute it to his passion'. He then asks to see Louis:

> He was standing with his elbows resting on the projection formed by the wainscotting, so that his body seemed to bend beneath the weight of his bowed head. His hair, which was as long as a woman's, fell over his shoulders and surrounded his face, which was perfectly white. He constantly rubbed one of his legs against the other with an automatic movement which nothing could check, and the continual rubbing of the two bones made a ghastly noise. Beside him was a mattress of moss, laid on a board. He was a remnant of vitality rescued from the grave, a sort of conquest of life over death, or of death over life. Suddenly Louis ceased to rub his legs together and said slowly, 'The Angels are white'.

The storyteller quotes Louis' writing, which shows excessive religious preoccupation and unmistakable disordered thought, then observes:

> I felt an extraordinary mental disturbance there, which went beyond the most fantastic effects caused by tea, coffee, opium, by sleep or by fever, mysterious agents whose terrible performances so often set our brains on fire. Perhaps I could have fashioned into a complete book those scattered fragments of thoughts, comprehensible only to certain minds accustomed to lean over the brink of an abyss, in the hope of seeing its base.

Nikolai Gogol, the great Russian novelist, published *The Diary of a Madman* two years after Balzac's *Lambert*. Gogol himself was tragically to succumb to what was probably severe depression leading to pervasive guilt, withdrawal, despair and death by self-starvation. *The Diary* paints a frenzied picture of insanity. Gogol has no romantic illusions, portraying a terrifying illness with poignant accuracy. The final plea of the madman's monologue, uttered in an asylum, is heart-rending:

> Mummy, save your poor son! Shed a tear on his poor battered head and look how they are tormenting him! Press your orphan boy to your breast! There is no place for him on earth! He is persecuted! Mummy, have pity on your sick little child!

Another great French writer to record sensitive observations of insanity was Guy de Maupassant. In his short story, 'The Horla' (the name probably a contraction of the French word for outsider), he gives a vivid and telling self-description:

> I ask myself whether I am mad. As I was walking just now, in the sun by the riverside, doubts as to my own sanity arose in me, not vague doubts, such I have had hitherto, but precise and absolute doubts. I have seen mad people and I have known some who were quite intelligent, lucid, even clear sighted in every concern of life, except at one point. They could speak clearly, readily, profoundly, on everything, till their thoughts were caught in the breakers of their delusions and went to pieces. There, they were dispersed and swamped in that furious sea of fogs and squalls which is called madness . . . Was it not possible that one of the imperceptible keys of the cerebral fingerboard had been paralysed in me? . . . By degrees however, an inexplicable feeling of discomfort seized me. It seemed to me as if some unknown force were numbing and stopping me, preventing me from going further and calling me back.

Eventually the narrator comes to believe that he can fend off his persecutor only by setting fire to his house. But his torment persists to the final lines: 'No—no—there is no doubt about it—he is not dead. Then—then—I suppose I must kill *myself*!'

The sheer numbers of mentally ill people, living, or rather barely surviving, in the burgeoning slums of eighteenth-century cities demanded action. An institutional solution was developed—the asylum (from the Greek *asulon* meaning 'refuge'). With the best of intentions, the asylums built on the outskirts of cities or in rural settings were planned to be havens in which the insane could receive humane care. In the serenity of the countryside, and through carrying out simple tasks, they could be distracted from their emotional torment and find purpose and dignity 'far from the madding crowd'. Daniel Defoe was not convinced: 'This is the height of barbarity and injustice in a Christian country, it is a clandestine Inquisition, nay worse'.

In the asylum, whatever its merits, the psychiatric profession evolved as a branch of medicine. The accumulation of thousands of patients provided the first opportunity to study and classify mental illness. For example, Emil Kraepelin, working in an asylum near Munich, identified dementia praecox at the turn of the century (differentiating it from manic-depressive insanity). This was further refined into the disorder we know today as schizophrenia (a word coined by the Swiss psychiatrist Eugen Bleuler in 1911).

Psychiatrists, faced with an overwhelming number of suffering patients, sought 'great and desperate cures' to temper the ravages of severe mental illnesses, particularly schizophrenia. Henry Rollin, an English psychiatrist and historian of his profession, captures the intense zeal:

> The physical treatment of the frankly psychotic during these centuries makes spine-chilling reading. Evacuation by vomitoria, purgatives, induced sneezing and sweating, blisters and bleeding were considered essential. Flagellations and flogging were recommended in certain conditions. There was indeed no insult to the human body, no trauma, no indignity which was not at one time or other piously prescribed for the unfortunate victim. Not one of these so-called remedies has the remotest rational basis, but if the practitioners who prescribed these remedies were sincere, then they were not mountebanks.

For example, malaria therapy as a treatment for general paralysis of the insane—syphilis affecting the brain—was introduced in 1917 by the Viennese psychiatrist Julius von Wagner-Jauregg, earning him a Nobel Prize.

The first widely available and effective physical treatments were developed in the asylum. By contrast, innovative psychological therapies evolved in the community; Freud's great contribution of psychoanalysis was the forerunner of multiple 'schools' of psychotherapy. The discovery in 1938 of electro-convulsive therapy (ECT), for example, by Cerletti and Bini, two Italian psychiatrists, led to a dramatically effective treatment for people with severe depressive illness. ECT was rapidly adopted everywhere as a major treatment. But its history vividly illustrates a typical pattern of treatment practice in psychiatry, with initial unbridled enthusiasm later tempered by a lengthy process of scientific evaluation. Exactly the same can be said for psychosurgery, which is surgical procedures on the brain to modify psychiatric symptoms. This was pioneered in 1936 by a Portuguese neurologist, Egas Moniz (another Nobel Prize winner) and a surgeon, Almeida Lima. It has been a source of controversy ever since. Regrettably the negative image of both treatments still hampers their usefulness for carefully selected people.

The Second World War led to a flurry of new treatments for war-related psychological disorders, driven by the need for a prompt return of soldiers to the battle-field. Active psychotherapy, combined with short-term use of sedatives, brought startling results and a new sense of optimism, which laid the foundation for widespread treatment outside the asylum.

A momentous breakthrough was the discovery in 1949 by John Cade, a distinguished Australian psychiatrist, of lithium as a treatment for mania. Major tranquillisers, the so-called neuroleptics, followed three years later in Paris, when Jean Delay and Paul Deniker noted that a drug which effectively calmed patients undergoing surgery also dramatically reduced the torment of psychotic people, but without excessive sedation. Shortly after this, Nathan Kline, working in a vast mental hospital in rural New York State, discovered that a drug being tested for its effect in tuberculous patients had an anti-depressant action—the forerunner of the anti-depressants. These drugs transformed the practice of psychiatry dramatically. The prestigious journal *Science* has depicted these developments as one of the twenty great scientific discoveries of the century.

Unwittingly, the spread of asylums from the mid-nineteenth century triggered the movement of psychiatry away from the mainstream of the medical profession. This unfortunate divorce was reflected in the term 'alienist' for those who practised in the remote asylums. Asylums also turned out to be seriously detrimental to many 'inmates'. They fostered profound dependence, and put the mentally ill out of sight and consequently out of mind. Public loss of interest and political neglect became the norm. Indeed, the asylum may paradoxically have decreased tolerance of the mentally ill, who could be so readily 'put away'.

The effects of separation from broad society should not be underestimated. The shadows of this era still linger in patients and their families fearful of seeking early treatment because of the reputation of the brooding building on the hill. The stigma of being put away still runs deep. The combination of disenfranchised patients, psychiatric hospitals run for the benefit of staff, inadequate inspection by outside agencies and government bodies, and a chronic lack of resources led at times to quite disgraceful conditions.

The conditions are evocatively described in the Australian classic, *The Fortunes of Richard Mahony*, by Henry Handel Richardson. We read of the author's father's decline and death probably from general paralysis of the insane, a form of neurosyphilis, at that time afflicting a sizeable proportion of patients in the asylums. Richard Mahony, previously a gynaecologist, had succumbed to mental illness, been certified and detained in an asylum. Toward the end of the novel his wife makes the journey from the country-side to see him:

> She hung her head, holding tight, as if for support, to the clasp of her sealskin bag, while the warder told the tale of Richard's misdeeds. 97B was, he declared, not only disobedient and disorderly, he was extremely abusive, dirty in his habits (here the catch of the handbag snapped and broke), would neither sleep himself at night nor let other people sleep, also he refused to wash himself, or to eat his food . . . But she had to keep a grip on her mind to hinder it from following the picture up: Richard, forced by this burly brute to grope on the floor for his spilt food, to scrape it together and either eat it or have it thrust down his throat . . . she had heard from Richard about the means used to quell and break the spirits of refractory lunatics . . . There was not only feeding by force, the straitjacket, the padded cell. There were drugs and injections, given to keep a patient quiet and ensure his warders their freedom: doses of castor oil so powerful that the unhappy wretch into whom they were poured was rendered bedridden, griped, thoroughly ill.

Eventually, by persuading Richard's influential friends in Melbourne, Mrs Mahony was allowed to take him home where he was nursed until his death a few weeks later.

Psychiatry was created and practised in asylums, apart and alienated from the rest of medicine and society. In the grim asylum, people were shut away and forgotten. The community could put insanity and melancholy out of sight and mind. Attendants and asylum doctors were also separate from the rest of the community, often living with their families in the hospital grounds. Asylums originally built for hundreds of people were holding thousands by the Second World War. Few people were discharged; many stayed for decades. Family contacts were often lost, especially as the asylum was frequently a long way from the patient's home.

The bleakness of these originally tranquil settings made the community terrified of approaching them. Patients were objects of fear, to be avoided. Families could hide the fact that a relative was resident in an asylum. People sought help from such places only in extreme situations. Families are still discovering unknown sisters or aunts, now elderly, living in country hospitals and often clearly marked by the years of institutionalisation.

## Mental illness today

Massive changes in the care of mentally ill people have taken place in the second half of the twentieth century. Closure of the asylums began in earnest in the 1960s, and required transfer of hundreds of thousands of 'long stay' patients to alternative accommodation. This process of 'de-institutionalisation'—the movement of patients from hospital into the community—continues unabated. Specialist care beyond the hospital is now more readily available. But the process is challenging all contemporary societies, as it is far more costly than politicians and social planners have realised.

Mentally ill people and their families still face the ordeal of stigma, as psychiatric illness is still seen as shameful. Fears associated with the history of the asylum are a continuing influence. People may hesitate to bring symptoms to medical attention or to accept referral to psychiatrists. Stigma also affects recovery since the prejudice of others and the person's own expectations affect opportunities for work and social contact.

The massive movement of psychiatrists and their patients out of the institutions has brought an unexpected expansion of psychiatry's territory. The community has gradually come to recognise and accept this vastly increased role. Up to one in five adults experiences an identifiable psychiatric illness in any year. While most go to their family doctors for help, some move on to specialist mental health care.

The range of illnesses seen by psychiatrists differs markedly from that seen in general practice and general hospitals. Psychiatrists are concerned with people with relatively uncommon psychotic and severe mood disorders, with marked personality disorders, and with co-morbidity (the concurrence of two or more psychiatric conditions, or of a physical and a psychiatric condition). For instance, dependence on alcohol occurs in association with other psychiatric illnesses in a high proportion of people using mental health services.

Despite this progress, the news media run many graphic, often sensationalist, stories revealing the deficiencies of mental health care. This no doubt reflects society's increased expectations, and justifiably so, for competent, comprehensive psychiatric services. The challenges to create a just, equitable system are immense, at times overwhelming. Yet, while an ideal mental health care system remains elusive, underlying principles do exist. They are perhaps best spelt out in the 1992 United Nations Charter on the Rights of Mentally Ill People, which has prodded societies around the world to focus attention on reform.

Finally, in this brief historical account, community expectations have also led to increased funding for research into mental illness, which has gathered considerable momentum. Similarly, lobby groups comprising patients, their relatives and friends have emerged as a vital force in securing funds for research, better conditions for patients and the public acceptance necessary to eliminate the stigma of mental illness.

The story of psychiatry provides a rich tapestry for understanding the place of mental illness in society. The middle of the twentieth century was a watershed, hopefully marking the end of centuries of ignorance and neglect and the beginning of an era of enlightenment in which modern science, art and ethics in psychiatry will provide a solid foundation for the next century.

# 2    *Making Sense of a Life*

Vincent Van Gogh, in 1879 at the age of twenty-six, began to preach in the Borinage, a deprived mining area in Belgium. He evangelised unrelentingly. He gave away his possessions (including his bed), lived in a dirty hovel, wore shirts he made of sackcloth, and subjected himself to severe privation. Ten years later, he sliced off the lower lobe of his left ear and gave it to a prostitute saying, 'Keep this object carefully'.

How can we make sense of such behaviour? Psychiatrists attempt to do so by using a number of perspectives, two of which—understanding and explanation—are discussed below. No single perspective can provide a complete account of a person's psychological state.

Daily, each of us tries to make sense of our own behaviour and that of others. We may not give much thought to how we do this, but we are adept at the task, sufficiently so as to feel we understand what 'makes them tick'. The means we use are based on our ability to empathise with the experiences of another—we are able to put ourselves in their shoes and to imagine how they feel. The information we use includes their statements about what they believe, feel, perceive, intend and so on and, of course, the reasons they themselves give for behaving as they do. We also take into account their past experiences, their habitual ways of feeling and thinking and their current circumstances. We then arrive at a 'commonsense' understanding of why a person has reacted in that way to that event.

This way of reasoning approaches the other person's world from the inside. It seeks meaning in behaviour and builds up an understanding based on links between experiences and events. The same event, for example the failing of an exam, may have a different meaning for different people depending on their previous experiences, aspirations, competing interests, and so on. This approach handles information that is intangible: the contents of the mental world of others, their thoughts, motives, feelings, and so on. Our understanding seems inbuilt; connections may seem obvious, compelling or satisfying as a narrative or life story. As the German philosopher and psychiatrist Karl Jaspers put it:

> We can understand directly how one psychic event emerges from another. This mode of understanding is only possible with psychic events. In this way we can be said to understand the anger of someone attacked, the jealousy of the man made cuckold, the acts and decisions that spring from motive.

A well-developed capacity for understanding is a good start, and an indispensable tool for the psychiatrist, but it has major limitations. It is not so useful when the experiences and behaviours of people are not on the face of it meaningful and when the sequence of mental events is incomprehensible.

In such situations, the experiences and behaviours of the person are studied not from the inside but from the outside, using explanation rather than understanding. For example, psychiatrists recognise delusions by features they have in common regardless of what they are about. Thus, a person may be concerned about being persecuted, but what makes this concern a delusion rests on specific qualities of that belief—that the person holds it with absolute conviction, without adequate reasons, and stubbornly resists clear evidence that the belief is ill-founded.

This is essentially the scientific study of disease. Abnormal mental states are regarded as diseases and their cause sought in the disruption of a person's biological, psychological or social functioning. This explanatory perspective has resulted in important discoveries about mental illness, including the classification of psychiatric disorders (see Chapter 4), the role of genetic factors, the effect of disturbed brain function on mental states, and helpful treatments. The perspective aids diagnosis of a specific disorder, which in turn provides information about cause, outcome and effective treatment, and applies to the group of people who share it.

Let us see how both understanding and explanation are used by psychiatrists to illuminate the intriguing story of Vincent Van Gogh. We turn to him not only because he was a great artist but also because his life has been so richly documented both in letters in which he expressed much about his inner life, and through descriptions by others. Excellent biographies have also been published. The major dates and events in Van Gogh's life are shown on pages 13–15.

## Vincent Van Gogh's life history

| Age | Date | Event |
| --- | --- | --- |
| | 1853 | March 30: Born in Zundert, Holland; birth occurred one year to the day after his mother gave birth to a still-born son, also named Vincent |
| 11 | 1864 | Oct: Sent to boarding school in Zevenbergen |
| 13 | 1866 | Sept: Sent to new school in Tillburg |
| 16 | 1869 | Mar: Left school, returned home |
| | | July: To The Hague as apprentice to Goupil's, art dealers; arranged by uncle Vincent, a partner |
| 20 | 1873 | Jan: Goupil's Brussels branch |
| | | June: Transferred to London branch |
| 21 | 1874 | June: Proposal of marriage to Eugenie Loyer, but rejected; lost interest in art dealing; solitary, absorbed in religion |
| 23 | 1876 | Mar: Dismissed from Goupil's due to poor performance |
| | | Apr: Obtained post as assistant teacher at small school in Ramsgate |
| | | July: Became a 'sort of curate' under a Methodist minister at Isleworth |
| | | Dec: Returned to Holland with intention of becoming a pastor |
| 24 | 1877 | Jan: Job in bookshop in Dordecht |
| | | May: Moved to Amsterdam commencing studies for entrance to the faculty of Theology at the university |
| 25 | 1878 | July: Abandoned studies in Amsterdam |
| | | Aug: Went to mission school in Laeken |
| | | Nov: After a three-month trial period, failed to be accepted |
| 26 | 1879 | Jan: Appointed as unqualified mission preacher in the poor mining district of Borinage |
| | | July: Dismissed because of excessive self-sacrifice and embarrassing behaviour |
| | | Aug: 'Vagabond' existence, unable to settle; regarded himself as an 'outcast and a tramp'; a period of silent misery |
| 27 | 1880 | Aug: Decided to become an artist |
| | | Oct: Lived in Brussels, mainly drawing |
| 28 | 1881 | Apr: Returned to parental home, now in Etten |
| | | Aug: Rejected by widowed cousin, Kee Voss; family scandal |
| | | Dec: Left home again, moving to The Hague where he briefly stayed with a cousin, Mauve, a painter; tense relationship |
| 29 | 1882 | Apr: Met an alcoholic and pregnant prostitute ('Sien'), lived with her and devoted himself to her and her children |
| | | July: Began painting seriously in oils |

## Vincent Van Gogh's life history (continued)

| Age | Date | Event |
|-----|------|-------|
| 30 | 1883 | Sept: Broke with Sien; moved to the bleak environment of Drenthe, followed by lonely wandering<br>Dec: Returned to father's home, now in Neunen, where he remained for the next two years; relationships remained strained; distressing affair with Margot Begemann resulting in her suicide attempt; painted productively |
| 32 | 1885 | Mar 26: Father died<br>Nov: Moved to Antwerp |
| 33 | 1886 | Jan: Registered as a student at Academy of Art in Antwerp<br>Mar: Left Academy; moved to Paris to stay with brother Theo (an art dealer) for almost two years; during this period met a group of modern painters including Gauguin, Toulouse-Lautrec and Emile Bernard; brief period in Cormon's studio; began drinking heavily; many quarrels |
| 35 | 1888 | Feb 20: Moved to Arles in Provence<br>May: Took rooms in the Yellow House<br>Sept 20: Gauguin visited Arles following invitation from Van Gogh; relationship soon became tense<br>Dec 23: Van Gogh sliced off part of his ear and deposited it with a prostitute; hospitalised the next day under Dr Rey |
| 36 | 1889 | Jan 7: Discharged from hospital<br>mid-Jan: Theo engaged to be married to Johanna von Bonger<br>Jan 21: His friend the postman, Roulin, transferred to Marseilles<br><br>Further episodes of mental illness requiring re-admission: 4–19 Feb; 26 Feb to mid-April<br><br>Mar 19: Put in a cell in hospital after a petition alleging that he was a dangerous madman was presented by neighbours and upheld by the Mayor; rejected by local villagers<br>Apr: Theo married; Johanna pregnant soon after<br>May 8: Of his own free will, decided to enter the Saint-Paul-de-Mausole asylum at nearby St Remy-de-Provence where he stayed for a year<br><br>Further episodes of mental illness: 8 July to mid-August; 24 Dec to 1 Jan 1890; 23–30 Jan; mid-Feb to mid-April |
| 37 | 1890 | Feb 1: Theo's son born, named Vincent<br>May 17: Left St Remy; spent four days in Paris with Theo |

| Age | Date | Event |
|-----|------|-------|
| | | May 21: Moved to Auvers-sur-Oise, just north of Paris, under the supervision of Dr Gachet who had a special interest in art |
| | | July 27: Vincent shot himself; died two days later |
| | | Theo died six months later of chronic nephritis; psychotic at the end |

## The case history of Vincent Van Gogh

Vincent was born to an austere Dutch middle-class family. His father, a pastor of limited talent, was consigned to obscure parishes. His mother married late and was a strong woman, unusually gifted in writing and painting. From his family tree on page 16, note particularly those named Vincent and Theo, and their relationships. Two professions dominate, the clergy and art-dealing. The family tree also reveals a striking family history of mental illness. Van Gogh's uncle, also named Vincent, was subject to nervous complaints, frequently fleeing to the southern sun to recuperate. A family history of epilepsy existed on his mother's side.

Accounts of Van Gogh's childhood are inconsistent. Some suggest an unremarkable child, others portray him as solitary, 'not like other children', and estranged from his family. He was passionate about nature. He briefly attended the village school and then from eleven to sixteen was educated in boarding school. His progress seems to have been unexceptional, but he read prolifically and became a gifted linguist.

His career was most unsettled, despite excellent connections. Through the mentorship of his wealthy uncle, Vincent, he became an apprentice art-dealer. The prospect of inheriting his uncle's mantle was obvious. However, after rejection in love by Eugenie Loyer, his landlady's daughter, he lost interest and became fanatically religious. In England he began to preach. Attempts to study theology in Amsterdam and later to become an evangelist through a mission school were unsuccessful, largely through his provocative behaviour. Still determined to become an evangelist, Van Gogh was appointed as a lay preacher in the district of Borinage. But his extreme self-martyrdom proved unacceptable to his superiors and he was soon dismissed. He then withdrew into solitude and spent almost a year in silent misery. In 1880 he emerged from this period of what he termed 'moulting' and announced his intention to become an artist. Studies in conventional

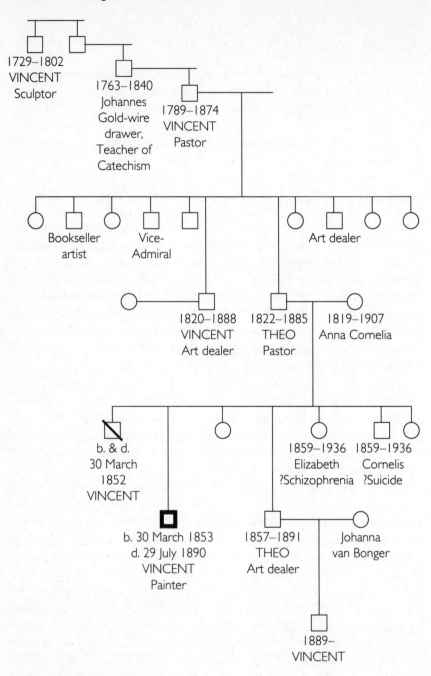

Vincent Van Gogh's family tree

academies were broken off because of further disputes. He returned to his parents' home for two years, then lived with his brother Theo (who had become a successful art-dealer in his uncle's footsteps), then moved to Arles and finally to Auvers-sur-Oise. He painted prolifically. Over eight hundred paintings are catalogued, most dating from the last seven years of his life.

Van Gogh's only enduring, close relationship was with Theo, although this was not free from recriminations on Van Gogh's part. They corresponded frequently from 1871, and by 1886 he was entirely financially dependent on his brother.

His four important relationships with women all ended in 'shame and humiliation'. In London a passionate proposal of marriage was rejected by Eugenie Loyer, who was already engaged to another. In 1881 he fell in love with Kee Voss, a widowed cousin. He was again rejected, and his stubborn persistence resulted in intense family bitterness. The following year he formed a liaison with an unmarried, pregnant prostitute, 'Sien', already the mother of a 5-year-old girl. Sien was described as unbalanced in mind and 'forsaken like a worthless rag'. Despite his care, she lapsed into her old ways and he felt no choice but to leave her. In 1884 he was subject to the infatuation of Margot Begemann, a lonely, melancholic spinster ten years his senior. She wished to marry him but her family bitterly disapproved. In the ensuing crisis she attempted suicide and was sent to a sanatorium.

Other intense relationships did not survive. The most crucial was with the artist Gauguin in Arles, where after two months the atmosphere between them was described as 'electric'. It culminated in Gauguin's plans to depart and a severe episode of mental disturbance in Van Gogh.

Van Gogh complained that he was ugly and coarse ('as thick skinned as a wild boar'). He felt unloved and inferior. From the age of twenty he was regarded as an 'eccentric', and at times as a 'madman'. He was impetuous, moody and obstinate. Yearnings for human ties were constantly frustrated.

Numerous references testify to his self-abasement and melancholy. There were prolonged periods of misery as in 1879. Van Gogh's accounts of his mood are vivid: 'a terrible discouragement gnawing at one's very moral energy ... fate seems to put a barrier to the instincts of affection, and a flood of disgust rises to choke one'; 'I am a prisoner in I do not know what horrible, horrible cage'; 'stultified to the point of being absolutely incapable of doing anything'. Depression occurred with some regularity in the winter.

There were also times when he felt remarkably energetic: 'The emotions are sometimes so strong that one works without knowing one works'; 'Ideas for my work come to me in swarms'; 'I go on like a steam-engine at painting'; 'I am working like one actually possessed, more than ever I am in a dumb fury of work'; 'I only count on the exaltation that comes to me at certain moments, and then I let myself run into extravagances'. But after such bursts of energy, depression inevitably followed. He neglected his appearance and physical welfare. He exposed himself to the elements in Herculean hikes, sometimes slept in the cold, and often ate little. In Paris, and later in Arles, he drank heavily: 'If the storm gets too loud, I take a glass too much to stun myself'.

## His medical and psychiatric history

Van Gogh suffered from gonorrhoea in June 1882 and required a three-week admission to hospital. He may also have suffered from syphilis in 1886. He often complained of physical symptoms including stomach trouble, anorexia, dizziness and headaches.

At least seven episodes of severe mental disorder occurred between 24 December 1889 and mid-April 1890. The first followed his stormy relationship with Gauguin in Arles, when he sliced off part of his left ear and deposited it with a prostitute. Most attacks began abruptly, with confusion accompanied by frightening auditory and visual hallucinations, then gradually improved over a few weeks, but at least one lasted two months. His talk was rambling and there were delusions of an 'absurd religious' nature and of being poisoned. He could be aggressive without provocation, at least on one occasion because of delusions of persecution by the Arles police. He made frenzied attempts to eat his paints and to drink turpentine or lamp kerosene. During recovery his mind was 'foggy' and there was a partial loss of memory. He later described these experiences as 'frightening beyond measure' and the thought of recurrences filled him with a 'fear and horror of madness'. There were associated 'moods of indescribable anguish', and he was sometimes observed to sit immobile for many hours. At times he rejected all food. He voluntarily spent a year in a mental asylum although for most of this time he remained very productive. Finally, at the age of thirty-seven, he committed suicide.

## What can psychiatrists make of all this?

Psychiatrists will see in this story unusual behaviour which might prove understandable, but also aspects better accounted for by an unravelling of its causes. Van Gogh's disturbances of mood, the 'ear episode', the psychotic episodes and his suicide are the subjects of particular interest.

Let us start with his mood and personality. From the age of twenty he suffered from swings of mood, predominantly depression but also excitement. In an effort to understand these, various psychological interpretations have been proposed. One of his biographers gives a fascinating account which would closely reflect the psychiatrist's construction. Van Gogh's childhood was dominated by the stillbirth of his older brother, Vincent, one year to the day before his own birth. His mother continued to grieve the loss and was not able to commit her love to the new child. He had to replace, and compete with, an idealised lost child whose tomb he saw every day in the adjacent graveyard. This led to a profound sense of inferiority, of being unloved and unlovable, and a sensitivity to rejection.

This was later played out in, and reinforced by, his unsuccessful love affairs. These failed relationships were followed by depression associated with self-punishment and estrangement from an apparently rejecting world. At the same time he continued to crave intimacy, but with intolerable demands on others since he sought the kind of unreserved love that had been denied him earlier. He began to seek solace in a loving God, which required further suffering through self-denial and service to others. In this manner he could also give to those rejected like him the love he had never himself received. Van Gogh's estrangement from his family is further supported by the absence in his letters of affectionate remarks about his mother and by the omission of his family name when signing his paintings.

Van Gogh began to identify with Christ—who also suffered, was rejected and misunderstood, and was devoted to the oppressed. This provided the comforting possibility of remaining aloof from mankind yet eventually of being universally loved. The liaison with Sien can be understood as a consequence of his poor self-regard. But she was also his Mary Magdalene, outcast and wretched, the whore who would be transformed by compassion into a 'good' woman. He rejected the conventional church and its hypocritical 'Pharisees', like his father. Periods of exaltation and frenzied work accompanied spiritual labours. Finally, Van Gogh's decision to become an artist represented a fusion of his, and his family's, spiritual and artistic heritage. His extraordinarily intense immersion in his painting, often associated with a numbing of his senses through starvation, exposure, exhaustion and alcohol, acted to ward off distressing feelings.

This interpretation, based on understanding, clarifies many aspects of Van Gogh's personality but does not seem adequate to account for his intense mood swings nor their seasonal fluctuations. At times he was virtually paralysed, oblivious to his surroundings, stared bleakly into space, and stopped eating. At other times his mind was in tumult, he dressed outlandishly, and talked and laughed embarrassingly; then he worked frenetically at strange projects, such as a simultaneous translation of the Bible into four languages (instead of attending to his job in a bookshop).

Van Gogh described his moods as sudden 'unaccountable but involuntary emotions'. Others did not doubt that he had at these times passed from 'eccentricity' to insanity. The psychiatrist would now turn to the explanatory perspective—proposing a biological basis for his vulnerability to mood swings and, at times, clear manic-depressive illness (see Chapter 8). His experiences and behaviour are consistent with typical features of what psychiatrists now recognise readily as depressive and manic episodes. Genetic factors may have played a part, while unhappy events and physical ill-health may have been important triggers. But meaningful connections do not end here. Understanding comes back into play as the psychiatrist appreciates how Van Gogh's awareness of his vulnerability to these uncontrollable spells and to the frequent jeers of people around him may well have increased his sense of inferiority and alienation.

Van Gogh's mutilation of his ear is perhaps the most tantalising episode of all. None of the many interpretations fully accounts for this bizarre act. A psychotic illness is the likely explanation for the form his mental state assumed. It was probably sparked off by heavy consumption of absinthe (an alcoholic drink containing a neurotoxin, thujone, known to be associated with mental disturbances). Van Gogh's poor nutrition and physical self-neglect may also have contributed. His apparent loss of memory for the episode is consistent with this explanation, as it is with his doctor's diagnosis of epilepsy.

Nonetheless, we must consider the timing and the content of his 'madness' as well as its form. Van Gogh's vulnerabilities were exposed in his deteriorating relationship with Gauguin. The weather was miserable and the two spent a number of enforced days in close proximity in the 'Yellow House'. Christmas was always a dangerous time. Vincent probably also knew about his brother Theo's prospective marriage, and could see the implications of this for his continued support. Immediately before the episode he had quarrelled with Gauguin, throwing a glass of absinthe at him, and later he was reported as having threatened him with a razor. Gauguin, like so many others, had 'betrayed' him. In guilt, Vincent directed his anger inwards, mutilating himself.

Why the ear? Why did he present it to a prostitute? Several explanations are possible, all of them equally plausible. Bullfights, a popular pastime in Arles, culminated in the ear being sliced from the vanquished animal to be presented by the toreador to his favourite lady. Stories about Jack the

Ripper's dismemberment of his prostitute victims, sometimes involving an ear, appeared in the local paper at the time. Gauguin was a great success with the prostitutes of Arles and the ear may have represented for Van Gogh a 'gift'. He was preoccupied with the story of Christ in the Garden of Olives (Gethsemane), and actually destroyed two canvasses on this subject because they so frightened him. In this episode of betrayal, the disciple Peter cut off the ear of Malchus, a servant of the high priest who had come to seize Christ. It is also possible that Van Gogh was attempting to excise the apparent source of auditory hallucinations which he thought of as a 'diseased nerve'.

## Why the psychotic episodes?

There were obvious sources of stress in Van Gogh's life at the time. Largest among these was the threatened loss of Theo's support, undivided until then and on which he was entirely dependent. In quick succession between January and April 1889, Theo had become engaged, married and an expectant father. Yet Van Gogh was not, as we might expect, preoccupied with this situation. Seeking solace in religion would not have been surprising given his past behaviour, but his religious ideas took a bizarre, frightening form which was incomprehensible to others and, in retrospect, to himself. These episodes thus appear non-understandable. Eventually Van Gogh believed himself unfit to govern his life and accepted the suggestion of a prolonged period of asylum.

A psychiatrist would now look to the forms of the breakdown in terms of our classification of illness. A definite diagnosis is difficult to make but a disordered brain is possible in view of the confusion, loss of memory and brief duration of the episodes. Absinthe may again have been implicated, especially as most recurrences followed visits to Arles. Further severe depressive episodes may also have occurred. Schizophrenia is very unlikely, as there was no deterioration in his personality, and he remained extraordinarily productive—and his paintings showed no evidence of the loss of control or disorganisation we would expect.

## The suicide

Let us now try to reconstruct Van Gogh's mental state at the time of his suicide. Depressed moods continued in Auvers. A month before his death he wrote, 'My life is threatened at the very root, and my steps are also wavering'. The famous painting *Crows over the Wheatfields* carries a chilling atmosphere of evil foreboding, but this was not his last canvas. He had lost faith in the ability of his medical attendant, Dr Gachet, to help him, and described Gachet as being as sick as he was. This was important because the fear of a recurrence of his madness plagued him, and he might have felt an impending relapse. There were inexplicable explosions of anger directed at Gachet, during one of which he feared that Van Gogh might perhaps use the pistol—which he eventually did, but upon himself. These incidents are reminiscent of his hostility towards Gaugin and it is possible that he had indeed relapsed.

The threatened loss of Theo's support had become more urgent. Theo now had a child with the perhaps ominous name of Vincent who, to make matters worse, had fallen ill. Theo's own health was declining (he died six months later); he had money worries, and was thinking about quitting his job. Although repeatedly begged by Van Gogh to spend his vacation at Auvers rather than in Holland, Theo declined. Van Gogh had on several occasions declared that his 'life or death' depended on Theo's help. He could not easily express his resentment openly, and it is understandable, particularly in the light of previous self-destructive acts, that he turned his hostility inwards again.

For the first time, Van Gogh had received praise for his painting. His response shows how events desirable to one person may have a disturbing meaning for another. He wrote, 'But when I had read the article I felt almost mournful, for I thought: I ought to be like that, and I feel so inferior. My back is not broad enough to carry such an undertaking'. Guilt-ridden, he could not tolerate success; it was yet another burden to endure.

## Blending understanding and explanation—the hallmark of the good psychiatrist

It is clear from this story that there are limits to the method of understanding. Sometimes, despite conscientious attempts to find meaning in a particular experience or behaviour, a barrier is encountered. The person's behaviour seems not to emerge coherently from what has gone before. At this point the psychiatrist is forced to conclude that it is meaningless, non-understandable, 'crazy', and that the person has become mentally ill.

There can be no proof that a particular understanding is 'correct'. It is an interpretation which looks different to different observers. Equally plausible interpretations may be constructed, depending on the prominence given to certain aspects. However, a good interpretation is not a fiction either. It can be tested against the evidence on which it is based, to see how it fits the 'facts'. Inconsistencies are sought in the same way as a barrister attempts to undermine an apparently plausible account by a witness during cross-examination. A convincing interpretation will survive close scrutiny, and one may be chosen as superior to its competitors.

Understanding may also change as new information comes to light. A new behaviour may force a change in the interpretation so that previous behaviours take on a different meaning. This makes the new behaviour consistent with what has gone before. And, new information may lead to a deeper understanding, of greater subtlety. The experienced psychiatrist, through scrutiny of many stories, becomes aware of a wider range of meaningful connections and is skilled at drawing out significant information about the person's mental life and behaviour.

It is important to recognise that the logic underlying understanding does not lead to the formulation of general principles nor is it a reliable way of predicting future behaviour. People with similar experiences may share more or less similar patterns of meaningful connections, but there will always be variation and for some the patterns will be quite different. Such patterns assume the status of maxims or proverbs (such as 'Absence makes the heart grow fonder') and are widely recognised in literary and artistic themes (consider Othello's jealous rage or Hamlet's indecisiveness). We will make many allusions of this kind in the pages ahead.

On the other hand, the methods of science have made a crucial contribution to psychiatry, and will continue to do so through the rapid progress being made in, for example, the neurosciences. However, this approach also has its limitations despite the claim that only through this method can 'real' knowledge be acquired.

Science may have useful things to say about people who find themselves in predicaments easily understood in terms of life circumstances (for example, grieving the loss of a near one). But such a person is better understood in psychological terms, and more appropriately helped through such means. Even when a person suffers from a clear-cut mental illness, the nature of which is best elucidated through explanation, contact with them is made through the psychiatrist's sense of that person as a subject rather than an object. It is essential to understand what it means for the person to have the experiences arising from the illness. Even if an important treatment is the prescription of a specific drug, compliance with it will often be determined by the quality of the relationship between patient and psychiatrist. The impact of the illness on the person and their family will also be best appreciated through understanding.

# 3  *What Causes Mental Illness?*

We used the story of Vincent Van Gogh in the previous chapter to outline the complementary perspectives of understanding and explanation in the approach to mental illness. Understanding is the 'art' which helps the psychiatrist to appreciate the person's experience. Explanation uses the methods of science to unravel the causes of psychiatric disorders. A good psychiatrist applies both, in seeking a complete picture.

## One cause or many?

Diseases in medicine generally are seldom due to a single cause. The tubercle germ is a necessary cause of tuberculosis. Similarly, a fall is an obvious reason for a fracture. But neither condition arises entirely from a single cause. For instance, the woman infected by the germ was a refugee from a war-torn country, malnourished for many months and exposed to severe privations. The man who fell and fractured his wrist was drunk at the time, and his subsequently discovered misuse of alcohol could be traced to problems in his personality related in turn to an emotionally chaotic upbringing. Each condition was the culmination of a series of causes, not a single one.

Psychiatric disorders are even more likely to have multiple causes. Indeed, there are always a number of interrelated factors operating in sequence or concurrently. In assessing their patients effectively, psychiatrists tease out as many of these factors as possible; they then reassemble them in planning appropriate therapy. Our understanding of factors which give rise to psychiatric disorders is steadily increasing, with exciting findings relating to both causes and treatment.

The pattern of symptoms often suggests the predominance of a particular causal factor. For example, in a confused, disoriented person with impaired memory, the basis is likely to be disturbed brain function. However, other factors may emerge when the psychiatrist conducts a comprehensive inquiry. Consider this example:

> *Kylie became morose following the break-up of an intimate relationship. At first sight, her disappointment in love was probably the major reason for her mood change. However, there were other contributing causes which she may never even have considered. In fact, it emerged in the psychiatrist's deft probing of her background that this was not Kylie's first broken romance. She had had several affairs. Each break-up seemed to be the result of an uncompromising attitude to her partner. This pattern in turn appeared linked to an emotionally cold environment in her family of origin typified by lack of intimacy between the parents, parents and children, and the siblings. Moreover, two of her paternal uncles had suffered from severe depression, this suggesting a family predisposition.*

Bearing this young woman in mind, we can readily see how the psychiatrist applies what is called a *bio-psycho-social approach*. Indeed, in considering causes of psychiatric disorders, the responsible factors may be many but fall into three main categories:

- *biological factors* arising from the physiology and biochemistry of bodily systems, or from genetic endowment;
- *psychological factors* usually derived from upbringing, emotional experience and interaction with people;
- *social factors* arising from the person's cultural environment and current life situation.

In most cases, more than one set of factors contribute. Let us consider each category in turn.

## The biological causes

At the end of the nineteenth century when the microscope revealed for the first time that the basis of much physical disease lay in abnormalities of the cells of various bodily organs, it was hoped that a similar basis in disturbance of brain cells would be found for psychiatric disorders. This hope, while realised for some conditions such as dementia, has not been fulfilled for many others. But the search continues unabated, boosted by improving technology and emerging tantalising clues, such as a specific type of brain shrinkage in schizophrenia demonstrated by new brain imaging methods (see page 160).

Biological causes are either inherited or acquired. The many acquired causes include hormonal disturbances, nutritional deficiencies, brain tumours and therapeutic and illicit drugs. The most convenient way to look at these biological causes is to tease out genetics, and then biochemical, physiological and pathological disturbances of the brain.

*Genetic factors*

Some disorders are transmitted by genes passed down from one generation to another. Where a disease occurs more often in the families of patients than in the families of unaffected people, it strongly points to heredity. Through family studies, the means of inheritance may become clear and an expectancy rate of the disease among relatives of patients may be calculated. Such studies have been done for conditions like schizophrenia (see page 160) and the mood disorders (see page 103) and they demonstrate a genetic factor.

The study of twins is an important method of investigating the genetics of any disease. The relevance of inheritance can be established by comparing the difference in the rates at which a disorder occurs in both twins (concordance rates) between identical (monozygotic or MZ) twins and non-identical (dizygotic or DZ) twins. The genes of MZ twins are identical whereas those of DZ twins are no more alike than are the genes of other siblings. So, if the concordance rate for an illness is higher among MZ than DZ twins, this strongly suggests that inheritance is a prominent part of the cause.

Because twins are usually raised in the same environment, studies of adopted twins are a useful way of sorting out the effects of genes and upbringing. If the concordance rate for an illness is higher for MZ twins raised together than for MZ twins raised apart, it is likely that rearing influences are significant.

Because adopted children receive genes from the family of origin, and have their environment moulded by the family of adoption, much can be learnt by studying them. In a study of the children of schizophrenic mothers, for example, those who were adopted before the age of two were assessed on various criteria of mental health and ill-health. They were then compared with adopted children whose natural mothers did not have psychiatric illness. Children of schizophrenic mothers had a higher rate of various mental health problems, of psychiatric disorders including schizophrenia, and of criminal behaviour. In other words, they were more vulnerable to psychological disturbance in general.

*Biochemical factors*

Investigation of various chemical substances in the brain is handicapped in a number of ways:

- it is obviously difficult to study the living brain, and investigating chemicals elsewhere in the body, like blood and cerebro-spinal fluid or post-mortem tissue, has limitations;
- producing a model psychiatric state in an experimental animal is problematic for obvious reasons;
- in people receiving treatment, the question arises as to whether biochemical changes are the cause or the effect of their disorder.

However, the evidence is clear that biochemical abnormalities are associated with certain psychiatric disorders.

Neuro-transmitters (chemical messengers) in the brain have been especially well studied (see page 268). Certain disorders are possibly due to their abnormal action. For instance, the chemical activity of the neuro-transmitter dopamine is affected in schizophrenia—there appears to be too much of it. Most of the effective anti-psychotic drugs used to treat this illness act primarily by blocking dopamine's action.

In depression, there seems to be too little of another group of neuro-transmitters, the monoamines, at one or more sites in the brain. In manic states, on the other hand, there appears to be too much. This evidence suggests a possible link between monoamines and mood disorders. One group of anti-depressant drugs blocks the action of the monoamines, allowing other chemicals to activate neighbouring nerve cells. The positive effect of all anti-depressant treatments, including drugs and electro-convulsive treatment (ECT), may involve their increasing the sensitivity of the brain to monoamines.

*Brain functioning*

Some functions of the brain can be investigated, particularly its electrical activity. Electro-encephalographic (EEG) studies measure electrical discharges of the brain. Studies of, for example, people with schizophrenia show intriguing findings—faster activity in acute schizophrenia and slower activity in chronic cases, especially in the front part of the brain. This is thought to correlate with the relatively reduced blood flow also found in the frontal lobe of these people.

## Changes in the brain

Most psychiatric conditions—including psychoses such as schizophrenia and severe mood disorders—are not associated with microscopic brain changes. But for 'organic' psychoses like dementia, changes in the brain are typical.

In Alzheimer's disease, the most common dementia, changes are obvious and the basis for the symptoms, which include degeneration and loss of nerve cells and the deposition of a protein substance between cells in the shape of plaques. The contribution of genetics to diseases of the nervous system is illustrated in the link between Alzheimer's and Down's syndrome. People with Down's syndrome who live beyond middle age often develop Alzheimer's disease.

## The psychological causes

### Early life experience

Proverbs such as 'The child is the father of the man' and 'As the twig is bent, so is the tree inclined' point to an age-old recognition that a person's experience in childhood has an effect throughout life. Early life experiences are pivotal in the formation of personality. Childhood psychological difficulties are closely associated with emotional disorders in adulthood. The British psychiatrist John Bowlby, for instance, studied the effects of maternal deprivation on young children and concluded that the prolonged or recurrent absence of a consistent mother-figure led to later difficulties in forming affectionate bonds and a tendency to anxiety and depression.

### The contribution of psychoanalysis

Sigmund Freud, the founder of psychoanalysis, proposed a continuum of severity between influences that shape personality development and those that cause emotional disturbance. He saw human behaviour as arising from unconscious drives whose expression both contributes to personality development and is influenced by early and current life experiences.

These instinctual forces, beyond a person's awareness, are active from infancy. They are pleasure-seeking (Eros) or destructive (Thanatos) in form, and reside in that part of the psyche labelled by Freud as the id. The ego, the executive function of the mind which provides a sense of self, deals with the external world as well as with internal psychic conflicts. As a person is socialised by family and society, he or she develops a conscience, of

William Hogath's engraving of a scene in Bedlam, London's notorious asylum (from *The Rake's Progress*, 1735).

A lecture on hysteria by the French physician, Jean Martin Charcot (after a painting by Andre Brouillet, 1887, in the Musée de Nice).

The Bethlehem Royal Hospital, typical of the asylums in which psychiatry was born (an engraving by Robert White, *c.* 1700).

The 'gallery for women' in the same hospital (from the *Illustrated London News*, 1860).

A magnetic resonance imaging (MRI) scan showing different areas of the brain (Mental Health Research Institute).

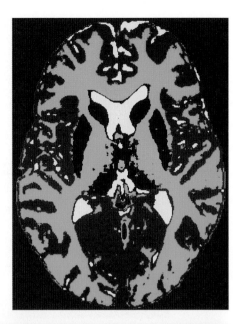

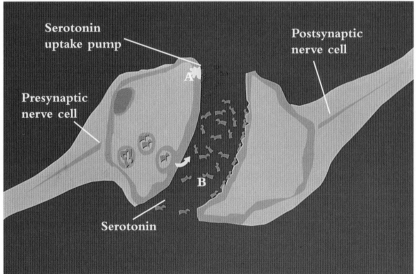

One group of anti-depressants, the SSRIs (*see* page 111), acts by preventing the uptake pump (**A**) from removing serotonin from the synapse (the space between the nerve endings). The resulting higher concentration of serotonin in the synapse (**B**) leads to more of the chemical messenger reaching the postsynaptic nerve cell (Mental Health Research Institute).

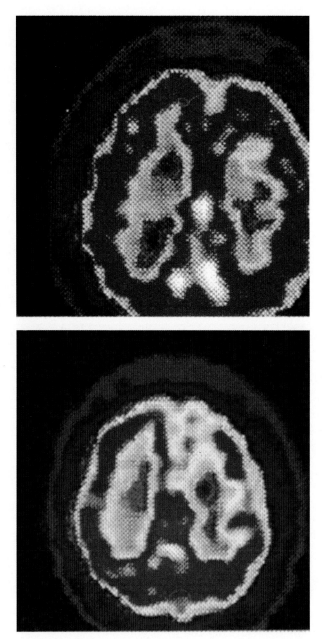

Good blood flow to the outer rim of brain tissue (red), shown in the top brain scan, contrasts clearly with the reduced blood flow (yellow) of a person with dementia in the scan below (Royal Melbourne Hospital Illustration Department).

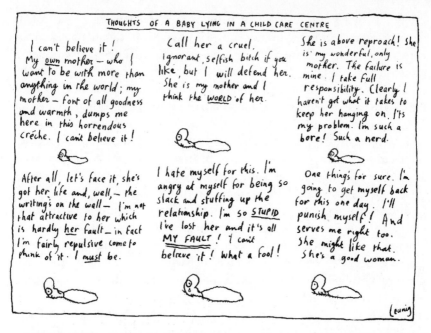

THOUGHTS OF A BABY LYING IN A CHILD CARE CENTRE

I can't believe it! My own mother — who I want to be with more than anything in the world; my mother — font of all goodness and warmth, dumps me here in this horrendous crèche. I can't believe it!

Call her a cruel, ignorant, selfish bitch if you like, but I will defend her. She is my mother and I think the WORLD of her.

She is above reproach! She is my wonderful, only mother. The failure is mine. I take full responsibility. Clearly I haven't got what it takes to keep her hanging on. It's my problem. I'm such a bore! Such a nerd.

After all, let's face it, she's got her life and, well, — the writing's on the wall — I'm not that attractive to her which is hardly her fault — in fact I'm fairly repulsive come to think of it. I must be.

I hate myself for this. I'm angry at myself for being so slack and stuffing up the relationship. I'm so STUPID I've lost her and it's all MY FAULT! I can't believe it! What a fool!

One thing's for sure. I'm going to get myself back for this one day. I'll punish myself! And serves me right too. She might like that. She's a good woman.

(leunig)

which the superego is the unconscious component, comprising parental values, ideals and prohibitions.

According to Freud, a troubled mind results when the ego is challenged from one or more of three sources:

- the id seeking expression (for example, a child's nightmares reflect his attempts to deal with murderous rage towards his mother following her incessant, carping criticism);
- demands of the superego (for example, a young woman from a traditional family develops anxiety in the face of her sense of absolute obligation to remain in a patently destructive marriage);
- perceived threats from the outside world (for example, a woman experiences acute terror upon discovering a breast lump).

The ego may be more or less able to withstand these challenges depending on the nature and sturdiness of its defence mechanisms.

Freud's theory of personality development uses strong bodily metaphors, dividing the first six years of life into oral, anal and phallic stages. This is followed by a relatively 'quiescent' or latent phase. According to his theory, unresolved difficulties in one or more of these personality development stages predispose the person to psychological disturbances in adulthood when issues similar to those originally faced are encountered.

In the oral stage, from birth to about eighteen months, the infant depends on a mother-figure not only for physical nurturance but also for consistent emotional care. The infant needs to feel neither at risk of being abandoned nor engulfed by the carer. Difficulties at this point predispose the infant to fear for survival, which may manifest in various ways in adult life and which is reflected in inappropriate mistrust of others. A person may go to great lengths to please others so as not to be abandoned (dependent personality) or, conversely, avoid intimate relationships altogether (schizoid personality), may seek solace in 'oral' behaviour like bingeing and alcohol misuse or take pleasure in displaying a hostile attitude towards those who get too close ('biting the hand that feeds you').

In the anal stage, from about the second into the third year, the child comes to recognise the reality of separateness from the mother and of an emerging independence. Curiosity and pleasure in asserting this autonomy may conflict with concerns that such behaviour may incur parental displeasure. This underlies the 'power battles' over such matters as toilet training and feeding, which are typical of this stage. The legacy in adulthood of these early difficulties are fear of losing control over feelings, especially through outbursts of anger. Such problems may lead to vulnerability to depression in response to failure to live up to one's own or others' expectations or to compulsive behaviour, rigid attitudes and a devaluation of emotional in favour of overly rational ways of behaving (obsessive personality).

The next stage, the phallic, continues into the fifth or sixth year. The focus of the child's interest shifts from a two-person relationship (mother–child) to the complexity of a three-person relationship (mother–father–child). This coincides with interest in the sexual organs, their functions, and differences between the sexes. To the needs of the oral stage (to be nurtured) and those of the anal stage (to be approved of) are now added unconscious desires for affection from the opposite-sex parent (the Oedipal complex). This leads to a futile set of circumstances: rivalry with the same-sex parent who is simultaneously loved by the child. The development of the superego (conscience) through identification with the values of both parents helps resolve these difficulties. Problems in this stage may manifest in adult life as sexual anxiety, concern about sexual identity, and fears about attractiveness or worth to others.

The latency phase lasts from the fifth or sixth year to puberty. The child turns its attention to socially sanctioned activities outside the home, including relationships and athletic and academic pursuits.

Erik Erikson, a brilliant 'Freudian', extended Freud's theory by considering several other developmental phases as part of the life cycle. Puberty, marked by maturation of the genitals and the hormonal changes that go with it, leads to the resurgence of sexual and aggressive forces. However, the child now has socially permissible ways of expressing them, as well as the capacity for abstract thought and aesthetic pursuits. Emotional independence from parents is facilitated by strong relationships with peers or with the idealisation of non-parental adult figures like rock stars, a teacher or a political hero. The tasks of this stage are to establish a secure personal identity, accept adult roles, and develop the capacity for a mature sexual relationship and the ability to care appropriately for one's own children. Failure leads to complex difficulties in one or more of these spheres of adult life.

The stages of development, the tasks to be accomplished and the psychological problems which may ensue are summarised in the table below.

**Freudian stages of personality development**

| Stages | Age | Developmental tasks | Possible psychological problems |
|---|---|---|---|
| Oral | birth to 18 months | • satisfaction of dependency needs<br>• development of trusting relationships | • fear of abandonment<br>• lack of trust<br>• overeating<br>• alcoholism<br>• lack of impulse control |
| Anal | 18 months to 3 years | • autonomy and control of own body<br>• managing a two-person relationship, that is, with mother | • fear of disapproval<br>• obstinacy and stubbornness<br>• power conflict over control, shame and guilt<br>• concern over body<br>• obsessive compulsive behaviour |
| Phallic | 3–4 years to 5–6 years | • appreciating gender differences<br>• coping with being part of a three-person relationship<br>• development of sexual identity and mastery of environment | • sexual anxiety<br>• inappropriate use of sex in dealing with residual problems from earlier stages of development<br>• fear of loss of self-esteem<br>• inappropriate competitiveness |
| Latency | 5–6 years to puberty | • control of sexual and aggressive forces through sublimation and peer relationships | • impaired creativity and poor development of social skills |
| Genital | puberty to adulthood | • establishment of personal identity<br>• adaptation to social expectations and social values | • 'identity crisis'<br>• complex psychological problems in adult life |

As mentioned earlier, psychological problems may occur if the ego is challenged from one or more of three sources: from id forces, from super-ego demands, and from threats from the external world. If these challenges cannot be met or if the ego perceives a threat to its integrity, anxiety or other distressing feelings result. This then serves as a signal to the ego which sets up various strategies, the so-called defence mechanisms, to deal with the demands experienced. Since these strategies operate unconsciously, the person reacts deliberately but is unaware of the underlying discomfort—and may only become conscious of motives and defences at a later point or during psychotherapy. These defences were originally described by Freud and later elaborated by his daughter Anna Freud, a child psychoanalyst. Strategies vary, according to the stages of psychosexual maturity and the particular situation. Some are used by 'healthy' people, particularly the 'mature' ones, while others are used more commonly, or more obviously, by psychotic people. A wide range of these defences operate. They are described in Chapter 6, where examples are also provided.

## A cognitive approach

Cognitive theory, which deals with the interplay between learning, infor-mation processing and experience, is another major approach to the under-standing of mental illness. According to this view, a psychiatric disorder can result from inappropriate and inflexible ways of viewing and responding to the world, derived usually from past, especially childhood, experience.

The person's experiences, in childhood within the family, at school, with peers and in various social groups, all add to the mosaic of factors contributing to patterns of thinking (called schemas). If these experiences are in some way negative or traumatic, learning and hence normal devel-opment may be distorted. The resulting disturbed ways of thinking then continue to influence later experience. Abnormal ways of thinking become solidly entrenched and additional problems accumulate, further disabling the person. Development can be interrupted and behavi-our become so dysfunctional that diagnosis of a psychiatric disorder is appropriate.

We'll use depression as an example. The person with depression views the world pessimistically. Aaron Beck, the American psychiatrist who devised cognitive theory, highlights three streams of 'depressive cogni-tions', involving the person, the world and the future. For example, if the person fails in a task, negative thoughts may include, 'I am always a failure in anything I do'; 'There is nothing that can change this, it's hopeless', and 'I will always fail'. These distortions are accompanied by unwarranted and self-critical inferences, such as, 'If I fail no-one will like me and I will never be happy'. The depressive 'schemas' may have originated in that person's early development from limited opportunities to succeed and from pervasive criticism.

## The social causes

It is self-evident that conditions prevailing in society influence the lives of people and thus affect their mental health. One critical way to study the social factors implicated in psychiatric disorders is to examine their pattern of distribution in the community (the technical term is epidemiology). Epidemiological research has identified specific social aspects which relate to certain disorders: age, sex, marital status, socio-economic status, emotional support and life events. These sorts of factors do not pinpoint precise causes, but they do indicate factors that may be contributing and therefore should be looked at. For example, we know that 90 per cent of people with anorexia nervosa are female, mostly in their adolescence or early adulthood; this make us curious about what specific factors may have caused this striking pattern.

The picture of suicidal behaviour in a community provides another example of the relevance of epidemiology. Whereas people who attempt suicide, usually as the proverbial cry for help, are mostly women in their teens and early twenties, those who actually kill themselves tend to be men in their sixties and beyond. This does not of course mean that young women do not suicide or that older men do not make attempts. And the person who has 'completed' suicide is likely to have been single, divorced or widowed, and to have suffered a painful chronic illness.

Social scientists have studied some key social factors in order to deepen our understanding of their potential to cause mental illness. Unemployment, for example, correlates with physical and psychiatric ill-health. Moreover, it is not only the health of the unemployed person that is affected but also that of family members. Lack of a job is linked to a higher rate of depression and the worsening of physical conditions like asthma and heart disease.

The social status of people with schizophrenia has been particularly well researched. It is more prevalent among poor people, and various ideas have been offered to explain this link. The 'breeder' argument is that factors like social hardship, poverty, inadequate obstetric care and increased exposure to infection all contribute to a greater likelihood of a person developing schizophrenia—in other words, these factors are conducive to the 'breeding' of schizophrenia. Conversely, the 'drift' argument is that a schizophrenic person is unable to function at the level required to remain in his or her original social group or to move upwards. Instead, there is a decline, a downward drift.

The research of an eminent British sociologist, George Brown, and the Australian psychiatrist, Scott Henderson, highlights the importance for mental health of social groups to whom a person relates. These groups provide basic support for a person encountering the ups and downs of life, especially in times of crisis. The social networks of people with psychiatric illness tend to be impaired. For example, women are more likely to become depressed if they do not have support from a partner, family or friends.

We have all experienced the impact of major life events on our well-being. Indeed, studies show that such events, or indeed their possibility, are commonly reported by psychiatric patients in the period leading up to their illness. The greater the number of 'life changes' the more likely is physical and/or mental ill-health to occur. Interestingly, in a group of United States Navy recruits, those with higher scores on 'life changes', as assessed by their answers to questionnaires, experienced more minor physical illnesses.

One critical life event is migration. Adjusting to a new country undoubtedly is a common source of stress. Climate, food, language and customs are often unfamiliar. Special attention has been paid to the psychiatric consequences. Soren Ødegaard, a Swedish psychiatrist, found that Swedish migrants to the United States were more likely to develop schizophrenia than were their compatriots who had not migrated or than Swedes born in the United States. Similar findings have been made in other parts of the world. But the significance of migration as a cause of mental illness remains unclear. It may be that people who are poorly adjusted to their own environment choose to migrate, and so transfer a vulnerability to their new country.

The complexity of human behaviour is clearly illustrated by differences in the response of migrants over the short versus the long term. In a study of migrants to Australia, Southern European women were apt to develop depression not upon their arrival but some fifteen years later. This was possibly because initially they were busy helping their husbands and children to settle. More than a decade later, their husbands were economically established, had acquired some English and had mostly adapted to the new life. And their children had learned to speak fluent English at school, made a network of new friends and integrated into the Australian way of life. The women, lacking the same opportunity to learn English or to move beyond their ethnic community, found themselves isolated and without a role.

Finally, we need to comment on the tantalising observation that certain clinical syndromes occur in specific cultural settings. They were once thought to be due to local cultural factors. An example is koro, which occurs most commonly among the Chinese. A man feels that his penis is shrinking into his body and believes that this signifies impending death. Severely anxious, he cries out for help and the community rallies to his aid. Research does not confirm such a relationship, and several so-called 'exotic' syndromes are widespread and universally recognised but with 'cultural colouring'. Koro, for example, is merely another form of panic.

## The mosaic of causes

While all these factors, whether biological, psychological or social, may operate separately or in combination, they may also apply at different times. They may predispose a person to illness, precipitate it or perpetuate it, depending on their timing in relation to the illness, as shown in the table on page 36.

Predisposing factors are those that exist long before the onset of illness. For example, specific inherited personality traits may make a person vulnerable to certain disorders. Then adverse early-life experience may lead to a deep-seated sense of insecurity, which again makes for vulnerability.

Precipitating factors are those that make an impact just before the symptoms appear, whether as part of a new condition or a relapse of a previous illness. They are regarded as responsible for the illness occurring at the time it did.

Perpetuating factors are those that prevent or delay the resolution or improvement of symptoms. For example, a family that criticises their ill relative has a negative influence on that person's recovery from an episode of schizophrenia.

There are distinct advantages in considering these three timing factors in conjunction with the biopsychosocial ones, as shown in the table. They interweave to form the particular pattern of a person's illness.

Mrs A's story illustrates the interweaving of many factors. We have teased them out and presented them in the second table.

*Mrs A became intensely depressed two months after her husband's death from cancer. She discovered that he had been heavily in debt from the failure of his business and accepted that she would have to do what she could to settle these debts. She had had an episode of depression eight years earlier, after she was*

**The interweaving of typical biopsychosocial factors with time**

|                 | Biological                                           | Psychological                                                  | Social                                                       |
| --------------- | ---------------------------------------------------- | ------------------------------------------------------------- | ----------------------------------------------------------- |
| **Predisposing** | • genes<br>• mother's alcoholism<br>• maternal health in pregnancy | • upbringing<br>• parental strife<br>• personality traits     | • cultural demands<br>• poverty<br>• migration              |
| **Precipitating** | • trauma<br>• infections<br>• illicit drugs          | • bereavement<br>• exam failure<br>• being jilted             | • retirement<br>• being robbed<br>• stock-market loss       |
| **Perpetuating** | • malnutrition<br>• poor sanitation<br>• dependency on drugs | • bad marriage<br>• conflict with neighbours<br>• delinquent offspring | • demands at work<br>• refugee status<br>• financial obligations |

robbed on the street one night. Twelve years before the present illness Mrs A had been depressed for no apparent reason. She had required treatment in hospital on both these occasions. When Mrs A was a teenager, her mother had been depressed and been treated in hospital.

The recent death of her husband and the robbery eight years earlier were events which contributed to Mrs A's episodes of depression at those times—they were precipitating factors on each occasion. But she had been depressed for no apparent reason twelve years earlier. She had probably inherited a tendency to depressive illness (her mother had suffered from severe depression)—a predisposing factor. Her husband's legacy of debts with which she had to grapple was a continuing source of concern and no doubt contributed to the persistence of her depression—it is a perpetuating factor.

**The specific factors in Mrs A's illness**

|                  | Biological                   | Psychological                                                            | Social                          |
| ---------------- | ---------------------------- | ----------------------------------------------------------------------- | ------------------------------- |
| **Predisposing** | • positive family history    | • robbery eight years earlier<br>• neglect from a depressed mother      |                                 |
| **Precipitating** |                              | • death of husband<br>• financial stress of funeral expenses            |                                 |
| **Perpetuating** |                              |                                                                         | • heavy debts left by husband   |

There is no better summary of the complex mosaic of multiple factors involved in psychiatric illness than in this conclusion of a taskforce convened by the National Institute of Mental Health in the United States, the nerve centre of American psychiatric research, in 1995:

A full understanding of mental health and illness requires a research perspective that includes not only genetic, biochemical, and neurological factors but also the interpersonal and cultural environments in which people live and the mental processes by which they comprehend that world, interpret their experiences, and plan their actions.

# 4  *Defining Mental Illnesses*

Psychiatry is the branch of medicine that deals with the diagnosis and treatment of mental illness. The fundamental question of what is and what is not mental illness is complicated and contentious. Most of us experience emotions such as anxiety or depression at some stage in our lives, but they do not amount to a psychiatric disorder. Such emotional responses are entirely understandable in the light of life's ups and downs. As not all unpleasant emotions are due to a psychiatric disorder, psychiatrists at times help people who do not suffer from a diagnosable illness but who nevertheless experience substantial distress or dysfunction.

The following widely accepted definition of a psychiatric disorder helps to distinguish between it and what we might call emotional problems of living: a psychiatric disorder is a psychological 'syndrome' (or pattern) that is associated with distress (unpleasant symptoms) or dysfunction (impairment in one or more important areas of functioning) or with an increased risk of death, pain or disability.

Most psychiatric disorders are defined as syndromes (see page 40), with the pattern of symptoms, their onset and progress being used to distinguish between them. But the view that each disorder is a distinct disease has been criticised as reflecting an overly restricted medical model which cannot be applied to psychiatry. Other models have been proposed as mentioned earlier in Chapter 3.

Some experts consider that mental illness can be confirmed only with objective evidence of disturbed psychological functioning, whether of thinking, learning, remembering or feeling. Behaviour which is deviant is seen as indicating a mental illness only if it is associated with such disturbed functioning. In a much-quoted statement Sir Aubrey Lewis, a leading figure in British psychiatry, commented: 'If non-conformity can be detected only in total behaviour, while all the particular psychological functions seem unimpaired, health will be presumed not illness'. The risk of applying a label of mental illness inappropriately is sharply illustrated in Emily Dickinson's poem:

*Much madness is divinest sense*
*To a discerning eye;*
*Much sense the starkest madness.*
*'Tis the majority*
*In this, as all, prevails.*
*Assent, and you are sane;*
*Demur,—you're straightway dangerous,*
*And handled with a chain.*

A sociological model of psychiatric disorder, known as 'anti-psychiatry', has gone so far as to question whether mental illness exists at all, and suggests that psychiatry is nothing more than an instrument of society which 'labels' certain people as having a mental illness in order to control them.

The vast majority of psychiatrists reject this radical view and support an expanded concept of disease—using the so-called 'biopsychosocial model'. This model, which is the basis of our approach in this book and which is described in Chapter 3, looks not only at symptoms but also at a person's total psychological and social world.

## Why is classification necessary?

Classifying mental illness is vital to the proper practice of psychiatry, despite the possible misuse of diagnostic labels and the pigeon-holing of people. In psychiatry, as in other fields of medicine, it is used to group various disorders on the basis of their similarities and differences. Classification is important for both patient and psychiatrist for these reasons:

- it makes for effective communication both between mental health professionals and between them and patients and families;
- it provides a framework for the study of the outcome of mental illnesses, which gives patients and families some idea of what to expect;
- it allows for prediction of the effects of treatment and helps patients and families to understand the rationale for selecting one treatment over another;
- it facilitates scientific research into possible causes of psychiatric disorders and, indirectly, their treatment—with obvious potential benefits for patients.

In medicine it is possible to classify on the basis of known physical causes of disease. For example, the provisional diagnosis of a heart attack—based on the typical pattern of severe chest pain of sudden onset, associated with sweating and nausea—can be confirmed by specific tests such as the electro-cardiogram (ECG) and raised levels of certain enzymes in the blood. But in psychiatry the causes of most disorders remain unknown, and no such objective tests are readily available for most of the conditions dealt with. Classification is therefore based on clinical features and how they cluster together.

The 'complaints' made by a person seeking medical treatment are called *symptoms*—they may be physical such as pain or palpitations, or emotional such as sadness or intrusive thoughts. The findings of the doctor are referred to as *signs*—which again may be physical like an irregular heart rate, or an abnormal mental state like disorientation in time and place. A cluster of symptoms and signs occurring together is called a *syndrome*. If a particular cluster occurs regularly and shows a distinct pattern of progression and response to particular treatment, this forms the basis of a syndrome as a specific *disorder*—which is then incorporated into a formal classification.

Traditionally, medical classification is arranged so that there is no overlap between categories of disorders. This is difficult to achieve in psychiatry as, in individual cases, more than one diagnosis may well apply.

Of the many available classifications of psychiatric disorders, two are widely accepted. The *International Classification of Diseases* published by the World Health Organization (WHO) is in its tenth edition (1992) and is known as ICD-10. The *Diagnostic and Statistical Manual of Mental Disorders*, published by the American Psychiatric Association (APA), is in its fourth edition (1994) and is known as DSM-IV.

The basis for classification within ICD-10 can be traced to 1885, when the Congress of Mental Medicine, held in Antwerp, established a committee to develop a classification 'which the various associations of alienists [an old term for psychiatrists] could unite in adopting'. This was a radical step. Until that time, all systems stemmed from the theories of an assortment of influential leaders in psychiatry. At the International Congress of Mental Science, held in Paris in 1889, eleven categories were adopted. Following publication of the seventh edition of the ICD in 1955, the World Health Organization invited Erwin Stengel, then Professor of Psychiatry in Sheffield University, to establish principles for a truly international system. His report formed the basis for subsequent versions of the ICD.

But marked differences in diagnostic practice were still apparent—the result of psychiatrists having differing theories of the nature of psychiatric disorders. Dissatisfaction with this state of affairs led the American Psychiatric Association in the mid-1970s to explore a new approach. Its three innovations were classification according to observable clinical features, the use of specified criteria to improve diagnostic agreement between psychiatrists, and a 'multi-axial' system. The multi-axial system provided for a more comprehensive evaluation, including any physical conditions, the role of life stress factors and the level of psychological and social functioning.

## The essence of ICD-10

Certain core groups of psychiatric disorders are part of all classification systems. Psychiatrists use these groups, but recognise that they in no way do justice to the complexity of either the clinical picture or the uniqueness of the suffering person. For one thing, more than one diagnostic category is often applicable (for example, mood disorder *and* alcohol abuse).

Let us look at the World Health Organization's classification. The ICD-10 contains ten main groups. These groups are then subdivided further. So, for example, organic disorders include Alzheimer's dementia, vascular

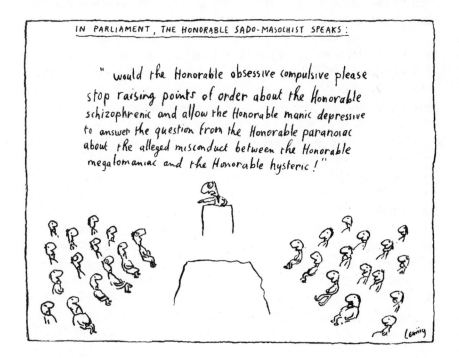

dementia, other forms of dementia, delirium, other mental disorders due to brain damage, and personality and behavioural disorders due to brain disease or brain damage.

We now provide a brief account of each of these ten groups. We deal with each of these diagnostic categories in detail in separate chapters of this book.

*Organic disorders*   Here the person's psychological state or behaviour are affected by a recognisable physical process, involving either the brain (for example, tumour, injury, stroke, Alzheimer's disease) or the body as a whole (for example, liver failure, thyroid deficiency). They have a common cause in disturbance of the brain. It is 'primary' if directly affected or 'secondary' if the disease process indirectly influences brain function (see Chapter 14).

*Misuse of drugs* (prescribed or illicit)   This can directly produce a range of psychiatric states which affect the brain. Alcohol is certainly the most common example world-wide. Other drugs commonly misused include benzodiazepines (tranquillisers), marijuana, amphetamines and heroin. Their effect can take many forms, ranging from the easily reversible state of intoxication to permanent loss of memory and of other higher mental functions. The best known of the syndromes in this group is the state of addiction—the psychological and physical dependence on a particular drug (see Chapter 13).

*Schizophrenia and related delusional disorders*   These are the classical psychoses. The word 'psychosis' has a long history, but psychiatrists now regard it as too vague and ill-defined to be useful. In essence, it means the impairment of psychological function to a degree that grossly interferes with the person's ability to maintain contact with reality and consequently to meet the demands of everyday life. In schizophrenia, the person's thinking, perception and emotional state are highly disturbed, leading to a sense of fragmentation of the self (schizophrenia literally means split mind). In delusional disorders, the main features are bizarre, unrealistic thoughts, most commonly the conviction that one is being persecuted or hounded (paranoid psychosis) (see Chapter 12).

*Mood disorders*   Here, the basic disturbance is a major change to either depression or elation (mania) associated with a variety of symptoms like abnormal thinking (for example, inappropriate pessimism in depression and unbridled optimism in mania) and level of activity (for example, apathetic inertia in depression and inexhaustible mental and physical energy in mania) (see Chapter 8).

*Neurotic disorders*   Like 'psychosis', the term 'neurosis' is enveloped in mists of ambiguity. Coined in the early nineteenth century by a Scottish neurologist, William Cullen, to refer to so-called nervous disorders of psychological origin, the word has been applied so widely (and disparagingly) as to be meaningless. In ICD-10 it is used to more specific purpose. It covers the states of anxiety—including phobia, panic and obsessive-compulsive disorders; conditions linked to severe stress like that resulting from a major trauma (such as torture or rape); and to physical disorders which have a psychological origin (Cullen's original group) (see Chapter 7).

*Behavioural syndromes associated with physiological disturbances*  These cover the three basic biological functions of eating, sleeping and sexuality. In each case a wide variety of problems may arise as a result of psychological factors going awry. The most clear-cut example of this association is anorexia nervosa where profound disturbance in appetite and weight occur, even to the point of death through self-starvation, without a physical cause. Insomnia is another example. Its outcome is less serious, but it is extraordinarily common in the community and a source of much distress (see Chapter 10).

*Disorders of adult personality*  Controversy persists as to whether these are really psychiatric conditions. People described as having these disorders have ingrained and enduring behaviour patterns, with inflexible responses to a range of personal and social circumstances. They perceive, think, feel, and relate to others in ways that differ significantly from those of the average person in the same culture. Such patterns tend to be stable and to encompass many aspects of psychological functioning including feelings of distress and problems in social relationships. The character traits of people with these disorders are clearly present to some degree in everyone. The term 'personality disorder' is used if these character traits lead to detrimental outcomes and are of long standing (see Chapter 11).

*Mental retardation* (or intellectual disability)  This covers all those long-term situations in which development of the mind has been arrested or is incomplete. Mental impairment, ranging from mild to severe, in such areas as thinking, reasoning and language, and social functioning is the result. The best-known example is Down's syndrome (mongolism), which is the result of an inherited chromosomal abnormality. (We do not deal with intellectual disability in this book).

*Disorders of psychological development, and childhood behavioural and emotional disorders*  These are the two principal conditions occurring in childhood and adolescence. The former is divided into specific areas (such as reading, writing and language) or generalised areas (such as autism). The latter is a hodge-podge, made up of diverse categories linked to particular areas of disturbed childhood functioning, which include hyperactivity, conduct disorder (such as oppositional defiant disorder), emotional disorder (such as social anxiety), tics (Tourette's disorder) and mixed emotional/behavioural disorder (such as bed-wetting) (see Chapter 15).

## How the classification is used

The usefulness of the ICD-10 classification is clearly illustrated by the story of Jill.

*A 28-year-old woman was brought by a girlfriend to the emergency department of a general hospital with self-inflicted superficial lacerations of both wrists. Following an argument with her boyfriend three days earlier, Jill had been tearful, unable to sleep, and 'too upset' to go to work. She decided to cut her wrists because her boyfriend had not called her since the argument. She then telephoned her friend to tell her that she was 'going to die', and it was this friend who brought her to hospital.*

*Jill described frequent episodes of feeling depressed over many years, each usually lasting for several hours and precipitated by conflict with boyfriends or family members. However, she had not experienced significant sleep disturbance, reduced appetite or weight loss at any time. She conceded that she was an 'emotional' person most of the time. Her many relationships usually ended in conflict and a dramatic gesture on her part—including suicidal behaviour.*

*At first Jill was tearful, but soon became animated. She told her story with dramatic flair, and seemed to want to impress the psychiatrist with the intensity of her distress. She described herself as making friends easily—she was a 'people person'. At the same time it seemed that her friendships were superficial and short-lasting, and that others thought her inconsiderate and immature. She found it easier to 'make friends' with men than with women, and apparently considered other women as rivals for her boyfriend's attention.*

*In making a diagnosis, the psychiatrist would first consider the episode which brought Jill to the hospital, and then whether or not she has a disorder of personality. Although describing herself as having felt depressed from time to time over many years, those episodes were brief and not associated with features of 'clinical depression' (see Chapter 8) such as diminished appetite, weight loss or disturbed sleep. Thus, she does not meet the criteria for a mood disorder.*

*The episode which led to the self-harm, precipitated by the argument with her boyfriend and associated with crying and inability to work over three days, indicates a diagnosis within the Neurotic and stress-related disorders—more specifically, of an adjustment disorder (a brief depressive reaction). (See Chapter 7 for a detailed account of this group of disorders, which are commonly encountered in psychiatric practice.)*

*Jill's description of long-standing patterns of behaviour and of relating to others suggests a personality disorder, although there is not enough information to make a definite diagnosis. The psychiatrist would be cautious about this diagnosis because personality disorder is a long-term pattern of behaviour which needs specialised and correspondingly long-term psychotherapy.*

*In fact, the psychiatrist began brief counselling to deal with the adjustment disorder and took the opportunity, in a planned way, to assess any other under-lying personality features. During the sessions, it became very clear to both Jill and the therapist that several traits in her personality had led to a pattern of continuing difficulties in her life, especially regarding relationships, both general and intimate. They agreed that a longer course of psychotherapy was warranted (see Chapter 21).*

This brief clinical account leads us to look at how psychiatrists go about the dual tasks of assessing and treating patients.

# **5** *The Psychiatrist at Work*

The key tool that the psychiatrist uses in everyday work is the clinical interview. The psychiatrist's purpose is not only to hear the person's story, assess the mental state and make a diagnosis, but also to understand the individuality of that person and the reasons for seeking help at this time. The interview is vitally important in establishing a trusting relationship. It is the crucible in which all subsequent treatment operates. Central to this relationship are the hope of receiving help, a supportive association with a dependable professional, an opportunity to share problems and a source of reliable advice.

Respect for the dignity of patients is paramount in medicine generally, but especially for mentally ill people, who are so vulnerable to stigmatisation and disempowerment. Psychiatrists are often confronted with issues relating to respect for autonomy, particularly when weighing up the need for compulsory treatment. Should people be forced into hospital? Should they be compelled to receive treatment? Should they be allowed to act on suicidal wishes? Generally, psychiatrists respect the person's civil rights except when those rights conflict with the doctor's duty of care. For instance, compromise is necessary for people who are not in full control of their faculties (such as the demented or psychotic), or who need protection against their own harmful impulses (such as the severely depressed and homicidal).

Confidentiality, which is one aspect of respect for privacy, is central to the relationship between psychiatrist and patient. The Hippocratic Oath stresses that 'Whatever in connection with my professional practice or not in connection with it, I see or hear, in the life of men, which ought not to be spoken abroad, I will not divulge, as reckoning that all should be kept secret'. This is particularly important in psychiatry, given the intensely personal nature of material revealed. Confidentiality cannot always be absolute, but its breaches must be rare, and made only in order to safeguard the patient's interests and the safety or interests of others.

When interviewed, the person may well be embarrassed, ashamed and fearful of humiliation at a time of marked vulnerability. A courteous, tactful, accepting attitude on the part of the psychiatrist will foster trust. Time is essential, and rushed interviews inevitably jeopardise a sensitive approach. Unfortunately, psychiatrists often have to make the best of less than ideal conditions. The setting may be inappropriate (for example, a busy hospital emergency department or a police station) or there may be a lack of resources (for example, pressures on staff because of long waiting lists).

The psychiatrist will begin the interview by explaining its purpose, then listen empathically to the person while observing his or her behaviour and emotional responses and monitoring the developing relationship. The psychiatrist's apparent passivity may provoke anxiety in the patient. But the process (which can include purposeful silences) is indeed active. The psychiatrist is constantly alert to the person's story and needs and, even if not firing a volley of questions, will be using a set of strategies to help the flow of information. Asking the person to 'go on' or to 'say more' are simple examples, as is repeating the person's last phrase as a question. Non-verbal gestures—such as a receptive nod of the head, a facial expression of increasing interest, and leaning forward—are commonly used.

As the interview unfolds, the psychiatrist begins to explore a range of areas, first in a non-directive manner and then using direct questions to clarify details. Eventually, 'closed' questions, answered by 'yes' or 'no', can search out vital information which may not yet have emerged. While the story is being sought, the psychiatrist seeks to understand the person's circumstances. The problems facing a young mother soon after the birth of her first child are of course different to those of an elderly man who has just lost his wife.

Some aspects of the interview call for special sensitivity. For example, when inquiring about sexual experience the psychiatrist must use considerable tact. Due to guilt and embarrassment, people may hesitate to talk about extramarital affairs, homosexual experiences, sexual fantasies and impotence. Probing these areas will wait until later in the interview or another occasion. Other areas of potential sensitivity include trauma, such as sexual abuse or the death of a sibling. If the person is tearful, the psychiatrist acknowledges the distress and encourages the person to express feelings further, within the security of a growing trust.

The psychiatrist virtually always raises the topic of suicide, even though it may seem irrelevant at first. Self-destructive impulses are very common in psychiatric illness. Given the profound nature of questions of life and death, this approach must be gentle (see Chapter 19).

No two interviews are ever the same. Apart from sensitivity, the psychiatrist's awareness of the powerful, potentially disturbing effects that psychiatric illness has on communication leads to different approaches. For example, an obsessional person needs to provide a highly detailed and intricate factual account but tends to maintain control over feelings, and the psychiatrist will allow for this. On the other hand, a person who is suspicious and angry due to the illness may cross-examine the psychiatrist and question his or her motives. While it would be natural to react to this hostility, the psychiatrist must recognise the person's underlying desperate need to retain control—in this instance by seeking, at appropriate points, the person's permission to continue their discussion.

If a person is inattentive, forgetful or confused, the psychiatrist attempts to establish his or her grasp of the surroundings and then moves promptly to gather information from a relative or carer. This is because a person with impaired cognitive functioning, such as in dementia, may not tolerate a lengthy interview due to mental fatigue. Questions to the elderly are put clearly and explicitly, as there may be a hearing, visual or other loss.

The presence of a psychosis such as schizophrenia or mania requires a special set of skills. They are used to make sense of someone who is showing agitated or bizarre behaviour, who is preoccupied with thoughts entirely unrelated to the task at hand, and whose communication would be unintelligible to the ordinary person. Interviewing in these circumstances may look disorganised to the observer, as the psychiatrist has to gather information piecemeal, as it is offered.

People with poor or no English need sensitive attention. While some information may be picked up from observation, a professional interpreter is usually needed for a detailed interview, although a family member may have to play this role. Differences in values, culture and socio-economic background can be as great a barrier to communication as is a foreign language. Psychiatrists must modify their style to 'join' effectively with their patients.

Psychiatrists rely heavily on the co-operation of relatives. Patients rarely set out to mislead, but self-observation is notoriously unreliable in many people with a psychiatric disorder, and the perspective of someone close provides invaluable information about the patient, the illness and its impact. However all observations are coloured by emotions and may be biased, and the psychiatrist must appreciate the potentially devastating effect that a serious psychiatric illness has on the family, and its influence on their objectivity.

Given a fundamental responsibility to the patient and a wish to help family members, the psychiatrist may be caught in a cleft stick. Every effort is made to seek the patient's consent to approach the family and to exercise discretion about confidentiality and family secrets. Only in the rare instance does the psychiatrist bypass the patient (see Chapter 18).

## What is covered in the interview, and why?

After asking for the person's name, address, age, marital and family status, occupation, and how they came to be sent there, the psychiatrist turns to the person's concerns, gathering details about the following:

- The main problems and when they began, how they progressed and what is happening now. A beginning point (for example, the first symptom or events such as the death of a spouse) in the story is identified. The psychiatrist then clarifies the nature and severity of any stress factors in the person's life, and how they are being dealt with.
- Details of the effect of the problems on the person's life (for example, work, relationships, ability to care for oneself).
- The treatment, if any, to this point, including what has been tried, by whom and with what results.
- The relationship of the psychiatric features to any relevant medical condition (the psychiatrist's medical training comes into play here).

This case history illustrates the ground covered in a typical interview:

*Lee was a 45-year-old married mother of three children, working as a computer programmer. She was referred by her family doctor following a suicide attempt. She described six months of depressive symptoms which began two months after she had separated from her husband. She experienced lowered mood, inability to take pleasure in her usual daily activities, loss of weight, feelings of worthlessness and insomnia. More recently she had had trouble concentrating on her work because of intrusive suicidal thoughts. Two weeks before, Lee had stopped work and was having increasing difficulty caring for herself and her children. Five days later she was taken by her eldest daughter to her doctor who, following a sensitive appreciation of her plight, diagnosed her as suffering from a depressive illness, prescribed anti-depressant medication and made arrangements for her to see a psychiatrist. The day before the appointment she had, while alone, taken an overdose of the tablets and left a note describing herself as a 'failed wife and mother'.*

Since many psychiatric illnesses recur, the link between the current episode and any previous ones is strong (see Chapter 22). This is why psychiatrists enquire about previous illnesses, as well as about admissions to hospital and treatments received. If, as in the following case history, a person refers to a 'nervous breakdown', then a thorough description of symptoms and of past treatment is documented, as this term can cover every situation from two days sick leave for anxiety to a long period of hospitalisation for psychosis.

> *A woman described her treatment in psychiatric hospital ten years previously for a 'nervous breakdown'. The psychiatrist found evidence that this had been a manic illness, in that she was excitable, euphoric, heard voices and thought she was Jesus Christ. She was treated with a tranquilliser for six months and took part in a group programme. She had been well since.*

A focus on any medical illness, past or present, follows logically, particularly when it relates to the present psychiatric condition. A full list of medications is always recorded as part of this assessment.

> *A 55-year-old woman had a debilitating form of rheumatoid arthritis which was compounded by a state of despair because of an increase in pain and disability and reduced response to her anti-rheumatic medication. But her despair had increased immediately following the introduction of a new drug and, given this drug's potential to induce a depressed mood as an occasional side-effect, her medications were reassessed and the likely offending drug withdrawn.*

'The patient who has the illness is more important than the illness the patient has.' This saying sums up the importance of the person's family and personal background, which are a wealth of information. A person's life-story begins with the family of origin—a description of parents and their relationship; siblings, their order of birth and the nature of their relationships; the family atmosphere especially as it affects and is affected by the patient; and any history of psychiatric illness in any family member. The person's life story is a hallmark of the psychiatric case history.

The psychiatrist gathers a range of information in order to build up a picture of the uniqueness of the person and his or her world—a sort of vivid biography. While no list can be complete, this is the kind of information recorded, with different emphasis in each case:

- complications of the mother's pregnancy, feeding problems, achievement of normal 'milestones';
- childhood hyperactivity, bed-wetting, phobias, friendships and play, major childhood illnesses like asthma;
- school performance, disciplinary trouble, peer relationships;
- adolescence adjustment difficulties;
- employment record and satisfaction;
- age at first menstruation, menstrual problems, age and complications of menopause;
- sexual attitudes, activities, orientation and dysfunctions;
- courtship, relationship with spouse or de facto, state of current marriage, any past marriages or divorces;
- children and their relationship with the patient;
- social network—family and friends.

Here are two examples of the pictures built up by this process:

*An 18-year-old student sought help for a bout of severe bingeing and vomiting. She was the youngest of three daughters. Her mother was a 45-year-old primary school teacher and her father a 50-year-old electrician. Both were described by their daughter as strict, a result of their strong religious beliefs. She stressed that their marriage was 'a farce—they never talked or touched'. The atmosphere was usually tense. She was not close to either parent but did confide in her sisters until they left the family home a year earlier.*

*A young man was referred by the university counselling service because of difficulty in concentration and abrupt deterioration in his marks. He was extremely shy, had been a loner throughout school and as an adult had no friends. He had never had a girlfriend, had not had any sexual contact and pursued solitary activities including model-making. He had little contact with his family—'I'd rather be alone, people don't interest me'. But his lack of social contact did trouble him—'Maybe I shouldn't be like this'.*

Often the psychiatrist will draw a family tree to keep track of the detail of family relationships (see Vincent Van Gogh's family tree on page 16).

## Examination of the mental state

While drawing out the life story, the psychiatrist's second task is to examine the person's mental state—that is, the person's current psychological functioning. The history may date back for years, but the mental state provides a snapshot of how that person is at the present time. The history may be vague or in some instances even impossible to obtain, but the mental state can always be assessed. The psychiatrist depends on the mental state evaluation in just the same way as the doctor in general medicine relies on the physical examination to support the history.

To begin with, careful note will be taken of the person's general appearance and behaviour, from dress and grooming to demeanour, eye contact, over-familiarity, withdrawal and so on. Even apparently trivial behaviours—'closes his eyes when talking about his wife', 'paces around the room' or 'laughs uproariously at his own joke'—provide clues to the person's personality and disorder.

*A 45-year-old overweight woman was dressed in brightly coloured clothes, wore heavy make-up and had purple-coloured fingernails. Her general personal care was clearly inadequate, her hair unwashed and tousled. Her movements were rapid; she had trouble remaining seated and constantly fidgeted throughout the interview. Her manner lacked appropriate restraint, as she winked and tried to touch the psychiatrist. All these behaviours alerted the psychiatrist to her likely manic state.*

Because of its critical importance in communication, the psychiatrist pays particular attention to the rate, volume, quality and tone of speech.

*He displayed minimal spontaneous speech and answered questions briefly. When he did speak, he did so slowly with long pauses and in a soft voice. This pattern was a reflection of his exceeding shyness which suggested a diagnosis of an 'avoidant' personality style (see Chapter 11).*

As speech reflects thought, both are examined closely together. Two aspects in particular are carefully teased out—form and content. Form refers to the organisation of thought, to how logical it is. The typical abnormality is the thought disorder in schizophrenia, where loose links between thoughts amount in severe cases to incoherence.

*The thoughts were highly disorganised, with evidence of loose associations, jumping from one idea to another and the occasional made up word: 'In the case of cats, it is always to be said. Why did you go? Following the archensivism, God will triumph and yesterday the car improved'.*

Content covers aberrations of thinking of various types, such as phobias, obsessions, overvalued ideas and delusions. The latter are false ideas, held with unshakeable conviction, which do not fit with the person's cultural background. For example, a patient may firmly believe that the CIA is plotting against him and ruining his business, or a mother may hold the horrid thought that her new-born baby is a devil that must be destroyed.

Disturbed perception—of one or more of the five senses—is the most significant feature of the mental state in a range of severe mental illnesses. The key abnormalities are hallucinations and illusions.

### Mini-mental state testing

#### Orientation
What is the (year) (season) (date) (day) (month)?
Where are we: (country) (town) (hospital) (ward)?

#### Registration
Name three objects. Allow one second to say each. Then ask the patient to repeat all three. Repeat them until the patient learns all three.

#### Attention and calculation
Serial 7s (that is, subtract 7 from 100 and keep subtracting 7 from the answer you get). Stop after five answers.
Alternatively, spell 'world' backwards.

#### Recall
Ask for the three objects repeated above.

#### Language and copying
Name a pencil, and watch.
Repeat the following: 'No ifs, ands or buts'.
Follow a three-stage command: 'Pick up a paper with your right hand, fold it in half and put it on the floor'.
Read and obey the following: CLOSE YOUR EYES.
Write a sentence.
Copy a design.

*A man described hearing two male voices arguing with each other, commenting on his actions and commanding him to do things like 'punch your brother' (auditory hallucinations). He heard them often during the day, every day, and at times they led him to assault his brother. He often looked over his shoulder during the interview, appearing to respond to the voices.*

Every psychiatric illness has some effect on mood and emotions. Their quality, range and appropriateness are therefore of particular relevance. We are all familiar with the many types of emotions. The terms used by psychiatrists to describe mood include elevated, depressed, suspicious, irritable, guilt-ridden, anxious and perplexed. And the mood may be labile (swinging), restricted in scope, blunted or flat. The appropriateness of the mood to the person's circumstances is all-important.

> *She felt unhappy and pessimistic, conveying a doleful demeanour. She did not respond to any humorous comment and displayed a restricted emotional range.*

Our higher mental functions are extremely vulnerable to psychiatric disturbance, particularly in conditions associated with brain damage such as dementia and head injury. Neuropsychologists usually assess these functions, but the psychiatrist will use basic tests to check them. Problems occur in such areas as concentration, orientation for time and place, recent and remote memory, intellectual ability and judgement (capacity for rational decision-making). One popular test used particularly in the elderly is the mini-mental state examination (see the table on page 53).

Finally, the psychiatrist forms a judgement as to the person's attitude to and understanding of their mental illness, its cause, consequences and treatment. This judgement is one of the most important, because it will determine to what extent the person can be a 'partner' in the treatment.

> *He experienced florid, elaborate delusions (that the police wanted to detain him because of his 'exceptional powers' to tune in to their coded messages) and auditory hallucinations, and showed a complete lack of insight into his current condition. He repeatedly insisted that he was 'perfectly well', did not require medication and was only in hospital because the government and police had conspired to imprison him; he intended to contact the media to expose this 'devilish' plot and demanded his discharge. In a situation like this one, the psychiatrist may be forced to impose treatment against the person's will but in his best interests (see Chapter 18).*

## Physical examination

Because physical and mental illness often go hand-in-hand (an obvious example being alcoholism), a thorough physical examination is essential, although it is not necessarily conducted by the psychiatrist. Sometimes it is more appropriately done by the family doctor or specialist physician.

## Bringing it all together

All doctors, including psychiatrists, will summarise details of a person's history and the results of the examination so as to crystallise their thoughts in preparation for diagnosis and planning treatment. Who is this person? What is his or her problem? How and why did it arise? The answers to these essential questions are brought together in a summary, like this one:

> *A 45-year-old, previously well, married lawyer had gradually developed a series of bodily symptoms whose cause remained a mystery to her doctors. These had occurred in the setting of major losses, including the death of her sister to whom she was very close. She had a family history of major mental illness, her mother having suicided when the patient was ten. She had few friends and an unsupportive husband.*

The next step is making a diagnosis, which is a judgement about which condition represents, most accurately, the person's clinical features. When this is not feasible because the assessment is complex or incomplete (for example, a full series of neuropsychological tests is needed), the psychiatrist juggles a set of so-called 'provisional diagnoses' until a definitive judgement can be reached.

As in the rest of medical practice, diagnosis points to 'prognosis', which is the short-hand prediction of the likely outcome of the person's condition, with or without treatment. In psychiatry, this is by no means clearcut. Many factors play a role, such as personality, the degree of social support, co-operation with treatment, continuing stress, and complicating aspects such as drug or alcohol abuse. Prognosis is often conditional on one or more of these factors so that, even though the natural course of the illness may be favourable, those factors may affect the outcome adversely. Summing-up the prognosis as simply 'good' or 'bad' fails to do justice to the intricacy of prediction in the field of human behaviour. If questioned, the psychiatrist is likely to list both positive and negative prognostic features and bring these together. For example, a person's youth and solid personality prior to the illness are positive factors, but the severity and persistence of his hallucinations in the absence of any major precipitating stress does not encourage optimism. Predictions are therefore tentative.

## The psychiatrist's 'formulation'

Psychiatrists have been the first to recognise the inadequacy of a diagnostic label to capture the richness of a person's condition. They have compensated for this by various means, particularly the 'diagnostic formulation'. This is an account which builds on the summary by adding a discussion of the causes that predispose, precipitate and maintain the illness. All these elements, along with empathic understanding and attempts at explanation, are brought together to make sense of the patient (see Chapter 2).

This ability to 'formulate' is one of the consummate skills a psychiatrist has to master. The following case history illustrates the process:

*Mustafa, a single, 25-year-old storeman and the eldest son in a Turkish family, presented with an eighteen-month history of altered eating behaviour and subsequent weight loss to the point of physical collapse. His symptoms developed in the context of family conflict although there was no family history of psychiatric illness.*

*After failed out-patient treatment, Mustafa was admitted to a psychiatric unit with continuing weight loss and prominent suicidal ideas. A diagnosis of anorexia nervosa was arrived at, based on his failure to maintain body weight appropriate to age and height, a morbid fear of gaining weight and a disturbed body image (he regarded himself as obese). The plan of management was to set immediate objectives including close observation, particularly since he expressed suicidal ideas. This was judged as best done in hospital because of concern about Mustafa's deteriorated physical state. A thorough physical investigation was done, as was correction of nutritional and metabolic deficiencies. After his psychiatric and medical safety had been attended to, a re-feeding programme was proposed during which his relationship with the psychiatrist would be consolidated and his family assessed.*

Following on from this summary, and from details of past and proposed treatment, the psychiatrist's 'formulation' would look something like this:

Although anorexia nervosa is rare in young men its emergence in this case is understandable. Major family issues, particularly the importance of traditional and cultural values, are central in appreciating his condition. Mustafa's illness evolved in the context of long-standing family disharmony. The clash between cultural tradition and assimilation had led to immense tension between son and father. Mustafa's divided loyalties meant that he was a partial member not only of his family but also of the Turkish community. On the other hand, his position in the Australian community, as an immigrant whose primary language was Turkish, was ambiguous.

Thus, Mustafa found himself precariously straddling two cultures with no opportunity to discuss his concerns, resulting in ever-increasing distress. His personality while well-balanced was not assertive or extroverted, and so expression of his frustration in a hostile family was not possible. Furthermore, such expression may have been culturally inappropriate.

Mustafa's view of himself as 'too fat' may have been precipitated by prevailing Australian attitudes. His dieting may also have been a means of rebelling against a Turkish culture that tends to associate a large physique with strength, prosperity and attractiveness.

As he saw himself reflected as a failure in the eyes of his father, his 'success' as a dieter may have perpetuated this behaviour. It was difficult to give up something in which he had finally succeeded. And his illness had a major impact on the family. While they were busy caring for him as the ill member, this may have served as a distraction from issues revolving around his striving for independence and their difficulties in responding. His illness could also be seen as expressing the family's troubles. His indirect ventilation of anger toward the family may also have perpetuated the pattern, as unexpressed anger is often a prominent emotion in anorexia nervosa.

This formulation is many-layered, relatively complex and tentative. By no means is it the last word or in fact the 'truth' but rather a framework to guide the psychiatrist's work with both patient and family. It will have to be revised as the clinical picture becomes more elaborate.

## How does the psychiatrist tackle therapy?

Having completed a formulation as illustrated in Mustafa's case, how does the psychiatrist set about this task? The first step is to devise a treatment plan using the biopsychosocial framework in which immediate, short- and long-term strategies are mapped out and, just as importantly, to convey this to the patient.

The rights of the patient to be fully informed about his or her condition and its treatment, in terms he or she understands, is implicit in the duty of doctors to obtain informed consent. The patient is familiarised with the nature, purpose, benefits and risks of the proposed treatment, and of any alternative ones. Limits of confidentiality are specified. Care is taken to ensure that consent is freely given, without duress. If a patient is not competent to provide consent, it is usually obtained from a close relative or guardian.

Informed consent in relation to any medical treatment is problematic, but especially so in psychiatry. Can people lacking professional knowledge ever be fully informed about a proposed treatment? The person's mental state may interfere with comprehension, or make it impossible. The psychiatrist will therefore determine whether a person is sufficiently competent to make an informed judgement about a proposed treatment and, if not, will assume this responsibility. Consent is particularly important when the treatment is known to produce marked side-effects, for example, the risk of a serious disorder of bodily movement with the long-term use of anti-psychotic medication.

The particular problems affecting respect for autonomy and informed consent are sharply drawn in psychiatry when people simply must have medication as part of their long-term care. Medications may cause unpleasant side-effects and some disorders may result in poor judgement and loss of insight, so that people fail to appreciate the need for treatment or do not believe it will help. Some conditions, like mania, are 'pleasant' and people may resist treatment in order to hold on to their feeling of euphoria.

The process of treatment varies considerably from one person to another. For instance, the emphasis is quite different for a person presenting for the first time than for one suffering recurrence of a long-standing disorder. Who treats, where they treat and the ingredients of treatment given depend on the nature and stage of the illness, the person's strengths and vulnerabilities, available social supports and current stressful factors.

## Where and by whom?

People may receive treatment from a psychiatrist in a variety of settings ranging from a quiet office to the hectic atmosphere of a hospital admission unit. The psychiatrist may function individually or as a member of a multidisciplinary team with, for example, psychologists, nurses, occupational therapists and social workers.

Most psychological distress is initially dealt with by the family doctor, who determines whether referral to a mental health specialist is called for. Common reasons for choosing a psychiatrist are that diagnosis is uncertain, that the person has failed to respond to initial treatment, or that a co-existing medical condition is complicating treatment.

A major decision for the psychiatrist is whether admission to hospital is warranted. Several factors operate in this judgement. Perhaps the most crucial is the need for a protective, supportive situation for people who may be extremely perplexed, disorganised, depressed, psychotic or dangerous, or the need to remove them from a destructive social environment. In-patient care provides a structured setting in which acute symptoms can be treated and attention given to the overall welfare of the person and their family.

Other reasons for admission are less urgent, such as to permit a detailed assessment or to begin or continue complex treatment.

Long-term institutional care has become relatively rare. When required, it is more commonly delivered in community residential settings. Such care is needed by people who, because of the enduring effects of their illness, loss of social skills and marked dependency, cannot cope independently or are liable to be exploited by others (such as ruthless landlords).

## Compulsory treatment

People with mental illness may be deprived of their liberty and treated against their wishes. This is a remarkable situation, unlike any other area of medical practice. In rare cases, people who are infectious, like those with tuberculosis or cholera, may be detained to protect others. But compulsory treatment of the mentally ill is an everyday issue. In the not too distant past, virtually all psychiatric admissions to public hospitals were involuntary and, though psychiatry has moved rapidly towards a state where mentally ill patients are treated similarly to any other patient, the spectre of compulsion still looms.

Why are mentally ill people subject to laws which override their civil liberties to an extent only matched in convicted criminals? The first answer is that it is in their best interests. Mental illness affects the capacity to judge what is in one's interests. Thus, depressed people often consider themselves guilty and worthless, see no future and believe that this is an accurate judgement rather than the product of an illness. In this state of mind they may attempt suicide or make no effort to care for and feed themselves. The psychiatrist, aware that such people will take an entirely different view when the depression lifts, accepts a duty to protect them from themselves and to promote recovery by offering treatment even in the face of resistance. Given that the world is full of people who act against their own best interests, concern for the mentally ill relates to the fact that it is not the person but rather the disorder itself which generates self-damaging behaviour. The second reason for compulsion is that psychiatric disorders may lead to behaviour endangering those with the disorders and others.

Suicide was a criminal offence until relatively recently, and those who attempted it could be detained under criminal law. It is a small step to confine those who threaten the act. The common law confers the right, if not the duty, to prevent people harming themselves or others, and mental health law is an extension of this. Society's long-standing fear of the mentally ill contributes to its willingness to compel treatment.

Mental health laws vary in terms of when compulsory treatment is justified. They usually allow compulsory treatment of people considered a danger to themselves or to others. Some laws require concrete evidence of aggressive or suicidal behaviour. But most consider potential risk, such as people stating their intent to harm themselves or others, or making preparations by, for example, accumulating lethal substances.

Detention in the interest of the person's 'health' is a more difficult matter. Some laws do not define health, whereas others provide criteria in terms of people's inability to care for themselves to the point where their health and safety are threatened. The 'health' criterion is controversial in that it provides wide powers of compulsion on the basis that anyone with a treatable psychiatric disorder impairs his or her health by refusing help.

## The procedure of committal

The usual practice is that an application for committal is made by a relative or other concerned person. It may be a member of the public, or a professional such as a social worker, or a police officer. The application has to be supported by recommendations from one or more medical practitioners, in some cases specifically a psychiatrist.

Short-term committals lasting from two to seven days are intended for urgent admission of the acutely disturbed person for assessment with or without treatment. Extended committals lasting usually from two to six weeks are intended for assessment and treatment. Many mental health laws also provide for long-term committals which allow supervision and compulsory treatment of people, both within hospitals and in the community. These sometimes impose treatment on people who are relatively stable on the assumption that they will deteriorate without such treatment.

Safeguards to protect patients' rights have been an important development in mental health law. Tribunals automatically review all committals, and patients can appeal to them for reassessment. These tribunals (often called mental health review boards) usually have legal, medical and lay representatives, though sometimes the role is given solely to a judge. By contrast, a new legal formalism, particularly in the United States, has introduced elaborate 'due process' procedures, similar to criminal procedures. In some US states, full judicial hearings are necessary for all but brief emergency committals, with lawyers, juries, judges, rules of evidence and right of appeal. These trials are costly and, despite attempts to prevent it, often marked more by form than by content.

Committal removes the right of people to determine their place of residence and treatment. Many laws place constraints on seclusion, psychosurgery (see Chapter 20) and electro-convulsive therapy (ECT) both for committed patients and, to some extent, for voluntary patients. In the case of ECT the objective is to ensure that it is properly and appropriately used, but in some parts of the United States and Europe it is effectively outlawed.

## The multi-disciplinary approach

People have complex and varied needs, and a multi-disciplinary approach has been devised to meet them. A range of mental health professionals— psychiatrists, psychiatric nurses, clinical psychologists, occupational therapists and social workers—contribute their complementary skills in both assessment and therapy. The psychiatric nurse may play a pivotal role in carefully observing the person's mental state and behaviour; the psychologist may be involved in testing mental abilities; the occupational therapist may assess vocational and living skills, and the social worker may investigate the family circumstances.

In the past, the person's family, both immediate and extended, were not seen as potential aides to the professional team, but psychiatrists are drawing them increasingly into this role. This is particularly so in the era of deinstitutionalisation, when psychiatric hospitals have been shut down and their patients transferred to 'facilities' in the community—often the family home. Hundreds of thousands of such people now depend increasingly on family caregivers. This is not to disregard the need of family members for support in their own right or for bolstering of their capacity as continuing carers. Families of people with long-term conditions are particularly in need. The demands and difficulties of frequently recurring or worsening illness are enormous.

That people take an active part in their own care—to which many professionals contribute—is fundamental to the notion of treatment. And self-help groups, which may include family members, are a valuable support to professional treatment. They offer strength in numbers and reduce feelings of isolation, alienation and stigma. In Australia, for instance, the first such group, GROW, began in 1957. Many have developed since then, such as the Schizophrenia Fellowship, the Obsessive-Compulsive Support Group and the Agoraphobia Support Group. Groups for relatives include the Association of Relatives and Friends of the Emotionally and Mentally Ill (ARAFEMI).

## How long should treatment continue?

The pattern of mental illness may take several forms. It may be brief with full recovery from symptoms. Recovery may be followed by recurrent episodes. It may be long-term, either stable in nature or relentless in its progress.

For people with an illness from which full recovery is expected, the psychiatrist intervenes actively to identify and possibly remedy the factors causing the illness, to shorten the episode, and to minimise or prevent complications. By contrast, people with a stable or progressive condition need continuing treatment to limit symptoms, to provide support especially at times of stress, and to minimise deterioration. For illnesses which recur, long-term treatment focuses on maintaining health between episodes and preventing relapse.

Let us consider the following case and its treatment to illustrate these points:

*A middle-aged man with symptoms of depression also describes problems with his marriage; he has recently begun treatment for high blood pressure, and admits to drinking excessively to 'block out problems'.*

Immediate aspects of this man's treatment include:

- determining whether treatment for the blood pressure is a factor in the onset of the depression (some anti-hypertensives, as we have noted, can cause depression);
- estimating his alcohol intake and judging its effect on his physical health;
- assessing his physical health generally (physical illness may accompany depression);
- assessing the severity of the depression, particularly the risk of self-neglect or suicide;
- searching out details of treatment of any past episodes of depression;
- interviewing his wife about the mood change and their marital difficulty, with particular attention to exploring cause and effect.

If the man is severely depressed, he will be admitted to hospital for further evaluation, to ensure his safety, to help him give up alcohol, and to begin treatment.

His initial treatment in hospital will include:

- treating alcohol withdrawal, should its symptoms emerge;

- prescription of anti-depressants if the diagnosis of depression is confirmed;
- individual psychotherapy to explore contributing stress factors;
- psychotherapy with the couple to clarify and lessen difficulties in their marriage.

His continuing treatment may include:

- further prescription of anti-depressants to prevent relapse, with its possible long-term use if he has had previous depressive episodes;
- individual psychotherapy to encourage and assist more fundamental change in his personality, supported by couple therapy if conflict continues.

In this chapter we have set out the psychiatrist's tasks in general terms. In the following chapters, which deal with the wide variety of psychiatric disorders, we will look at how particular illnesses are assessed and treated.

# 6  *Coping with Stress*

In some psychological conditions, symptoms clearly result from stressful life events. They may range from mild anxiety to a temporary mental breakdown. Before describing this group of illnesses we must explain what we mean by 'stress', 'crisis', 'coping' and 'defences'.

## Stress

This word comes from the Latin '*stringere*', which means to draw tight or compress. It has been commonly used since the seventeenth century to describe human experiences of hardship, adversity or affliction. It conveys the idea of being subjected to extreme forces, of resisting their distorting effects in an effort to maintain physical and psychological well-being, and ultimately of returning to the original state. Stress usually refers to actions or situations that place excessive physical or psychological demands upon people and threaten to unbalance them. Major life events are sources of stress to which we must adjust.

## Crisis

Related to stress is the notion of life crisis—which in psychological terms is an imbalance between the demands presented by a particular problem and the resources available to deal with them. Our usual methods of handling the situation do not work, and neither do attempts to minimise the problem. There are two kinds of crisis—developmental and accidental. Transitional periods in the life cycle—such as adolescence (vividly illustrated in J. D. Salinger's *The Catcher in the Rye*), mid-life and retirement (beautifully captured in the film, *On Golden Pond*)—are typified by emotional upheaval, which leads to a loss of personal equilibrium. These developmental crises are predictable and experienced by everybody. Accidental

Back to Normal.

crises, on the other hand, are associated with sudden, unexpected and distressing life events involving loss, threat or conflict, and our psychological reactions to them.

Crises, while they do overlap, can usefully be divided into the following categories:

- Loss, which covers a wide range of life events both physical and abstract, including loss of a loved one, of one's health, of a bodily part or function (for example, following a stroke), or even of one's sense of pride and self-confidence. The typical reaction is grief, in which a shifting between psychological states is experienced.
- Change, in which new life circumstances such as marriage, retirement or migration throw up difficulties and so threaten our psychological well-being.
- Interpersonal relationships, where difficulties either in the family or beyond, intimate or superficial, are the source of substantial stress.
- Conflict, where we are immobilised by a dilemma and unable to choose between options for fear of making the wrong decision. The conflict may operate beyond our immediate awareness. Hamlet's indecisiveness is a perfect example:

*Whether 'tis nobler in the mind to suffer*
*The slings and arrows of outrageous fortune,*
*Or to take arms against a sea of troubles,*
*And by opposing end them?*

## Coping

The strategies we use to grapple with a crisis are called coping mechanisms. They help us to reduce our distress and to adapt more effectively. Coping is a problem-solving effort which enables us to return to a balanced state so as to be able to face and manage the continuing tasks and challenges of life.

In order to cope with stress, we must first be aware of the nature of the stress and of its implications. 'Coping' comes from a Greek word meaning to strike. This suggests a deliberate response and covers a range of activities from everyday, realistic problem-solving to more elaborate manoeuvres. Skilled coping is a flexible, rational attempt at mastery.

Coping has been classified in many ways, depending on whether it is cognitive (that is, adopting a specific way of thinking), or behavioural (that is, taking a certain action). However, people in crisis usually resort to several strategies, a blend of the cognitive and the behavioural. These are some common examples of coping strategies:

- realistically avoiding the source of stress, either by distraction or withdrawal;
- seeking appropriate help from family, friends or professionals;
- reducing tension and other unpleasant stress-related emotions by using various methods of relaxation;
- recognising the challenging features of a stressful situation;
- applying problem-solving manoeuvres—identifying the problem, clarifying its nature, mapping out possible options for dealing with it, choosing the most appropriate option and monitoring its effectiveness;
- drawing on past experience relevant to the stress;
- using humour to achieve a more balanced perspective ('It could be worse');
- adopting a stoical attitude ('What will be will be, getting upset won't help').

Despite this array of options, when we are faced with a major crisis where intense feelings predominate, the coping skills of even the most psychologically robust person may well become less flexible and adequate.

# Defence

Defence, which is a form of coping, has developed a specific meaning derived from its origins in psychoanalytic theory (see Chapter 3). The so-called 'mechanisms of defence' are unconsciously determined—that is, they are beyond our immediate awareness. We consciously choose and voluntarily implement the coping strategies described above, but we are not directly aware of the defences we use. Except for a small group of 'mature' mechanisms, they tend to operate inflexibly. They protect us from unpleasant emotions such as anxiety, guilt and shame, which are themselves the result of conflict or other forms of threat. Defences also provide a breathing space, particularly in an emergency, so that other methods of coping can be explored. Judging whether a defence helps or not can in some circumstances be very difficult.

Defences have been classified in various ways, first by the child psychoanalyst Anna Freud, the daughter of Sigmund Freud. Freud himself recognised the vital role of defences in maintaining psychological balance, and he described several types. But it was Anna Freud who expanded this work

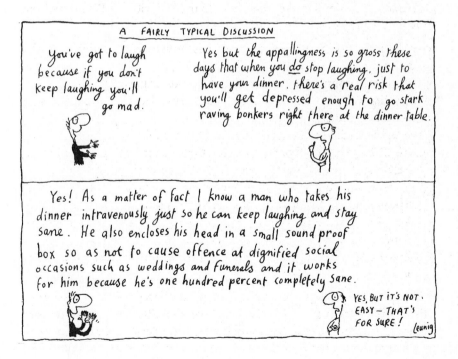

A FAIRLY TYPICAL DISCUSSION

You've got to laugh because if you don't keep laughing you'll go mad.

Yes but the appallingness is so gross these days that when you _do_ stop laughing, just to have your dinner, there's a real risk that you'll get depressed enough to go stark raving bonkers right there at the dinner table.

Yes! As a matter of fact I know a man who takes his dinner intravenously just so he can keep laughing and stay sane. He also encloses his head in a small sound proof box so as not to cause offence at dignified social occasions such as weddings and funerals and it works for him because he's one hundred percent completely sane.

YES, BUT IT'S NOT EASY — THAT'S FOR SURE!

leunig

and systematically grouped the defences. In her classical text, *The Ego and the Mechanism of Defence*, she took each defence in turn and vividly showed how they operate in everyday psychological life and in abnormal mental states. Freud, the proud father, acknowledged her contribution in this charming quote:

> ... the ego makes use of various methods of fulfilling its task, i.e., to put it in general terms, of avoiding anxiety, danger and unpleasure. We call these devices defence mechanisms. Out knowledge of them is as yet incomplete. Anna Freud's book (1936) has given us our first insight into their multiplicity and their manifold significance.

An ingenious system building on Anna Freud is that of George Vaillant, an American psychiatrist, who has contributed much to our understanding of defences. He groups them according to their level of maturity, ranging from 'psychotic' (level 1) through 'immature' and 'neurotic' to 'mature' (level 4). The mature mechanisms closely resemble the coping strategies already described. Since Vaillant's scheme is complex we will list only some representative examples, with brief illustrations from everyday life or from a medical setting:

*Denial* is the process by which we minimise unacceptable thoughts, feelings or impulses, and so keep distressing and threatening aspects of reality at bay. For example, a woman told that she has a terminal illness behaves as if she is unaware of the diagnosis, or a man returns to strenuous work following a severe heart attack, against medical advice.

*Repression* is the mechanism by which an unacceptable impulse or idea, or a painful emotion, is pushed out of consciousness and so is actively forgotten by being excluded from awareness. The repressed material is still active, and continues to affect our behaviour. Common examples are when we forget a well-known name, particularly when the name has some unpleasant association—or are unable to recall a vivid dream we had last night.

*Regression* is the return to an earlier stage of psychological functioning. We behave in ways more appropriate to that stage, usually child or infant-like, when there were no responsibilities and when dependence on a parental figure was appropriate. For example, a 5-year-old boy reverts to thumb sucking and babble talk upon the arrival of an infant sibling—a reflection of his jealousy and feelings of rejection.

*Rationalisation* is plausible but invalid thinking used to avoid stressful reality. For example, a man in a coronary care unit declares, on the death of a neighbouring patient, 'He was very old and I suppose too frail to deal with his heart attack'. Or someone facing retrenchment murmurs, 'I'm sure Mary was fired because she wasn't up to the job'.

*Intellectualisation* is the reliance on a bland account of an important personal matter with much attention to trivial detail and avoidance of expression of feelings in order to keep them at bay. For example, a woman talks about her illness as if she was reading about it in a dry textbook—as if it was not really happening to her.

*Displacement* is the redirection of feelings towards an object, person or situation that is less threatening than the actual source of the feelings. This eases the distress, although the underlying issues persist. For example, a woman awaiting the results of the biopsy of a lump in her breast tells her surgeon, 'I don't know whether you noted my husband in the waiting room; he's a very sick man, he has terrible asthma. I'm really worried about him'. Or a mother, whose marriage is full of tension, is constantly focused on her daughter's handling of school pressures.

*Projection* is the unconscious attribution of our own unacknowledged feelings, thoughts and qualities to other people. Disturbing feelings such as shame, fear and disgust are avoided by projecting them on to others. For people with schizophrenia, projection takes the form of frank delusions, that is, false beliefs held with conviction and usually concerned with persecution. In most situations, it is a tendency to see our own distress through others. For example, a renal dialysis patient who states, 'I have to conceal my shunt because people are disgusted by it', is really saying, 'I am disgusted by my shunt'. Or a woman with a lump in her breast who exclaims, 'I don't like the expression on your face, you look very concerned', is really saying, 'I suspect something awful, and I am very concerned', and so avoiding learning the truth.

*Introjection* is the taking on of qualities of either a feared or an admired person. Thus a young man takes on the characteristics of his deceased father to lessen his sense of loss and to relieve any tension arising out of mixed feelings towards his father.

*Sublimation* is satisfying an impulse by transforming it from a socially unacceptable to a valued form of activity. So, for example, an unconsciously angry man excels in vigorous contact sport.

*Reaction formation* is the conversion of an unacceptable unconscious impulse into its opposite form. Thus a man contemptuous of his own emotional weaknesses might become a counsellor of the sick.

*Compensation* or *counter-dependency* is an extreme form of denial, which usually shows in the way in which a person acts. With an intense need to be active, energetic and joyful, the person 'compensates' for limitations imposed by illness by 'going flat out'. For example, after a heart attack and having been near to death, a man takes on extra responsibilities at work and plays new sports, reassuring himself that he is fully alive and will remain so. His reprieve makes him live life to the full. A bereaved woman instead of grieving the loss of her husband indulges in many more social activities than before his death, and so avoids the distress of mourning.

## Adaptation, or bringing it together

'He knows not his own strength that has not met adversity' wrote the dramatist Ben Jonson nearly four hundred years ago. His observation about our everyday responses to life events lies at the heart of a model devised by the American psychiatrist Gerald Caplan. The model brings together the concepts of stress, crisis, coping and defence.

When we are dealing with normal situations, Caplan assumes that we operate consistently and with minimal strain. When faced with circumstances requiring a response, we bring into play both habitual and previously effective coping mechanisms. Before we make this response, we experience a state of increased tension which helps us to resolve the issue and thus return us to a balanced state. A crisis occurs when an imbalance develops between the difficulty and/or importance of the problem and our habitual problem-solving responses. If a new stress, either developmental or accidental, cannot be dealt with by these usual means, tension escalates further and we feel lost, helpless and ineffective. The persisting tension then stimulates us to call upon our reserves—our internal and external resources—and we attempt new methods of problem-solving. We may, for example, define the problem in a new way so as to find different features that we can then approach. We may decide that certain goals are unattainable and, by trial and error, identify new goals worth pursuing.

Our own resilience and the social support available to us play a crucial role in crisis. Resilience is our capacity to act with determination in the face of adversity, to call on a range of useful coping strategies, and to enlist mature defences. By contrast, vulnerability is a state of inadequate resilience—our ability to battle 'a sea of troubles' is diminished and we depend on more immature defences.

Social support is the aid provided by our immediate and extended families, by our community of close friends and colleagues, and by the broader human network in which we function, including professional and non-professional helpers. The availability, adequacy and helpfulness or otherwise of social support are powerful factors in either enhancing or worsening the effects of stress.

We may well be able to deal with the problem by drawing upon our various resources. And our success will, as Ben Jonson implied, increase our resilience and our capacity to cope with future stress. But if we cannot manage the problem, or we avoid it by such means as giving up, tension mounts further and leads to psychological disorganisation. This in turn diminishes our resilience to future stress, and leads to the clinical conditions soon to be described.

This model, which describes how we deal with the ups and downs of everyday life, was then applied by Caplan to the treatment of psychiatric illness. He highlighted the contributions of primary, secondary and tertiary prevention (see Chapter 23). Primary prevention ensures a good outcome by providing skilled intervention at the time of crisis. Secondary prevention attempts to limit the role of the factors that have precipitated the crisis when their role in initiating or aggravating the crisis is known. Tertiary prevention seeks to reduce deterioration of an established condition by concentrating on the factors that maintain that condition.

A typical response to crisis is the sequence of reactions which follow the loss of a loved one through death. The experience of bereavement is accompanied by grief, a process clearly divisible into a series of phases, which we describe in Chapter 8.

## Stress and psychosomatic illness

While stress is commonplace in everyday life and contributes to the cause or to the persistence of many psychiatric conditions, it is in relation to physical illness that it has attracted most attention. This is especially so in certain medical illnesses which are usually labelled 'psychosomatic'.

The concept of psychosomatic medicine was initiated by doctors who observed the profound effect of emotion on a range of medical conditions and developed theories to explain their relationship. Central to their thinking was the detrimental effect that stress clearly has on health and well-being.

One theory, put forward in the 1930s, suggested that particular life events, psychological conflicts, emotional states and personality styles relate to specific medical illnesses. The most influential view of this theory came from the American psychoanalyst Franz Alexander. He suggested that typical conflicts arouse anxiety in particular people. This triggers defences, with associated physiological changes affecting particular bodily organs. In those people with an 'organic weakness', continuing repressed conflict leads to pathological changes. For instance, a conflict about dependence–independence manifests as a continuing wish to be looked after, causes increased flow of acid in the stomach and ultimately peptic ulceration in those people with a genetic predisposition to high acid secretion.

Although this theory is not much favoured today, the idea that particular people are vulnerable to particular illnesses persists in medical thinking. The most notable example is the relationship suggested between Type A behaviour (characterised by drivenness, competitiveness and an urgency to get things done) and a tendency to heart disease.

A contrasting theory holds that cumulative stress increases a person's vulnerability to illness but that its form will depend on several factors, including those that are well recognised in medicine as causing disease. Pioneering work in this field was done by two American researchers, Thomas Holmes and Richard Rahe. They devised an ingenious method to quantify stresses by achieving a consensus about the relative severity of a wide range of life events. Death of a spouse, for example, was ranked as the most traumatic of the forty-three items in their list.

## Stress and physical illness

Just as life events and psychological factors have major effects on health, so the experience of medical illness can lead to profound changes in a person's emotional state. These effects have been labelled 'somato-psychic' (to contrast with the term 'psycho-somatic'). They are common in general hospital settings as people attempt to come to terms with illness ranging from the sudden and life-threatening to the chronic and disabling. Somato-psychic reactions bring much distress in their own right as well as interfere with the ability of people to comply with medical treatment.

People with physical illness face stresses imposed by the condition's inherent pain and incapacity, by the threatening hospital environment, and by discomfort involved in investigation and treatment which can be painful, even mutilating (for example, the surgical removal of a breast). Perhaps the main source of stress is the uncertainty posed by illness—its severity, the possibility of death, long-term effects and the overall outcome.

Psychological reactions include both the defences we have discussed (such as denial, regression and rationalisation) and coping strategies like seeking relevant information, turning to others for support, setting realistic goals, adopting a stoical attitude or finding meaning in the experience.

Maladaptive responses that may occur include demanding or aggressive behaviour, depression, anxiety, dependency and withdrawal. A failure to comply with treatment may result from any of these reactions. Certain services in the hospital—including intensive care, coronary care, cancer wards and burns units—present specific problems, both in the nature of the conditions treated, and because they are highly stressful environments.

## Adjustment disorders

Adjustment disorders are the result of major life changes leading to continuing distressing circumstances. Exceptionally traumatic life events may produce an acute stress reaction (see below).

As we pointed out earlier, life events may precipitate and contribute to the continuation of a wide range of mental illnesses. The link between stress and illness is not always clear and often depends on a person's vulnerability. Thus susceptibility is again a factor, as is social support, in determining whether or not stress is managed successfully.

The key feature of adjustment disorders is an ineffective reaction to an identifiable stress. The reaction occurs within a few weeks of the experience of that stress and persists for several months. As mentioned earlier, crises are of two sorts. They may be developmental (such as starting school, leaving home, getting married) or accidental (threatening and unexpected events such as car accident, robbery, rape). These events may be single or multiple, episodic or continuing.

The following terms are used by psychiatrists to cover the variations they see in their clinical practice: adjustment disorder with anxious mood, with depressed mood, with physical complaints, with withdrawal, with work and/or study difficulties, and various combinations of these. The entire range of psychiatric symptoms described in later chapters may occur as a result of stress, and they may be of mild, moderate or severe intensity. Associated symptoms impair people's everyday functioning at work and in their social and intimate relationships, and are disruptive and distressing to them.

It is not surprising that adjustment disorders occur at any age, as we face developmental and accidental crises throughout our lives. People with these disorders often turn not to the psychiatrist but to the family doctor, community health centres, student clinics and a variety of other counselling services.

### Acute stress reactions

This is a temporary but severe state which develops in a previously well person in response to exceptional stress, and which usually subsides within hours or days. The stress may be an overwhelming trauma involving serious threat to a person's security or safety or that of a loved one (such as a natural disaster, war or physical assault) or an unusually sudden, threatening change in circumstances (such as multiple bereavement in a car accident).

Immediately afterwards, a sense of unreality prevails. The person is dazed and disoriented, and the mechanism of denial is obviously in play. A mix of emotions quickly takes over, including grief, fear, despair and anger. Over the next few days or weeks, the person works at understanding and coming to terms with the event, after which a new level of adaptation is reached. The stages of denial, emotional arousal, 'working through' and resolution are basic responses to a variety of stressful circumstances.

The most disruptive reaction is a state of acute psychosis (see Chapter 12) in which the person loses touch with reality. This is what many people refer to as a 'nervous breakdown'. Its features are like those of any psychosis—that is, delusions, hallucinations and bizarre behaviour—but they occur suddenly in a person exposed to severe trauma. Symptoms vary considerably, fluctuate in intensity and usually subside when exposure to the trauma ceases or within a few weeks of the experience.

Here is an example of the rare but dramatic acute stress reaction which presents as psychosis:

*Jane was the 35-year-old wife of a diplomat on an overseas posting. The couple had been posted a year before her breakdown to a politically unstable African country, but she had managed to adjust to her new circumstances. This adjustment began to fragment when a political crisis occurred; Jane felt herself floundering in her efforts to cope. The outbreak of civil war proved to be the straw that broke the camel's back. She became acutely disturbed one evening, publicly accusing her husband of being a spy for one of the warring parties. She heard voices passing secrets to her, and made an attempt on her life in response to a voice commanding her to slash her throat as the only way to stop the war. Within a week of being sedated and evacuated to her home country, Jane's symptoms disappeared completely and she could barely recall the details of her ordeal. In discussion with a psychiatrist she was able to put this ghastly episode in perspective, recognising that her coping strategies had been challenged and then overshadowed by the frightening events. She had regressed to a 'primitive' emotional state in which everyone was a threat to her, even her husband.*

## Treatment and long-term problems

The expected improvement of adjustment disorders and acute stress reactions does not imply that treatment is not important. On the contrary, intervention at the time of the crisis makes for the best possible outcome and minimises the risk of future vulnerability. The tasks of treatment are to deal with acute symptoms, and to help the person return to a balanced state or to a workable level of adaptation to a continuing stress, such as the restrictions imposed by a stroke. The key is that people are offered support while they mobilise their own resources to achieve these goals. The approach is practical and brief (see page 289). Limited changes in a person's environment may help, but the glib suggestion of 'taking a few days off' is unlikely to do much good.

Group psychotherapy, particularly for people who have experienced a common stress (such as a community disaster), can be valuable. Sharing memories of the experience in a supportive group brings effective release of intense feelings. For a person to go back over the trauma and look at their psychological responses and at possible alternatives is also useful. Simply to repeat the details of the stressful experience helps to make the unmentionable acceptable.

Medication may help but is usually used sparingly. Temporary use of drugs to reduce anxiety and to allow sleep may be needed, but anti-depressant tablets are not generally required. Drug treatment may be necessary to tide a person over the turmoil of a psychotic experience.

Both adjustment disorders and acute stress reactions are understandable responses to severely stressful situations, and they usually subside with time. But occasionally they persist and merge into more sustained psychiatric conditions. They then become less understandable as they continue long after the stress has faded. Post-traumatic stress disorder (see Chapter 8) is the name given to a delayed and/or drawn out response which lasts for months or even years, either because the stress itself was so traumatic or damaging (for example, torture, rape, natural disaster, multiple bereavement or war experience) or because a person is particularly vulnerable.

A person who has not made the adjustment will repeatedly relive the trauma through memories which intrude in dreams or when awaking. It is likely that their emotions and personality will be dulled, and that they will be having difficulties with their relationships. They may be fearful and inclined to withdraw. The 'flashbacks' are best understood as repeated, unsuccessful attempts to master the traumatic experience.

Our recognition of post-traumatic stress disorder since the Vietnam War has highlighted the critical importance of skilled, psychological intervention at the time of trauma, or shortly afterwards, so that people can work through the experience and so lessen the risk of later problems.

## Conclusion

In this chapter we have looked at how best to understand common reactions to stress. We have also described a group of conditions to which we are all susceptible, and which many of us have actually experienced when buffeted by the ups and downs of life. They are understandable responses, whether the stress is catastrophic or a fairly predictable part of the life cycle. We have presented them as a stepping stone to considering more complex psychiatric conditions, many of which seem bewildering at first encounter but all of which involve, in one way or another, people struggling to adapt to life circumstances and/or to their illnesses.

Anxiety marks this painting of a narrow, dangerous road leading nowhere.

A cry for help from a woman imprisoned within a cage.

# **7** *The Spectrum of Anxiety*

Men during numberless generations have endeavoured to escape from their enemies or danger by headlong flight or violently struggling with them . . . And now, whenever the emotion of fear is strongly felt, though it may not lead to any exertion, the same results tend to reappear through the force of inheritance and association.

This is Charles Darwin's eloquent account, in *The Expression of Emotion in Men and Animals*, of the very understandable emotion of fear. Fear is a normal emotional response that prepares us for realistic, anticipated dangers, and so has obvious survival value. Anxiety, on the other hand, feels like fear but occurs in the absence of danger, which is why we find it so puzzling. Both fear and anxiety are decidedly unpleasant, as they combine a sense of foreboding and physical discomfort which may affect any part of the body.

Anxiety is regarded by psychiatrists as a disorder when a person experiences a group of symptoms, both bodily and psychological, whose core is either an intense and paralysing sense of fear or a more sustained pattern of worrying. These symptoms occur in the absence of any threat or are grossly disproportionate to a threat. They restrict and hamper the person's normal life, do not lessen with reassurance, and may be accompanied by thoughts and actions which are exaggerated or even ridiculous. For example, many people fear spiders and snakes but few will stop walking in the bush in case they encounter one. Fear of flying is widespread but few people would not take an overseas holiday for this reason alone. An example of anxiety which even the sufferer knows is silly is the person who has trouble leaving the house for fear the gas has been left on, and must repeatedly check to ensure it has been turned off.

These are the meanings of the key words used to describe anxiety disorders:

• *Fear*  An unpleasant feeling that is a normal response to realistic danger.

- *Anxiety*  Similar to fear but experienced in the absence of a specific danger and usually in response to anticipated problems.
- *Phobia*  A disproportionate fear of an object or situation which cannot be reasoned away and leads to avoidance of the feared stimulus.
- *Panic*  A sudden upsurge of intense fear, usually accompanied by both fearful thoughts and bodily symptoms of anxiety, and lasting only minutes.
- *Obsessions*  Distressing, repeated and persistent ideas, thoughts, impulses or images experienced as intrusive and senseless which cannot be resisted.
- *Compulsions*  Repetitive actions which must be carried out even though the person knows they are ridiculous or excessive, as not doing so will increase the level of anxiety.

Some anxiety disorders can be clearly understood by everyone. Immediately after a car accident, it is natural to feel apprehensive about driving a car, to experience anxiety, lowered mood and nightmares and to avoid the scene of the accident. But we would find it puzzling if these symptoms persisted for months or even years as they do in the clinical syndrome known as post-traumatic stress disorder.

All negative emotions affect the way we see the world. Anxiety produces a heightened awareness of physical or psychological danger. People who feel generally anxious make assumptions which lead them to interpret a wide range of situations as threatening. The anxiety then focuses their attention on aspects of the world that they view as hazardous, and so the pattern is entrenched. For example, people who suffer from panic interpret bodily sensations as indicating that they are dying. Breathlessness points to impending death, palpitations to a heart attack and dizziness to collapse. Both external stimuli (for example, returning to a place where panic occurred previously) or internal stimuli (thoughts, images or bodily sensations) may bring on an attack. Once this tendency has developed, people invariably become vigilant about monitoring their physical state and noting sensations of which they would not normally be aware.

Anxiety disorders are marked by psychological symptoms which reflect mental disturbance, and by somatic (bodily) sensations and experiences. The central psychological symptom is fear—of dying, of losing control, of being trapped, of embarrassment, of humiliation or of losing one's mind. The fear may be more vague—a sense of foreboding, a worried expectation that something terrible is about to happen. Closely linked with this is a state of inner tension and restlessness, an endless and hypervigilant scanning of what is seen as a threatening world. Some people experience actual distortions of the sense of self (depersonalisation) and of the world (derealisation); they feel unreal and/or perceive the world as weird and strange. Understandably, higher mental functions such as attention, concentration and thinking are disturbed. Sleep provides no escape from this uneasiness and disquiet—a pattern of insomnia, restless sleep and vivid dreams is typical.

Physical experiences cover all systems of the body—anxious people may feel their heart beating rapidly and chest pain, or experience laboured breathing or a sense of not being able to catch their breath. Dry mouth, nausea and diarrhoea are experienced by people who tend to respond to stress with their gut. Others have muscular tension, headaches and general aches and pains. Yet another group of symptoms relate to the nervous system—dizziness, faintness and pins and needles.

These psychological and bodily disturbances are common to many other mental illnesses, particularly depression. In fact, many depressed people describe the anxiety and associated agitation as more distressing than the feeling of sadness. Psychotic people may also experience intense anxiety as their world fragments and they sense the terror of 'falling apart'. Anxiety is often both the cause and effect of alcohol and drug abuse. People use chemicals to blot out anxious feelings, but the anxiety worsens during withdrawal or abstinence. Also, a range of medical conditions may be accompanied by anxiety. It may arise from the person's concern about the possible implications of illnesses (such as cancer), or it may be part of the condition itself (as in the case of excessive thyroid function), or the result of its treatment (for example, steroids make many asthmatic people inexplicably anxious).

## One anxiety or many?

Anxiety disorders have long been grouped as a category of the neuroses. That word was introduced in 1772 to refer to a group of puzzling disorders which, for want of a better explanation, were thought to be due to malfunction of the nervous system. In everyday speech, to say that someone is neurotic is highly insulting, but psychiatrists still use the word in a technical sense to decribe a class of mental illnesses which have no physical basis and where sufferers recognise unwanted feelings, thoughts and other experiences as their own. The anxiety disorders are the commonest form of neuroses.

But is there one, or many? Some professionals consider that there are several separate anxiety disorders, including panic, agoraphobia and obsessive-compulsive disorder. Others see these disorders as expressions of a common underlying condition, a 'general neurotic syndrome'. As support for this view, they point to the fact that these disorders frequently co-exist, and often change from one to another over time. For example, people may have obsessive-compulsive symptoms in adolescence, then develop agoraphobia in middle age, and general anxiety after retirement. This debate is far from academic since different forms of anxiety disorders require specific treatments.

Anxiety disorders occur throughout life. One in six people will develop one or other form at some point. Specific phobias (for example, fear of spiders) are the most common, although people with them rarely seek professional help either because they are embarrassed about it or because the feared situation can be easily avoided. Obsessive-compulsive disorder used to be considered the most rare, but with a lifetime risk of around 3 per cent this is in fact not so.

Panic with agoraphobia and simple phobia are more common in women than in men, whereas social phobia is evenly distributed. Anxiety may start at any time in life in stressful circumstances, but the fully fledged disorders usually begin before middle age.

The usual pattern is a long-term course marked by worsening in the face of stress, particularly for generalised anxiety disorder. It is not uncommon for people with agoraphobia to say that they are never free of it. Social and specific phobias tend to persist unless treated. Most people with obsessive-compulsive disorder have episodes of symptoms and can function reasonably normally, but a third never fully recover.

## What causes anxiety disorders?

There are many explanations, ranging from the theories of Freud to today's biological models. Freud had an intriguing but now largely discredited view that these disorders arose when sexual energy became blocked and was then channelled into anxiety. But in some forms, for example in obsessions and phobias, this anxiety is transferred on to a seemingly harmless object, situation or idea which could then be acted on (for example, through repeated thoughts or rituals as in obsessive-compulsive disorder) or avoided (as with phobias), and so the person becomes not a helpless victim but an active participant. Freud later suggested that anxiety lay at the core of most neuroses, weaving its influence in multiple ways. He pointed out that both pressures from within the psyche at an unconscious level and demands of the outside world could lead to intolerable conflict, resulting in the development of symptoms.

Learning theorists have suggested that conditioning and reinforcement contibute to anxiety states. They argue that faulty learning has occurred— that fear which is appropriate in one situation has become linked to a relatively harmless or non-threatening situation, or has been exaggerated or generalised to a range of circumstances. For instance, a student who fails in an examination becomes anxious about all examinations and, even worse, becomes fearful of all circumstances in which he feels his abilities (academic, sporting, social, occupational, and so on) are being tested.

In complete contrast, existential theory which developed over the last half-century has it that all forms of anxiety have at their core a fundamental concern (the German word 'angst' is often used in this context) about life ending. People who cannot accept the prospect of a state of non-being 'deceive' themselves by converting their angst into a range of neurotic symptoms.

In opposition to these psychological perspectives, researchers have since the 1980s sought to identify brain disturbances which might underlie anxiety disorders. A genetic factor is likely to operate. In obsessive-compulsive disorder, for example, about 20 per cent of first-degree relatives (parents, siblings, children) have also suffered from the condition. Twin studies, which show a rate of 40 per cent in identical twins, also point to a hereditary contribution. Investigation of brain neuro-transmitters suggests that there is dysfunction of certain chemicals in panic and obsessive-compulsive disorders, and this is supported by the finding that only one class of anti-depressants (the SSRIs) is effective for obsessional symptoms (see Chapter 20).

Particularly tantalising is evidence that certain parts of the brain are overactive in obsessive-compulsive disorder. Some people seem to have a specific biological vulnerability to anxiety. They are much more likely to respond with acute anxiety and even panic to a range of stimuli, including drugs (such as caffeine), overbreathing, and infusion of certain chemicals. It is as if the brain is set at a more highly tuned level so that its readiness to respond to danger is accentuated.

We will now look at the various forms of anxiety disorder, distinguished by the prominence of certain clinical features. General anxiety disorder is, as the name suggests, the most diffuse. Panic disorder is similar, but occurs as relatively brief, intense attacks. Three related groups of irrational fears are specific (such as spiders), social (for example, eating out) and agoraphobia (for example, shopping in a supermarket). In obsessive-compulsive disorder, anxiety is recurrent, with intrusive thoughts and associated ritualistic behaviour. And post-traumatic stress disorder is a collection of particular anxiety symptoms following a severe trauma like rape.

## General anxiety disorder

The person with this disorder is the typical 'worrier'. Worry punctuates everyday life time and time again—worry about job, children, marriage, finances, leaking roof, health, and a myriad other trivial and non-trivial matters. With this worry comes a wide range of anxiety features described above, including bodily tension, hypervigilance and physical symptoms. These physical symptoms lead to endless medical consultations and tend to obscure the central disorder. Special tests are often done to investigate headaches, chest pain or diarrhoea. When these draw a blank, the spectre of stress is invoked and anti-anxiety drugs often prescribed. These drugs may then bring problems in their own right. More appropriate treatment combines explanation, support, careful limiting of medical investigations, and avoidance or only short-term application of drugs.

All of us experience some of these anxiety features when we are subject to intense or prolonged stress. The concept of general anxiety disorder is confined to the 5 per cent of people who suffer these symptoms for years, often starting in childhood or adolescence. The disorder tends to smoulder on throughout life, becoming more intense when stress factors such as parenthood impinge.

## Panic disorder

Panic disorder, which affects 1 to 2 per cent of the population in any one year, has similar symptoms to general anxiety disorder, but they are experienced much more abruptly and unexpectedly. Spontaneous attacks of anxiety occur without warning and for no apparent reason. In a typical episode the person feels sudden, overwhelming fear and a variety of the physical symptoms described above. The fear is of collapse, going mad, losing control or dying, or a vaguer sense of imminent catastrophe. Episodes last for seconds to minutes but occasionally for an hour or more. They occur every other day on average but the frequency varies considerably. People are often convinced that they have a physical disease. Medical investigations which find nothing wrong do not reassure them, because the bodily symptoms are so overwhelming. It comes as no surprise that panic disorder leads to the 'panic prone person' who tends to avoid situations in which the attacks are triggered. When extreme, the avoidance is labelled agoraphobia (see phobic disorders below).

*A 33-year-old woman experienced a sudden 'strange' feeling while driving. She became intensely fearful, and just managed to reach her destination, quivering with relief that she had reached the safety of home. Her family doctor referred her to a specialist who, despite a normal electro-enchephalogram (a test of the brain's electrical waves), made a provisional diagnosis of temporal lobe epilepsy. He suggested that she might need an anti-epileptic drug, and warned her to take care while driving. She promptly concluded that she was an 'epileptic' and could have a 'fit' at any moment. She refused to go out, stopped work and avoided friends. Several further episodes of the same fear finally resulted in her seeing a psychiatrist who, with the benefit of hindsight in regard to the course and pattern of the condition, diagnosed panic disorder.*

## Phobic disorders

Although fear of catastrophe is a hallmark of panic, psychiatrists have found it helpful from a therapeutic point of view to demarcate another set of anxiety states—the phobic disorders—in which the experience of fear is dominant. But in these states the fear is focused, which allows a pattern of avoidance to develop. The three phobic disorders are specific phobia, social phobia and agoraphobia.

Specific phobia affects about one in ten people, and the common objects or situations include spiders, snakes, lightning, thunder, flying, driving, heights, lifts, blood or injury. The sequence is predictable. People know what they fear, even experiencing anxiety at the thought of it, and 'help themselves' by carefully avoiding all possible contact with the object or situation. This disorder was previously referred to as 'simple' phobia, but this downplays the disruption that the irrational fear can cause to a person's life. Think of the businessman who needs to travel regularly but is afraid of flying, or the woman who procrastinates in visiting the dentist, petrified of injections. This degree of fear is quite different from ordinary apprehension about encountering such things as snakes and spiders—which we would not go to excessive lengths to avoid.

*A young woman requested treatment for a fear of feathers. She had always been fearful of birds, particularly of their feathers. Not only did she avoid going out if she saw or heard birds in the area but she was constantly on the look-out for feathers which might be blowing about. She could not visit areas like parks where there might be birds. A programme of graded exposure, first using video and later having her handle feathers, was helpful. She was finally able to watch the horror movie* The Birds *without anxiety.*

Social phobia is like a specific phobia but the fear is focused on social situations. This calls for a different approach to treatment. Socially phobic people describe anxiety in many circumstances. They fear what others may think of them, especially of appearing ridiculous. They avoid eating or drinking in public in case their hands shake, they feel nauseous or vomit or are unable to swallow. Others are concerned about blushing or sweating in company and so avoid speaking in public or performing any transactions (such as signing a cheque or handling money). These difficulties often begin in adolescence, with marked social isolation continuing throughout adulthood.

*A 40-year-old woman complained of a fear of vomiting. Since childhood she had been worried about doing this in front of others and looking stupid. So she avoided holidaying with friends, travelling in other people's cars, eating out in company or inviting friends for a meal. By the time she finally sought treatment, her everyday activities and those of her family had become extremely limited.*

Agoraphobia, which tends to start in the early twenties, was first described in 1871 as the 'impossibility of walking through certain streets and squares, or the possibility of doing so only with resultant dread of anxiety'. A frequent misunderstanding is that agoraphobia is a fear of open spaces, but the Greek word '*agora*' refers to the market-place and other places of assembly. The most restrictive form is a fear of venturing into a public place alone. Some people are anxious on their own even in the familiar surroundings of their home. People avoid situations in which they feel trapped—such as shops, queues, theatres, public transport, bridges or tunnels. The fear may be so pervasive that they become entirely housebound.

Strategies that people often use to reduce the fear of having a panic attack include travelling with a companion, using a train which stops frequently, shopping late at night when the supermarket is virtually empty, and sitting near an aisle in a theatre. They may enlist relatives, friends and neighbours to run messages, shop or take the children to school. Research has shown that recruiting these same people may help the person to 'unlearn' this avoidance behaviour.

*A 45-year-old married man experienced his first panic attack at the age of twenty. He drank heavily, which he said controlled the anxiety. After a driving infringement he stopped the drinking, and described a worsening of the panic attacks. Soon he was unable to drive on freeways, or to enter lifts or shop. He carried a mobile phone at all times in case he needed to summon help. He insisted that his wife also carry a phone and inform him of her movements. He became increasingly anxious about his 13-year-old daughter, refusing to let her go out with friends lest a 'disaster' befell her.*

## Obsessive-compulsive disorder

There is yet another way in which anxiety may become focused, but a more accurate description would be channeling. The anxiety is directed into a particular form of thinking (obsessional) coupled with predictable and understandable behavioural responses (compulsions).

Obsessive-compulsive disorder is characterised by either obsessions or compulsions or, more commonly, both. Obsessions are repeated, intrusive thoughts, impulses or images which the person knows are silly but is helpless to resist. The obsessions often revolve around highly distressing sexual activities; spiritual themes; uncertainty about whether one has taken adequate precautions such as switching off the gas or the iron; being dirty and/or contaminating others; and harming others, including loved ones (they do not, in fact, harm others). People make attempts, though futile and intensely frustrating, to ignore, suppress or neutralise the obsessions.

John Bunyan, the author of *The Pilgrim's Progress*, gives a graphic account in his autobiography of his 'spiritual' obsession:

> ... Sometimes again, when I have been preaching I have been violently assaulted by thoughts of blasphemy and strongly tempted to speak the words with my mouth before the Congregation ...

Compulsions are repetitive, stereotyped behaviours performed in response to the obsessions. The person seems to have no option but to pursue ridiculous behaviours in an effort to reduce the anxiety produced by the obsessions. Checking, washing, counting and hoarding offer relief but only for a while. Soon, the troublesome obsession reappears, and with renewed vigour. Boswell described his friend Samuel Johnson's repetitive rituals when crossing any threshold:

> ... for I have upon innumerable occasions observed him suddenly stop, and then seem to count his steps with a deep earnestness; and when he had neglected or gone wrong in this sort of magical movement, I have seen him go

back again, put himself in a proper position to begin the ceremony, and having gone through it, break from his abstraction, walk briskly on, and join his companion ...

The lifetime risk of obsessive-compulsive disorder is about 2 per cent, usually beginning in early adulthood, and following an intermittent, often unpredictable, course. Often, but not always, it occurs in people with obsessional personalities—those who live an orderly, highly organised life. Obsessional traits can help to prepare people for the ups and downs of life. It is when they become intrusive and disruptive of everyday life that we use the diagnosis of obsessive-compulsive disorder.

*A 35-year-old woman consulted her family doctor complaining of lack of energy and apathy. Her 'cleaning' rituals had so exhausted her that she could only muster the energy to 'decontaminate' two of the five rooms in her home. She had always been house-proud and liked orderliness and predictable routines. After the birth of her first child, these previously reasonable traits got entirely out of control. Having touched a surface she had to disinfect it repeatedly, in a highly ritualistic way which took several hours. But she was still tormented by the fear that her children would be contaminated by the 'dirt' and contract a deadly illness. The unfortunate children were drawn into these rituals, being literally scrubbed daily to remove all trace of the supposed faeces contaminating their buttocks. Despite being fully aware of how distressing this was for them, she was powerless to do otherwise. In any event, the compulsive act brought only short-lived relief from the obsession—sometimes a few minutes only.*

## Post-traumatic stress disorder

Unlike all the previous categories of anxiety, this one does have an identifiable cause. The condition we now know as post-traumatic stress disorder has long links with the effects of war, and has been variously experienced and described in many wars. Physical and mental exhaustion was noted in soldiers during the American Civil War, 'irritable heart' in the Crimean War, 'shell shock' during World War I and 'battle fatigue' in World War II. The disorder is remarkably well portrayed in Pat Barker's trilogy about World War I and its aftermath, based on the historical character, Dr W. Rivers. He struggled to bring relief to the soldiers severely traumatised in the trenches in France, among them the poet Wilfred Owen. Owen wrote about his own experience in several powerful poems, including 'Mental Case':

*Therefore still their eyeballs*
*shrink tormented*
*Back into their brains,*
*because on their sense*
*Sunlight seems a blood-smear*
*Night comes blood-black*
*Dawn breaks open like a wound that bleeds afresh.*

Civilian disasters such as bushfires, earthquakes and floods have since been noted to lead to post-traumatic stress disorder. The effects of severe trauma affecting an individual rather than a community (such as witnessing or being the victim of a violent crime or rape) can also produce this disorder.

The person has invariably been involved in a distressing event beyond the range of usual human experience. Typical symptoms are reliving the trauma, having the event penetrating into consciousness unmercifully, the numbing of emotional response, hyperarousal and avoidance of situations even remotely associated with the original trauma. The diagnosis is often complicated by other behaviours, particularly the misuse of alcohol and drugs, adopted in a desperate attempt to dull the intrusive symptoms.

*A 22-year-old chef was caught up by chance in a shoot-out. He witnessed the brutal murder of a young woman, although he himself was unharmed and even returned to work the next day. However, in the weeks that followed he became increasingly irritable, depressed and anxious. He was so highly aroused that he could not stand the noise of traffic and jumped at any loud sound. Moreover, he could not tolerate the hustle and bustle of the restaurant's kitchen and began to stay home. He would intermittently and unexpectedly see the scene replayed in his 'mind's eye'. His sleep was much disturbed, and punctuated by terrifying nightmares. He felt guilty about the woman's death and believed he should have done more to save her. He avoided the scene of the crime to protect himself from becoming intensely distressed. He was convinced he should have 'coped' better. Previously a lively extroverted companion, he gradually withdrew from his friends, ultimately becoming a virtual recluse. He started to drink heavily, which seemed his only way to deal with his painful thoughts.*

## Treatment of the anxiety disorders

Whatever form the anxiety takes, the psychiatrist will first take a careful history from the person (and other appropriate people), ensure that a phys-ical examination has been performed and arrange any tests to exclude a physical cause. If other psychiatric symptoms are present, especially depression, it is necessary to establish whether anxiety is the primary disorder. The psychiatrist looks for factors which aggravate and maintain the disorder, since they will be a focus for treatment. These factors include interpersonal conflict, major life events, and excessive use and/or withdrawal from caffeine, nicotine or alcohol.

The effects of the disorder on the person and the family are of course explored, since they may be considerable. For instance, the child whose mother is housebound or who spends several hours a day washing her hands and checking cannot be unaffected. Likewise, a spouse may have to make considerable adjustments to accommodate his partner's multiple phobias. Paradoxically, however, the illness may 'suit' the family—an emotionally insecure husband, for example, feels safe that his wife is confined to the home. Family and friends may be heavily caught up in their symptoms. If it appears that they are encouraging dependency and blocking improvement, their involvement in treatment becomes vital.

> *A 24-year-old woman had symptoms of panic disorder. Her father had taken to accompanying her to college and all social activities in case of an attack. The father had recently been retrenched and felt a failure. His daughter's symptoms had given him an 'occupation' and a sense of being needed. In parallel with his daughter's treatment, the father was advised about the nature of the disorder and alternative strategies for his daily activities were devised.*

Since many people hold unrealistic beliefs about their physical state (which is related to the anxiety symptoms), an important part of their treatment is to reassure them that they will not die or go mad, and to explain the nature of the condition. For example, hyperventilation is often not recognised as a cause of many of the symptoms. It is helpful to clarify which ones are produced by over-breathing and to actually demonstrate in the psychiatrist's presence how symptoms can be produced voluntarily by such over-breathing. This is the first step in mastering controlled breathing, by slowing the rate and avoiding overly shallow or deep breathing.

More general relaxation training may help. Learning to achieve a state of calmness offers people a sense of control over bodily symptoms and a welcome alternative to a perpetually worried psyche. This can be achieved in many ways. The benefits of meditation and yoga have been known for centuries. More recent methods centre around alternately tightening and relaxing groups of muscles, known as systematic relaxation. This technique is often combined with visual imagery. People are encouraged to imagine a scene which, from their own experience, is tranquil and calm. Common images are beach scenes, gentle rolling waves, shady glades or billowing clouds—which may be complemented by tape recordings of soothing music or sounds of nature, like bird calls.

Psychoanalytically oriented therapy had its heyday in the 1950s and 1960s and forms of it are still relevant in selected cases. Freud's classical case histories (such as Little Hans and the Rat Man) centred around phobic and obsessional symptoms which he thought had symbolic significance and were therefore open to his approach. But while such symbolism is clear (for example, the obsessional person with thoughts of harming others is often grappling with powerful underlying aggressive drives), drawn out psychoanalyses have not been effective.

The cognitive and behavioural approaches deal directly with symptoms. Therapy aims to improve people's psychological (and thus social) functioning, as well as to find more effective ways of coping with stress. A combination of these approaches is now the mainstay of psychological treatments. First, peoples' irrational beliefs and false assumptions are identified, and then they are guided to challenge these and to replace them with a more realistic view of themselves and their world.

*A 21-year-old student gradually developed a fear that she would faint while on public transport. Although she had never actually done so, and accepted the therapist's explanation for her symptoms, her level of anxiety still rose dramatically when she boarded a bus. As part of therapy, she was provided with a cue card which read, 'You have never fainted. What you are feeling is anxiety and it will not make you faint. Anxiety goes away. Sit on the bus and wait'. She read this card repeatedly while waiting for the bus and was able to get on and prove to herself that she would not faint.*

Specific behavioural techniques can be combined with the cognitive approach in particular anxiety disorders. Once panic attacks are controlled, 'graded exposure' to the feared situation helps people with related agoraphobia to overcome avoidance. Simple phobias can be effectively treated in this way. As the words suggest, the person is gradually brought into contact with the object or situation which brings on the anxiety. In 'systematic desensitisation', the original form of this therapy, fearful stimuli were arranged in order from mild to severe (for example, in the case of fear of flying, from viewing a photograph of a plane, through visiting an airport to an actual flight). People are first trained to relax and then led through these steps until each has been mastered. The purpose is to bring the person into contact with the feared stimulus in order to break the pattern of avoidance which is the main cause of the disability.

In the past, the very opposite was done. People were immersed in the very worst of their fears, and their pleas for relief were ignored. This seemingly cruel procedure was intended to prove that people could both survive the ordeal and recognise the irrationality of their fear. The process was obviously unpleasant, and the outcome equivocal.

For people with social phobia, a helpful set of strategies known as social skills training has been developed. People can improve their social interaction by learning, for example, how to initiate and sustain conversation, how to read non-verbal cues and how to be appropriately assertive.

Obsessions may respond to the simple and specific technique of 'thought stopping'. People learn to recognise when their thoughts are becoming obsessional and to counteract this pattern of self-absorption by sheer willpower. Another technique is 'thought satiation', in which people are forced to think continuously about the obsession.

Another form of behavioural therapy is modelling based on imitation. The therapist clearly demonstrates that the feared stimulus is harmless. In the case of a phobia of mice, for instance, the therapist confidently handles a mouse in the presence of the person, who is encouraged to do likewise.

Hypnosis would seem to be a reasonable treatment for some of the anxiety disorders given that, in the suggestible hypnotised state, a fear can be induced and just as readily eradicated. However, it has proved of limited value and has not been popular among psychiatrists.

Drugs may be used for the more severe cases of any anxiety disorder to complement explanation, reassurance and cognitive/behavioural strategies. The benzodiazepines have been widely used in the past but, because they are addictive, they should be used for short periods only. The main advantage is that their effect is rapid. Anti-depressants have specific roles. One of the tricyclic group, imipramine, is particularly effective in preventing panic attacks, and another group, the SSRIs, seem to alleviate the symptoms of obsessive-compulsive disorder. Beta-blockers, which prevent physical symptoms of anxiety such as tremor, sweating and palpitations, help to reduce the anxiety in specific or social phobias (see page 273).

Obsessive-compulsive disorder may be so unresponsive to years of both psychological and drug therapies that the psychiatrist has no alternative but to recommend the radical procedure of psychosurgery (see page 277). A highly specific part of the brain is 'destroyed' in order to relieve the person of the tortured self-concern which can be typical of this disorder.

Because family members can powerfully reinforce the maladaptive behaviour, they are now actively recruited into treatment programmes. For example, relatives may be advised how to help the phobic person to tackle the avoidance, which is the core of the disability, by encouraging him or her to confront the fearful situation rather than giving the usual reassurance—in other words, being 'cruel to be kind'. One of the best-developed family-based therapies is so-called 'spouse-aided therapy', in which the spouse, usually the husband, is helped by the therapist to play a central role in implementing and maintaining the treatment strategies. It may well be used as a model for the treatment of many other psychiatric conditions.

## Conclusion

From a world in which social structures and customs have served us reasonably well for much of the century, we are being hurtled into the relatively unknown. We are all in a state of 'future shock', as the sociologist Alvin Toffler starkly puts it. As family, work, leisure, information technology and so on all change dramatically, we are vulnerable to a time of escalating anxiety. We began this chapter with Charles Darwin, and will close with him. Human beings seem to respond to the new with a combination of curiosity and fear. But, when the unfamiliar is all about us, and change occurs at such a rapid pace, will we adapt well or will anxiety become the dominant condition of the new century? The question is a profound one for which we cannot pretend to have an answer. But, as the American psychiatrist George Vaillant suggests, we have certain 'mature' coping mechanisms available to us (see Chapter 6). One of these is anticipation—preparing as much as we can for future happenings. We will comment on this and associated coping strategies in the last chapter of this book, as part of our thinking on preventing mental ill-health and encouraging psychological well-being.

# 8  The Highs and Lows of Mood

I have of late—but wherefore I know not—lost all my mirth, foregone all custom of exercises; and indeed it goes so heavily with my disposition that this goodly frame, the earth, seems to me a sterile promontory; this excellent canopy, the air, look you, this brave o'erhanging firmament, this majestical roof fretted with golden fire—why, it appeareth no other thing to me than a foul and pestilent congregation of vapours.

Shakespeare's *Hamlet*, Act 2, Scene 2

## When does low or high mood become abnormal?

We all have good and bad days—that's normal. Indeed, it is not unusual for our mood to vary considerably in the course of a single day. In response to the ups and downs of life, we experience joys, disappointments, success and failure. And our mood may also be affected by many physical factors, like premenstrual hormonal changes, viral infections (the flu virus is a common culprit), alcohol and drugs.

There is no precise dividing line between ordinary sadness and what psychiatrists call 'clinical depression'. They use this term when lowered mood persists, brings intense distress, and interferes with the person's ability to cope with the ordinary demands of living, whether of work, study or personal relationships. This lack of a clear division is typical of many areas of our mental health. It is equally the case with, for example, anxiety, phobias and obsessions. Similarly, many physical disorders—such as high blood pressure, diabetes and osteoporosis—are also on a continuum from close to normal to what we call illness.

Clinical depression is a syndrome—in other words, a group of symptoms and observable mental and physical signs that commonly occur together. At least two weeks of lowered mood is regarded as the minimum period to warrant the diagnosis. Most people have experienced symptoms for much longer before they consult their doctor. People with milder forms may not feel bad all day but still describe a dismal outlook and a sense of gloom. They may be cheered by a positive experience but are then dragged down by even a minor disappointment. The degree of severity extends from mild, blurring into ordinary sadness (minor depression) to extreme (major depression), where the risk of suicide is high and health may be seriously affected by poor nutrition and self-neglect. A severely depressed person may also lose touch with reality and be buffeted by hallucinations and delusions.

These criteria for diagnosing clinical depression may seem rather technical but behind them lies a state of mind of tragic proportions that has always ravaged humankind. Richard Burton, in the first detailed description, *The Anatomy of Melancholia,* published in 1621, makes this powerful comment:

> Being then it is a disease so grievous, so common, I know not wherein to do a more general service, and spend my time better, than to prescribe means how to prevent and cure so universal a malady, an epidemical disease, that so often, so much, crucifies the body and mind.

A persistent heightened mood occurs far less commonly than clinical depression. There is a similar continuum, with milder states difficult to disentangle from normal joy. Moderately severe (hypomania) or very severe forms (mania) are more clear-cut—then, the person's behaviour has serious consequences if treatment is not promptly initiated. Most people with mania also suffer depressive swings at other times as part of the condition of bipolar mood disorder (previously known as manic–depressive illness).

Depression requiring professional help is common. The rate of major depression over a person's lifetime is as high as one in four women and one in eight men. But many of these people remain undiagnosed and untreated. Bipolar mood disorder is much more rare, with a lifetime rate of under 1 per cent. The two forms may occur at any age but the usual age of onset is in the late twenties; they are far less common during childhood. Over half the people who have an episode of disordered mood suffer from one or more recurrences. So, it seems that there is a continuum of possible moods in everyone.

## What is clinical depression?

*Tom a 32-year-old bus driver, went to his family doctor complaining of tiredness and disturbed sleep over the previous six weeks. His appetite was poor and he had lost three kilograms. Although well-liked and highly regarded at work, he felt incapable of performing his duties and suspected that his workmates were ignoring him. He denied any previous emotional problems. His wife was expecting a baby but this was planned and they were both delighted about the prospect of parenthood. There had been no tension between them but he had lost interest in their sexual relationship. His father had had an alcohol problem and deserted the family when Tom was four years old. A maternal aunt had once been treated in a psychiatric hospital and had suicided later.*

*A physical examination was normal, as were tests to exclude any physical illness (especially an underfunctioning thyroid, any infection or anaemia). The doctor prescribed anti-depressant medication, provided encouragement and reassurance, and arranged to review Tom the following week.*

*Tom disappeared a few days later. With the aid of the police he was found comatosed in his car, which was parked in a deserted paddock. An empty bottle of whisky and an empty packet of anti-depressant tablets lay by his side, as well as a note to his wife expressing his regret at leaving her and the baby. A hose had been connected to the exhaust but, luckily, loss of consciousness had prevented him from starting the ignition. He was most fortunate to survive this determined suicide attempt.*

*Admitted urgently to hospital, the psychiatrist diagnosed major depression of so serious a degree as to warrant electro-convulsive therapy (ECT). Together with general psychological support and the use of anti-depressants, he responded extremely well. He was able to return to work six weeks later. Tom suffered two further depressive episodes during the next two years but his wife alerted the psychiatrist, as planned, at the first appearance of symptoms. He was again treated effectively with ECT. Due to Tom's vulnerability to these serious episodes, lithium was prescribed, a treatment designed to reduce the rate of recurrence (see page 275). He was still well and free of any serious mood swings after twelve years.*

As is obvious from Tom's case, where his life was almost lost, depressed people feel so miserable that they view the future with despair. They judge their circumstances to be hopeless, believing their prospects are bleak or that they burden their family and others. Friends or relatives usually reveal a more favourable picture, but depressed people persist in seeing their situation in the blackest of terms. They often describe their mood as one of endless misery, quite different from ordinary sadness. People who have also experienced bereavement say that grief is consolable (see page 104), whereas when they are clinically depressed they feel utterly forlorn and beyond comforting. Given this state of despair, it is not surprising that depressed people are unable to take any pleasure in their usual activities— as is illustrated poignantly by Hamlet's account at the beginning of the chapter, or vividly in Theophile Gautier's poem, 'Tristesse' (Melancholy).

> *April is back,*
> *the first rose,*
> *with its lips half-parted,*
> *smiles at the first fine day,*
> *the blessed earth*
> *opens and burgeons,*
> *everything loves, everything enjoys,*
> *alas! there is a fearful melancholy in my heart!*
>
> *The drinkers in merry mood*
> *in their rosy songs*
> *celebrate beneath the vine-trellises*
> *wine and beauty,*
> *the joyful music*
> *with their clear laughter*
> *scatters itself through the air,*
> *alas! there is a fearful melancholy in my heart!*
>
> *In scanty white dresses*
> *the young maidens*
> *go away under the arbours*
> *on the arms of their swains,*
> *the languorous moon*
> *silvers their long-held kisses,*
> *alas, there is a fearful melancholy in my heart!*
>
> *For my part, I no longer love anything,*
> *neither man nor woman,*
> *neither my body nor my soul,*
> *not even my old dog:*
> *go and say that they are digging*
> *beneath the pale turf*

*a nameless grave,*
*alas! there is a fearful melancholy in my heart!*

Loss of interest touches everything, ranging in degree from an unwillingness to join in everyday activities such as sport or hobbies, through neglecting oneself and one's family, to not caring whether one lives or dies. Severely depressed people cannot concentrate, stop working and neglect personal hygiene. Irritability is common and may cause alienation from family and friends. If the condition remains untreated, physical health may suffer. Extremely depressed people can even die from starvation or dehydration.

People with milder depression highlight their misfortune. Those more severely affected tend to experience a sense of guilt and feelings of failure. They blame themselves for the situation they are in, regarding themselves as bad and undeserving of care. Guilt may reach the proportions of delusion, with people convinced they have committed crimes or horrible sins. Rarely, such people take their own lives as well as those of their family in order to 'save them from a world of evil'.

Suicide is obviously the most serious outcome of clinical depression. Of all people suffering clinical depression, two-thirds have suicidal ideas or thoughts of dying, and 15 per cent take their own lives. Those lost to depression include many a famous figure: Vincent Van Gogh (as we noted in Chapter 2), Ernest Hemingway, Sylvia Plath, Primo Levi, Virginia Woolf, Robert Schumann and many more. Other forms of self-harm such as wrist-slashing may also occur. Depressed people run a greater risk of accidents, possibly due to poor concentration or because they do not care whether they live or die.

John Stuart Mill, the nineteenth-century philosopher, captures the despair which overwhelms even the most rational mind, with suicide the only means of relief. In his *Autobiography* he poignantly shares his descent into hopelessness:

It was in the autumn of 1826. I was in a dull state of nerves, such as everybody is occasionally liable to; unsusceptible to enjoyment or pleasurable excitement . . . the whole foundation on which my life was constructed fell down . . . At first I hoped that the cloud would pass away of itself; but it did not. A night's sleep, the sovereign remedy for the smaller vexations of life, had no effect on it . . . Hardly anything had power to cause me even a few minutes oblivion of it. For some months the cloud seemed to grow thicker and thicker. The lines in Coleridge's 'Dejection'—I was not then acquainted with them—exactly describe my case:

*A grief without a pang, void, dark and drear,*
*A drowsy, stifled, unimpassioned grief,*
*Which, finds no natural outlet or relief*
*In word, or sigh, or tear.*

... there was no one on whom I could build the faintest hope of assistance. My father, to whom it would have been natural to me to have recourse in any practical difficulties, was the last person to whom, in such a case as this, I looked for help. Everything convinced me that he had no knowledge of any such mental state as I was suffering from, and that even if he could be made to understand it, he was not the physician who could heal it.

Mill's feeling of isolation is echoed by the novelist William Styron in *Darkness Visible*, a powerful account of his own depressive experience:

Depression is a disorder of mood, so mysteriously painful and elusive in the way it becomes known to the self—to the mediating intellect—as to verge close to being beyond description. It thus remains nearly incomprehensible to those who have not experienced it in its extreme mode, although the gloom, 'the blues' which people go through occasionally and associate with the general hassle of everyday existence are of such prevalence that they do give many individuals a hint of the illness in its catastrophic form.

Although depression is foremost a disturbance of emotion, bodily changes may predominate. A group of so-called 'vegetative' symptoms occur in severe cases. Less interest in food is common, leading to substantial weight loss in the severe forms. Marked sleep disturbance, particularly early morning waking (typically about three o'clock), also points to a severe state. Difficulty in falling asleep is more typical of milder cases. Hypersomnia or excessive sleep is another kind of disordered sleep. Other changes include variation in mood intensity, the morning being the worst time with improvement towards evening (diurnal variation); the slowing down of thinking and movement, sometimes to the point when speech may be impossible to follow (retardation); a sense of restlessness which causes people to pace up and down, wring their hands and pull their hair (agitation).

Rarely, there will be psychotic symptoms like delusions and hallucinations. The delusions typically contain themes of worthlessness, guilt for sins committed, persecution or nihilism (a belief that the person does not actually exist). Hallucinations are usually auditory, located within the head, and referred to as 'voices of conscience'. These psychotic features parallel the severity of the depression, and cease when the person recovers.

All sorts of symptoms may mask an underlying depressed state. For example, depressed adolescents may exhibit disturbed behaviour, truancy, sexual promiscuity or poor academic performance. Elderly people may focus on physical symptoms like constipation and weakness, or show excessive concern over their general health. Pain may dominate the picture. These situations have been referred to as masked depression, but the term is misleading as careful enquiry usually uncovers the depressive symptoms. Sometimes the person may not refer to sadness, although appearance and behaviour—withdrawal, poor sleep, weight loss, or no interest in life—indicate otherwise.

*How does the depressed person look?*

It is easy to spot a severely depressed person. He or she looks downcast and has a drawn appearance, furrowed brow and stooped posture. There may be evidence of poor self-care and loss of weight. Activity is often slow with limited spontaneous movement and speech. Or the person may be extremely agitated with hand-wringing, restlessness and pacing.

People with milder forms appear less miserable, and the change in mood is apparent only to family or friends. Depressed people often shed tears and tell of frequent, spontaneous periods of crying. But tearfulness in itself is neither an indicator of depression nor more likely to occur in severe compared to milder forms. Indeed, more severely depressed people may be quite unable to cry and show little in the way of emotional response, which is blunted or flattened.

Less affected people often find relief at being able to 'get things off their chest', particularly if given the chance to vent their feelings. On the other hand, people with severe depression find little or no benefit in sharing their experience. They may have minimal insight into their circumstances, failing to understand that they are suffering from an illness and are in need of treatment. Instead, they may believe their condition to be justifiable punishment for their 'misdeeds'.

## Mania—the other side of the coin

*Alex, a 28-year-old teacher, was referred to a psychiatrist by a police doctor after he had assaulted the school principal. The principal had confronted Alex following reports that he had made sexual advances to several female students. He had recently bought an expensive car he could ill afford and announced his plan to lecture at prestigious overseas universities. On admission to hospital (compulsorily, because of his total lack of insight into his condition) he was irritable, excessively active and brimming with grand ideas. He proudly spoke of his influential political contacts and of his intention to issue Supreme Court writs against the principal and the doctors. His speech was so rapid at times that it was barely intelligible. He had not been mentally ill in the past but his mother had been hospitalised for a mood disorder after the birth of his younger brother. Alex was immediately treated with an anti-psychotic drug while in a supportive ward environment, and made a full recovery within three weeks. Sadly, he was not able to return to his previous job: the ugly force of stigma had triumphed. However, with the help of his psychiatrist he managed to re-establish his career elsewhere and put the unpleasant experience into perspective.*

Such an episode of abnormally high mood usually begins rapidly, over a matter of days. It may follow a depressive period and can, paradoxically, be triggered by treatment with anti-depressant drugs. People report feeling unusually happy and optimistic. Their sense of self is highly inflated, many regard themselves as unusually gifted, and there is an obvious grandiosity to their manner. This euphoria has an infectious quality. However, if their wishes are thwarted, they may become prickly and irritable, even aggressive. They are excessively energetic, hyperactive and barely sleep. Speech is rapid, loud and pressured, with jokes, puns and plays on words. In more severe cases, speech is so fast that an almost continuous flow of ideas occurs ('flight of ideas'), with jumps from one thought to the next—speech may become incomprehensible. Judgement is so very distorted that the social consequences can be devastating. People spend vast sums of money, drive recklessly, make foolish business decisions or perform sexual indiscretions. Delusions such as a belief of having extraordinary power, or hallucinations like hearing God assign them a special mission, occur in especially severe states. All these abnormalities improve rapidly as the mood disturbance resolves.

Spike Milligan vividly portrays the essence of mania in conversation with the psychiatrist Anthony Clare, who records it in his book, *Depression and How to Survive It*:

The best scripts I wrote were when I was ill. I've just recalled this—the ones that I wrote best were when I was ill—a mad desire to be better than anybody else at comedy, and if I couldn't do it in the given time of eight hours a day I used to work 12, 13 and 14 . . . I was four feet above the ground at times, talking twice as fast as normal people. Working on this with great fervour to write this stuff . . . I once did write 10,000 words in one day, like Balzac! I was pressured inside. I couldn't sleep. I just wrote and wrote. I couldn't sleep. I just couldn't stop, couldn't control it.

Occasionally, in what is known as a mixed affective state, people experience features of both depression and mania in a single episode. They have a dejected mood but are grandiose and hyperactive and may have flight of ideas.

## Types of mood disorder

Since antiquity, some extremes of mood have been considered illness. In the Old Testament, the Book of Samuel tells of Saul's tendency to depression, which was responsive to music: 'And it came to pass, when the evil spirit from God was upon Saul, that David took a harp, and played with his hand: so Saul was refreshed, and was well, and the evil spirit departed from him'.

Hippocrates was the first, in the fourth Century BC, to describe 'mania' and 'melancholia'. The idea that disordered mood does not take a single form is therefore centuries old. The Roman physician, Arataeus (120–180 AD), first referred to 'endogenous' and 'reactive' types, suggesting that some forms were biologically based whereas others were due to psychological and social factors. The famous German psychiatrist, Emil Kraepelin, distinguished what he called manic depressive insanity from dementia praecox (later relabelled schizophrenia) according to the course and outcome of the illness. The former was episodic with recovery between attacks, the latter a progressive decline. Today, psychiatrists have built on this distinction, and further noted that some people may suffer from either depressed or manic swings (called unipolar mood disorder) or experience both over time (bipolar mood disorder).

Mood disorders are now observed to be a group of conditions with certain similar, overlapping features. The several classifications devised emphasise different aspects, including the clinical features, the severity, the course of the illness, its response to treatment and the psychological factors that precipitated it. For example, the chief criteria for a major depressive episode in DSM-IV (the American system described in Chapter 4), are listed in the following table.

## Criteria for a major depressive episode (DSM-IV)

At least five of the following have been present during the same two-week period and represent a change from previous functioning; at least one symptom is depressed mood or loss of interest or pleasure:

- depressed mood (or irritable mood in children or adolescents) most of the day, nearly every day;
- marked loss of interest or pleasure in activities most of the day, nearly every day;
- significant weight loss or weight gain when not dieting (for example, more than 5 per cent of body weight in a month), or decrease or increase in appetite nearly every day;
- insomnia or alternatively excessive sleep nearly every day;
- agitation or retardation nearly every day;
- fatigue or loss of energy nearly every day;
- feelings of worthlessness or excessive or inappropriate guilt (which may be delusional) nearly every day;
- diminished ability to think or concentrate, or indecisiveness, nearly every day;
- recurrent thoughts about death and suicide.

A major depressive episode usually begins gradually, over weeks. Some people recover completely and only suffer a single attack during their lifetime. Over half will have one or more recurrences but are usually symptom-free between episodes. Sometimes many years will pass before a relapse, but other people have only a brief respite. Typically the period between episodes diminishes with age. Untreated mania lasts about three months, and untreated major depression between six and twelve months. Major depression with prominent 'vegetative' features is referred to as melancholia, and major depression with psychotic symptoms as psychotic depression.

Some people experience depression regularly during autumn or winter with recovery in spring and summer (seasonal affective disorder). Others have intense episodes of depression lasting only a few days and occurring about every three weeks—their symptoms tend to be severe and often involve suicidal thinking.

To refer to 'minor' depression is not to minimise its importance, as it can thoroughly disrupt a person's life, including work performance and interpersonal relationships. In the past, this form was called reactive depression, to emphasise that mood responded to environmental influences. Also, milder types of depression are often accompanied by so-called 'neurotic' features, notably anxiety (see Chapter 7). Such features may also be part of major depression.

Dysthymic disorder is a continuing 'low-grade' depressive state, more common in women than men, marked by an extremely pessimistic view of life and of the future, low self-esteem, indecisiveness and lack of energy. It usually begins in late adolescence or early adulthood, adversely affecting study or adjustment to work. Clear-cut bouts of depression, breaking the long, continuing dysthymic pattern, may move the person to seek professional help.

Cyclothymia is a pattern where people experience distinct, but relatively mild, mood swings. But the changes may disrupt their lives with harmful effects on career and relationships. The swings are largely not influenced by life events.

Finally, lowered mood clearly resulting from well-defined stress such as a marital break-up or loss of a job is referred to as an adjustment disorder with depressed mood (see Chapter 6). As the stress lessens, so do the symptoms.

## What causes mood disorders?

There has been much research, and it points to many potential causes within three broad groups—biological, psychological and social. One group will be more important than the others in any particular form of disordered mood.

### Biological factors

The fact that disordered mood runs in families suggests that genes play a role. Their contribution is particularly well established in bipolar disorder. For example, twin studies show a high concordance rate in identical twins compared to non-identical twins (see page 26).

A pioneering theory to explain mood disorders was based on the observation that Reserpine, a drug widely used to reduce high blood pressure and which causes depression in some people, lowers certain chemical messengers in the brain. By contrast, anti-depressant drugs increase their level. Later research reveals a more complex picture, with various abnormalities in the function of these chemical messengers. These defects show in changed levels in the blood, urine and the fluid surrounding the brain. Post-mortem examination of the brains of suicide victims known to have suffered depression confirms the dysfunction.

As chemical messengers influence the secretion of hormones, endocrinal abnormalities might be expected in people with mood disorders. People with certain endocrinal disorders, particularly an underfunctioning thyroid or an overfunctioning adrenal gland, often experience a mood disturbance. Brain–thyroid and brain–adrenal links have been intensively studied and a series of abnormalities revealed, although they are not consistent. In fact, the most widely studied blood test to assist in diagnosing depression is hormonal—the dexamethasone suppression test (DST). Although an abnormal DST is more likely to occur in people with depression than with other psychiatric disorders, it is unfortunately only of limited value as a diagnostic tool.

## Psychological and social factors

People with certain personality traits, especially if dependent and obsessional, are more vulnerable to developing depression, but it occurs in even the most well-adjusted and sturdy of us.

Loss of a parent during childhood is associated with an increased risk of depression in adult life, but the link may be non-specific since such loss is also linked with other disorders, including alcoholism and anti-social personality.

One life experience that has been intensively studied and is intimately linked to depression is the death of a loved one. Grief and depression share some features, but grief differs in being a normal response to loss with the psychological purpose of enabling the person to adapt. Uncomplicated grief typically follows a broad pattern. The first effect, stunned disbelief, which is really a state of shock, is followed by recognition of the reality of the loss and the first painful feelings. People who are grieving will, like people with clinical depression, experience intense sadness, helplessness, disturbed sleep, loss of interest and social withdrawal. But grief does have distinctive features. The bereaved person is preoccupied with the dead person and may even imagine seeing or hearing them. The person may lose interest in food, but marked weight loss is rare. Any guilt concerning the deceased (for example, not having done enough for them in a terminal illness), does not extend to feelings of failure and worthlessness.

'Working through' the loss and surrendering ties with the deceased will happen gradually. This 'grief work' entails a step-by-step accommodation of the intense emotions experienced and concludes with a phase of resolution. The bereaved person finds ways to accept and live with the loss and restructures their world accordingly. So normal grief is limited by time. Given support from family, friends (and sometimes professionals), the bereaved person will accept his or her sense of loss. Recovery does not mean forgetting the deceased; rather, memories are no longer accompanied by emotional turmoil. The past is recalled with sentimental pleasure while, at the same time, new interests and friends are cultivated.

C. S. Lewis' well-known account of his personal agony after losing his wife, *A Grief Observed* (now filmed as *Shadowlands*) illuminates the essence of grief, especially when he rails against fate and tells how grief pervades everything:

> They tell me H. is happy now, they tell me she is at peace. What makes them so sure of this? I don't mean that I fear the worst of all . . . But why are they so sure that all anguish ends with death? . . . Why should the separation which so agonizes the lover who is left behind be painless to the lover who departs? . . . Sometimes it is hard not to say 'God forgive God'. Sometimes it is hard to say so much. But if our faith is true, He didn't. He crucified Him.
>
> We are under the harrow and can't escape. Reality, looked at steadily, is unbearable . . . How often—will it be for always?—how often will the vast emptiness astonish me like a complete novelty and make me say, 'I never realized my loss till this moment'? The same leg is cut off time after time. The first plunge of the knife into the flesh is felt again and again . . . Grief is like a long valley, a winding valley where any bend may reveal a totally new landscape.

This brief account of grief helps us to an understanding of the psychoanalytic view of depression which suggests that it may be a form of abnormal grief. Grief responses are not confined to death. They may, for example, follow a break-up of a relationship, the loss of job, diminution of status or deterioration in health. These are all experiences of loss and may be accompanied by the psychological reactions of grief. Even the shattering of an ideal can cause grief in the broader application of the concept.

Psychoanalytic theory further holds that basic personality is shaped during the very early years of life (see Chapter 3). Disruptions at this time, particularly in the infant's relationship with its mother or other primary caregiver, sensitise the person to loss during adulthood and make for a greater vulnerability to depression. That person will experience ambivalence in relationships and is too dependent on others for support, guidance and confirmation of self-worth. If such a vulnerable person experiences bereavement, the deceased is no longer available as a support to bolster self-esteem. And the bereaved person's ambivalent feelings towards the lost person intensifies, with a hostile component so difficult to acknowledge that it is redirected at the self. The anger then shows itself as guilt and self-recrimination.

Apart from a depressive outcome as outlined above, death of a loved one may lead to a decline in mental and physical health. Sometimes, although a person may realistically appreciate that death has occurred, they may not acknowledge it emotionally, and a delay or absence of grief will follow. That person may suffer physical complaints whose cause is unclear, and which resemble those of the deceased during the terminal illness. A severe or prolonged grief response may lead to clinical depression with guilt, suicidal ideas and 'vegetative' symptoms (see page 98). Uncommonly, a psychotic illness is precipitated by bereavement, usually in the form of a paranoid reaction.

Stress deserves special mention in considering the causes of depression. Depressed people often experience major stressful life events immediately before their illness. It had been thought that this pattern was more typical of milder 'reactive' forms of depression, but stressful events accompany severe depression just as often. Stress may also precede the beginning of other psychiatric states like schizophrenia and anxiety, and some physical disorders like asthma and peptic ulcer. An underlying vulnerability to a particular disorder is probably the crucial factor. Stress is a personal experience—what one person finds unnerving may not be perceived as such by another. And stress is so common that it may simply coincide with the beginning of depression.

Behavioural theories to explain depression arose from animal experiments. If an electric shock is applied to an animal, it will attempt to escape. After repeated shocks, with no means of escape, the animal will eventually give up, in a state of helplessness resembling depression. Similar helpless states may arise as part of the human condition. It is further suggested that repeated setbacks pave the way for pessimistic patterns of thinking—a so-called 'negative cognitive set'. People in this situation will view the future in a bleak light and so misinterpret life events and deprecate themselves (see page 32).

## Physical illness and depression

Physically ill people commonly develop depressive symptoms—at the rate of about a third of all medical in-patients and out-patients (see page 72). The link here between mind and body may be confusing, as some general symptoms of a physical illness may be very like depressive features. Tiredness, insomnia, anorexia, weight loss, apathy and loss of libido are common both to many physical disorders and to depression. For instance, the first phase of an illness such as glandular fever may be misdiagnosed as low-grade depression—as may the early stages of cancer. As an example, for months a 25-year-old man with lymphoma of the stomach felt low in mood and energy, lost interest in everyday activities, and even reached the point of having suicidal ideas. It was routine tests during his admission to a psychiatric ward after an impulsive overdose that revealed the truth of the matter.

The fact that serious physical illness is a critical life event and therefore a substantial source of stress is another complicating factor. The physically ill may suffer many losses, including physical function, a bodily part or organ, self-esteem, earning capacity and friends. In fact, grief reactions are a normal response to illness, and their severity is usually consistent with the degree of stress. If the reaction is so marked and/or persistent as to interfere with recovery, it is regarded as a disorder in its own right and termed an adjustment disorder with depressed mood (see page 73). Symptoms of anxiety often accompany these reactions. A person who is predisposed to depression may also suffer a major depressive episode precipitated by a physical illness.

The biological effects of a physical disease may directly cause a depressive syndrome known as an organic mood disorder. A classical example is depression following an endocrine abnormality like thyroid under-functioning. Conditions affecting the central nervous system, such as stroke, Parkinson's disease, multiple sclerosis and epilepsy, may also have this effect.

Drugs which act on the brain's chemical messengers (such as the anti-hypertensive Reserpine, referred to on page 103) can cause depression; indeed suicide has been reported following the use of Reserpine. Steroid medication may cause disordered mood (usually depression, occasionally mania). Many women on oral contraceptives experience mildly lowered mood, and may choose not to continue taking the drug for this reason. Depressive symptoms have been implicated as a side-effect of many medications, such as antibiotics, analgesics, anti-convulsants and drugs used to reduce high blood pressure, but their precise role is not clear.

The doctor may have difficulty in determining whether depressive symptoms are a direct result of a physical illness, are simply coincidental, or are due to a drug. If a drug has recently been prescribed and depressive symptoms follow, it is assumed to be the cause and the person is switched to another medication. When the drug is withdrawn, the depression should subside or disappear. On the other hand, if a person has been on a particular medication for months or years and then becomes depressed, the drug is unlikely to be responsible.

## Treating the depressed person

The psychiatrist will make a thorough evaluation, including past psychiatric history, prior suicide attempts, previous psychiatric treatment and its response, family history and current physical health. At the heart of this pursuit is consideration of biological, psychological and social contributions. Information about current life circumstances and recent stress is central in assessing psychological and social factors. Physical examination may suggest the need for investigations such as thyroid function tests, blood examination and CT scan of the brain. In assessing the severity of depression and the risk of suicide, an interview with a family member or friend helps, as someone who has known the person can gauge the level of change. This assessment is a crucial part of treatment, particularly because of the risk of suicide. These following questions are always considered: Is there a suicide risk? Does the person's mood vary with environmental influences? Is the mood disturbance an 'understandable' response to life circumstances? Is there evidence of 'vegetative' symptoms such as weight loss? Does the person express inappropriate guilt? Are there psychotic symptoms?

*Psychological treatments*

People with mild depression are helped by a brief course of psychotherapy (an average of 10 to 20 sessions). There are several forms of effective psychological therapy (see Chapter 21). For instance, therapists using a

Misery and loneliness are portrayed by this sad little girl exposed to the elements.

A depressed and bowed man trudges along a dark, lonely road.

cognitive approach carefully tease out negative thoughts, attitudes and beliefs. By completing a daily diary, the person monitors his or her mood and identifies responses to life events. The therapist challenges the validity of any negative thinking by asking the person to judge its appropriateness, and also encourages a more realistic interpretation of life situations. The person may be given specific tasks from which to gain a sense of mastery.

Interpersonal therapy, another well-researched form of brief psycho-therapy for depression (and other conditions), focuses on the here and now and particularly on current family and social relationships by emphasising 'interpersonal learning'. The rationale is that emotional distress commonly arises from complications in these relationships. Crisis intervention is appropriate when the depression began recently and is linked to an obvious stressful life event. People with long-term depression, poor self-esteem, conflicted relationships and pervasive self-defeating attitudes may benefit from intensive psychoanalytically oriented therapy, either individually or in a group. Depressed people with marked marriage or family problems may be helped by one of several types of family therapy.

*Physical treatments*

People with more severe forms of depression usually do not respond to psychotherapy alone, although it is helpful in combination with medication or electro-convulsive therapy (ECT), and after recovery. Whether or not a person is hospitalised depends on their level of social support, physical health and degree of suicide risk. A serious suicide risk calls for urgent referral to a psychiatrist. If the person cannot recognise that he or she is ill and refuses treatment, compulsory care (see Chapter 18) and close nursing observation are essential, indeed can save life. Because it takes at least two to three weeks before people respond to anti-depressants, ECT may be recommended. ECT is very safe and effective. The widespread myth that it is dangerous and barbaric could not be further from the truth. We remember a leading British psychiatrist declaring in a teaching session that, if he were unfortunate enough to suffer severe depression, he would want to be hooked up without delay to the nearest ECT machine! The main unwanted effects of the treatment—headache, confusion and memory impairment for recent events—are fortunately short-lived (see Chapter 20).

Most people with moderately severe depression are treated with anti-depressant medication and supportive care, with no need for hospitalisation (or ECT). The anti-depressant drugs fall into three main groups: the tricyclics, monoamine oxidase inhibitors (MAOIs), and so-called second generation drugs. The chemical names of these drugs and the usual dosage range are listed in the following table.

**The anti-depressant drugs**

| Drug | Usual dosage (milligrams per day) |
| --- | --- |
| **Tricyclics** | |
| Amitriptyline | 100–250 |
| Clomipramine | 100–250 |
| Desimipramine | 100–250 |
| Dothiepin | 100–250 |
| Doxepin | 100–250 |
| Imipramine | 100–250 |
| Nortriptyline | 50–150 |
| Trimipramine | 100–250 |
| **MAOIs** | |
| Phenelzine | 30–90 |
| Tranylcypromine | 20–60 |
| **Second generation** | |
| Mianserin | 30–120 |
| Moclobemide | 300–600 |
| Fluoxetine | 20 |
| Paroxetine | 20 |
| Sertraline | 50–200 |
| Venlafaxine | 37.5–150 |

Many studies have confirmed that these drugs are effective. Two-thirds of people respond well to them. There is little evidence that one anti-depressant is more helpful than another, although there is some doubt about the value of the MAOIs. The choice is really based on side-effects. Most people tolerate tricyclics, but a third suffer some side-effects and about one in ten who use the drug will stop because of them. Common unpleasant side-effects are dry mouth, constipation, blurred vision, drowsiness, weight gain and dizziness. The more sedating anti-depressants are taken at night to aid sleep.

MAOIs are only prescribed by experienced psychiatrists. Their side-effects include dizziness, insomnia and sexual impotence. The most serious complication results from their interaction with certain chemicals (tyra-mine) in food and other drugs, resulting in a rapid rise of blood pressure. People treated with a MAOI must therefore keep a strict diet, particularly avoiding mature cheeses, red wine and certain drugs. Fortunately, this last complication has been overcome through advances in drug development; the modern MAOIs do not affect blood pressure. The earlier forms are only prescribed when absolutely necessary.

Suicide risk is a crucial consideration when using the older anti-depressants as they can be lethal when taken in overdose. Tricyclics are toxic to the heart in excessive dose, even causing death from an irregular heart rhythm. For people over 55 years, an electro-cardiogram is per-formed before starting treatment with a tricyclic.

Newer drugs, the so-called second generation anti-depressants, have fewer side-effects and seem to be much safer in overdose. If there is heart disease, these are the drugs of first choice. The best known are the selective serotonin re-uptake inhibitors (SSRIs). The first one of these to be discov-ered, fluoxetine (Prozac), has received widespread publicity. As the name suggests, the SSRIs probably act by blocking the re-entry of the chemical messenger, serotonin, into the brain cell from which it was released, and so permitting more to pass to another cell and activate it.

For the treatment to be effective, an adequate dose must be taken and for a long enough time. There is a great deal of individual variation in tol-erance of these medications. People taking a tricyclic for the first time are warned about side-effects, taking alcohol and possible effects on driving. One approach is to start with a low dose and, if the drug is well tolerated, to increase by small amounts every two to three days to a standard dose. Mild side-effects are usual, and indeed their absence may suggest inade-quate levels of the drug in the body. People usually are instructed to take the medication before going to bed, to improve sleep and minimise drowsiness during the day. They will be seen at least weekly until there is a definite improvement. An adequate trial requires four to six weeks of med-ication at an appropriate dose. If there is an insufficient response, a higher dose is tried, provided the person tolerates the drug (the higher the dose the more likely the side-effects). If there is no improvement within four to six weeks, other treatments will be considered.

This approach may vary, depending on the type of anti-depressant drug prescribed. The SSRIs, for instance, are usually taken in a single dose, in the morning, because of the possible side-effect of insomnia. The MAOIs may also produce insomnia but, because their effect is short-lived, they are best taken in the morning and at lunchtime.

To be effective, drug treatment for a depressive episode must continue for six to nine months after improvement. The anti-depressant is then gradually withdrawn. People with recurring major bouts of depression often need regular medication, sometimes for years, or they may be advised to start taking it again at the earliest sign of relapse. Lithium is often used for long-term depression to help reduce the number of episodes.

## Treating mania

People with hypomania or mania are treated in essentially the same way as those with an acute psychosis. The first step is to rule out organic conditions, including drug-induced states. For reasons of safety, most people need admission to hospital which, because of their lack of insight, may be involuntary. The mainstay of drug treatment are anti-psychotics like Haloperidol and Chlorpromazine. Lithium is another effective anti-manic drug at relatively high concentrations, but it is slow to act. ECT may be needed occasionally, for particularly severe cases.

In the long-term, most people with bipolar mood disorder take lithium, as it often reduces the rate of recurrence. It succeeds in preventing both mania and depression in up to 80 per cent of affected people. Carbamazepine and Sodium Valproate, which are actually anti-epileptic drugs, are also useful in prevention and may be substituted if lithium fails or causes excessive side-effects.

## Conclusion

The story of mood disorders and their treatment mirrors the story of modern psychiatry in one significant way. The consignment of people to the gruesome fate of months of sheer agony has been replaced by early detection and effective treatment.

The distress of hundreds of thousands of people has been eased by the discovery of and continuing advances in anti-depressant drugs and the development of specific psychological treatments. The causes of the various forms of mood disorders are still unclear, but there are grounds for optimism here as researchers tackle the subject on all fronts—biological, psychological and social.

# 9 *Mind Talking Through Body*

Many people who suffer physical symptoms and ill health actually have emotional problems but are experiencing them through the body. They may or may not have a medical condition, but even if they do it is not enough, in their doctor's judgement, to fully explain the health problems. Such situations of psychological distress are all too common in medical practice. They affect about a quarter of people attending family doctors, but are still a puzzle to both patient and doctor (see Chapter 3).

Two words are often used to describe these situations. In hysteria (an ambiguous word but one with a rich history), there are physical symptoms but no physical disease. In hypochondria, people are preoccupied with a fear of having, or conviction that they have, a serious illness.

Bodily symptoms with an emotional basis may also be part of the so-called psychosomatic illnesses, where medical conditions are certainly present but are heavily influenced by psychological factors (see page 71).

In all these conditions, bodily symptoms arise from, or are accentuated by, emotional forces of which the person is mostly unaware. Defence mechanisms that are deployed at an unconscious level transform the emotional state into bodily dysfunction, and this shows itself as physical symptoms (see page 67). People interpret these physical symptoms in vastly different ways. One person, for instance, may readily put a headache down to stress while another is convinced that it is due to a brain tumour.

If symptoms are under voluntary control, then the person is regarded as faking illness or malingering for an obvious purpose. It might be a student trying to avoid the pressures of an examination, or a person determined to gain financial compensation after a minor accident.

## Why the mysterious leap from mind to body?

This is how many observers have described the puzzling transformation of one form of experience into another—the emotional into the bodily.

Personality factors and defence mechanisms have been particularly valuable in helping us to understand the process, but the most illuminating concepts have come from medical sociologists. Their ideas of the 'sick role' and 'illness behaviour' provide a useful social and cultural perspective from which to approach the subject. In all societies, people who become ill are granted certain privileges—exemption from work and other responsibilities and offers of care by family and friends. They are also expected to meet certain obligations—to seek medical help and to accept the recommended treatment in order to recover as soon as possible.

'Illness behaviour' describes people's responses in the 'sick role', particularly how they perceive, evaluate and act on bodily symptoms. These responses vary greatly, from the stoical to the dramatic, from communicating distress in words to displaying it through gesture and action. People who exaggerate physical symptoms and are preoccupied with them have been described as showing a form of 'abnormal illness behaviour', at least in the eyes of the doctor. When such behaviour is combined with denial in the face of obvious psychological distress, at least to others, then the psychiatric states described below come into play.

Some of the variation in people's responses is linked to social factors and may be particular to an ethnic group, social class or a family. Social context is relevant generally—for example, a severe injury in a football match may go unnoticed whereas a relatively trivial injury at work may bring intense distress. Similarly, a work injury may be a badge of honour in one family, a symbol of weakness in another.

## Who is predisposed to talk through their body?

People with exaggerated symptoms often share certain personality traits, although it is difficult to know whether these have always been there or have resulted from prolonged distress. Dependency, or the tendency to be too needy and demanding of others, is a good example. Masochism, or obtaining satisfaction through painful experience, is another trait which may work strongly against a return to health. People often relieve feelings of guilt by finding in 'suffering' a sense of punishment.

Anger is very common. It may be directed either externally, say to medical staff for their 'uselessness', or inwards, when it may take the form of 'refusing' to take medication, co-operate with treatment, undergo necessary surgery or ultimately get better. Analgesics have no effect on pain, prescribed medications produce intolerable side-effects and even surgery fails to bring relief.

These sorts of patients challenge the doctor, who feels inadequate. They continue to return for treatment until there is little or nothing else to try. This sometimes leads to desperate measures like surgery, which in turn may bring their own complications. Generally, such people are long suffering. They may, if delicately questioned, tell of having had their own needs unmet as children when they had to care for a younger or ill sibling or an ill parent. They came to deny their own needs and grew up into 'compulsive carers', overly responsible and tending to others. Then, often triggered by a minor illness or injury, their role is radically reversed. Quite unexpectedly, as they are oblivious of their underlying psychological needs, they become long-term users of health care.

One way to bring all these elements together is by applying psychoanalytic ideas. Freud believed that the 'somatising' response is an unconsciously determined manoeuvre to deal with a deeply embedded psychological conflict. The symptom that arises symbolically reflects that conflict—in essence, it is a disguised form of it. The reduction in anxiety that results from this compromise solution (the somatising response) is called 'primary gain'. 'Secondary gain' refers to the more obvious advantages of physical illness such as sympathy, care and relief from responsibility. Our modern term, 'somatisation', encompasses Freud's somatising response, which is the tendency to experience and communicate emotional distress as physical symptoms.

Anna O., perhaps the most important case in all of psychoanalysis, is highly relevant in this context. She was treated by Josef Breuer, a celebrated physician in Vienna, in the early 1880s. Freud became involved as a close colleague and friend of Breuer's in trying to unravel her seemingly inexplicable physical symptoms. Their jointly written book, *Studies in Hysteria* published in 1895, was the outcome of this pioneering clinical research. Anna O. helps us to understand the conversion of emotional conflict into bodily symptoms. A young attractive woman, she had nursed her dying father and in the process developed a number of physical symptoms including nervous crying, paralysis of her limbs and her neck, a squint, difficulty in talking, and a problem with swallowing.

In treatment with hypnosis, Anna O. re-experienced the intense feelings she had had while at her father's bedside. In recalling, in the hypnotised state, these experiences in which her symptoms had originally occurred it became clear how each one of them related to actual events surrounding her relationship with her ill father. Through this sort of detective work, Freud and Breuer were the first to propose that psychological factors, operating unconsciously, could affect bodily function, so mimicking physical disorders. Soon, Freud advanced this thinking by emphasising the sexual nature of the underlying psychic conflicts, and so shaped the long-term direction of psychoanalysis. Although the sexual dimension did not find favour with many of Freud's contemporaries (a position which still holds today), his fundamental contribution to the understanding of hysterical phenomena remains as compelling as it was a century ago.

One of our own patients throws further light on the influence of the psyche on bodily function:

> *Werner, a 35-year-old teacher of the intellectually disabled, awoke one morning with a paralysed right arm after observing his wife flirting with a close friend at a staff party the evening before. When tests in hospital ruled out a stroke or other physical disorders, a psychiatrist was consulted. In discussion it soon emerged that the symptom represented both Werner's wish to hit his wife and the unaccept-ability of this behaviour given his religious upbringing and moral standards. He had grown up in a puritanical environment. His parents had been members of a fundamentalist sect, and the children were expected to conform to the sect's tenets—notably, the expression of any emotion was frowned upon. Always resentful of these constraints, Werner had unwittingly channelled his anger into dedicated involvement with a disadvantaged group.*

## The family as a crucible

A somatising response (somatisation) tends to 'run in families', probably due to their original illness behaviour and their beliefs about illness. For example, people who as infants or children suffered the loss of a key figure tend to remain particularly sensitive to how family and friends relate to them. Following a later experience of loss, they may show their distress in the form of either psychiatric or physical symptoms. Then, the care given by family and health professionals may become an alternative source of gratification that compensates for the earlier loss but paradoxically per-petuates the symptoms.

To understand the meaning of an illness for a particular person, the doctor has to appreciate that early experience of illness and the way it was handled in the family may powerfully determine later illness behaviour.

## How the psychiatrist approaches somatisation

Somatisation is a feature in many psychiatric states, but sometimes the physical symptoms are so prominent that the underlying psychological disorder is hidden, or masked. So depressed people often experience fatigue, constipation, aches and pains, and preoccupation with physical symptoms (see Chapter 8). In people with anxiety disorders, bodily changes (such as palpitations and the shakes) may predominate (see Chapter 7). Loss of weight is central to anorexia nervosa (see Chapter 10). Less commonly, unexplained physical symptoms like an unshakeable belief that one's intestines are rotting occur in the psychoses as the content of bizarre delusions (see Chapter 12).

A regular dilemma for the psychiatrist (and for any doctor) is to determine whether a set of physical symptoms are mainly physical or psychological in origin. In our view, this is a meaningless distinction, as in most illnesses both these elements, together with social factors, make a combined contribution. In practice, the real task is to sort out to what extent each one of these three elements bears upon a particular disorder. The following case is a typical clinical conundrum:

*Mrs J, a 74-year-old woman with previously documented angina, had been living alone since the death of her husband eighteen months previously. Her daughter telephoned to say she was going overseas. Mrs J immediately developed chest pain and feelings of panic. On admission to hospital it was unclear whether the symptoms were an episode of angina, conversion of her concern about being left on her own into chest pain, chest discomfort typically associated with anxiety, or malingering—that is, simulation of angina in order to gain her daughter's attention. All were possible in the circumstances.*

## Hypochondriasis

The hallmark of hypochondriasis is the fear of having, or the belief that one has, a serious disease, when a thorough clinical check-up does not support the diagnosis of a physical disorder that would account for the symptoms. Over three hundred years ago, the French playwright Molière gave a vivid account of this human malady in his satire, *Le Malade Imaginaire*. The central character, Argan, is so thoroughly and incessantly preoccupied with matters of ill health and disease that his life is consumed by them, with unpleasant results for his family. At one point, Argan rebukes his daughter like this: 'Ah! She has entirely put me . . . out, and I shall want more than eight doses of medicine and 12 enemas to put all this right'.

The hypochondriac is imprisoned by morbid preoccupations. There is no room for a commonsense view or even a touch of humour. Indeed, these health preoccupations and resistance to reassurance make the person the butt of humour. A wizard of Id cartoon illustrates this nicely. The nurse informs the doctor that the hypochondriac has arrived for a consultation. 'Why are you so concerned about your health?', the doctor asks (rather naively, one would think). 'Death runs in our family', the patient responds in all seriousness!

People with hypochondriasis are on a never-ending vigil in obsessing about every detail of bodily function, being exquisitely sensitive to physical sensations, which they interpret as evidence of a serious disease. But this behaviour occurs in many situations, especially in the elderly and as a response to actual physical disease. A specific diagnosis of hypochondriasis is made when these concerns linger on for months despite repeated medical reassurance. The person may worry about multiple diseases or fix on a single condition. For instance, in 'cardiac neurosis' the person's fear is of having heart disease; in 'cancer phobia' the concern is of a hidden tumour. This is the classical hypochondriacal pattern:

> Mrs P, a 77-year-old married woman, consulted her family doctor in a state of agitation, complaining of headache and dizziness and convinced she had a brain tumour. Her fears were calmed temporarily after a thorough physical examination. The doctor's sensitive inquiry drew out the following story. Mrs P was the youngest of a family of ten children. Since her father's death when she was fifteen and her sisters' departure from home, she had had to care for her mother. Mother had died of cancer six months previously. A brother and a niece had also died of cancer, while one of her own daughters had survived it in childhood. In the preceding month both of her unmarried daughters had revealed plans to leave home. The doctor concluded that all these stresses had led to marked anxiety and hypochondriacal concerns. A sense of potential abandonment had highlighted Mrs P's own emotional needs for others, which had been inadequately met as a child. Her fears were closely associated with her experience of family members suffering from cancer and her mother's fatal illness.

## Conversion disorder

Psychiatrists apply this diagnosis when a person's loss of, or alteration in, bodily function suggests a medical disorder but thorough clinical examination reveals no evidence of such and the symptoms appear to be a response to stress. The symptoms are typically, although not necessarily, related to the nervous system—for example, paralysis or inability to speak (as in the case of Anna O.). A seeming lack of concern (so-called '*la belle indifférence*') about the symptoms was described originally as a central feature, but is not always present.

Conversion disorders were much more common in the nineteenth century, reflecting their close links with social and cultural factors. That they are more common in women, and in developing countries, also points to socio-cultural influences.

The diagnosis is always difficult to make, as it involves a judgement that symptoms are not physically determined. A complicating issue is the person's typical response: 'So, you think its all in my head!' The possibility arises if the doctor's findings on physical examination do not match any known patterns of bodily dysfunction—for example, paralysis of a limb with nothing to indicate damage to the nerves supplying the affected limb. The likelihood of a conversion disorder is strengthened by a story of psychological stress preceding the onset of the symptom.

*Claudia's 8-year-old son had died tragically in a boating accident. At first, she was grief-stricken, cried uncontrollably and experienced vivid images of the accident. On the morning after the funeral she complained of weakness in her legs to the extent that she found it difficult to walk. Physical examination by her family doctor revealed normal neurological functioning, including reflexes and sensation. Claudia's symptoms were no doubt due to a conversion disorder, the translation of grief into bodily weakness. The significance of the death was intensified by the difficulty she had had in conceiving her son and by the memories reawakened in her of her husband lost five years previously in a car accident. As in many of these cases, Claudia did not share this pivotal information with her doctors as she was so preoccupied with her 'paralysis' and worried that multiple sclerosis might be the culprit.*

The commonest form of conversion disorder today is somatoform pain disorder, where the main symptom is obviously pain. The pain is severe and prolonged, and no adequate physical cause can be located.

*Linda, a 36-year-old woman, fell at work and since then had had unremitting back pain, unrelieved by medication. At first no physical changes were found. However, following her fourth series of x-rays in eighteen months, the third orthopaedic surgeon she consulted diagnosed a slipped disc and recommended surgery. When reviewed two years after the operation by a psychiatrist, Linda was still physically disabled, entirely dependent on her husband, and thoroughly demoralised. He drew out a story which gave him a good understanding of her plight. As a child she had been responsible for her younger sister when both parents had worked. Following primary school she had been sent to boarding school, a move she resented bitterly. After completing a university degree Linda joined the public service and was soon promoted to a managerial position. She then became attracted to, and soon married, a man much younger than herself. Thus, with her emotional needs in childhood unmet, she responded as an adult by striving for positions of superiority (and therefore invulnerability) in both work and marriage.*

*A minor event, the fall, forced Linda to resume a dependent role. Her doctors experienced many negative feelings about her, seeing her as punishing and belittling. The psychiatrist put this understanding to effect in psychotherapy where she was encouraged to address the issue of her anger toward her parents and associated guilt. This, combined with a physical rehabilitation programme, led to gradual improvement.*

## Neurasthenia

This disorder has had a long, chequered history. The main features are general fatigue and difficulty in concentration, with physical symptoms such as dizziness and muscular aches—often accompanied by anxiety and depression. Neurasthenia is not often diagnosed today, but many of its features resemble those of chronic fatigue syndrome. Debate now rages about whether chronic fatigue syndrome, together with myalgic encephalitis and repetitive strain injury, are physical or psychological in origin.

## Psychogenic amnesia and fugue

Although confusing to the general public, psychiatrists include within conversion disorders a number of psychiatric states in which psychic conflict of one kind or another is transformed not into physical symptoms but rather into particular disturbances of mental functioning such as loss of identity or of memory. Dissociation, a term coined by the great French psychiatrist Pierre Janet, is used to cover the unconscious process involved.

A typical dissociative state is psychogenic amnesia—that is, psychologically induced memory loss in contrast to the common brief amnesia following concussion. A sudden inability to recall basic personal information is its hallmark. Related is depersonalisation, in which people feel unreal, detached from themselves, as if in a dream-like state. Less common but most dramatic is psychogenic fugue, where typically the person wanders away from home without any sense of who he or she is and is found days or weeks later—in rare cases having assumed a totally new identity.

Although depersonalisation is experienced by many people during anxiety-provoking events, amnesia and fugue usually occur only in extremely stressful situations such as war or disaster. These psychological states may also occur in the face of overwhelming internal unresolvable conflict. The case of Sophia is a perfect illustration:

> Sophia a 21-year-old student from a traditional Greek family, was found by police wandering in the centre of the city, confused about who she was. When brought to the hospital emergency department, it emerged that she was totally amnesic—she could not remember her name, where she lived or any details about her family.
>
> Over the next three days, Sophia gradually recovered her memory by which time the police had located her parents. When she was more 'accessible', her story enabled the psychiatrist to make sense of the psychologically based amnesia. Her boyfriend had been pressing for them to begin a sexual relationship on the grounds that they were 'serious' about each other. Sophia was inclined to agree to this, but the prohibition of pre-marital intercourse by her parents and their culture led to an intense internal conflict. Her desire to satisfy her boyfriend's wishes seemed irreconcilable with her loyalty to her family. Hopelessly stuck, her mind resorted to an unconscious manoeuvre which enabled her to 'forget' not only the dilemma but her entire identity. Involvement of the family allowed an open exchange of feelings about Sophia's dilemma, which paved the way for a reconciliation.

Multiple personality disorder, in which two or more personalities appear to function alongside one another in the same person, but quite separately and without one being familiar with the others, is a rare and fascinating form of severe dissociation. It is a source of intense controversy, with the mental health professions quite unable to agree even about whether such a condition exists at all. Some say that the disorder results from early life trauma, particularly sexual abuse, which is forgotten for a time but may be recovered through sensitive psychotherapy—the so-called repressed memory syndrome. Others contend that such memories are the products of the therapist's imagination and influence rather than memories of 'actual' events.

## Psychosomatic disorders

In contrast to all the above conditions, psychiatrists often assist in the treatment of people with psychosomatic disorders—that is, those in which psychological factors appear to play a causal or aggravating role in an actual physical disease. Several medical conditions have been labelled psychosomatic, including high blood pressure, asthma, dermatitis, ulcerative colitis, peptic ulcer and rheumatoid arthritis. After decades of meticulous studies, the link between *specific* psychological conflicts and these conditions has not been found, indeed has been abandoned (for example, the association claimed between a frustrated wish to be fed and nurtured, and peptic ulcer). On the other hand, stress generally does appear to trigger and/or aggravate any medical disorder. For example, an interaction between a driven, ambitious personality (sometimes referred to as Type A), work stress and coronary heart disease is well established, especially as demonstrated in a most comprehensive study of thousands of men in Framingham, in the state of New York.

The fact that emotions can trigger common bodily changes like rapid heart rate, elevated blood pressure and increased gastric secretion is one clue as to how stressful states may often bring on or worsen medical conditions. Further evidence for this psychosomatic link is that psychotherapy enhances biological treatment in tackling medical symptoms—for example, anti-inflammatory drugs in rheumatoid arthritis and bronchodilators in asthma. Asthma is perhaps one of the most clear-cut medical conditions in which psyche and soma intersect.

> *Sylvie, a 45-year-old woman with a history of intermittent asthma since her teenage years, developed more severe and more frequent attacks despite maximal drug therapy. Inquiry revealed a pending divorce and increasing repressed hostility towards her estranged husband. Treatment involved helping Sylvie to become aware of her anger and to express it, but in the context of a therapeutic relationship. She also became aware of long-concealed resentment towards her parents over the deprivation she felt following their divorce when she was a young child. The psychological dimension of treatment led to better control of her asthma by standard doses of anti-asthmatic medication.*

## Treating both soma and psyche

Ideally, all doctors should treat both the body and the mind, with the balance between somatic and psychological treatment varying according to individual circumstances. With people who speak through their bodies, the doctor seeks to shift their preoccupation from the exclusively physical to the psychological (and the social) and to assist them to wrestle, and come to terms, with the latter more adaptively. The sensitive doctor does this without challenging the legitimacy of the physical symptoms. In general, the more sudden the onset of the physical changes and the clearer their link with psychological stress the better the outcome. On the other hand, long-standing forms of somatisation are most resistant to change.

Confrontation virtually never succeeds. Rather, the doctor carefully poses the question whether a physical condition exists or not. The doctor's purpose is to determine if there is an adequate physical basis to explain all the symptoms, as well as to gain the person's confidence that the complaints are being taken seriously and not being dismissed as trivial or, even worse, as 'neurotic'.

The snags in this process can be formidable. Repeated use of complex investigations is likely to reinforce the person's conviction of a bodily disturbance, even when the doctor suspects a psychological basis. Errors are made in both directions. People who do not have a bodily disease may, for instance, end up being referred for surgery, whereas others diagnosed as 'hysterical' may turn out to have a real physical disorder. Over-investigation is encouraged by a generally increasing reliance on technology among doctors, combined with a demanding or anxious patient and the possibility of being sued for negligence. A valuable rule of thumb for both patient and doctor is that once a 'workup' is complete, no further tests are done and treatment proceeds on the basis of psychological counselling, review at regular intervals, and drug treatment as appropriate. However, the doctor remains alert to the possibility of a new medical disorder emerging.

The place of drugs is complicated. Unfortunately, somatising people are often sensitive to the side-effects of almost all medications, and drugs like anti-depressants are poorly tolerated. And, because of a concern about addiction, drugs for anxiety and insomnia are prescribed with excessive caution. Drug treatment of enduring psychogenic pain is problematic as it tends not to respond to conventional methods. People with pain from any cause need analgesics. However, those with predominantly psychogenic pain are prescribed strong analgesics rarely, if at all, again because of their addictive properties. Indeed, the key to treatment of chronic pain is not medication but attention to psychological and social issues.

*Mr S, a 60-year-old married man, had developed irritable bowel syndrome ten years previously following an extra-marital affair. He consulted his family doctor because of a recent onset of severe and disabling headache; he had been thinking of telling his wife about the affair after she had suffered a mild stroke. Neurological examination and investigations were all normal. However, Mr S's headaches persisted, along with lowered mood, loss of interest and pleasure in everyday activities, slowness in thinking, feelings of remorse and early morning waking. A biopsychosocial approach was adopted, to excellent effect. This combined continued drug treatment for the irritable bowel, judicious use of analgesics for the headache, a course of anti-depressant medication (biological) and individual and marital psychotherapies (psychological).*

The contribution of biological, psychological and social factors is well illustrated in Mr S's case. The possible presence of depression or anxiety is relevant because they are both readily treatable. Depression, which commonly occurs alongside physical symptoms, varies from grief over the loss of bodily functions to sustained, generally depressed mood. Many people who are not fully aware of their inner emotional state may still benefit from specific anti-depressant or anti-anxiety treatment.

If doctor and patient have conflicting approaches to the problem, then psychological and social treatment may be hampered. Indeed, they may clash over the basic question of whether the condition is physical or psychological, much to the patient's dismay. When the doctor focuses on psychological matters, the patient may vehemently resist. In any event, the doctor should strive to understand the patient's point of view through empathy and discussion of practical difficulties imposed by the illness. Trust is a key to the sharing of personal dilemmas and concerns whether at work, in marriage or in other relationships. Mr S's case shows how psychotherapy may relieve symptoms in people who accept that approach. Gains are made by shifting the focus from symptoms to adaptive coping. This overcomes the impasse and gives the person an opportunity to set achievable goals and to improve functioning and self-esteem. In more severe cases, compromise rather than cure is the only realistic option.

A striking feature of treatment is the large number of professionals who may become involved, including the family doctor, physician, surgeon, psychologist, social worker, physiotherapist, occupational therapist and psychiatrist. Such a cumbersome team may not work in unison. Opinions will differ and individuals may even offer contradictory advice. Ideally, one professional co-ordinates an agreed-on plan of treatment, most conveniently the family doctor. A role for the psychiatrist usually emerges when either formal psychiatric illness is suspected or the frustrations of other professionals reach a crescendo!

## Conclusion

The sheer complexity of the link between psyche and soma, the mind and the body, has been reflected in our own difficulty in presenting the ideas in this chapter any more clearly. Despite a century of scholarly interest and research effort, the somatisation and psychosomatic groups of disorders remain a source of bafflement and frustration. However, one thing is abundantly clear—mind and body cannot be separated from each other. They are inextricably bound together, whether in health or illness. The psychiatrist's understanding of this will, at least, enable the adoption of a coherent therapeutic approach in trying to meet the challenge of the somatising response.

# 10  *Eating, Sex and Sleep*

Having looked generally at mind/body relationships and seen how inter-connected they are, we will now turn to three areas of bodily functioning —eating, sleeping and sexual behaviour. They warrant special attention because they are basic to biological integrity and full of meaning and symbolic significance. As a result, these three functions are especially sensitive to becoming disturbed by psychological factors. Minor disturbances are commonplace—such as temporary insomnia due to stress. More serious disordered function is less common but tends to reflect deep, underlying emotional imbalance. So, it is no surprise that the psychiatrist is enlisted in trying to understand and deal with what, on the face of it, are physical complaints.

## EATING DISORDERS

Concern about the size and shape of our bodies is widespread in Western society. Equally common is a concern about what we eat. In fact it would be the rare teenage girl who has not experimented with dieting. The model, Twiggy, from the era of the 1960s, and Kate Moss in the 1990s, demonstrate how an inappropriately slim body can capture the imagination of a society, particularly through the focus of the media. This is mostly of no great consequence, being simply one facet of the surrounding culture. However, dieting can go drastically wrong, even to the extent of becoming a life-threatening illness.

Anorexia nervosa is one of the most dramatic of all psychiatric dis-orders. The typical picture is of a girl inexplicably starving herself, at times to the point of death. Its central feature is severe weight loss in the relent-less pursuit of thinness. Although widely regarded as a contemporary condition, a similar clinical picture has been noted for centuries. In the Middle Ages, cases of weight loss, celibacy and asceticism in young women were taken as evidence of sainthood. The first clear description of anorexia nervosa dates back to 1689, but the syndrome was established through the accounts of Pierre Lasègue in Paris and William Gull in Oxford (who gave the condition its present name) some two centuries later.

By contrast, the history of the other common eating disorder, bulimia nervosa—that is, binge eating and vomiting—is brief. The syndrome was first outlined in 1979, reflecting then its 'epidemic' proportions and the accompanying professional interest in its treatment. It is possible, however, that features of the syndrome go back hundreds of years: St Catherine of Siena made herself vomit as a form of repentance in the fourteenth century, while St Mary Magdalen de Pazzi exhibited a pattern of over-eating followed by vomiting in the early seventeenth century.

These two principal disorders of eating occur mainly in young women, usually starting in the late teens. Abnormal patterns of eating are in fact extraordinarily common in young women. Fortunately, most are transitory and do not progress to the clear-cut disorders to which we now turn.

## Anorexia nervosa

Self-induced weight loss, intense fear of becoming fat and cessation of periods (amenorrhoea) are the three core elements of anorexia nervosa. Weight loss is usually achieved through starvation—following up on a strongly held, distorted view of the body's weight and shape—as well as through over-exercising and vomiting. A weight of 15 per cent below the standard for age and height is the commonly applied criterion for the condition, while amenorrhoea is defined as missing more than two consecutive menstrual periods. People typically fear gaining weight, even if substantially underweight, based on a grossly distorted perception of themselves as larger than is actually the case. They report feeling fat even when at an extremely low weight; on objective psychological tests they overestimate their current size. Associated with the starvation is an unusual fascination with food—its preparation, consumption and disposal. This includes avoidance of eating in company, odd eating practices such as cutting food into minute pieces, eating slowly, drinking large amounts of water, spicing food heavily and hoarding or hiding food.

Other symptoms may include depression, particularly in the severely underweight person, exercise rituals, loss of sexual drive and insomnia.

Physical signs may include slow heart rate, cold extremities, low blood pressure, swollen legs and a fine downy hair on the face and trunk. Starvation has dramatic effects on the body. Of the various hormonal and metabolic changes that occur in eating disorders, most are a direct result of weight loss. Fortunately, most changes are reversible, except for long-standing osteoporosis (bone thinning due to lack of calcium).

All these features are important in establishing the diagnosis, since weight loss can also point to several serious psychiatric and physical disorders. For example, in severe depression with pronounced weight loss, the person has a genuine loss of appetite and is not anxious about body image. Or a schizophrenic person may have marked weight loss because of a conviction that food is poisoned and unsafe to eat, but will not hold the attitudes to eating and weight that are typical of anorexia nervosa. People with physical illnesses may experience weight loss without the other symptoms. Someone with an overactive thyroid gland, for instance, may lose weight despite normal eating but, again, without the attitudes to the body typical of anorexia nervosa.

## Bulimia nervosa

The key difference between anorexia and bulimia is that weight is generally not lost in the latter. In fact, the core symptoms are repeated bouts of uncontrolled over-eating, an intense fear of gaining weight and attempts to limit its increase through extreme weight control strategies. The disorder typically begins with dieting in an attempt to lose weight. The person's compulsions to 'give in' to urges to eat is followed by vomiting, spontaneous or induced, to get rid of that food. Over-eating involves large amounts of high-calorie foods—chocolate and cakes are common—and may only end through abdominal discomfort, pain and vomiting. Binges are triggered by stress, and tend to occur in cycles. The manoeuvres people use to lose weight are self-induced vomiting, purging with laxatives or fluid tablets, and intensive exercising. Although people are anxious about weight gain, weight remains normal. Amenorrhoea occurs in a third of people with bulimia.

## Causes of anorexia and bulimia

There are various causes of both anorexia and bulimia nervosa. Eating disorders are five times more common in family members of anorexia nervosa patients than in normal families, which suggests a genetic factor. Moreover, twin studies show a concordance rate of 50 per cent for anorexia nervosa in identical twins compared with only 5 per cent in non-identical twins (see page 26).

Triggers such as being teased about weight and difficulty in intimate relationships point to a psychological contribution. Whether specific stress factors apply is less clear. A personality dominated by perfectionism may be significant. Psychoanalytically oriented therapists have suggested that anorexia nervosa develops as an unconscious manoeuvre to avoid facing the challenges of moving to emotional and sexual maturity. Obviously, an emaciated girl stands little chance of being regarded as sexually attractive. On the other hand, family therapists highlight recurring patterns of relating in families with an anorexic member—parental over-protection of the children, over-involvement in the affairs of one another, rigidity in ways of thinking and inability to resolve conflict. Family dysfunction of this kind is certainly observed, but it is unclear to what extent it precedes the anorexia nervosa or results from the family's struggle to cope with an anorexic member. Peter Dally's observations reflect the intrinsic complexity:

> An adolescent's refusal to eat with her family . . . reflects her inability or refusal to communicate her deeper and still unacceptable feelings. In turn, parents and other eating companions feel puzzled, hurt and rejected by such behaviour, then angry, and ultimately helpless. A vicious circle quickly arises and the family flounders in disarray around the patient, whose triumph is always tinged with guilt.

The increasing number of people seeking treatment has brought speculation that social influences are relevant. As mentioned earlier, the widespread Western emphasis on a slim body shape may be relevant, particularly as in non-Western cultures where such attitudes are uncommon, eating disorders are rare. Additional evidence of a social role comes from groups such as ballet dancers, models and athletes who are under constant pressure to maintain a trim body—for example, anorexia nervosa is estimated to affect about one in ten dancers. When they are removed from this influence, spontaneous improvement tends to follow. Adolescent dieting may be the key ingredient in these social circumstances. Indeed, girls who diet have a massive, eight-times greater risk of developing an eating disorder than those who do not.

## Treatment and outcome of anorexia and bulimia

The psychiatrist first establishes the diagnosis by excluding other conditions which may mimic an eating disorder, and looks at the extent of psychiatric and physical problems. A key factor is the degree and rate of weight loss. Nutritional treatment is the first core element for anorexia nervosa, followed by psychological therapies like those also necessary for bulimia nervosa.

In severe cases of anorexia nervosa, people must be admitted to hospital so as to restore their weight. Many in-patient programmes adopt a behavioural approach in which weight gain is reinforced by incentives such as increased social contact (for example, with family and friends) and freedom of movement. Beyond this, treatment may include strict bedrest, isolation and occasionally feeding through a tube passed into the stomach.

Because of the role of psychological factors in triggering the illness as well as in recurrences, one or more forms of psychotherapy are used. Lasègue wrote that he 'placed in parallel the morbid condition of the patient with the preoccupations of those who surrounded her'. The need to attend to complex family relationships in anorexia nervosa is extremely important. We still don't know whether specific patterns of family interaction predispose people to anorexia, but the value of family therapy has been confirmed by research. After weight restoration, people in their teens who have not been ill for long are particularly likely to benefit from such family intervention. Individual psychotherapy is more suited to adults who live away from their families (see Chapter 21).

The most effective treatment for bulimia nervosa is cognitive-behavioural therapy—on the basis that a person's false and distorted ideas about weight and body shape perpetuate the abnormal behaviour (see page 291). The person is advised about good patterns of eating, monitored through the use of a diary, trained to control bingeing and to avoid dieting. Anti-depressants of a particular type have been used in bulimia nervosa, usually as a subsidiary treatment (see page 270). For people with marked depressive symptoms, anti-depressants may be essential to curb self-destructive feelings.

In anorexia nervosa, we look at the outcome from several perspectives—the persistence of the condition, any continuing psychological and social difficulties, and mortality. Half of the people treated recover, a quarter retain some symptoms, and the remaining quarter do not respond. Since it may take a few years to achieve a positive result, there is no cause for pessimism early in the treatment. On the other hand, poor outcome correlates with severe weight loss, long-lasting illness, an older age of onset and marked family dysfunction. Mortality has declined in recent years from 15 per cent to a third of this, probably due to more effective treatment. Half of these deaths are suicides, and others are due to complications of starvation.

In bulimia nervosa, the outcome is not clear-cut. The persistence of illness is similar to that of anorexia nervosa, with half of those affected recovering well and a quarter remaining afflicted.

## Obesity

We all know how people turn to food as a source of comfort at times of emotional distress. Whether this behaviour, if continued long-term, leads to obesity is controversial. The medical consensus suggests that obesity is the end result of an interplay of many biological, psychological and social factors. This very common problem is not usually viewed as an eating disorder. It has simply come to be seen as a feature of contemporary life, especially in the West. Although it rarely involves risk to life or seriously impairs health, repercussions in the severe case can be serious. We need only to consider diseases closely associated with obesity, such as cardio-vascular disorders like angina and heart attack, or stroke.

Unlike anorexia and bulimia, obesity is not seen as the province of the psychiatrist. Rather, it is dealt with by self-help groups, organisations like Weight Watchers, and in rare cases by health professionals ranging from dietitians to surgeons (the latter may, for instance, staple the stomach to reduce its capacity).

## SEXUAL PROBLEMS

Sexual identity and sexual function are an intregal part of the human experience. During the twentieth century the contribution of Freud, who brought sexuality into the human psychological arena, and the pioneering work of William Masters and Virginia Johnson in describing both normal and abnormal sexual function and the treatment of the latter, have helped to draw the whole subject into a medical framework. The psychiatrist, as a part of this, plays a pivotal role in providing psychological understanding and treating many problems—ranging from sexual identity problems (uncertainty about gender) and sexual dysfunction (disturbed sexual performance) to the so-called paraphilias (deviant sexual behaviour).

## Sexual identity

Gender identity is all about the sense of being male or female. For most people, biological sex and gender identity are in harmony with each other. Sexual development is shaped by both biological processes and environmental experiences including family and social influences and cultural norms and expectations.

Problems of gender identity may stem from clear biological abnormalities (for example, a child born with deformed genitalia), early treatment of which can minimise long-term harm. On the other hand, a person may be convinced that he or she has been born the wrong sex, and may seek a change to what feels natural (trans-sexualism).

Trans-sexuals, who are usually male, ultimately become so desperate that they see the only remedy as changing their gender through surgery. Before this drastic step, they may have lived a heterosexual life, but this is always unrewarding and soon abandoned. They may also have had homosexual relationships. Not surprisingly, they will be emotionally unstable and have personality difficulties. Most people are not operated on either because their plight is not sufficiently convincing to the doctors or because the treatment facilities are not available. Some psychiatrists believe that surgery is always inappropriate and argue that psychotherapy should be offered instead to 'normalise ideas and behaviour'. However, there is no doubt that many people have adapted well to their 'converted' gender and live stable lives. One such person is the well-known British author, Jan Morris, who writes in her book, *Conundrum*:

> But it all seemed plain enough to me. I was born in the wrong body, being feminine by gender but male by sex, and I could achieve completeness only when the one was adjusted to the other . . . I believe the trans-sexual urge, at least as I have experienced it, to be far more than a social compulsion but biological, imaginative and essentially spiritual too. On a physical plane I have myself achieved, as far as is humanly possible, the identity I craved . . . So I do not mind my continuing ambiguity. I have lived the life of a man, I now live the life of a woman, and one day perhaps I shall transcend both, if not in person, then perhaps in art. If not here, then somewhere else . . .

## Sexual dysfunction

Sexual feelings increase powerfully in early adolescence. A lack of sexual feelings is usually abnormal and professional help may be needed, but it is common for people to be inhibited in their sexual expression for social, cultural or religious reasons. With good health and regular sexual practice, both sexes can remain active until late in life—although a decline in performance does accompany ageing. When a person seeks help for sexual difficulties, the family doctor or psychiatrist clarifies the nature of the problem: how it began and its pattern (gradual or sudden onset, precipitating circumstances, changes in severity and/or frequency over time); sexual behaviour before the problem arose; the person's views of the matter, including motivation for change; and the effects of any previous treatment.

The problem may have always been there (primary dysfunction), or may have followed a period of normal function (secondary dysfunction). This distinction is important for the purposes of treatment. The most common problems for men are lowered sexual drive, difficulty in achieving or maintaining an erection and ejaculating prematurely. For women, they are lowered sexual drive, painful intercourse and inability to experience orgasm.

## Problems for men

Little or no sexual activity, or lack of drive are usually the result of stress, depression, long abstinence, increasing age, poor physical health or a non-conducive environment (such as lack of privacy). Many physical conditions can reduce or abolish sexual drive—including infection, kidney failure, hormonal imbalance, neurological disturbance, the effects of surgery, malnutrition and drug side-effects.

Impotence is the failure to achieve an erection, or to keep one until intercourse is completed. Some men will never have achieved an erection sufficient for vaginal insertion, whereas others will previously have had a normal sexual pattern. Selective impotence may occur when a person is potent with one partner but not with another (although not easily able to admit to this). Impotence is rare in young men. Its frequency rises with age so that, for example, four in five men over eighty are impotent. Lifelong impotence is much more commonly associated with the previously mentioned medical conditions than with purely psychological factors. Impotence which follows a normal sexual pattern was once considered almost entirely psychological in nature, but it is sometimes linked with physical causes, the best example being diabetes.

Premature ejaculation occurs with minimal sexual stimulation before, during or soon after penetration. It often begins with a man's very first attempt at intercourse or after long abstinence. It may develop after surgery or diseases affecting the genitalia, or due to psychological factors including anxiety and hidden hostility towards his partner.

Retarded ejaculation is a delay or an absence of orgasm in an otherwise physically normal process. Orgasm may occur in other situations like masturbation, but not during intercourse itself.

## Problems for women

As with men, a lowered interest in sexual activity is usually due to stress, depression, age, physical ill health and so on, as outlined above. Sexually inhibited women may fail to achieve orgasm (inorgasmia) for both physiological reasons (for example, vaginal lubrication may be absent) and psychological reasons (such as conflict about their sexuality). Oestrogen deficiency may produce difficulty for women with a previously normal sexual pattern, especially in older women or those who have had their ovaries removed. Absent or delayed orgasm may be part of quite normal sexual arousal. Some women experience orgasm outside intercourse but not during it—which may be due to a couple's poor sexual technique. Unlike men, most instances of life-long lack of orgasm have no physical basis. Problems with a previously normal sexual pattern may be due to conditions like diabetes or the side-effects of drugs. Psychological factors include unresolved sexual conflicts, problematic gender identity, sexual abuse during childhood or an inability to relax. The outlook for women who have never experienced orgasm is optimistic. The outlook for later problems will depend on the treatment of the particular psychological or physical factors.

Vaginismus occurs when the spasm of the muscles of the woman's vagina makes intercourse difficult or impossible. Various gynaecological conditions may be responsible, or it may be due to anxiety about sexuality or pregnancy, a strained relationship, ignorance about anatomy and physiology, or fear of injury.

## Drugs that may cause dysfunction

Many drugs can cause loss of libido, interfere with erection or ejaculation in men, and delay or prevent orgasm in women. If drugs are the cause, the effects are mostly reversible when the drug is stopped or the dose decreased. Drugs for high blood pressure probably interfere with sexual function more than any other type, but dysfunction that occurs with one anti-hypertensive may not recur when the person is switched to another.

Anti-psychotics and anti-depressants may interfere with sexual function due to their disruptive effects on the neuro-transmitters which pass between nerve cells and are necessary for normal sexual function. Some anti-depressants can actually cause difficulty with ejaculation or inorgasmia, and others may affect libido and potency.

## Treatment of sexual dysfunction

The first step will be the taking of a comprehensive sexual history, and a medical examination. Special tests are sometimes necessary, particularly to determine the level of hormones. Once the possibility of a physical disorder is eliminated or treated, psychological and social factors will receive attention. In general, both partners participate wherever possible, but this is complicated to arrange in some cultural groups. It is surprising how widespread are myths and misconceptions about normal sexuality. Education therefore is often the key. Particular forms of psychotherapy may be helpful. A behaviourally oriented or cognitive approach (see Chapter 21) stresses a move away from preoccupation with 'performance' to the enjoyment of sexual activity, improving the relationship between partners, and encouraging relaxation in the intimate situation. Authors like Alex Comfort in his *Joy of Sex* guides have helped to spread information and helpful advice to a great many people.

Although hormones are widely prescribed, their use has little or no effect on potency unless testosterone is low, or absent. But administration of testosterone to men or oestrogen to women whose own levels are low may lead to dramatic improvement. Brief use of benzodiazepines or alcohol in moderate amounts can be helpful in promoting relaxation. For severe impotence, there is a place for self-administered injections of a drug to maintain erection prior to attempting intercourse.

## The paraphilias or sexual deviations

Controversy surrounds the question of the boundaries of 'normal' sexual behaviour. Is sexual behaviour which differs from socially acceptable norms abnormal? Where should the limits of such norms be drawn and by whom? Should variations from what is regarded as 'normal' necessarily be labelled as deviant? Debate about these issues is highly charged—as is clear in the changed medical and social attitude towards homosexuality since the 1960s. Homosexuality was categorised as a paraphilia until the 1970s when, through professional consensus, it was deleted from official psychiatric classifications. The concept of homosexuality where a person is 'uncomfortable' with his or her orientation is still classified as a psychiatric condition, although arguments continue in medical, religious and legal spheres about whether or not it should be.

The main feature of the paraphilias, which occur almost exclusively in men, is an intense sexual urge and fantasy involving either non-human objects or suffering and humiliation of the person or their partner, or children or other non-consenting persons. Paraphilias reflect an intensity of certain aspects of normal sexuality, or a grossly inappropriate choice of sexual object. If a person has acted on one of these urges or is distressed by thinking about them, then the diagnosis of a psychiatric disorder is appropriate. But we must remember that human beings may harbour a rich fantasy life without corresponding action. For most people, such fantasies accompany normal sexual arousal.

Behaviour of this kind is usually not harmful to the person or to others, except, importantly, in relation to psychological and sexual risks, especially for children. Some cases of paedophilia physically harm children through penetration or in the course of restraining them. The level of emotional harm in the victim may obviously be extremely high. Murder for sexual gratification, particularly serial killing, has a morbid fascination for the public, as reflected in the popularity of films and books like *Silence of the Lambs*.

The paraphilias take many forms including exhibitionism, voyeurism, fetishism, cross-dressing, frotteurism, paedophilia and sadism. Other types of unusual sexual behaviour occur—especially centring on self-stimulation —but we don't know how often since most of it takes place privately and, if not distressing, may never come to professional attention.

*Exhibitionism* is a relatively common sexual deviation, mostly in men in their twenties. It takes the form of penile exposure to strangers, perhaps accompanied by masturbation or spontaneous orgasm during or after the event. Typically, no further sexual activity is attempted, as the person's wish is to be seen, not to make physical contact. Victims are usually female, both children and adults. Although many incidents involve passive, sexually inhibited males, this is by no means the rule.

*Voyeurism*, which often accompanies exhibitionism, is the observation of unsuspecting women either naked or engaging in sexual activity, or in the context of excretory functions. The person experiences intense sexual gratification, perhaps explaining why he may go to great lengths to achieve his ends.

*Fetishism* involves the use of non-living objects for sexual arousal, commonly women's clothing. Underclothing, shoes, and occasionally rubber or plastic items are favoured. The objects are used for masturbatory purposes or, less commonly, to enhance conventional sexual behaviour. Cross-dressing is part of a complex pattern of deviant sexual behaviour. It can also be a feature of a gender identity problem like trans-sexualism.

*Frotteurism* concerns men deriving gratification from touching and rubbing their genitals against anonymous, unsuspecting women in crowded places or from touching the breasts and buttocks of others.

*Paedophilia* refers to sexual activity with pre-pubescent children by an adult. Particularly in the case of girls, a male friend of the family or a relative, rather than a stranger, is commonly involved. But strangers are more frequent in the homosexual situation. Such behaviour may be a product of relationship, marital or sexual problems within a family, often associated with substance abuse. Behaviour involves fondling, having the child touch the genitalia, and masturbation, but attempts at penetration vary with the age of the child.

*Sadism* covers acts in which inflicting psychological or physical suffering is sexually exciting. In masochism, the person is humiliated, beaten, bound or otherwise suffers to achieve sexual gratification.

## The principles and results of treatment

The first step is to establish whether the abnormal sexual behaviour is part of a psychiatric illness. 'Pure' paraphilias, which usually accompany sexual development from puberty, need to be distinguished from those that begin at a later time and are mostly related to other conditions. The chance of change toward socially acceptable norms is greater if the person has experienced normal heterosexual arousal in the past and is strongly motivated to be rid of the deviant behaviour.

Many drugs have been used in the case of male offenders, including oestrogens as a form of chemical castration. Oestrogens do reduce libido but often with feminising effects which tend to generate new problems, especially in prison settings. In some European countries and parts of the United States, surgical castration has been carried out. While this may meet society's needs for retribution, it raises profound ethical quandaries. Anti-psychotic drugs have been used because they have the side-effect of dampening down libido. Anti-male hormone drugs have also been given, with reports of effective outcome. Drugs to suppress libido do not work consistently since human sexuality is to an important degree psychologically driven. In any case, suppression does not alter the direction of sexual behaviour but only helps to minimise the urge.

Various forms of psychotherapy, either individual or group, can be helpful, but they are relatively ineffective in serious cases. Family support is pivotal, and the outlook better when the offender's family remains intact. So intervention is designed to improve family cohesion and to reduce the problems in relationships which may trigger the paraphilic behaviour.

Psychosurgery, which destroys a selected part of the brain (see Chapter 20), was previously used for aggressive sexual offenders when it was thought that abnormal function of that part was linked to sexual drive. This treatment is now rarely, if ever, applied.

Generally speaking, the results of treatment are uncertain. Evaluating the benefits is tricky, particularly as people's self-reports are unreliable (the accuracy of their reports does improve substantially when confidentiality is assured). The hazardous nature of some paraphilic behaviour may lead to imprisonment or other forms of constraint in order to protect society. But for people with other paraphilias, prison serves little if any purpose, apart from society's need for revenge. One recent innovation involves the victim confronting the offender so that he may see the effects of his behaviour on others.

## SLEEP DISORDERS

> *O sleep! O gentle sleep!*
> *Nature's soft nurse, how I have frighted thee,*
> *That thou no more wilt weigh mine eyelids down*
> *And steep my senses in forgetfulness?*
> Shakespeare, *Henry IV, Part Two*

We spend one-third of our lives asleep. The link between sleep and good health is so clear that many social customs have developed around sleep. In psychiatry, sleep disturbance is a key to the diagnosis of many disorders, while dreaming is a window into the unconscious in psychotherapy. What are the main sleep disorders? They divide into two broad groups. In the first, the problem is in the amount, quality and timing of sleep, while in the second the disturbance is an abnormal event occurring during sleep (for example, sleep-walking, nightmares and night terrors). The first group includes insomnia, hypersomnia (excessive sleep) and disorder of the sleep–wake schedule (by, for example, shift work and jet lag), any of which may relate to an underlying psychiatric disorder or a physical condition, or be a problem in its own right, independent of any other condition.

## How do psychiatrists assess disturbed sleep?

Psychiatrists will be looking for answers to these questions: What has been the sleep pattern and when did this begin? Were there any stresses at that time? What makes the symptoms better or worse? How does the sleep problem affect the person's life? What is the person's typical daily schedule? Does the person have healthy sleep habits? Is there a family history of similar complaints? What treatments have been tried previously and with what effect? Information from a bed mate or other family member is always helpful, as is a sleep diary and, in more complex cases, sleep laboratory studies.

## Insomnia

This is the most common sleep complaint. Whether it is occasional or long-standing, insomnia is not a medical condition in itself but only a symptom. We define it as the person's own sense that they have insufficient or non-restful sleep. It has traditionally been classified into difficulty in falling asleep (initial insomnia), difficulty in remaining asleep (middle insomnia) and early morning awakening (terminal insomnia).

A third of the people who have responded to community surveys complain of difficulty in sleeping during the previous year, and half at some time in their lives. Sleep problems increase with age. Younger insomniacs more often have difficulty falling asleep, while for older people staying asleep or early waking are the problems. Women of all ages have more trouble with sleep than men. If insomnia is only one of many symptoms of a psychiatric or physical condition and does not predominate, it is important to establish the contribution of the underlying condition. Occasional sleep disturbance is part of everyday life and not an illness.

Most people with continuing insomnia become obsessively preoccupied with the sleep disturbance, denying any associated emotional problems. In order to unravel the latter, the family doctor or psychiatrist notes personality features, what has been happening in their lives and how they have been coping overall. More errors are made in approaching insomnia by a superficial consultation and quick prescription of a hypnotic drug than in any other aspect of sleep disorder (a staggering 5 per cent of the adult population rely on sleeping pills).

People with long-term insomnia often develop complex rituals associated with going to bed, report stressful events around its onset and have been prescribed sleeping pills by their family doctor. They may show anxious, depressed or hypochondriacal personality traits, and they seem to have higher states of arousal, with heart and respiratory rates above the normal. They consistently overestimate the degree of their sleep disturbance. Unhelpful behaviour patterns play a critical role in perpetuating the insomnia, and a fear of sleeplessness reinforces the original difficulty. Environmental cues which may heighten arousal and hinder healthy sleep include bedtime behaviour like reading and lying awake in bed.

*Mrs W, a 60-year-old widow, complaining of poor sleep for five years, insisted that she could not possibly manage without sleeping pills. Although she had first developed insomnia after her husband died, she believed she had grieved satisfactorily. She had, for instance, pursued new interests and friendships and returned to work. Her only problem, Mrs W insisted, was her sleep. She regularly took a benzodiazepine but still awoke at four o'clock and was restless after that. Her family doctor had prescribed such hypnotics whenever she requested them. It was not until a locum doctor saw her that she learned that her insomnia was paradoxically related to the benzodiazepines (a well-recognised complication of their long-term use). Mrs W was gradually weaned off the drug and, with careful attention to healthy sleep habits, her insomnia settled within three weeks.*

Insomnia can be associated with many medical conditions. Pain, shortness of breath, fever (and pregnancy) are common examples. Sleep disturbance is common in most psychiatric states, particularly mood disorders (both depression and mania), anxiety disorders including post-traumatic stress disorder, and anorexia nervosa.

Treatment is directed towards factors that have predisposed a person to insomnia, then trigger and sustain it. A behavioural program, which is the mainstay of therapy, involves practising healthy sleep habits (see the table below), relaxation methods and a focus on coping skills.

The role of hypnotics, or sleeping pills, is controversial. They do provide relief, but in other than short-term use the risk of developing dependence on them is always present. A hypnotic taken during a long flight or a brief period in hospital is reasonable. The snag, however, is that a person may develop tolerance (the need to raise the dose in order to achieve the same effect) to a benzodiazepine within only two weeks. Since rebound insomnia on withdrawal of the drug is common, people should expect a few restless nights. In any event, any short-term hypnotic needs to be accompanied by the common-sense sleep practices listed in the following table.

### Healthy sleep habits

- Keep regular sleep hours:
  - go to bed and arise at consistent times;
  - maintain consistent sleep times, including on weekends;
  - use rituals involving washing, brushing teeth, pyjamas as behavioural cues.
- Exercise daily but not too close to bed-time.
- Avoid daytime naps.
- Ensure bedroom is comfortable (sound, light, and temperature).
- Avoid alcohol, caffeine, tobacco, excessive liquid intake and heavy meals before sleep.
- Plan the evening to include a winding-down phase before retiring.
- Go to bed only when sleepy.
- Use bed for sleep, not watching television, reading or worrying.
- If unable to sleep, go to another room and engage in a boring activity (like ironing) and return to bed only when sleepy.
- If in bed for more than ten minutes without falling asleep, get up again; repeat this step as often as necessary during the night.

These healthy sleep habits make for sound sleep. If they are not followed, insomnia may continue or worsen. These strategies also tend to break the learned link between lying in bed and not sleeping. Reading, watching television, eating or worrying in bed are common associations. In their place the practice of relaxation, meditation and self-hypnosis can help by reducing anxiety. Worrying thoughts can be suppressed by imagining pleasant scenes such as waves gently rolling in to the shore. If these strategies fail, psychological treatment may be necessary to address factors like a continuing inner conflict. The person is helped to discharge emotions during the day rather than have them expressed through tension at night. Attention to relevant family and marital problems can help, as can assistance with relationships generally.

## Hypersomnia

Excessive sleepiness is a problem for a much smaller proportion of people (about 1 per cent). Again, a varied group of conditions, both physical and psychiatric, lead to this pattern. Among the most puzzling is narcolepsy, a condition related to dysfunction of the brain's sleep–wake mechanism.

People experience excessive daytime sleepiness with 'attacks' of sleep, together with temporary paralysis and vivid visual hallucinations on falling asleep. The paralysis is often triggered by emotions and varies from weakening at the knees to complete physical collapse. Narcolepsy is life-long, mostly starting in adolescence or young adulthood. A genetic factor is probably the cause, but the condition can also follow head injury, multiple sclerosis or a brain tumour.

Sleep apnoea is a condition in which breathing stops repeatedly for several minutes during sleep, mainly in obese men with poor respiratory function. Daytime symptoms include sleepiness, fatigue, irritability, headache and poor concentration. Daytime sleepiness is frequently incapacitating and may lead to job loss, marital and family problems, poor school performance in children, and a perception by others of laziness. Resulting anxiety and depression, even despair, are common. Symptoms during sleep include snoring, restlessness, sleep-talking and sweating.

## Events disturbing sleep

These events include sleep-walking, nightmares and night terrors—and possibly sleep-talking, snoring, teeth-grinding and bed-wetting.

Sleep-walking typically occurs during the first third of the night. The person's behaviour over about ten minutes is complex, with utterances and usually with the ability to move around furniture. Up to a third of healthy children sleep-walk, declining to 1 per cent of adults. It often runs in families. The important condition which looks like sleep-walking is a form of epilepsy (known as partial complex seizures) which typically involves repetitive automatic movements and much confusion on awakening.

Nightmares are extended, frightening dreams, common in children and reported as an annual event by one in three adults. The word comes from the Sanskrit, 'mara', meaning the destroyer. Stress increases the rate of nightmares. A severely traumatic event, such as a brutal war experience, followed by recurrent nightmares in which the frightening circumstances are relived, is the hallmark of post-traumatic stress disorder (see Chapter 7). Nightmares are also more common in other forms of anxiety disorder, in depression and in withdrawal from alcohol and other drugs acting on the brain.

In night terrors an abrupt wakening from deep sleep during the first third of the night is heralded by a loud piercing scream followed by a feeling of panic. Intense sweating, and rapid heart rate and breathing accompany the fear of attack by a person or animal, of being trapped, falling, dying or choking. It occurs in 5 per cent of children (rarely in adults), who belong to families with a record of night terrors or sleep-walking.

Shakespeare wrote insightfully in *Macbeth* of the states of mind which lead to these disturbed patterns of sleep. Lady Macbeth reveals her torment in repetitive sleep-walking and sleep-talking, and Macbeth himself draws a link between his overwhelming guilt (following his murder of Duncan) and his unremitting insomnia when he laments:

*Methought I heard a voice cry, 'Sleep no more!*
*Macbeth does murder sleep,' the innocent sleep,*
*Sleep that knits up the ravell'd sleave of care,*
*The death of each day's life, sore labour's bath,*
*Balm of hurt minds, great nature's second course,*
*Chief nourisher in life's feast.*

# 11 ▌ *Disturbance of Personality*

One of the most controversial areas in psychiatry is the concept and treatment of disturbed personality. Part of the controversy arises from the many definitions of 'personality'. This in turn creates difficulties in drawing boundaries for the 'normal' personality, beyond which an individual's behaviour leads to problems for that person and for others. A useful definition of personality refers to a person's unique enduring, deeply ingrained qualities and corresponding patterns of behaviour, including the way that person relates to, perceives and thinks about the world and himself or herself.

Social forces exert an important influence on the evolution of personality. Culturally based differences in child rearing may explain marked variations in adult behavioural responses. Some cultures reward qualities which others condemn, so leading to personality styles which are determined by those cultures. The stiff upper lip of the English is a sharp contrast with the emotional volatility of the Italians!

The quest to determine the nature and type of these qualities has been vexed. Indeed, one observer has suggested no less than 18 000 potential candidates! Consider for a moment what such a list would include: extroverted, gregarious, sociable, curious, frugal, harsh, callous, irresponsible, immoral, envious, obstinate, cautious, optimistic, fearful, shallow, buoyant, flamboyant, happy-go-lucky, enterprising, creative, boring, excitable, immature, impulsive, extravagant, adventurous, persistent, reflective, rational, orderly . . . the list is virtually endless. The psychologist Gordon Allport was the first to point out, in the 1930s, the many definitions of personality —he located over fifty in the scientific literature of the time.

What can we do in such circumstances? One main scientific approach has evolved over the last half-century to bring order to this overwhelming picture. In brief, the aim is to group personality traits systematically in order to reduce them to a manageable number of distinct, so-called 'dimensions'. A linked task is devising measures so that people can be rated on these dimensions and their personality profile mapped out.

The American psychologist Raymond Cattell pioneered this method of clustering in the 1940s by studying thousands of American students and then applying elaborate statistical techniques to the data. Arising out of his work is a set of sixteen primary and eight subsidiary factors—which are set out as 'bipolar scales' with the extremes of the dimension at either end. For example, Cattell's sixteen-primary-factor questionnaire includes introversion–extroversion, dominance–submissiveness, emotional stability–neurotic emotionality, adaptable–rigid and venturesome–timid.

Other psychologists have found this far too unwieldy. Professor Hans Eysenck of the Institute of Psychiatry in London, for instance, reduced the personality dimensions to only two, namely stability–neuroticism and introversion–extroversion. Like many other personality researchers, Eysenck used a range of explicit and implicit questions requiring yes or no answers. Questions covering the stability–neuroticism dimension include 'Do you often worry about things you should not have said or done?' and 'Are you an irritable person?' Examples of introversion–extroversion questions are 'Do you enjoy meeting new people?' and 'Do you have many different hobbies?'

The challenge of producing a coherent array of traits which capture the richness of personality continues, with distinguished contributors wrestling with the subject. The popular figure in the 1990s seems to be five, with the so-called five-factor model in the ascendancy, as shown in the following table.

**The five-factor solution to grouping personality traits**

| High degree of | | Low degree of |
|---|---|---|
| anxiety, tension, irritability, perfectionism | **1 Neuroticism** | blandness, lack of concern |
| excessive talking, inappropriate self-disclosure, attention seeking, over-dramatism | **2 Extroversion** | social isolation, lack of zest, inhibition, shyness |
| eccentric thinking, rebelliousness, fantasising, impracticality | **3 Openness** | low tolerance of others, emotional blandness, conformism, aesthetic insensitivity, narrow interests |
| gullibility, indiscriminate trust, candour, openness to manipulation | **4 Agreeableness** | cynicism, suspiciousness, quarrelsomeness, arrogance, exploitativeness |
| over-achievement, workaholism, compulsiveness, over-scrupulousness | **5 Conscientiousness** | under-achievement, disregard of rules, aimlessness, lack of self-discipline |

A much more refined and comprehensive approach to what distinguishes one person from another links dimensional traits with biological attributes. An American psychiatrist, Robert Cloninger, has shown persuasively that this can be done. In his psycho-biological model, he differentiates between two broad groups of characteristics: temperament and character. Temperament refers to dimensions which we inherit independently, show early in life and involve unconsciously determined ways of learning and developing habits. Character, by contrast, matures in adulthood, influences social and personal effectiveness and relies on our capacity to learn from experience.

The four dimensions of temperament are novelty seeking, harm avoidance, reward dependence and persistence. People scoring highly on novelty seeking are ready to explore their environment in response to cues, make decisions impulsively and avoid frustration. Harm avoidance covers pessimism, worry and fear of uncertainty. Reward dependence is about reliance on the approval of others and the need for social attachment. And persistence, as the word suggests, entails perseverance and resoluteness.

The three dimensions of character are self-directedness, which is self-determination and willpower; co-operativeness, which is the acceptance of others; and self-transcendence, which suggests a sense of spirituality.

So far, we have looked at the attempt to bring some sense of order to the range of normal personality types. People at the extreme ends of the personality dimensions that have been identified are of particular interest to psychiatrists, since they tend towards patterns of behaviour marked enough to affect their lives significantly. Psychiatry at the coal-face rather than in its research function has always had to deal with people who have been labelled as disordered in their personality (in addition to a disordered mind as in psychosis, or a disordered intellect as in intellectual retardation).

This apparently reasonable system of grouping personality types by dimensions immediately throws up the controversial question of when a personality pattern crosses the boundary from the normal to the disordered (if indeed such a boundary exists at all!). While this debate continues, psychiatrists must take a pragmatic position—even if only because they are consulted by people whose personality traits lead them to have troubled lives. In general, these people show inflexible, maladaptive patterns of behaviour which impair their functioning in relationships, work and play. Indeed, their long-standing traits disrupt various vital parts of their lives and, because of poor coping with everyday ups and downs, they may also cause much distress.

The psychiatrist will try, as with any patient, to understand why these people are behaving in particular ways, rather than use the label of personality disorder to trivialise or, worse, dismiss their problems. Unfortunately the term 'personality disorder' tends to be used in a derogatory way, which is paradoxical as the people so called are in real need of help. Indeed, they are highly vulnerable to the full range of psychiatric disorders, which are often difficult to detect as they may be masked or coloured by the personality structure. The psychiatrist needs a depth of understanding to unravel the specific contribution of the personality factors, since they will greatly affect the person's outcome and treatment.

## Types of disordered personalities

Interest in disturbed personality has a long history, with clear descriptions found in great literary works. We have only to think of a Charles Dickens character like Fagin, or a Shakespearean one like Iago. Efforts were made in the nineteenth century to study and understand a group of people who, while appearing to be normal in every other way, showed patterns of behaviour which suggested the absence of conscience—that is, lying, stealing, assaulting, even killing—without any remorse whatsoever. Dr John Prichard of Bristol was one of the first to suggest, in 1835, that this pattern might be an illness in its own right, perhaps due to an aberration of the moral centre of the brain. 'Moral insanity' was the term he gave to this new 'condition'. Included among its features were 'angry and malicious feelings, which arise without provocation' and elicit 'the greatest disgust and abhorrence'.

This questionable business of creating a psychiatric condition based on behaviour alone—which makes it essentially a social construct—has continued for a century and more to bedevil not only psychiatry but society as a whole. The profession (along with other social institutions, particularly the legal system) has wrestled with the thorny problem of whether people labelled as psychopathic are responsible for their actions. To put this dilemma most starkly, Does the psychopath who kills without remorse deserve the death sentence or treatment? (see Chapter 18).

The psychopath was soon joined by other categories of personality disorder, culminating in the 1920s when a renowned German psychiatrist, Kurt Schneider, grasped the nettle and attempted to bring order to the chaos. His classification has survived more or less intact and forms the core of the section on personality disorders in the International Classification of Diseases of the World Health Organization. The 1992 version (ICD-10) subdivides the disorders into eight types: paranoid, schizoid, anti-social, emotionally unstable, histrionic, obsessional, anxious and dependent. The classification of the American Psychiatric Association (DSM-IV) more usefully groups them into three 'clusters', each with an underlying theme (an approach popular with psychiatrists). In addition, each disorder has certain criteria:

- Cluster A is marked by odd, eccentric behaviour; it includes schizoid, paranoid and schizotypal disorders.
- Cluster B is marked by dramatic, explosive, emotional and erratic behaviour; it includes histrionic, anti-social, narcissistic and borderline disorders.
- Cluster C is marked by anxious, fearful, dependent and introverted behaviour; it includes avoidant, dependent, obsessive-compulsive and passive-aggressive disorders.

## What leads to personality disorders?

Just as we are all fascinated about what makes someone the person he or she is, so many theories compete—genetic, temperamental, psychological and social—as to the basis of personality disorders. Animal breeders can select for desired behaviour patterns through controlled breeding, which suggests that aspects of personality may well be inherited. Evidence for a genetic contribution comes from comparing twins—identical twins have higher concordance rates for personality traits than do non-identical twins. Certain personality disorders seem to occur more often in biological families. More evidence for a genetic basis comes from studies on what happens to children of an anti-social parent who are adopted by 'normal' families—they tend to have a higher rate of anti-social behaviour than their step-siblings.

Physical damage like brain disease (tumours and infection) early in life may be associated with disordered personality. People with anti-social personalities have been the group most closely studied, and investigations have shown irregular brain waves and minor neurological abnormalities. Clearly, such physical changes may greatly affect a child's behaviour, which in turn may lead to learning or relationship difficulties, all these features combining to produce anti-social traits. Similarly, brain damage resulting from severe head injury may be followed by marked personality change.

Several theorists suggest that personality disorders are mainly psychological in origin. Psychoanalysis, for instance, sees personality development as resulting from the interplay between basic drives (sex and aggression) and ways of dealing with them. Since these drives are primitive in type, their expression may not mesh with family and wider social expectations.

The person may then deal repeatedly with the resulting conflict in one of many ways—for example, by blaming others (paranoid response) or by developing theatrical, attention-seeking behaviour (histrionic response). The dominant response moulds the emerging personality (paranoid and histrionic personality disorders respectively in these examples). Another example is that people who have been emotionally deprived during the early years of life often have difficulty in forming trusting relationships in adult life.

A derivative school of psychoanalysis, self-psychology (Heinz Kohut, an analyst from Chicago, was the pioneering leader), introduced the idea of personality deficit. They argue that normal human development requires a consistent empathic response from the principal caregiver, usually the mother, towards her baby and, later, young child. If this response is absent or markedly distorted (for example, because the mother has chronic depression or an inadequate personality), an integrated sense of the self fails to evolve, which in turn results in one or other form of severe personality disorder (see particularly borderline and narcissistic types on pp. 152 and 153).

## What brings people to psychiatric attention?

Psychiatric help is usually sought at a time of crisis such as loss of a loved one, marital conflict, tussles at work or financial pressure. Various offences, such as assault, drink-driving and shop-lifting, may lead to the courts referring the offender for treatment. Or, personality-disordered people may need help with an associated psychiatric disorder, to which they are particularly vulnerable. Whatever the circumstances, people are often brought by distraught relatives or friends.

The psychiatrist will take a detailed history from the person and from relevant other people (usually family and friends) in order to capture a complete picture of the person in his or her environment. An account of childhood and early relationships within the family and with significant other people is particularly important, as are the methods of dealing with conflict and perceiving current problems. This emphasis on gathering information about many aspects of the person's life contrasts with a symptom-focused approach—to, for instance, psychotic disorders. Relationships, self-esteem, motivations and ambition, for example, are considered.

Pinpointing the specific personality disorder requires the identification of particular life-long, maladaptive patterns of behaviour. A cross-sectional snapshot is not enough. For example, a severely depressed executive in charge of a large company may be utterly reliant on family and professional staff for even the most trivial decision. These dependent features could be part of the mood disorder or reflect a dependent personality disorder. Talking with the person alone may not give enough information to tease out the diagnosis. Since people are not always the most objective observers of themselves, the psychiatrist needs additional observations from parents, siblings or friends.

A further source of knowledge is the psychiatrist's reactions to the person. Take the histrionic type. Because people in this group are typically shallow, vain, demanding, dependent and sexually provocative, the psychiatrist may well feel manipulated and come to resent the person's behaviour. The borderline personality tends to idealise or denigrate rather than see people as mixtures of both positive and negative qualities. A common result, within a hospital, is splitting, in which certain staff are treated with great reverence and respect whereas others are severely criticised and devalued. The two staff groups may (if they have no insight into what is happening to them) come to 'verbal blows' about how best to approach the person.

## Specific personality disorders

We will now give brief accounts of each form of personality disorder covered in the three clusters of DSM-IV, together with case examples.

### Cluster A

The ordinary person undoubtedly considers this group as strange, unusual or eccentric. Although expressed in a variety of ways, the gist of the disorder is oddity. People in this group also tend to develop psychoses, either delusional disorder or paranoid schizophrenia (see Chapter 12).

*Paranoid* people have an unwarranted belief that others are deliberately untrustworthy. Unjustifiable jealousy is common, and these people hold long-standing grudges and react with hostility to perceived threat. They show few affectionate qualities, rarely have intimate relationships and view others as potentially devious. Not surprisingly, they are usually regarded by others as secretive, tense, litigious and angry. Their lack of basic trust makes them hypervigilant—especially in new situations where they assume that other people will conspire against them, and they may even experience some psychotic symptoms (see Chapter 12).

*Fiona complained that people at work disliked her and contemplated seeking legal advice as she thought that they wanted her to leave. She had repeated disagreements with the pay office about her salary and conditions. She felt that other people were inferior and that she had married a man who was socially and academically far less accomplished than herself. When she saw a psychiatrist, having been referred by her family doctor for 'problems at work', she was angry, rejected the help offered and complained bitterly about the rigidity of health professionals.*

*Schizoid* people are quite indifferent to others. They have few if any friends, preferring to live alone. They are unconcerned about the opinions of others. Since they are incapable of deep emotions, they come across as detached and distant. Because of poor social skills and their disinclination for intimacy, they rarely develop close relationships. They may succeed in work that requires relative isolation and tend to avoid occupations involving interaction with others.

*Marjorie, a nurse, worked the night shift in a small hospital. She lived alone with her six cats and saw her family only on Christmas Day, an event which she found most anxiety-provoking. Born of elderly parents, she had always been quiet and remote, a compliant child who seemed to need no company. In adult life she found it difficult to understand other people's need for friends and believed that an emotional life was 'unnecessary'.*

*Schizotypal* people have patterns of peculiar thinking, appearance and behaviour, but not to the extent encountered in schizophrenia. They have odd beliefs, are frequently suspicious, and may become excessively fascinated by magic and the occult. Although their speech is often vague and idiosyncratic, one can still follow their train of thought. They often dress eccentrically and are stilted in their mannerisms. They generally have no friends, as their lack of social skills and strangeness makes them anxious in unfamiliar social situations.

*Mr J lived alone following his retirement from a position as a clerk in the Public Service. In the belief that people looked strangely at him, he always wore dark glasses. As he grew older he became more reclusive. Although he wrote letters to all his previous doctors seeking treatment for his facial 'tics', he refused to consult them directly because going out was terrifying to him.*

## Cluster B

People with these disorders seem sometimes to be out of control. They are excessively emotional and act it out in ways invariably distressing to themselves and disturbing to others.

People with an *anti-social* personality disorder exhibit pervasive irresponsible and socially deviant behaviour. In their childhood, lying, truancy and vandalism are common. As adults, they cannot hold steady employment or keep intimate relationships. They are reckless and unable to plan effectively. They frequently break the law, are aggressive and show scant regard for the property of others. They rarely experience remorse for such anti-social activity. Abuse of both legal and illicit drugs to relieve feelings of tension, boredom or anger is common. The disorder most often occurs in men, and is quite common among offenders. There may be evidence of hyperactivity and conduct disorder (see Chapter 15) in the childhood of these people, and their relatives show a high rate of similar personality features, as well as substance abuse.

> *Joe lived in a de facto relationship with a woman with three children from a previous relationship. She had retreated to women's refuges many times in the wake of his violent outbursts. He had been institutionalised as a child after his father had been gaoled for assaulting the family. Joe had never held a steady job and was inevitably fired following an angry episode, sometimes going on the rampage. Apparently unconcerned at the havoc he caused, he pointed instead to his shabby treatment by others. On one occasion he had burnt down his employer's warehouse after being sacked, and was subsequently convicted.*

Perhaps the most challenging of all personality disorders, both for family and professional, is the *borderline*. The term reflects the position it originally occupied between neurotic and psychotic in terms of the severity of symptoms. People with this disorder lack a sense of self. They feel chronically empty and unclear about their identity, goals and values. Their relationships are typified by intense contrasts, either idealising or denigrating others. They are overwhelmed by terrifying feelings of abandonment if left alone, even briefly. They also experience intense, short-lived mood changes with depression, anxiety and anger prominent among them. Impulsiveness leads to such behaviours as substance abuse, recurrent suicidal attempts and self-mutilation (wrist-cutting is the most common). The tendency for people to inflict physical damage on themselves may paradoxically serve the purpose of proving that they are actually alive— capable of feeling. The response may counteract the characteristic continuing sense of inner emptiness. Depressed mood may be severe, leading to suicide in one in ten cases.

> *Alice had been raised in a chaotic household in which she had been physically abused by her mother and sexually abused by her stepfather. She 'escaped' at fifteen and supported herself to an extent but was also dependent on her sister. Following the sister's marriage, Alice took multiple 'minor' overdoses while*

*intoxicated. She also began to mutilate herself by burning her skin with cigarettes and cutting her abdomen with a razor blade. She developed intense but short-lived relationships with men, and was devastated when these ended. She would readily plunge into self-condemnatory despair. Her legal career was disrupted by many admissions to hospital where she poured out feelings of alienation and abandonment, and a fear that her needs would never be met.*

People with *histrionic* personalities (confusingly and disparagingly labelled 'hysterical' in the past) show exaggerated but superficial emotional reactions and attention-seeking behaviour. Acting vainly and egocentrically, they have a constant need to be conspicuous. Moreover, they have to be satisfied immediately. They also have a pervasive wish for novelty and excitement, this leading to a stormy interpersonal life. Any relationships often begin seductively and remain shallow and inconsistent. A variety of physical complaints, dramatically presented, are often a central feature.

*Paula was always in 'crisis'. She had left her marriage after years of turbulence in which she could never 'wring' from her husband the affection she believed due to her. On the other hand, she told others about her exemplary behaviour as wife and mother. She never felt appreciated in the workplace and changed jobs frequently. She always imagined that the next intimate experience would be the answer to her needs. When problems occurred, Paula would feel distraught but show no flexibility or perseverance; bitter complaints about the 'unreasonable and cruel treatment' she received at the hands of others would follow. Her children, weary of her 'excesses', left home as soon as they could, which led to further outbursts about her wretched lot. She was flamboyantly dressed even at her lowest ebb. She ingratiated herself with all who tried to help her, however ineffectual she felt them to be.*

People with *narcissistic* personality disorders have an exaggerated belief in their own importance, accompanied by an acute sensitivity to criticism. The combination leads them to experience considerable distress. Feeling special brings with it a drive for excellence but gross disappointment when the associated sense of entitlement is inevitably not acknowledged by others. Envy of others' accomplishment is intense, pushing the narcissist to seek increasingly ambitious goals. While constantly desiring reassurance, they respond to any slight by others with profound disappointment, rage or chilly withdrawal. They have major difficulties appreciating the feelings of other people, and this failure of empathy leads to dislocated encounters which invariably dissolve in ill-will.

*Stephen, a merchant banker, always believed that his next scheme would make him his fortune. He had little patience with the 'dreariness' of 'ordinary' people and would only befriend those whom he thought would advance his prospects. His endless preoccupation with his own successes combined with general thoughtlessness rapidly alienated other people, and he then reacted furiously at their lack of appreciation of his special qualities. He never found a woman worthy of him, consequently flitting from one relationship to the next. Always dissatisfied and never feeling that he had to offer anything more than his 'wonderful' self, Stephen was unable to understand why others could not recognise his charms.*

## Cluster C

These are people who in the past would have been considered 'neurotic'— the chronic worriers for whom life is a relentless trudge. They are the tense, fearful and 'unhappy' members of society who find coping with life's demands an ordeal.

People with *avoidant* personalities fear the negative judgement of others, and feel so inadequate in social situations that it inhibits their chosen activities. So, despite intense desire for approval, they have limited social relationships and work in situations which are not likely to bring unpredictable social exchange in case they might say or do something 'inappropriate'. They are often acutely aware of their own limitations but too anxious to advance beyond them. Depression, self-denigration and anxiety are common.

*Magda lived with her parents and had worked at the same secretarial job in a small office all her life. She had always been painfully shy and envied those she knew who had married and had families. She rarely visited her small circle of associates, too concerned that she might offend them with her intrusiveness. She had never holidayed away from her parents yet was an avid reader of travel books and dreamed of visiting exotic places. After her parents died she lived in the family home and, despite financial independence, remained unable to venture out into the world.*

People with *dependent* personalities submit to others and seem incapable of making decisions without advice and approval. They transfer responsibility to others, quite unable to work and live independently. They often feel anxious and frightened when alone. Consequently, they cling to established relationships and are concerned that they might end. They are very sensitive to criticism and often deny their own views rather than disagree with others. They have a general lack of self-esteem.

*Christina always sought 'advice'. She found it impossible to do anything without seeking approval—she could not even shop for clothes for her children without taking her sister along. Her husband was extremely demanding but she seemed oblivious to this and welcomed any opportunity to serve him and his extended family. She had always wanted to learn the piano but, since her husband thought this a frivolous pursuit, she abandoned the idea for fear he would disapprove of her spending time and money doing something for herself.*

People with *obsessive* personalities display a rigid perfectionism which interferes with their ability to complete anything. Rarely do their achievements or those of others measure up to their required ideal standards. Their preoccupation with rules, procedures and social order overrides efficiency and the pleasure of accomplishment or the company of others. They are often emotionally cold and judgemental. Their need for control leads to dealings with others being formal and unspontaneous. Problems are ruminated over with little likelihood of resolution, leading to further disorganisation which in turn causes more biting self-criticism.

*David, a successful lawyer, ran an independent practice because he was unable to delegate work. The only son of organised and distant parents, he had been meticulous as a child. He was a model student but had few friends since he was always preoccupied with homework or avidly collecting stamps. He did brilliantly at university but recalled the time as empty, with pressure of study leaving no room for participation in student life. David eventually married a librarian who shared many of his qualities. He found the arrival of children stressful as they disrupted his previously ordered life and gave him little pleasure. Whenever difficulties occurred he pondered over how he could control things or people better in future.*

People with *passive-aggressive* personalities resist the demands of others in all aspects of life. They are stubborn and appear intentionally forgetful and inefficient, usually causing inconvenience to others. They become sulky and resentful if criticised, and often feel that they are unreasonably treated. They have difficulty in accepting responsibility for the problems they cause and are more likely to see fault in others. Relationships are difficult, often stormy.

*Ed was always in strife with his wife, and crossed swords with his boss whom he felt made unreasonable demands. The electricity, phone and gas were cut off many times because, despite endless reminders from his wife, he 'forgot' to pay the bills. His employer found him constantly obstructive, but when confronted about his inefficiency he became argumentative and shifted the blame to others. Most of his friends had withdrawn from his company over the years, irritated at his inability to keep arrangements for social activities.*

## Principles of treatment

Treating any personality disorder is difficult. As disturbed functioning is long in the making and usually well entrenched, it does not respond to short-term or simple measures.

The choice of treatment is significantly influenced by the psychiatrist's view of which factors are related to the condition but, given the complexity of the picture, a range of interventions is always required. Most programmes combine treatments rather than rely on one type alone. Psychoanalytically oriented individual psychotherapy, cognitive therapy, behaviour therapy, group therapy and family therapy (see Chapter 21) and medication (see Chapter 20) may be used.

Diverse therapeutic approaches are used. The choice depends on a complex decision by the psychiatrist, requiring skill and experience. The severity of the disorder, the motivation and capacity of the person to engage in a psychologically oriented therapy, the fluctuating nature of the symptoms and the co-existence of a psychiatric disorder are all influential factors. Whatever form of psychotherapy is chosen, it proceeds over months, even years for more severely disordered people.

People diagnosed as borderline or narcissistic are of particular interest to psychoanalysts. Their preference is for a modified approach—setting clear limits and contracts, exploring childhood events and interpreting the evolving relationship between therapist and patient. The work involves a high level of skill to deal with the many dilemmas that will arise.

Supportive psychotherapy, required for the more severe forms of personality disorder, involves a focus on the person's strengths to make realistically attainable changes and to limit any self-destructive behaviour. Establishing a clear co-operative approach and providing a consistent structure are important ingredients.

Behavioural techniques such as assertiveness training, relaxation and problem-solving techniques may be helpful. Cognitive therapy is an important approach in management, particularly when depression is prominent.

Group therapy may be added to an individual approach when the person is likely to benefit from feedback from their peers. Family therapy involves a combination of supportive and interpretative strategies to gain the support of the family in order to help the person change and cope better with life's problems. Brief hospitalisation may help to defuse a crisis, but

A violent volcanic eruption painted by a person with mania.

The sense of being followed by a persecutor is often the essence of paranoid psychosis.

A sense of loneliness in a strange world is common to people with schizophrenia.

Hands shielding ears from the auditory hallucinations that can be a prominent feature of psychosis.

long-term admission tends to increase dependence on staff and so disrupt the person's coping skills.

Most psychiatrists agree that the mainstay of treatment of personality disorders is one or other of the psychotherapies. But skilful use of medication may be called for, both in the short and long term, and particularly in management of the borderline personality. Any drugs must be directed to symptom relief alone and not in the expectation of producing actual personality change. For example, people with borderline disorder may worsen in the face of marked stress and develop psychotic symptoms, in which case anti-psychotic drugs are a crucial addition to psychotherapy. Similarly, people with avoidant or dependent personalities may become anxious or depressed following a crisis, and anti-anxiety or anti-depressant drugs may then be necessary over the short term. In prescribing any drug, the psychiatrist stresses that the treatment is secondary to psychotherapy, or a temporary means to tackle an associated psychiatric disorder.

## Conclusion

We may have given the impression that all personality disorders are severe and difficult to treat. This tends to be the view of psychiatrists, since they usually see people at the extreme end of the spectrum. But the whole group is varied in at least two senses. Firstly, some disorders are generally less disruptive than others (for example, dependent, avoidant and obsessional). Secondly, in each of the nine groups many more people will be mildly rather than severely affected and will not attract the family doctor's attention, let alone that of the psychiatrist. Those people who do receive psychiatric treatment, whatever the degree of severity, may well be helped to lead less troubled lives.

# 12   *The Psychoses*

No man really knows about other human beings. The best he can do is suppose that they are like himself.

*John Steinbeck*

Although it may seem a trivial thing, the shift from indiscriminate use of the term 'madness' to the more specific 'psychosis' had profound implications for psychiatric practice. The word was introduced in 1845 by the Austrian poet and psychiatrist, Ernst von Feuchtersleben, to indicate a serious mental disorder affecting both body and mind. So, from the morass of human mental suffering was extracted a series of conditions which could be dissected and systematically studied.

But after a century and a half of painstaking inquiry, psychosis continues to be one of the most perplexing challenges confronting medicine, psychiatry and indeed society itself. Over the centuries and especially in this one, psychosis has formed a crucible for ideological debate about its basic causes. The forces fuelling the debate go to the very deepest levels of human thinking and mobilise powerful social processes of stigma and prejudice. The result of this confusion about the conditions encompassed by the term, and negative views towards the people afflicted by them, has been an unfortunate cycle of neglect punctuated by scandal and guilt.

The fundamental dilemma in psychosis is our difficulty in comprehending the internal world of people when they are literally mad. Our bewilderment and fear of losing our own sanity combine to reduce our willingness and capacity to understand, and empathise with, the psychotic person. This often causes us all, including psychiatrists, to seek explanations for the inexplicable behaviour. The history of psychiatry is riddled with such attempts, from the scientific to the bizarre, from witchcraft to viruses. Unlike other psychiatric disorders, a common-sense approach comes up against a chasm in our ordinary day-to-day experience.

## What is psychosis?

The word originally referred to a boundless range of mental disturbances. It now has a much more specific use, referring to a group of disorders in which misinterpretation and misapprehension of the nature of reality is the hallmark and is reflected in impaired perception (hallucinations), false beliefs and interpretations of the environment (delusions), and disorganised patterns of speech (thought disorder). A direct result of these defining features is that the person's competence as a person is called into question, at least temporarily, and so his or her status as a 'person' may be seen as undermined.

Psychotic disorders are a public health problem of major proportions. Rivalling other major diseases of modern times like diabetes and ischaemic heart disease in numbers and lifetime risk, they represent even higher economic costs to society. This is because they tend to begin in adolescence or early adult life, and the disability they bring is often prolonged, during the most productive period of adulthood.

Psychotic disorders, and particularly schizophrenia, have been seen as occupying a special place in psychiatry. In general, we do not consider psychotic people to be like ourselves. It has been argued that a psychiatrist's inability to understand a person's psyche suggests that he or she may be dealing with psychosis—in other words, that a subjective judgement points to the diagnosis. Karl Jaspers, an eminent philosopher and psychiatrist who developed this principle as part of existential philosophy, used the term 'abyss' to reflect our complete failure to be intuitive and sensitive to the plight of the psychotic person. This brings to mind Churchill's frustration in trying to grasp the Russian mentality: 'It is a riddle wrapped in a mystery inside an enigma'.

The Jasperian view has been challenged, notably by R. D. Laing, the radical psychiatrist who fostered the so-called anti-psychiatry movement. He most clearly recognised the dangers of giving up on the task of 'reaching' the person and of drawing inappropriate implications from a label of schizophrenia. As he put it:

> I think it is clear that by 'understanding' I do not mean a purely intellectual process. For understanding one might say love. But no word has been more prostituted. What is necessary, though not enough, is a capacity to know how the patient is experiencing himself and the world, including oneself. If one cannot understand him, one is hardly in a position to begin to 'love' him in any effective way . . . No one has schizophrenia, like having a cold. The patient has not 'got' schizophrenia.

He went on to propose a controversial alternative view, namely that the experience of psychotic people could be understood as a retreat into their own world in the face of intolerable reality.

Modern psychiatry does accept the Laingian position in one notable way. It uses the label 'brief reactive psychosis' (see page 168) for those psychotic states in which an obvious precipitant such as overwhelming and intolerable stress is thought to be a contributing cause. In observing Hamlet, Polonius obviously can attach some meaning to his seemingly bizarre behaviour when he observes:'Though this be madness yet there is method in it'.

## What causes psychosis?

For the psychoses overall, the conventional framework takes in the idea of vulnerability—which is defined as the tendency to develop psychiatric symptoms in the face of stressful life events. This stress–vulnerability model is appropriate in that it links biological predisposition on the one hand, and precipitating and perpetuating environmental influences on the other, to explain the onset and course of the psychotic state. Since psychosis is experienced only by a minority of people, even among those exposed to extreme stress, a specific vulnerability presumably operates. The greater this specific vulnerability, the less the stress required to trigger the disorder (this model is characteristic of many medical illnesses, for example, asthma).

A key biological vulnerability in this context is a person's *genetic* inheritance. Twin and adoption studies show a strong tendency for psychoses, notably schizophrenia and manic-depressive illness, to run in families. However, it is also clear from this type of research that genes alone are not enough to explain their development since, in the case of schizophrenia, in only 50 per cent of identical twins does the second twin also have the illness. And psychoses can occasionally result from a range of medical illnesses, for example epilepsy in which there is damage to a part of the brain. Overall, the evidence is clear that genetic vulnerability is a distinct risk factor for psychotic illness, even though in many cases no relatives share the condition.

*A disturbance in the development of the nervous system* could well be a key factor, according to recent research. Disordered function of nerve cells and their interconnections possibly distorts normal thinking and feeling. Brain-imaging studies of these changes demonstrate intriguingly in some cases that they predate the onset of illness. Major changes in brain structure during adolescence, a process known as 'pruning', are thought to play a role in the timing of onset of first symptoms.

*Complications during pregnancy and around the time of birth* occur in a proportion of those people who go on to develop schizophrenia. This suggests that subtle brain damage may lead to increased vulnerability, and supports the view that abnormal development of the brain is a key factor.

Controversial evidence suggests that a proportion of the psychoses result from the effect of *viral infection* on an immature brain. People born in late spring and early winter, or after a major viral epidemic, are somewhat more likely to develop schizophrenia later.

*Chemical changes* may underpin these disorders. The emergence of effective drugs for the psychoses, and research on their influence on brain neuro-transmitters, has naturally led to this notion. The best known is the dopamine theory of schizophrenia which points to dopamine (one of the neuro-transmitters) over-activity as causing the so-called 'positive' symptoms (that is, hallucinations, false beliefs and disturbed thinking patterns). The role of other neuro-transmitters is becoming better understood through study of new anti-psychotic drugs.

## The multiplicity of causes

Each of the psychoses may have a number of causes. The best evidence is the variety of medical conditions which can produce the organic psychoses. The term 'functional psychosis' as distinct from 'organic psychosis' is used to emphasise that no clear-cut brain dysfunction can be found—although, paradoxically, most psychiatrists believe that the functional syndromes are also associated with a disturbed brain. Where no such cause is obvious, varied tests of brain function have produced these findings: global (in some people) and limited patterns (in other people) of brain shrinkage (on brain-imaging procedures such as CT scan), and changes in blood flow to various parts of the brain. In addition, psychological testing of such mental functions as memory, concentration and information processing shows impaired ability to deal accurately with stimuli from the outside world. All these abnormalities, reflecting basic brain changes, have without doubt put an end to the long-standing debate as to whether psychoses are disorders of the brain.

Many life circumstances contribute to increasing a person's vulnerability to a psychotic illness, though the evidence is by no means clear-cut. Early life trauma, like child abuse or incest, particularly if severe and protracted, is an example of a general risk factor for psychiatric disorders in adult life. During the heyday of psychoanalysis, this source of vulnerability was thought to be the principal explanation for schizophrenia. Psycho-analytic theory then saw psychosis on a continuum with neurosis—it being a more severe form of neurosis. Poor self-esteem, and an incomplete sense of who one is, may be other general sources of vulnerability.

Reassuringly for many families already stigmatised by the fact of illness in a member, past theories that parents and families are capable of causing psychosis in relatives (for example, the so-called 'schizophrenogenic mother') are dead and buried. Certain personality types are probably more vulnerable to psychosis, particularly the socially withdrawn, the distrustful and the grossly unstable (see Chapter 11).

Gender influences vulnerability, and also has a marked effect on timing and severity. The peak age for the onset of schizophrenia is several years later in women (25–35 compared to 15–25 in men), and women usually respond better to drug therapy. Pregnancy tends to protect against psychosis, but the risk is higher than normal following birth (see Chapter 16). Symptoms tend to worsen before menstruation. The pattern of symptoms in schizophrenia also differs between the genders, with women more likely to be socially functional and less apathetic. In this case, but not other psychiatric states, female sex hormones give some advantage.

Several illegal drugs, especially amphetamines (speed) and hallucinogens (like LSD), cause psychoses in their own right. This may also be the case with marijuana (dope) but here the cause and effect relationship remains highly controversial. But we are certain that, in those people who are vulnerable to psychosis for other reasons, these drugs may influence the timing of onset and relapse, and the ultimate course of the illness.

Recent research has focused on the relationship of stress to the timing and outcome for psychotic disorders—in contrast to early studies which tried to show that stress could cause an illness like schizophrenia. Demanding life events—bereavement, a car accident, a bitter disappointment—may trigger relapse. Living in a continually stressful environment certainly predisposes a person to relapse, particularly in the case of schizophrenia. This is especially so when families are strained, in conflict or too closely involved with the person.

The broader social environment also appears to influence the course of psychotic disorders. Interestingly, people with schizophrenia do better in developing countries. A number of explanations have been suggested. Is it the lower expectation on members of such societies to 'perform'? Is it the apparently stronger sense of family cohesion? Is it a more accepting attitude by the community? These questions have thoroughly challenged both sociologists and psychiatrists.

## How do psychiatrists classify the psychoses?

Up to the late nineteenth century, psychiatrists lumped psychoses together, under labels like madman and lunatic. This 'unitary theory' was first challenged by Emil Kraepelin, a noted German academic psychiatrist and a masterful observer. He meticulously described the many features that were found in psychotic patients and attempted to find an underlying causal disorder in the brain. Failing to achieve this he turned to another method of classification based on the course of illness. He detected two main patterns: progressive mental deterioration, and a series of relapses with recovery between them. The first he labelled dementia praecox (renamed schizophrenia by his Swiss colleague, Eugen Bleuler, in 1911), the second manic-depressive psychosis. This model has out-lasted its competitors and is today the main way of classifying the psychoses. Contradictory findings—good outcome in up to a third of people with schizophrenia, and progressive decline in some manic-depressive people—have not shaken the Kraepelinian structure.

One unfortunate legacy of Kraepelin's achievement, probably one he did not anticipate, is the dehumanising effect of his labels—that is, the way the world has come to regard people with schizophrenia. They tend to be seen more as collections of symptoms than as human beings, belonging to a different 'species' and inevitably needing confinement in an asylum.

## The psychoses in general

Psychosis itself is defined by the presence of what have been called 'positive' symptoms—delusions, hallucinations and disorganised thought. Negative symptoms include blunting of feelings, constricted mental activity, poor motivation, diminished energy and social withdrawal. In addition, the full range of other psychiatric symptoms—anxiety, panic and hypochondriacal preoccupations among them—may occur in response to the upheaval which is part of the psychotic experience.

## Schizophrenia

People with schizophrenia typically experience bizarre delusions (false beliefs held with unshakeable conviction), particularly to explain disturbing, subjective experiences in which the person's mind or body seems to be influenced by external forces. Disorganised thinking and speech is also common, as are hallucinations, especially auditory. A change in the way the person experiences and expresses feelings is another core feature. The principal clinical features—as agreed in one widely used classification system—are reproduced in the table below. Not all of these are necessarily present and indeed the picture varies substantially. The diversity may be expanded by severe depression, even leading to suicide. Some people slide imperceptibly into psychotic disorder over months or even a couple of years (the so-called prodrome) while others make an abrupt, dramatic descent into madness. Similar variability characterises people's response to treatment, and rate and pattern of recovery.

### Core clinical features of schizophrenia

**Acute phase**

- delusions of a 'bizarre' type—that is, involving a belief that the person's cultural group would regard as totally implausible;
- prominent hallucinations (throughout the day for several days or several times a week for several weeks, each hallucinatory experience not being limited to a few moments; for example, a voice keeping up a running commentary on the person's behaviour or thoughts, or two or more voices conversing with each other;
- incoherence or disorganised thinking (such that it is difficult to follow the person's train of thought);
- flat, blunted or grossly inappropriate emotional response.

**Prodromal (preceding) or residual (succeeding) phases**

- social isolation or withdrawal;
- impairment in functioning as, for instance, wage-earner, student or home-maker;
- peculiar behaviour such as collecting garbage, talking to oneself in public, and hoarding food;
- impaired personal hygiene;
- blunted or inappropriate emotional response;
- digressive, vague, over-elaborate and circumstantial speech, or impoverished content of speech;
- odd beliefs or magical thinking influencing behaviour, for example, superstitiousness, belief in clairvoyance, telepathy, 'sixth-sense' and 'others can feel my feelings';
- unusual perceptual experiences, for example, sensing the presence of a force or person not actually present;
- lack of initiative, interests or energy.

Sandy Jeffs, an Australian university graduate in the humanities and a poet, has written vividly and honestly about her long struggle with schizophrenia. Her book, *Poems from the Madhouse*, has won two awards and her poems have appeared in many anthologies. She has the striking capacity to

convey the horror, the bewilderment and the suffering of the schizophrenic experience. As she herself puts it, 'I am one of the lucky ones . . .
so many are silenced by their illness'. This is her poem 'Psychotic Episode':

> *When the chilled, icy wind blew,*
> *in went I,*
> *into a world I knew nothing about,*
> *into a space for which I could*
> *never have prepared myself even if*
> *I had been warned of its existence.*
> *Down, down, down went I,*
> *tumbling into an abyss filled*
> *with a myriad spooks and phantoms*
> *which preyed upon my unsuspecting self.*
> *There was no room for rationality,*
> *only chaos upon chaos upon chaos,*
> *and flowing rivers of turbulent waters flanked*
> *on each side by Gothic mountains of angst.*
> *And I was immersed in something*
> *deeper than a huge black hole,*
> *from which I did not emerge*
> *until the haze was blown away*
> *by all manner of processes that acted*
> *upon my distraught, disturbed self.*
> *But as the wind wuthered about my cardboard face,*
> *a chill had set in and frozen my life force forever.*

Elsewhere, she gives rich descriptions of some of the clinical features listed
in the table opposite. Among her delusions have been these: 'Beethoven
had stolen the nine symphonies from me'; 'The devil had raped me and
was waiting for me every time I went to bed'; 'My friend was trying to
poison me with her pumpkin soup'. Her hallucinations have included
voices, visual images and smells:

> I hear voices which say different things. I hear voices which tell me among
> other things that I am evil, the most horrid person in the world—that I am
> capable of contaminating whole societies with my evil and I won't let people
> touch me for fear of causing their death. Imagine trying to have a conversation
> with someone while at the same time there is a person in each ear talking to
> you and saying different things. I have smelt God; I could never describe the
> smell but it was most sublime and at the time undeniably God.

She also recalls the initial phase of her illness, leading into her first actual breakdown:

> I had a history of psychological difficulties from the latter years of high school—depression resulting from an unstable home life. Early university days were also characterised by growing unusual behaviour (e.g. walking around the college corridors all night and sleeping all day . . . generally not coping with college life). I used to have 'turns' when I would thrash around violently and lapse into unconsciousness. These happened for quite a few years. When I was under quite a bit of stress I started doing crazy things. I thought I was a grand person who could do and say anything without any consequences. Eggs became important in the way they were arranged in the fridge because there was a great cosmic plan associated with their order. Finally I stopped talking, eating and drinking and retired to the bed of a person I did not even know. After some time I was taken to hospital and voices started to insinuate themselves in my mind. One of the voices was my father who would call me and I would answer. I began to hear voices that would tell me I was evil. This was the beginning of a terrible journey which has touched me with a profundity like nothing else I have known. My first diagnosis was hysteria and I was given Valium, but when the diagnosis of schizophrenia was made, my medication was changed to anti-psychotics. In one respect it was a relief to be given the label because it explained to me and my friends what my behaviour had been about . . . why I had been so bizarre . . . and that there was a possible way of ameliorating the condition with treatment. The first months of schizophrenia were frightening and bewildering because no one knew what was happening. People thought I was pretending or trying to manipulate the system. It turned out I was one of the lucky ones who responded to medication and had a reasonable outcome, but I cannot over-emphasise the fear of madness and its bizarre machinations and the reverberating consequences it has to all who come into contact with its spectre.

Despite Sandy's relief at being given a diagnosis, psychiatrists are reluctant to apply the label of schizophrenia until at least half a year has elapsed in case the psychosis represents a more benign, limited illness and to avoid the dreadful stigma unfortunately still attached to the term. This means that psychiatrists, paradoxically but not unwittingly, apply the term to a group of people who are more disabled and whose outcome tends to be worse, and so perpetuate an unnecessarily gloomy outlook. But even for these people, the fact is that the outcome still varies and is more positive, particularly over the long term, than is widely believed. A major study demonstrating this is the follow-up of a large group of patients who had been hospitalised for many years in an institution in the State of Vermont in the United States. When the hospital closed, many of them made a successful transition to community living, much to the astonishment of their professional carers.

The cumbersome term 'schizophreniform disorder' (that is, schizophrenia-like) is applied to people whose illness is abrupt in onset, respond well to treatment and do not go on to experience sustained symptoms. This diagnosis is much preferred to schizophrenia, with its sinister connotations.

## Psychotic mood disorders

Mood disorders are covered in Chapter 8, but mentioned here since in some cases of mania, depression or its combined form (as Kraepelin described), the disturbance is so severe that psychotic symptoms predominate. Particularly in depression, a gradual worsening of the mood state may lead to delusions of guilt and self-accusation. On the other hand, psychotic features develop abruptly in mania. The psychosis usually reflects the person's mood disturbance (is mood congruent) with the delusional belief, for example, that one has the power to influence world leaders (in mania). Less often, mood-incongruent delusions occur—those not clearly linked to mood—such as a conviction of being persecuted or of one's mind being interfered with by satellites.

Psychotic mood disorders are difficult to distinguish from schizophrenia and schizophreniform disorder, particularly in adolescence, which is a reason for frequent changes in diagnosis. When a person has both a mood disorder and psychotic features but there is no clear-cut relationship between them, the diagnosis of schizoaffective disorder is considered. In these people, schizophrenia and clinical mood changes appear together but have distinct courses. In others, episodes of illness occur with a mood disorder on one occasion and a schizophrenia-like disorder on another.

The psychiatrist's difficulty in establishing a clear diagnosis in the wake of an evolving psychiatric disorder experienced by a person for the first time is well illustrated in the story of Alex.

*Alex, aged nineteen and unemployed, was brought to the clinic by his parents who, with the help of their family doctor, had had to persuade him to come. He had been well until twelve months previously when, following success in his examinations and in gaining entry to university, he had left school.*

*During the first semester, Alex tended to spend much time on his own. Appearing preoccupied and moody, he became erratic in his attendance at classes, stayed awake at night and slept late into every day. Much to his parents' dismay he was uncharacteristically abusive to them. He began to use marijuana regularly. Alex failed dismally in every one of his subjects, the examiners struck by the incoherence and disorganisation of his answers.*

*Alex soon became more withdrawn and suspicious. He began to describe hearing voices which threatened to kill him. He tended to excitement, spoke rapidly and passionately, and did not sleep for days. He was incessantly active. His reckless driving brought him to police attention on two occasions. He proclaimed to the police that God had appointed him as the 'chosen' one. The parents' concern naturally escalated in the face of these increasingly bizarre changes. At first they sensed Alex was 'not quite right' but as his condition worsened they became convinced that something was horribly wrong. Gradually discarding a series of plausible explanations—'adolescent turmoil', transition from school to university and recreational drug use—the spectre of mental illness loomed larger. The family doctor was also uncertain at first, but after several months reluctantly reached a similar conclusion and confirmed the parents' worst fears. He then persuaded Alex to accept admission to hospital.*

*Physical illness and drugs were ruled out as a cause. With treatment the psychotic features and abnormally elevated mood resolved over the next few weeks. During this recovery Alex appeared stunned and demoralised. His emotional expression was blunted. He displayed no interest in activities like playing his guitar, a previously enjoyable pastime. He resented being a patient and denied that he had a psychiatric problem. He then became clearly depressed, continuously lamenting that 'my life is ruined'. Although anti-depressants and psychotherapy helped to alleviate this morbid state, he remained emotionally muted and withdrawn. He described not feeling himself, being 'cut-off' and as if 'living underwater'. This experience lasted for what to him and his parents seemed an eternity (in fact eighteen months), but gradually resolved. Eventually Alex returned to university, began to reconnect with family and friends and resumed a normal life.*

*In retrospect, the psychiatrist concluded that Alex had probably suffered an episode of bipolar mood disorder (see Chapter 8).*

## Psychosis as a reaction

Brief reactive psychosis is the only form of psychosis which is linked with a specific identifiable cause. Clear psychotic symptoms follow shortly after major stress, in presumably vulnerable personalities, the trigger being well beyond their customary life experience. Emotional turmoil, with fluctuating mood and perplexity, is a hallmark. Typically it lasts a matter of weeks, with full recovery. We give an example of this reaction on page 74.

## Delusional disorder

This condition, in which one or more false beliefs predominate but there are no other psychotic symptoms, tends to occur in the second half of life. It either develops abruptly or, more commonly, emerges slowly over months or even years. The beliefs may be of several kinds—for instance, erotomanic (that one is loved by a prominent person), grandiose (that one has special powers), morbidly jealous (that one's partner has been unfaithful), paranoid (that one is being persecuted) or hypochondriacal (that one has a serious illness). The delusion often evolves in a sensitive personality buffeted by everyday life stresses. It makes some sense and can be intuitively understood. Delusional disorders are thus a clear exception to the notion of the 'abyss' in psychotic illness, which helps the psychiatrist to distinguish them from schizophrenia. As their roots lie within the personality, they often resist treatment, particularly if the condition has evolved gradually.

## Principles in treating the psychoses

Since the whole experience of psychosis is typically a shattering one, sensitive and comprehensive treatment is essential if people are to survive and return to a meaningful life. Understandably, they have trouble accepting that they are ill and in need of care.

Some general principles of treatment apply to all forms of psychosis, but the details vary according to the diagnosis. We will focus on schizophrenia as it is so common and well illustrates the aspects of treatment that are part of good clinical care.

Within the biopsychosocial model we highlighted in Chapters 3 and 5, several avenues of treatment are available, depending on the phase of the illness. The first, and vital, step is to intervene promptly in order to relieve the person of the distressing, often terrifying, symptoms. If effective treatment is delayed, potential support from family and friends is sometimes lost forever. This is particularly so at the time of the first episode when everyone is confused and fearful, not knowing what to do. Similar failure to recognise the early signs of any later episodes may prolong the agony for both the person and family. The result is slower and less complete recovery, greater disruption to family life, impaired self-esteem, and reduced work prospects.

Acute psychosis, particularly when it shows for the first time, is a psychiatric emergency. The psychiatrist will initiate an active programme. The first step is to ensure the safety of the person and those around him or her by admission, if necessary, to a secure, non-threatening environment, usually a hospital ward. Sometimes compulsory hospitalisation is essential when people are a risk to themselves or to others through their inability to recognise that they are ill. Obtaining a detailed history and conducting a mental state examination is the next step. Physical examination and laboratory tests are necessary, partly to exclude rare but potentially remediable causes such as a brain tumour. The person's feelings, particularly of fear and hostility, are sensitively explored in order to gain trust and co-operation.

After this assessment, the first phase extends for days into weeks. Anti-psychotic medication is the mainstay of treatment (see page 268). These drugs are phased in gradually and kept to the minimum effective dose. The psychiatrist may turn to another type of anti-psychotic or increase the dose if the person does not respond or there are intolerable side-effects. The latter—particularly restlessness, involuntary and purposeless bodily movements and a 'spaced-out' feeling—can be most unpleasant and threaten a possibly fragile willingness to follow professional advice. To relieve associated anxiety, insomnia or depression, it may be necessary to use other drugs also, like lithium, anti-depressants and benzodiazepines (see Chapter 20).

When the psychotic symptoms die down, as they do in up to 90 per cent of people with a 'first episode' in response to medication and supportive care, other needs come into focus. The psychiatrist takes special note of the impact of the psychosis on the person's sense of identity and perception of his or her world, and on the family. This experience is influenced by many factors. In young people, for instance, their sense of who and what they are is fragile, and so they are reluctant to accept the idea that they are now psychiatric patients. Understandably, most reject the label completely or partially, at least at first, however some lose the sense of who they were prior to the psychosis, engulfed as they are by the intensity of their recent experience.

Education about the psychosis and psychotherapy are key aspects during and following recovery, particularly after the first breakdown. A critical need at the time is to combat the sense of demoralisation which is a predictable response to the dramatic disruption of life's pattern. Returning to an environment relatively free of stress, whether with family or elsewhere (a hostel or half-way house), is a major goal, as is the re-establishment or creation of meaningful social and work roles.

For about a third of people, there will be recurrences from time to time, and an underlying long-standing disability. Even in chronic forms of schizophrenia, however, relentless deterioration is unusual. While the first years may be tumultuous, the illness fortunately may improve with the passage of time. Remission may occur, even after many years. These patterns mean that long-term use of anti-psychotics, lithium and anti-depressants, in various combinations, forms the cornerstone of extended care in order to hold off the symptoms. To prevent relapse, it is vital for both person and carer to recognise early warning signs (the so-called 'relapse signature') and to seek professional help.

At its best, this treatment programme is a combination of a stable, caring living environment; a supportive partnership with experienced mental health professionals; and assistance to develop appropriate social and work activities. Although it may not be possible to achieve all these goals, the measures we have discussed can make an enormous difference to outcome and quality of life. Clearly, the contribution of the family in pursuing these tasks is central. Particularly for young people, the family is nearly always the most significant support when the psychosis first strikes and beyond. The family members are in crisis too, and need explanation and much support. They must be nurtured, and in many cases involved as partners in the therapeutic team.

Psychiatrists have been much influenced in recent years by a series of honest accounts by people and their families of their experience, including the stigmatising attitudes of society. Even mental health professionals, despite their training, have not always been free of prejudice. These personal testimonies are therefore all the more vital, especially in that they break long-standing taboos.

Anne Deveson, a prominent Australian journalist, broadcaster and writer, has contributed to this process of exposure by writing one of the most moving and courageous stories of her family's experience in dealing with the seven years of her son's battle with schizophrenia, culminating in his suicide. She gives the reasons for writing *Tell Me I'm Here* in the preface:

Jonathan is dead. But our stories need to be told. How else can we know that others tread the same pathways? How else can we find our healing? So I write this book for Jonathan, who was graceful and funny and lovely, but who for his last seven years lived a life of torment. I write it for those millions of others with schizophrenia, who daily walk a tightrope, courageously trying to balance between their world and ours. I write it for their families who struggle to hold on to hope when often they are scourged by despair, and who suffer from our ignorance and neglect.

This book is essential reading for any family grappling with the challenge of trying to help a family member afflicted with established schizophrenia. Although the outcome in Jonathan's case was tragic, Anne Deveson's searing honesty serves as a source of inspiration for both family and professional carers.

## Conclusion

For many people, psychotic illness is a tragedy and devastating in its impact. They see the only hope in discovery of the cause and a corresponding cure. While this wish is perfectly understandable, we need to remember that psychiatry now has enough knowledge and skill to provide effective comprehensive care for people across all phases of illness. The sad fact is that society has not shown sufficient will to commit itself fully to this task. But there are hopeful signs as a more informed and empowered consumer movement is linked to increased professional recognition of how to care for people and their families in the community setting.

# 13    *Alcohol and Drug Abuse*

Substance abuse, which covers a wide range of addictions and their associated physical, psychological and social problems, includes alcohol, opiates (for example, heroin), stimulants, cannabis (marijuana), hallucinogens and benzodiazepine tranquillisers. It often contributes to hospital admission, suicide, crime, marital disharmony and industrial accidents, and poses an enormous problem in contemporary society.

The move from medicinal to recreational use of drugs is best illustrated by the story of the opiates. These were used for medical purposes well into the nineteenth century. Morphine was isolated in 1803 and heroin in 1874. By the 1890s, however, opiates were increasingly recognised as dangerous drugs, because of their addictive potential. In recent decades their recreational abuse has reached epidemic proportion, spawning a drug counter-culture (particularly following the Vietnam War), drug-related crime, and the spread of AIDS and infective hepatitis. These developments have required increasing co-operation between governments, law-enforcement agencies and health services. The focus on either long-term hospitalisation or imprisonment has given way to out-patient treatment and a call for changes in drug legalisation.

On the other hand, recreational use of alcohol was spurred by its ready availability—for example, cheap gin in eighteenth-century England. The term 'alcoholism' was coined in 1849, and throughout the nineteenth century the temperance movement gained momentum. Prohibition in the United States, begun early in the twentieth century, failed and was repealed in 1933. This was the year of the founding of Alcoholics Anonymous (AA), which is still the principal support group. Today's trend is to lower per capita alcohol consumption, probably reflecting increased health consciousness among the affluent and educated.

## What is substance abuse?

A working distinction is made between substance dependence, or full-blown addiction, and substance abuse, which falls short of dependence. Substance abuse is typified by recurrent social, work, psychiatric and medical problems, or by use in hazardous situations such as while operating dangerous machinery. Examples would be a university student bingeing on amphetamine every weekend followed by a day of missed classes because of 'crashing'; and a middle-aged man repeatedly driving when intoxicated with alcohol. Substance dependence, on the other hand, is determined by the following criteria:

- the substance taken in large amounts, and over a longer period than intended;
- a persistent desire to use, and unsuccessful efforts to cut down;
- much time spent in obtaining, taking or recovering from substances abused;
- intoxication and withdrawal when there are social or work roles to be fulfilled, or when it is hazardous (for example, driving);
- important activities given up or reduced;
- continued use despite acknowledgement of a substance-related problem;
- marked tolerance, that is, increased need, or diminished effect with the same amount of the substance;
- symptoms on withdrawal of the substance;
- the substance taken to relieve or avoid withdrawal symptoms.

Assessment of substance abuse extends beyond distinguishing between dependence and abuse. It includes an estimate of the quantity used, diagnosis of related psychiatric and medical disorders, and attention to family, work and legal problems. These are the clinical states that commonly require medical attention:

- intoxication that may result in serious medical problems or even death;
- withdrawal, which is a typical set of physical and psychological symptoms (especially in the case of alcohol and other sedatives);
- delirium, characterised by disorientation for time and place, agitation and hallucinations;
- dementia, a diffuse loss of memory and intellectual function (occurring mainly in alcoholism);
- drug psychosis, usually transient (occurring mainly with amphetamines, cannabis and the hallucinogens);

- panic, frequently associated with stimulants like amphetamine, cocaine and caffeine, and with cannabis;
- flashbacks, the unwanted recurrence of an actual drug-effect (occurring with hallucinogens and cannabis).

## What causes substance abuse?

Several complex interacting factors—biological, psychological and social—contribute to the onset, course and outcome of substance abuse. Studies of twins point to a genetic factor in alcohol abuse. And people with strong family histories of alcoholism share certain biological traits, particularly the body's capacity to metabolise (break down) alcohol readily, so that they need ever higher 'doses' to feel its euphoric effect. Animal research confirms this biological factor—it is very easy to breed laboratory rats who are extremely susceptible to alcohol dependence, and to condition them to seek alcohol out.

In general, people use a substance either because it gives pleasure without obvious short-term harm or because it relieves pain in the widest physical and emotional sense. The search for the so-called 'addictive personality' has proved futile, since teasing out cause and effect is virtually impossible.

Factors that predispose people to substance abuse include previous deviant behaviour, delinquency, emotional trauma (such as violence, separation, loss, combat exposure, and incest and rape in women), psychiatric illness particularly mood disorders, and long-term painful physical illness. The psychological effects of alcohol and other drug abuse—which include low self-esteem, lack of assertiveness, guilt, shame and anger—further reinforce addictive behaviour. And mental illness commonly occurs in the wake of substance abuse.

The pattern of substance use is largely determined by its availability and by social attitudes. There is no doubt that the greater the access to alcohol and drugs, the greater the level of abuse. This is clear, for example, in statistics of deaths from alcoholic liver disease which increase when alcohol is cheaper and more widely available. The importance of a range of social forces is equally clear. Young people, for instance, are susceptible to peer pressure, reinforced by glamorous media advertising. Others at risk are socially isolated people, particularly in deprived urban environments where families are disrupted and drugs and alcohol are readily available. By contrast, but also at risk, is the so-called Type A personality—typically a driven, achievement-oriented man in whom personal expectations of success are paramount and social conventions to drink are common. Patterns vary from culture to culture. For example, the Irish typically binge, whereas the French tend to imbibe more continuously.

## The cycle of abuse

The 'career' of a person with substance abuse is determined by a web of personal and social factors. To make sense of it, we need to look at the addiction cycle and the family life cycle.

The addiction cycle has six stages—pre-initiation, initiation, continuation, escalation, cessation and relapse. Influential in the pre-initiation phase are anti-social behaviour, a family history of disharmony and substance abuse, and a deprived social environment. Initiation is linked to availability, experimentation, peer group pressure and self-medication of physical and emotional pain. Continuation is promoted by continuing stress leading to the development of a drug habit. Escalation is linked to inadequate coping and to crises related to substance use, and leads to dependence. Cessation, if it occurs, is temporary and related to periods of relief from stress. Relapse, triggered by a combination of demanding life events and poor coping, is usually typical of 'stable' addiction. Repeated cycles of abuse and cessation result in progressive ill health, and often in early death. However, some people achieve abstinence, even without professional treatment.

The family cycle runs alongside this addictive cycle and they intersect in recognisable ways. Addiction in early marriage, for instance, often leads to divorce but, should the marriage survive, the addicted person progresses to 'stable' addiction in mid-life. Mid-life crises may result in escalation of the abuse, often leading to marriage conflict and divorce. The pattern in later life is typified by either continuing addiction, stable abstinence or controlled drug use.

## Likely outcomes

Long-term follow-up studies suggest that about half the people who are substance abusers achieve stable abstinence. A major study of alcoholism in London, for example, showed that after ten years 40 per cent of people had a 'good outcome'—but half were still drinking uncontrollably.

Most of those who achieve abstinence make the decision independently. How they do it remains uncertain, but these seem to be important influences towards recovery:

- acquiring a substitute dependence such as compulsive working, exercise or eating;
- a consistent threat such as probation;
- a medical condition that deters continuing use;
- forming a new, supportive relationship or 'inspirational' group membership, the most effective of which is Alcoholics Anonymous (AA).

Some substance abusers simply become weary of their habit, realising that the many negative effects heavily outweigh any benefits. This change in attitude is often triggered by support from a key figure, often a respected friend, a doctor or an AA member.

## Seeking help

A key moment for anyone abusing alcohol or other drugs is when they seek help or are pressured to do so, often by a spouse or employer. Then a comprehensive assessment is crucial. It includes a thorough medical and psychiatric history, and meticulous physical and psychological examination, which focus on these points:

- The reasons for referral can be vital in planning treatment and rehabilitation (for example, many large firms have active programmes for early identification, and may insist that an employee seek help).
- The details of alcohol and drug use will include over-the-counter, non-prescription substances, given that multi-drug use has become the norm.
- Although people are often unable to explain why they use drugs, it is important to clarify where they are in the addiction cycle, and to pinpoint situations and emotions which reinforce the abuse.
- Some people will have legal problems and may seek a favourable court report, with the psychiatrist determining whether marked anti-social behaviour preceded or followed the onset of drug-taking.
- The question of whether psychiatric disorder was present before, or only after, drug abuse is of crucial interest.
- Examination of the mental state is possible only after any drug effects or intoxication have waned. In fact, the 'real' person may not emerge for weeks or even a few months.
- A thorough physical assessment is vital, including laboratory tests of liver and blood function.

## What can be done to help?

Treatment is a challenge due to two characteristics of substance abusers. They tend to deny the problem and so are unwilling to co-operate or waver in their commitment to deal with it. And they drop out from therapy in the face of even minor setbacks. Until the 1970s treatment was based more on ideology than on scientific principles. Treatment is nowadays rigorously evaluated, and so can be mapped out more accurately. Its components are:

- support during withdrawal, which may require medication;
- information about drugs of abuse and their effects, and about coping strategies;
- treatment of associated medical complications.

Treatment tends to be short-term, typically repeated over many years because of many relapses. The idea of a cure is not especially helpful since vulnerability to recurrence is life-long. It is therefore essential to help people minimise the harm they can do themselves as a result of the fixed habit, while maximising the quality of their lives between episodes.

Because of the difficulty in engaging the person's co-operation, a relationship of trust with the psychiatrist is pivotal in any programme of counselling. Skill in tactful confrontation is required, to deal with the ubiquitous denial, anxiety management, assertiveness training and social skills training. Positive feedback assists in bolstering the person's morale.

Recruiting the family may be pivotal because of their potential to aggravate or improve their relative's condition. Self-help groups are available, such as AA or NA (Narcotics Anonymous) for patients and Al-a-Non or Al-a-teen for spouse and children respectively. Families can be the focus around which effective treatment is built.

## Which substances cause the most problems?

*Alcohol*

Alcohol has always been viewed ambivalently because it can enhance the pleasures of life as well as cause immeasurable harm. Shakespeare knew this well:

> Come, come; good wine is a good familiar creature if it be well used . . .

> Oh God! that men should put an enemy in their mouths to steal away their brains: that we should . . . transform ourselves into beasts . . .

> *Othello*

Alcohol use ranges from occasional social drinking to severe alcoholism with medical complications. International recommendations on safe drinking are based on standard drinks or units and their alcohol content as shown in the table below. The blood alcohol level depends on the amount drunk, time taken to drink it, sex, age and stomach content. Safe drinking is up to four units a day for men, and two units a day for women. Harmful drinking is more than six and four units respectively. About one in five men and one in fifty women drink at an unsafe level, making alcohol by far the most abused substance in Western societies.

**A practical guide to standard drinks**

| Drink | Quantity | Standard drinks |
| --- | --- | --- |
| Beer (4.9% alcohol) | 200 ml glass | 1 |
| Beer (light) | 375 mls (1 can) | 1 |
| Wine (11.5%) | 90 ml glass | 1 |
| Fortified wine (18.5%) | 60 ml glass | 1 |
| Spirit | 30 ml glass | 1 |
| Beer | Stubbie | 1½ |
| Beer | Bottle | 3½ |
| Wine | Bottle | 8 |
| Spirit | Bottle | 25 |

People abusing alcohol follow a common pattern of substance abuse, only coming in for treatment when they are forced to do so. The usual reasons are medical, psychological, social or legal complications. People go to their family doctors with gastric upset, peptic ulcer, high blood pressure, the 'shakes' and sexual impotence. Accidental injuries during periods of intoxication (falls and road accidents) are common in emergency departments of general hospitals.

Social complications, like lateness or absenteeism at work, can push people to professional consultation. Coming up against the law is the fate for drink-driving and disinhibited behaviour while intoxicated (being drunk and disorderly). The social damage of alcohol abuse is particularly disastrous for the family, in the form of domestic violence, behavioural problems in children, financial embarrassment, and distress for the spouse (often associated with tranquilliser abuse or concealed alcohol consumption).

The precise relationship between psychological complications and alcohol abuse remains unclear but several obvious clinical pictures are recognised by psychiatrists. Given that alcohol has a temporary euphoric effect, it should come as no surprise that long-term drinking often leads to unstable mood. Most people treated for alcohol abuse are depressed. Although some improve within two or three weeks of withdrawal, many continue to experience lowered mood. Importantly, even when alcohol abusers are not clinically depressed, persistent gloominess and irritability tend to cast a pall over their lives and those of their families.

Between 15 and 25 per cent of suicides are committed by people who abuse alcohol. Only a small proportion of them are 'medically' depressed, but the disinhibiting effect of alcohol, together with the frequent crises which accompany its abuse, are key factors. Anxiety and panic are other common consequences whereas chronic social discomfort tends to pave the way for excessive drinking, a strategy used to lessen that discomfort. Alcohol abuse is also a major complication of the specific form of anxiety known as post-traumatic stress disorder (see page 86). The drug dampens down its distressing features, particularly the re-experiencing of the trauma. In Vietnam War veterans, for example, half of those with post-traumatic stress disorder were also abusing alcohol and other addictive drugs.

Alcoholic hallucinosis is a peculiar psychotic state which typically arises during the withdrawal period (see Chapter 12). Auditory hallucinations, or hearing voices which have a critical or intimidating quality, exert a dramatic but fortunately temporary dislocation of the person's life.

The most damaging psychological long-term effect of alcohol abuse is undoubtedly cognitive impairment, or brain damage, which if left unchecked leads to progressive dementia (see Chapter 14). There is no agreement about the claim that moderate drinking may give rise to this dismal outcome. The Wernicke-Korsakoff syndrome, named after two prominent Russian psychiatrists, is a particularly serious form of brain damage. Consisting of confusion, unsteady walking and disturbed vision, it results from a deficiency of thiamine (vitamin B6) which must be replaced immediately if serious memory impairment is to be avoided.

The sheer number of complications due to alcohol demands a range of treatments matched to the phases in which people come for help. These include detoxification, relapse prevention, strategies for controlled drinking, chemical aversion and self-help groups.

Detoxification, an unfortunately derogatory term, refers to the process of minimising the physical and psychological symptoms resulting from withdrawal. A specialised treatment setting is the best way to achieve this.

Admission to hospital is now necessary only if there are serious medical features such as delirium tremens (the DTs) (see Chapter 14). Diazepam, a tranquilliser, is the best treatment for withdrawal when medication is required, using progressively reduced doses over seven to ten days. Relapse is often associated with emotional states like boredom, anger and depression; with relationship conflicts; and with social pressure to drink. To prevent it, people are encouraged to take these steps:

- monitoring their own negative and pessimistic thoughts and feelings which often precede relapse;
- learning to identify personal and social situations in which there is a high risk of drinking;
- developing helpful strategies like avoiding usual haunts such as pubs, learning to say 'no', thinking afresh about life goals and adopting a more positive view of themselves;
- overcoming the usual vicious spiral of guilt, self-blame and return to uncontrolled drinking by finding more constructive ways to deal with a temporary lapse.

In chemical aversion a drug is prescribed that produces unpleasant effects like flushing, nausea and vomiting when alcohol is consumed. Disulphiram (Antabuse) is the most widely used. The medication works best as part of a well-supervised programme. Interest in aversive techniques has fluctuated over the years with many doctors reluctant to suggest a potentially unpleasant procedure.

Finally, there is Alcoholics Anonymous (AA), a worldwide social form of therapy. Many people view AA as the foundation on which they have built a life of abstinence. Their 'Twelve Steps' give a philosophical direction as well as practical pointers to recovery and better daily living. AA has proved so helpful to so many people that we reproduce its Twelve Steps below. The main value of AA is the strong bond forged between its members, who maintain a strikingly cohesive network based on loyalty, responsibility and obligation. But there is a warning—AA does not suit everyone, because it calls for a commitment to a strong philosophical position centring on 'spirituality'.

Continuing controversy surrounds the question of 'controlled' drinking. Its supporters believe that for people unwilling to abstain completely, a level of safe drinking is achievable. This approach applies best to drinkers early in their 'careers', before problems have become entrenched. The techniques resemble those used in relapse prevention, as listed above, with the additional tactic of specifying limits of consumption and circumstances in which drinking is allowed, and teaching strategies to help people stick to these goals.

### AA's 'Twelve Steps'

1. We admitted we were powerless over alcohol—that our lives had become unmanageable.
2. Came to believe that a Power greater than ourselves could restore us to sanity.
3. Made a decision to turn our will and our lives over to the care of God AS WE UNDERSTOOD HIM.
4. Made a searching and fearless moral inventory of ourselves.
5. Admitted to God, to ourselves, and to another human being the exact nature of our wrongs.
6. Were entirely ready to have God remove all those defects of character.
7. Humbly ask Him to remove our shortcomings.
8. Made a list of all persons we had harmed, and become willing to make amends to them all.
9. Made direct amends to such people wherever possible, except when to do so would injure them or others.
10. Continued to take personal inventory and when we were wrong promptly admitted it.
11. Sought through prayer and meditation to improve our conscious contact with God as we understood Him, praying only for knowledge of His will for us and the power to carry that out.
12. Having had a spiritual awakening as a result of these steps, we tried to carry this message to alcoholics, and to practice these principles in all our affairs.

## Benzodiazepines

In the 1960s a new drug looked set to revolutionise medical practice. It was remarkably effective for anxiety and stress and, unlike its predecessors (the 'nasty' barbiturates), seemed to be non-habit forming. The drug was Valium (diazepam), the first of a large group collectively called the benzodiazepines (see Chapter 20). Alas, this proved yet another mirage in the history of the search for *the* drug for the troubled mind. The medical profession and the public only become aware of their addictive potential after a long period of complacency was shattered by horrific stories of 'Valium junkies'.

It is estimated that 5 per cent of all medical prescriptions in Western countries are for benzodiazepines, while 2 per cent of people seen by family doctors are likely to be taking these medications long-term. Many of them were originally placed on these drugs for anxiety, symptoms of stress and insomnia. Before long they had become dependent, as was clear from the withdrawal symptoms they suffered on trying to quit the drug. These symptoms were often mistaken for a recurrence of the original complaint, and so the vicious cycle of prescribing and dependence continued. Fortunately, scientific studies and adverse publicity have led to less benzodiazepine use and a growing realisation that its use should be restricted to brief periods where rapid relief of anxiety and insomnia is needed—for example, in the midst of a severe crisis (see page 274).

Apart from addiction stemming from its prescribed use, usually in middle-aged or elderly people, benzodiazepines are popular street drugs among young people—who prefer potent forms of it, and also use a variety of other drugs.

Benzodiazepines are divided into two groups according to whether they are short-acting (4–6 hours) or long-acting (8–12 hours). Continuous users experience a withdrawal syndrome that peaks from two days (short-acting) to seven days (long-acting). The main symptoms are anxiety, a sense of unreality, depression, irritability, insomnia, bodily aches, nausea and diarrhoea.

Since epileptic fits may occasionally occur during withdrawal, severely affected people may need to be hospitalised, as with alcohol withdrawal. To overcome dependence, people need to learn other ways to cope with anxiety and stress (see Chapter 7). Self-help organisations like TRANX (Tranquilliser Recovery And New Existence) are similar to AA in their approach and effective in providing this help for at least a proportion of people.

## Opiates

This group of substances, which are among the most powerful drugs affecting the nervous system, has been of enormous value in the relief of severe pain. But it has also been a source of horrendous misery for millions of people who have become hopelessly addicted. Heroin, morphine, pethidine and codeine are misused because of their euphoric and sedative effects and their ability to blunt emotional pain. The intravenous route is usual (shooting-up) although the drugs may be smoked or swallowed. Abusers are mainly single men in their early twenties with a record of poor academic achievement and unstable employment. The socio-economically deprived are most vulnerable, with peer group pressure, family history of drug abuse and childhood trauma being important additional influences.

Signs of dependence are visible injection sites and hardened veins, intoxication (for example, pin-point pupils) and characteristic withdrawal features (such as nausea, cramps, gooseflesh, sweating, restlessness, watery eyes and nasal congestion).

People often receive help under legal pressure (or because of drug-related problems). They are best treated by a multi-disciplinary team used to the ups and downs of opiate abuse.

Withdrawal is best accomplished in a setting where the best possible support can be provided. Withdrawal over two to three weeks with methadone is a widely used method. After detoxification, follow-up individually or in a group emphasises relapse prevention, developing effective personal relationships, establishing membership of a 'healthy' social group, and securing a job. Self-help organisations such as Narcotics Anonymous (NA) may help in this process. Therapeutic communities such as Odyssey House, which offer rehabilitation over several months, emphasise the slow, difficult development of a sense of responsibility and self-esteem. However, success depends on commitment to treatment, and early drop-out is unfortunately common.

The major controversy in treatment revolves around the issue of maintaining the addicted person on a substitute form of opiate—that is, the ethical dilemma of prescribing another addictive drug. Methadone is that opiate; it is made in the laboratory and has the advantage of simple administration as a single, daily oral dose. Substitution therapy means daily administration indefinitely, even life-long, of a drug which removes craving for opiates and frees the person from the many troubles and dangers of securing their habit. Thus, methadone provides a breathing space for people to improve their physical, psychological and social well-being. Many people do well as long as they take the drug but there is, tragically, a marked relapse rate once it is discontinued.

Opiate addiction may result from treatment for severe pain. Appropriate prescribing of the pain-killer imperceptibly merges into dependence, with the doctor sometimes unaware this is happening. A special problem is 'self-medication' by doctors and their families.

### Stimulants

The most important examples are amphetamine and cocaine. Both can be taken orally or by injection, but cocaine is also frequently snorted or inhaled in the form of 'crack'. Stimulants produce a 'rush', a feeling of euphoria, disinhibition and great energy. A person may emerge from a period of use feeling relatively normal, but soon experience irritability, depression and insomnia lasting several weeks. These symptoms often pave the way for another 'run' of stimulant, and so the cycle repeats itself.

Stimulants are often associated with psychiatric states including anxiety, panic attacks and mood disorders. Paranoid ideas are common, ranging from passing suspiciousness to enduring delusions of persecution. As with alcohol, the disinhibiting effects of stimulants may lead to accidents, violence and crime.

Treatment follows the usual principles of substance abuse.

## Cannabis

Cannabis is the most popular recreational drug throughout the world. The two most common forms are marijuana (leaves and flowers) and hashish (resin). Usually smoked, it produces a feeling of well-being, disinhibition, distortions of body image and time, and enhancement of the senses. Physical effects may include rapid heart rate, low blood pressure, increased appetite and fluctuation in libido. Effects overall may last several hours. The withdrawal syndrome of insomnia, irritability, anxiety and sweating is relatively mild, not usually requiring treatment.

Cannabis use may be associated with psychiatric symptoms including anxiety, a sense of unreality and paranoid delusions. An acute psychosis may occur but is usually short-lived—however, in vulnerable people it may be indistinguishable from schizophrenia. Cannabis is also a notable cause of relapse in established schizophrenia. Long-term use may produce a so-called amotivational syndrome consisting of diminished drive, apathy and deterioration in lifestyle. This improves greatly if the person remains drug-free for several months.

## Hallucinogens

Of this range of substances, the best known is LSD (lysergic acid diethylamide), although mescaline, 'ecstasy' (a stimulant like amphetamine), and 'magic mushrooms' (psylocibin) are commonly used. Hallucinogens are usually taken occasionally, by people who take a variety of drugs. After enjoying great popularity in the 1960s their use waned, but a moderate resurgence has taken place in the 1990s.

A brief account cannot do justice to the variety of the psychedelic experience. Enhancement as well as distortion of all senses may occur, as well as changes in the experience of space, time and body. Some users report 'religious' experiences—an illumination of the meaning of life. It should come as no surprise, however, that hallucinations produce hazardous effects—anxiety, a sense of unreality, marked mood changes and, sometimes, delirium. Some users may develop an acute psychosis with visual hallucinations. Occasionally, a psychotic illness resembling schizophrenia develops. Death has resulted from risk-taking behaviour based on delusional thinking—for example that one can fly. The term 'flash-back' refers to the return of psychedelic drug-effects, which are experienced as unwanted and frightening. Because of the low potential for dependence, treatment is rarely sought for a psychedelic drug habit other than for bad 'trips'.

*Solvents*

These fall into two categories: commercial solvents, derived from petrol or natural gas (such as glues, lacquers, paints, cleaning fluids, petrol and butane) and aerosols (such as chlorofluorocarbons, or CFCs). Solvent abuse is seen in sporadic outbreaks in schools and among poorly adjusted adolescents, particularly in isolated rural settings.

Solvents have similar effects to sedative drugs—drowsiness, dizziness, lack of co-ordination, disinhibition, euphoria and perceptual distortions. Death may result from breathing difficulties or cardiac arrest, or as a result of bizarre, disinhibited behaviour. Treatment often involves dealing with the problems of the adolescent under-achieving at school and socially, and recommending healthier forms of recreation.

## Conclusion

It is a tragic reflection on our times that the international trade in illicit drugs is second only to that in armaments—hundreds of billions of dollars annually. At international, national and local levels, societies have struggled unsuccessfully to curb the raging epidemic of substance abuse. No matter whether substance abusers are considered victims or criminals, their ultimate fate is equally dismal. While the cacophonous debate is endless, psychiatrists can but attempt to shed light on the nature of the addictions through careful research, as well as offer their best available treatments—if not to cure, at least to ameliorate.

If the picture for illegal drug use is bleak, then the 'alcohol scenario' (and tobacco, for that matter) brings to mind the poet T. S. Eliot's remark, 'Man cannot tolerate too much reality'. Here too, the psychiatric profession is playing its part, particularly in striving to deal with the physical, psychological and social consequences.

# 14  *Mental Illness and the Brain*

It is no surprise that psychiatry as a professional discipline emerged from the world of neurology, which is the diagnosis and treatment of diseases of the nervous system. Psychiatrists, like their neurologist colleagues, searched for the origins of mental illness in the brain. In the mid-nineteenth century a surge of optimism coupled with a flurry of research took place as psychiatrists began to examine the brains of patients with a variety of psychiatric features in the hope of finding a pathological basis for what they observed clinically.

The underlying belief was that all behaviour, both normal and abnormal, was mediated by processes in particular areas of the brain. This is the origin of the concept of psychiatric organic diseases—that is, those diseases in which alterations occur in the structure of the tissues or organs (obviously, the organ concerned being the brain). Structural change was found only in the minority of disorders (for example, Alzheimer's disease). But the organic concept has been expanded to include disorders where the brain's *function* is adversely affected by 'toxins', produced either from within the body (such as excess thyroid hormone) or introduced from without (such as carbon monoxide poisoning as part of a suicide attempt).

A particularly intriguing example was the epidemic in the 1920s of a specific viral infection of the brain, encephalitis lethargica, which left its victims in a permanent state of torpor and withdrawal. Oliver Sacks has vividly told this story in his book *Awakenings*, later made into an emotionally powerful film.

The working distinction we make is between structurally based organic disorders (the dementias) and functionally based organic disorders (delirium), although the picture is far more complex. In this chapter we discuss these two disease groups, and briefly mention a miscellaneous group of psychiatric disorders in which brain dysfunction is fundamental (for example, multiple sclerosis).

## Delirium

Delirium is best described as an acute state of confusion. The word comes from the Latin '*de*', (off, away from) and '*lira*' (a ridge between ploughed furrows). Literally it means 'off the ridge' but more colloquially 'off the rails'. The classical example is delirium tremens, 'the DTs', caused by the withdrawal of alcohol in a heavy drinker. This begins rapidly, lasts from hours up to several days (occasionally longer) and fluctuates in severity. People experience a disturbance in consciousness, in the form of impaired awareness of the environment, and have trouble focusing and holding attention on their surroundings. They are disorientated in time and place and cannot recognise previously familiar people or remember recent events. Speech may be rambling, at times incoherent. People are often frightened as a result of persecutory delusions or horrific visual hallucinations of animals and insects.

Delirium of any kind tends to affect people at the extremes of life. Children are vulnerable, perhaps because of the immature state of their brains, as are the aged, especially those with an existing dementia. Delirium is also common among hospital patients. Between 10 and 20 per cent of older people in hospitals or nursing homes are affected to a greater or lesser extent.

Drugs and infection are common causes but a vast range of other physical problems may be responsible—for example, heart, lung or kidney failure; head injury and other brain damage; and epilepsy.

Complete recovery is the rule; examples include people intoxicated with or withdrawing from sedative drugs like benzodiazepines or alcohol. Delirium ends in coma and death in rare cases due to the severity of the underlying cause, such as terminal liver failure.

This is a typical example of delirium:

*Mr D, a 72-year-old previously well man underwent hip replacement surgery. On the evening following the operation, he became uncharacteristically abusive, began to shout incoherently and attempted to pull out his intravenous drip. Psychiatric assessment showed that he was totally disoriented for time and place, panic stricken and could not remember anything about his operation. Mr D believed that the nurses were poisoning him through the drip. He saw and felt ants crawling all over his body (visual and tactile hallucinations) and pointed to folds in the curtain as sinister figures plotting with the nurses against him (illusions). With appropriate treatment, correction of his electrolyte imbalance (together with breakdown and excretion of the anaesthetic drugs), Mr D made a complete recovery and only vaguely remembered his 'weird' experience.*

Most people need treatment in hospital while the cause is being sought (for example, urinary infection, pneumonia or electrolyte imbalance). A quiet, evenly lit environment with minimal distraction and maximal re-assurance is an essential part of care. Maintenance of fluids and nutrition are also important aspects of treatment. A tranquillising drug may be necessary, particularly if hallucinations or delusions are frightening the person. The core treatment is directed at the cause once this is identified—for example, antibiotics for pneumonia.

Following delirium, people may have baffling, unpleasant memories of their experience. Some may be embarrassed by reports of their behaviour, while others hold extraordinary beliefs about the treatment they received. Care during recovery includes repeated explanation and reassurance both to the person and to family members.

## The dementias

Dementia, a word which comes from the Latin term '*de mens*' (out of mind), refers to a group of conditions typified by impairment of memory and intellectual function and, ultimately, by personality change. People lose complex skills first, then routine functions as the condition progresses.

A sobering statistic is the rapidly increasing rate of the dementias with age, doubling every five years after the age of sixty. The best estimates suggest that Australia, for instance, had in the mid-1990s about 120 000 cases of dementia with at least a quarter of those people aged eighty-five and over. There is a direct link between the predicted rates of dementia and the predicted increase in the numbers of elderly people. In Australia, as in other developed countries, the growth of the elderly population as a proportion of the general population will be dramatic. This spectacular change has major social implications. Although most people who are mildly affected live in the community, up to half those with moderate and severe dementia are cared for in hostels and nursing homes. Indeed, well over half of the total number of nursing home residents have moderate or severe dementia.

Memory impairment is the key feature of dementia. People's ability to learn new information is reduced early and declines until they can retain virtually nothing for more than seconds. Their recall of events of the distant past is also disturbed and worsens over time, even to the extent of highly personal information like date of birth and names of spouse and children being forgotten. The process is like malfunction of a tape recorder where ability to record new information is steadily lost. Information already on the tape is wiped out at the same time, starting with recent material and progressing until the entire tape is wiped clean. Apart from memory, other mental functions deteriorate, including intelligence, language, calculation, orientation in time and place, and judgement. In the advanced stage, the person becomes a shell of his or her former self, requiring assistance in every activity of daily living—feeding, toileting and dressing. A full account of this distressing decline is given in Chapter 17.

Two diseases account for the majority of cases of dementia, but the numerous rarer causes are important in that some are reversible and others are inherited, and therefore can potentially be prevented.

## Alzheimer—the man and his disease

Alois Alzheimer is a prime example of a psychiatrist of the turn of the century who searched relentlessly for changes in the structure of the brain which might underly severe mental illness. He worked on syphilis of the brain, epilepsy, stroke and intellectual retardation. The fourth of November 1906 stands out as a key date in the history of dementia. On that day, Alzheimer presented a paper to his colleagues in which he described the case of a woman who, at the age of fifty-one, had gradually begun to develop an array of mental symptoms—jealousy of her husband, hallucinations, trouble in reading and writing, forgetfulness, poor judgement and, at times, delirium. Alzheimer had observed her closely over the five years immediately before her death as she deteriorated severely, becoming bedridden, mute and incoherent. He meticulously examined her brain following her death and found it to be shrunken and withered. Under the microscope he saw the loss of nerve cells and global degeneration. Four years later, his colleagues named the condition Alzheimer's disease in his honour.

Alzheimer's disease is a slowly progressive degenerative disease of the brain's outer layer (the cortex). A definitive diagnosis can only be confirmed by examination of brain tissue under the microscope after death. But most cases can be recognised in life, by the highly typical features and course of the illness together with the results of special tests. Characteristic deposits of a protein called amyloid are seen in the form of plaques between brain cells and as 'tangles' within the cells themselves.

The cause is still obscure but clues are emerging. Advancing age and a family history of dementia increase the risk. In recent years the amyloid protein found in the plaques has been shown to be part of a larger protein (APP—Amyloid precursor protein) which occurs in normal cells. It had been known for decades that the brain changes typical of Alzheimer's occur in all people with Down's syndrome (Mongolism) who survive to middle age. Down's syndrome itself is a genetic condition due to an abnormality of Chromosome 21. This link between the two conditions was finally explained by the realisation that a gene on Chromosome 21 controls the level of APP, with the amyloid deposits in Down's syndrome resulting from increased concentration of APP.

In a small percentage of cases Alzheimer's disease is directly inherited, but genetic factors cannot explain all cases. As in many medical conditions, it is likely that the cause is an interaction between genetic predisposition and environmental factors, which together take decades to produce the dementia. Advances in genetics research are opening up the possibility of testing for this vulnerability, bringing with it the uncomfortable dilemma of learning in advance that one may be a victim.

## Vascular dementia

The second most common type of dementia is vascular—that is, dementia arising from death of brain cells due to abnormalities in blood supply (cerebrovascular disease). Interestingly, this was also carefully described by Alois Alzheimer, in 1902. It is impossible to go past his original description:

> Sometimes a morose, tearful mood, sometimes tantrums of distemper, unwilling stubbornness, or perplexed restlessness occur. Quite frequently these states are followed by a striking lassitude and dull apathetic behaviour. A closer examination reveals that there are hardly any real deficits. The cause of the apathetic behaviour is an extraordinary impairment of comprehension, reasoning and retrieval. The condition shows marked fluctuations. The patient's sudden striking remarks about his person, situation and surroundings are quite surprising. The variations are fast and dazzling. Gradually, however, the deficits become more and more profound. Learning appears severely disturbed. Large islands of remote memories are preserved, but sometimes their shores have to be reached by circumstantial questioning. Thereby the severe weariness becomes obvious. The patient's interest wanders. Sometimes, however, a visit by relatives may arouse ideas and emotions which were deemed long forgotten. The patients' mood is mostly dull. I have never seen euphoria, but often tearful depression. Hallucinations and delusions occur mostly during transient states of excitement . . . Gradually a state of more profound and torpid mental impairment develops. Even in this profound state of dementia, the decay of personality is not uniform. Individual parts of the personality may remain strikingly preserved for a long time . . .

Usually there is a history of high blood pressure and/or strokes. Advancing age, diabetes and smoking increase the risk. Unlike Alzheimer's disease the onset is typically abrupt and takes the form of episodes of sudden deterioration with periods of improvement. Sometimes, one person has both vascular and Alzheimer's disease.

## Other dementias

Other dementias may result from head injury, poisoning from gas like carbon monoxide (for example, following a failed suicide attempt using car exhaust fumes) and AIDS. Some neurological diseases are characteristically linked to dementia. For example, about a quarter of people with Parkinson's disease are affected by dementia, while all victims of Huntington's disease, an inherited disorder consisting of writhing bodily movements, eventually become demented.

## Reversible dementias

The diagnosis of dementia is not necessarily one of despair but, alas, only a small proportion (probably less than 10 per cent of all dementias) can be reversed or, if the condition has been missed, improved with treatment. Those that can be reversed include deficiency of vitamin B12, alcohol abuse and hormonal disorders, especially under-functioning of the thyroid, and some infections (for example, encephalitis), and tumours of the brain.

## What can be done for dementia?

Assessment of dementia consists of a series of steps. First, the psychiatrist conducts a thorough mental and physical examination and takes a detailed history from someone who knows the person well. Any treatable causes are dealt with, such as removal of a brain tumour or replacement of Vitamin B12. Through co-operation with other health professionals (such as occupational therapists), the degree of disability in daily living activities is determined and note made of skills still preserved. The social worker looks at the help and support currently and potentially available to both the person and the carers. In many countries, specialised professional teams conduct these tasks (for example, Aged Care Assessment teams in Australia).

There is no cure for Alzheimer's disease, but vascular dementia may be slowed down if blood pressure is controlled and drugs to lessen 'blood stickiness' (such as aspirin) are given. Research since the 1980s has identified new drugs acting on the chemical messenger in the brain, acetyl choline, which plays a major role in memory and learning. These drugs block the enzyme that breaks down acetyl choline, so increasing its concentration in the brain. Results so far show that the drugs, while not being a cure, do slow down the mental deterioration. The pharmaceutical industry has thus been spurred to spend millions of dollars to create new compounds, many of which are now being evaluated.

Until more specific drug treatments become available, a range of drugs like tranquillisers can help lessen the symptoms (see Chapter 20). People with depressed mood may be helped by anti-depressant drugs, those with impaired sleep may respond to benzodiazepines, and aggressive outbursts may be damped down by anti-psychotics. However, all these drugs have the potential to harm, for instance by increasing confusion, and their use needs to be regularly reviewed. Perhaps more important than any of these medications is provision of care in the least restrictive and most humane environment possible, combined with support of the family.

Dementias in themselves shorten life but, because people with dementia tend to be old, most die from the common illnesses of ageing like heart disease and cancer. People who do not succumb to one of these illnesses tend to die of pneumonia because they become bedridden.

## How can we prevent dementia?

Since the cause of the commonest dementia, Alzheimer's disease, remains unclear, preventive strategies are difficult to come by. One hope is the early identification of people at risk and advice to them to avoid exposure to potential environmental factors. Both aluminium and zinc are suspect, but no hard evidence has yet emerged to incriminate them. Other possibilities include the development of drugs to stop or slow the deposition of amyloid or its precursor APP. An intriguing suggestion is the implantation of foetal brain tissue—which has already been attempted for Parkinson's disease.

More can be done for the less common dementias. High blood pressure is the main culprit in vascular dementia, and its early detection and effective treatment helps to reduce the incidence. Similarly, a decline in alcohol consumption should help reduce alcohol-related brain disease, including alcoholic dementia (see Chapter 13). Compulsory wearing of seat belts has lowered the rate of dementia due to head injury and this could decline further through road accident prevention. A ban on boxing would eliminate the late consequences of repeated head trauma. Safe sexual practice can help prevent infection with HIV and thus reduce the rate of dementia due to AIDS.

## Other psychiatric disorders due to organic disease

The full range of psychiatric symptoms can occur in association with bodily disease, whether in the brain or elsewhere. We now focus on the most common of these syndromes and diseases.

Anxiety, either of a general kind or in the form of panic attacks, and evident as inability to relax or concentrate, may be caused by a number of physical factors—drugs (for example, caffeine, cold remedies); withdrawal from alcohol, nicotine and benzodiazepines; hormonal diseases such as thyroid over-activity and lowered blood sugar in diabetes; and epilepsy.

Depression, too, may be closely associated with a medical condition (including hormonal over- or under-activity, undetected cancers, and infections, particularly influenza and glandular fever) or the drugs used to treat it (such as those for high blood pressure, oral contraceptives, anti-Parkinson medication and steroids).

The psychiatric symptoms may even reach psychotic proportions and resemble schizophrenia with delusions and hallucinations. This can occur in a wide range of medical disorders and their treatment—from stimulant drugs of addiction like amphetamines and cocaine, and hallucinogens such as LSD, to brain tumours and certain forms of epilepsy. We will now focus on the specific causes of brain dysfunction.

### Head injury

Behavioural disturbance following head injury may occur immediately or in the long term. In the former (concussion), the person may act more vaguely, concentrate poorly and be disinhibited or disorganised. Some of these features may last for days or weeks, often associated with irritability and fluctuating mood. This picture is often reversible as dysfunction of the brain recedes. Continuing difficulties point to actual damage, resulting from severe brain injury—which usually first shows as coma, followed later by irritability, explosiveness, poor organisational skill, apathy, inattention, impulsivity, disinhibition and poor judgement. Depression is common, affecting over half the people with severe brain injury, many of whom become suicidal.

Sometimes the entire personality may change for the worse. There may be enduring apathy, impulsivity, restlessness, and poor judgement with a failure to appreciate the likely impact of one's actions. The person may come into conflict with the law because of inappropriate sexual or aggressive behaviour. Although intellectual ability appears intact, the person is unable to function effectively. These behavioural changes bring severe stress to the family. Disappointments, altered roles and changed socio-economic circumstances often lead the family to become dysfunctional.

## Multiple sclerosis

This disorder of the nervous system, like many others, is often associated with an assortment of psychiatric symptoms at some time in the course of the illness. Disordered mood, depression or inappropriate euphoria are particularly common. These changes seem to result not so much from factors like loss of job and other social roles, impaired recreational or sporting skills and increasing physical dependency, but instead are linked to actual changes in the brain. Many people with advanced forms of the illness show abnormal functioning in thinking, learning and memory. A small proportion of them develop dementia.

## Parkinson's disease

As in multiple sclerosis, depression often accompanies Parkinson's disease and is probably linked directly to brain changes. This is of special interest since the chemical messenger, dopamine, which is deficient in Parkinson's, seems to be one of those that malfunctions in depression. Adverse changes including delirium, depression, psychosis and agitation may be closely related to the side-effects of anti-Parkinsonian drugs, in particular L-Dopa.

People may show cognitive impairment, though falling short of dementia. Again, anti-Parkinsonian drugs may be to blame. Dementia itself may occur in those with advanced Parkinson's, but in a distinctive way, referred to as 'subcortical'. Rather than the general intellectual impairment typical of Alzheimer's, people with Parkinson's experience slowing of performance, and difficulty in planning and organising and in using information.

## Epilepsy

The brain dysfunction underlying epilepsy is the key reason for the relationship between it and psychiatric complications. Disturbances in certain areas, particularly the temporal lobes concerned with memory and emotional regulation, are often related to psychiatric symptoms. These lobes are a common site of the abnormal electrical discharges which characterise epilepsy, and this accounts for the particular link between temporal lobe epilepsy and psychological disturbance.

Personality change—particularly pedantry, bad temper and extreme sensitivity—is common, although in this case the question as to whether this is a reaction to the experience of having epilepsy or results from underlying brain change remains controversial.

The association between epilepsy and psychosis is well recognised. A psychotic state that is indistinguishable from schizophrenia may arise many years after the onset of the epilepsy. Although people with epilepsy were traditionally seen as potentially violent, in reality they are not usually aggressive. Occasionally outbursts will occur as part of the brief delirious states that can immediately follow a fit.

Memory impairment is a common complaint in long-term epilepsy. In addition to the inevitable temporary amnesia during and following a fit, there may be more specific difficulties including defective memory for words or visual images. Anti-epileptic drugs, for example Phenobarbitone and Phenytoin, may also adversely affect memory and learning.

## AIDS

People's emotional reactions to a positive HIV result are like those to the diagnosis of any other life-threatening illness. Shock and disbelief give way to anger, guilt, fear of rejection, depression and withdrawal. Acceptance may eventually follow, marked by greater stability, but always with a degree of anxiety about the later developments of AIDS. Eventually, when AIDS develops, is progressive and the prospect of premature death looms, the person will experience anticipatory grief (see page 104), often intertwined with fear of the process of dying rather than of death itself.

Many people with HIV infection develop a psychiatric disorder, ranging across the spectrum from poor adjustment with anxiety and depressive features all the way to progressive dementia. Depression, with suicidal ideas (and perhaps actual attempts), is frequent. Occasionally people experience manic or other psychotic episodes, the result of either the disease or its drug treatment.

Of the organic mental illnesses, delirium is most common, its features ranging from apathy to agitation with paranoid delusions. Particularly distressing to loved ones is the so-called AIDS dementia complex, which may be the first sign of AIDS. As in other forms of dementia, forgetfulness, poor concentration, slow mental function, apathy and withdrawal may be easily misinterpreted as depression. The dementia is progressive if untreated, with severe cognitive decline within six months to two years. Modern drugs such as AZT have increased people's life expectancy significantly, with corresponding cognitive improvement.

## Stroke

The fact that disturbed psychological function is common following a stroke is not surprising given the extreme sensitivity of the brain to damage resulting from inadequate blood supply. Associated temporary or permanent amnesia is particularly disturbing, as are dramatic personality changes.

Psychiatrists have a marked interest in the depression which may follow a stroke since many studies show a clear relationship between the two in terms of the extent and site of the brain damage (the left, front part in right-handed people). Other factors contributing to depression include loss of independence, restricted activity and impaired judgement.

## Conclusion

Nineteenth-century psychiatrists were only partly successful in identifying and localising brain dysfunction as a basis for mental illness. The sub-specialty of neuropsychiatry which is their legacy takes in a large group of neurological and other medical conditions, some old ones (Alzheimer's disease) and some new (AIDS). The brain, an extremely sensitive organ, is easily buffeted by 'insults' from inside and outside the body, which show up in many ways. The disorders have been carefully identified, but specific treatments remain elusive. Our growing understanding of the brain's structure and function, together with dramatic technological advances, especially neuro-imaging, encourage us to expect therapeutic break-throughs in our lifetimes.

# 15   *Children and Adolescents*

Alas, it is a myth that childhood is the happiest time of one's life. In fact, many children will, at some time, have troublesome emotional or behavioural problems. Child and adolescent psychiatry, which deals with such problems, is distinctive in at least three ways:

- The huge changes during the years of childhood and adolescence mean that what passes as normal behaviour at one stage may be seen as disturbed behaviour at another. For example, distress on being separated from familiar caregivers is normal in toddlers and common in children starting school, but absence from school in an older child may point to serious anxiety.
- Children's dependence on their family evolves throughout childhood, with infants entirely reliant for survival, whereas adolescents are in transition between the family-based child and the young, autonomous adult.
- Children rarely seek professional help for themselves. Usually they are brought for help by concerned parents or teachers. While all parents worry at some time about their child's behaviour or development most do not seek professional assistance. Either the problem passes or they are reassured by the advice of family and friends. If the problem is severe or persistent enough, parents may consult an infant welfare sister or a family doctor, but only occasionally a mental health specialist.

About one in ten children and adolescents experience marked emotional and behavioural problems. Before mid-adolescence, boys are more affected than girls, and city more than country children. Those with a chronic physical illness are more vulnerable, particularly if the brain is involved or if they are intellectually disabled.

There is usually no identifiable physical cause for child and adolescent psychiatric disorders. Even though we are increasingly finding genetic and biological factors relevant in certain conditions, treatment is mainly by psychological means rather than by drugs. Parent counselling, family therapy and individual psychotherapy, both behavioural and psychoanalytically oriented, are mainstays, although medication has an important place in a few conditions.

The range of clinical problems fall into three groups:

- Developmental problems are those where psychological growth is derailed—for example, intellectual retardation, autism and specific distortions or delays of speech or language.
- Emotional problems show themselves directly as anxiety or indirectly as bodily dysfunction, usually in eating, toileting and sleeping.
- Behavioural problems, as the word suggests, take the form of disruptiveness, defiance or anti-social conduct.

Many children have mixed emotional and behavioural problems, and both are more common among intellectually disabled children.

## The critical role of development

The most dramatic changes in our lives take place between birth and early adulthood. Infancy—the first three years—is when the most rapid development in motor, language and intellectual skills occurs. Play, creativity and use of symbols begin, accompanied by a growing sense of physical, personal and sexual identity. From birth, an infant can attend, perceive and respond to the environment through behaviour and expression of emotion. This responsiveness powerfully triggers adult reactions—both positive love and caring, and negative emotions like distress and anger. Attachments to individual caregivers develop at around 4–6 months. Young children up to about five are the most vulnerable to family disruption and experiences of separation.

Interest is growing in temperament as a factor determining how a child relates to the environment. We define temperament in infants as being consistent patterns of response to themselves and to their world, whether of activity, persistence, emotional responsiveness, fearfulness or sociability. Infants with 'troublesome' temperaments are more likely not to fit well with their parents' expectations of the ideal child. It should come as no surprise that it is these children who may be brought to psychiatrists with emotional problems or disordered behaviour. As boys generally develop more slowly than girls and tend to be temperamentally more unsettled, they are more likely to have these difficulties.

Adolescence is at the other end of this time of great change. There are various opinions as to when it starts—at about ten years, or coinciding with either puberty or with the start of secondary school. The transition from adolescence to young adulthood is also ill-defined. In developed countries the long period of post-secondary education means that young people are often dependent on their parents well into their twenties. However, they become adults in the eyes of the law on their eighteenth birthday.

Contrary to popular opinion, most children negotiate their adolescence without major emotional turmoil. However, they do experience a range of intense feelings and their mood is often changeable. It is a time of marked transition that affects all areas of life. Erik Erikson, an eminent psychoanalyst, described in his classic book, *Childhood and Society*, the core task as establishing a sense of identity—awareness of one's separate and unique existence, and a sense of belonging to and identifying with a family, peer group, society and culture.

Physical and psychological changes are great. In general, adolescents are not daunted by their emerging sexuality and enjoy the associated bodily changes and intimate relationships. The key intellectual developments are the ability to think in abstract terms, to generalise from one experience to another and to appreciate the past and future. This often leads young people to challenge the beliefs and practices of their parents' generation.

About one-third of children move through adolescence smoothly, supported by good peer and family relationships. About half have periods of purposeful activity alternating with withdrawal, a tendency to become angry easily and to blame others. These adolescents are less confident and more prone to depression and anxiety. Concern over emerging sexuality hinders the development of their sexual relationships or, less commonly, leads to promiscuity. Their families are more likely to be affected by illness, parental conflict and divorce.

Serious turmoil with anti-social behaviour affects about a fifth of adolescents and is more common in poorer families and in families with parental mental illness and marital tension. Conflict with parents, low self-esteem, anxiety and depression are common. These adolescents often do less well academically, begin sexual relationships early, have difficulty forming stable friendships and struggle to develop a secure identity. A history of tumultuous development is often found among adolescents who later develop psychiatric, personality and social problems (such as homelessness).

## Development and clinical problems—the example of divorce

Divorce is experienced by many children—as it is the fate of up to a third of Western marriages. Significant stress factors for children are the preceding marital disharmony, the actual separation and its effects. After divorce, the child's stage of development greatly influences the experience of loss. Preschool children (3–5 years) may be confused about what has happened and preoccupied with fears of abandonment by the other parent. They may regress, behaving like much younger children; there may also be angry outbursts or demands for attention.

*After her father left the marriage Lucy, aged three, began wetting and soiling despite being fully toilet-trained. At times her speech was unclear. Her mother described tantrums and clinging to her 'like a shadow'. She became difficult at bedtime, screaming when her mother left the room, and needing her to return repeatedly before falling asleep.*

Young school-age children (6–8 years) may be extremely sad, feel torn by divided loyalties and yearn for their parents to be together again. They may also fear abandonment and neglect and blame one parent for the other's departure.

*Con, aged six, seemed unaware of his parents' unhappy marriage and his father's many affairs. His father had left for another woman after a failed attempt at marital therapy. Con stopped playing at home and school, sitting gloomily alone. His school work deteriorated sharply. When his mother found him hiding biscuits, he said he would need food when she also left. When reassuring Con that she was staying with him, he lashed out, crying: 'No, you should go away, because you made my daddy leave; then he can come back'.*

Older school-age children (9–12 years), being more mature cognitively and socially, can be more detached but may deal with their insecurity by aligning with one parent against the other, particularly when the latter finds a new partner.

*Danny, aged eleven, was a sullen youngster whose school progress was declining and who refused to see his father. The separation was instigated by his mother, and at first they had a co-operative arrangement for his care—which broke down when his father found a new partner. Danny angrily commented on this new relationship which he felt meant that he and his mother were no longer wanted.*

Adolescents (13–18 years) may find that divorce raises concerns about their own future relationships. Older adolescents may make a mature appraisal of their parents' situation but their anger may take the form of moral outrage. The experience may lead to disrupted emotional development or maladaptive patterns of behaviour, even delinquency.

> *Mario, aged eighteen, asserted that he could handle his parents' separation and divorce and the skirmishes which ensued because he was older than his sister and had developed a life of his own. He had shared with his girlfriend a fear that he himself might divorce one day and disappointment in his parents. He was highly critical of his parents whom he thought were acting irresponsibly, especially when they quarrelled. He went on to express his anger indirectly by petty thefts and rebellious behaviour in the classroom.*

The case of divorce illustrates clearly how, in children facing the same stress, psychological problems may show in many ways according to the child's stage of development.

## What does the child psychiatrist do?

The biopsychosocial model we discussed in Chapters 2 and 3 is central to the assessment of every child and adolescent who becomes emotionally distressed.

The biological dimension focuses on the child's birth and developmental history, any previous illnesses or current physical symptoms, and relevant evidence of psychiatric disorder in other family members. Physical examination and investigations may be necessary, depending on the particular problem. For example, a child whose problem is bed-wetting may always have wet the bed, or only after a recent stress such as parental separation. While the child is most unlikely to have a urinary infection or kidney dysfunction, these possibilities can be readily excluded by simple tests in order to set the minds of parents (and psychiatrist!) at rest. By contrast, a child with behavioural and learning problems who is 'going blank' several times a day would need more complex neurological tests to exclude a serious condition such as epilepsy.

The psychological dimension is concerned with the child's emotional state and cognitive abilities. The psychiatrist will usually assess these through direct observation and by asking parents and teachers for their views. The child's ability to relate to the interviewer, response to separation from the parents and current mood are all important. Younger children in particular may have difficulty telling others, even their parents, that they are anxious or unhappy. The psychiatrist therefore uses a number of indirect approaches—particularly drawing (say of a good dream and a bad dream) and play—to encourage children to share feelings and experiences. Many children find it easier to tell a story 'once removed'—that is, to tell how an imagined child may behave or feel in a situation that is like their own. Inviting a child to describe their 'three worst fears' or make 'three wishes' is usually very revealing.

> *Mary, aged eight, had abdominal pain and was missing school as a result. Given three wishes, her first was that her mother would stop worrying about her younger sister who was intellectually disabled. This turned out to reflect a constant concern about her mother's welfare and the translation of this anxiety into the 'tummy ache'. Her second wish was that her parents would stop arguing, and the third that they would all go on a wonderful holiday cruise.*

Older children and adolescents are offered the chance to be seen alone as well as with their parents. This is often the only way to explore sensitive subjects such as sexual abuse, suicidal thoughts and pregnancy. Deterioration in school work, withdrawal from social activities and 'rebellious' behaviour may be signs of underlying depression (although the depression may show in more obvious symptoms or attempted suicide).

The child psychiatrist may learn about the child's cognitive development from school reports and consultation with school teachers. In addition, by the simple task of the child drawing a person, his or her mental age, from 3 to 13, can be approximately calculated. If the child has considerable problems with learning and/or school achievement, a child psychologist will be asked to assess cognitive abilities including specific weaknesses which may need special help at school. Accurate diagnosis of any specific learning difficulty (such as dyslexia) is important as it should lead to remedial teaching, and relief of associated emotional difficulties.

The social dimension mainly involves looking at how the family might be triggering or maintaining the child's difficulties. For example, marital conflict, domestic violence and anti-social behaviour in other family members will have a bearing on a child who has been absconding from home or truanting from school. The psychiatrist will inquire about the parents' experiences in their own families, since these may be shaping the parenting style. Obviously of central importance is an account of the marriage including disharmony, conflict and separations. In meeting the family as a group, the psychiatrist can observe interaction at many levels between parents, siblings, parents and children, and parents and the child with problems.

The broader social situation is also considered. Cultural factors may, for example, affect adolescents from a different ethnic background who are torn between their parents' values and those of their peers. These issues may be less obvious but just as important for any adolescents who are at odds with the values of their friends on matters like smoking, drugs and sexual behaviour.

## PROBLEMS OF INFANCY AND EARLY CHILDHOOD (0–5 YEARS)

The most common problems are disturbances of bodily functions such as sleeping, eating and elimination, and those which are more serious and pervasive like autism. In all these instances, the psychiatrist pays close attention to the parents' functioning. Maternal depression is one notable example which, during the first year after birth, affects women directly as well as the rest of the family. It is often an unrecognised factor in feeding, sleeping and temperamental problems in young babies.

### Sleep disturbances

About one in ten children under school age have disturbed sleeping, and half of these have associated behavioural difficulties (see Chapter 10). Typically the child cannot get off to sleep, has a disturbed sleep pattern including nightmares, night terrors, sleep-walking, insomnia or, occasionally, too much sleep. Nightmares are common in the preschool years and are in fact anxious dreams. Night terrors, experienced by 3 per cent of young children, involve intense fear, screaming and an appearance of being awake but with no memory of it. Sleep-walking takes place in about 15 per cent of children and is more likely at times of stress—the child who is in a trance-like state for up to half an hour clumsily moves about and may say things that make no sense.

Poor sleepers are either children with family problems such as maternal depression and marital conflict, or those who are biologically vulnerable with a history of birth difficulties, developmental complications, awkward temperament and over-activity. Treatment ranges from attending to underlying problems like family tension, to introducing predictable bedtime routines and modifying behaviour by not responding to infant cries and gradually spending less time at the child's bedside.

A painting by an 8-year-old boy with severe anxiety.

A drawing by a depressed 7-year-old girl.

## Feeding and eating battles

Struggles between parent and child around feeding are common enough, beginning in the second or third year. When the child is temperamentally unstable and/or the parent intolerant of normal displays of self-will (part of the toddler's new sense of independence), the scene is set for a continuing conflict between distraught parent and defiant child.

Newborn premature babies have particular eating difficulties, and up to a third of them require several weeks of nasogastric or intravenous feeding. As they lack practice in swallowing and sucking, they will resist taking food by mouth. A more unusual condition is pica, which is the persistent eating of non-food substances such as soil—often associated with mental retardation or parental neglect. Prolonged ingestion of substances like paint, hair or grass may cause poisoning or intestinal obstruction.

## Bladder and bowel disturbance

All children will sometimes lose control of bladder or bowel function, but occasionally it becomes persistent and a matter of concern to both parent and child. Child psychiatrists can help by pinpointing exactly what is happening.

Children who have no physical disorders like urinary infection, epilepsy or diabetes, and who wet their bed or clothes, day or night, at least twice a month when aged 5–6 years, and once a month when older, are said to have functional enuresis. Enuresis is common. Untreated, it occurs in 15 per cent of 5-year-olds but only 3 per cent of 12 year-olds. Primary enuresis is a developmental problem in which the child has never been dry for a long period. It is not usually associated with emotional or behavioural problems, and it is distressing to both child and family. Like most developmental problems, it occurs more often in boys. There may be a genetic predisposition, and a family history of wetting is common. Secondary enuresis is wetting which follows a period of urinary control of a year or longer. It is often linked to disruptive family and life events, and accompanied by emotional and behavioural difficulties.

The psychiatrist will make a full inquiry, including a physical examination and urine testing. Behavioural treatment using a pad-and-bell alarm is most effective, particularly when a star-chart gives positive reinforcement. Parents help the child to use the toilet when the alarm goes off and reset it after changing the bed. Treatment continues until there have been at least fourteen consecutive dry nights. Tricyclic anti-depressants (see Chapter

20) are equally effective in the short term but associated with a high relapse rate. They are therefore useful when children sleep away from home.

A similar disorder of bowel function is called functional encopresis. The repeated passing of faeces into inappropriate places like clothing may be voluntary or involuntary. Encopresis occurs in 2 per cent of children aged 5–8 years, and is much more common in boys. It is often due to 'overflow' incontinence resulting from chronic constipation, which may be associated with a diet low in fibre and high in sugar, fever or anal pain. A number of children have an underlying abnormality of large intestinal function, with reduced sensitivity to dilatation of the rectum and difficulty in co-ordinating anal and abdominal muscles used to defecate. When parent and child are locked in a 'battle of the bowel', encopresis may follow. A punitive parental response undermines the child's desire to co-operate and increases fear of defecation. Some encopretic children have increased anxiety, low self-esteem and poor social skills, but these are usually due to the soiling which disrupts the child's life and causes embarrassment. Frequently, there is quite disturbed family dynamics in the case histories; the anger the child feels towards one or both parents needs to be carefully explored.

> *Sally was three when first admitted to the isolation ward of a rural hospital with suspected meningitis. Her mother was not allowed to visit for ten days. Eighteen months later, after a long history of intermittent diarrhoea, she went back to the same ward with a diagnosis of gastroenteritis. X-ray of the abdomen showed impacted faeces and led to the diagnosis of 'spurious diarrhoea' due to overflow incontinence. When asked specifically, her mother said that Sally had not wanted to use the toilet after her first hospitalisation and would occasionally pass large formed motions into her pants. Prior to that admission she had been making satisfactory progress with toilet training.*

Treatment involves high-fibre diet and oral laxatives for constipation and parental guidance to guard against any negative reaction towards the soiling. Rewards for regular toileting help too. In severe cases, hospital admission may be needed to empty a severely blocked bowel and to establish a regular pattern.

## Attachment problems

The normal bonding between parent and child, particularly between mother and child, may run off course, resulting in a clinging dependency or its more puzzling opposite—what child psychiatrists call reactive attach-ment disorder. In the 'inhibited' group, the infant consistently fails to begin or respond to social cues such as following faces or playing games like 'pat-a-cake' or 'peek-a-boo'. These children are withdrawn and apathetic, showing little spontaneity, curiosity or interest. Play skills and language development may be delayed and they may show self-absorbed behaviour such as rocking and head-banging. In the 'disinhibited' group, the child may be too 'friendly' and show affection indiscriminately, including towards strangers.

> Brian was an affectionate toddler who greeted every new adult entering the pae-diatric ward enthusiastically. He showed no preference for his mother, who didn't visit often. He was in hospital for investigation of his failure to thrive and at the time of admission he had cigarette burns on both hands. A diagnosis of reactive attachment disorder secondary to parental abuse was made.

This behaviour is typically a response to inadequate care in which the child's physical and emotional needs have been neglected by parents or there have been repeated changes in caregivers—for example, many foster-home placements. The child may fail to grow and gain weight—'a failure to thrive'—in response to serious distortions in the child–parent relation-ship. Reactive attachment disorder may be so severe as to be confused with mental retardation or autism.

In treating these children, the aim is to provide care appropriate to their development and protective measures to ensure their safety. Assistance with parenting, including joint hospitalisation in a mother–infant unit, may be necessary. Sometimes, however, the child must be removed from parental care before work with the family can begin. This intervention is crucial because of the possibility of long-term consequences, the most serious of which is the tendency for these children to reproduce their experience when rearing their own children, despite all their good intentions.

## Autism

More common in boys than girls, so-called pervasive developmental dis-order is a serious condition characterised by disturbed verbal and non-verbal communication, social interaction and play behaviour. It is usually associ-ated with some intellectual disability. Autism is the most common form (called Asperger's syndrome when language and intellectual skills are bet-ter developed). These typical signs are usually clear before the child's third birthday:

- delayed and abnormal language and speech (for example, repetition of phrases);
- impaired social responsiveness (children are aloof and avoid eye contact);
- ritualistic behaviour (for example, rocking, pacing up and down);
- intolerance of change;
- limited ability to start creative play.

Parents of autistic children were once described as cold and unresponsive, leading to the child's failure to form social relationships. In hindsight this judgement is totally unjustified. It is now widely accepted that the disorder is due to a brain defect, but its nature is still a mystery. If a parent seems to lack warmth, it is an entirely understandable reaction to an unresponsive child. Research shows a genetic factor in some families, an association with intellectual retardation and epilepsy (one in five retarded, autistic children suffer from epilepsy) and non-specific abnormalities of brain function.

It is crucial that autism is diagnosed early, and that educational and behavioural management programmes are begun. Autism is life-long but at least two-thirds of children go on to live independently or in a supported community, and can participate in special occupational programmes. A few are even able to work in ordinary employment. The outlook is best for those with higher IQs who develop functional speech. A typical autistic adult is well played by Dustin Hoffman in *Rainman*. In this film, the character is discharged to the care of his brother, who is more and more amazed at the selective mental capacities—for example, a photographic memory—of someone who nevertheless has severe intellectual retardation. Oliver Sacks has also brought the autistic condition to life in his engaging book *An Anthropologist on Mars*.

## PROBLEMS OF PRIMARY SCHOOL CHILDREN (5–12 YEARS)

Freud called this stage the latency period, which he saw as an inactive time in between the massive changes in infancy and early childhood and the turmoil of adolescence. Later observers have rejected this view. For example, Erik Erikson, one of Freud's students, highlighted the 'busy-ness' of the time when children are actively learning to master the basic tools of their society. In developed countries, great emphasis is placed during this period on formal learning in school, especially of 'the three Rs'. Failure at this task is, in Erikson's terms, associated with 'a sense of inferiority'.

So, it is at this time that children are brought to psychiatrists, among other professionals, with learning problems. These are often associated with behavioural difficulties, which show themselves in four main ways: attention-deficit, oppositional and conduct, and specific developmental disorders. Children with these conditions, particularly boys, make up a large proportion of the children referred to child psychiatrists, which reflects the concerns of parents and teachers. In addition, a number of other specific disorders show themselves at this stage of child development—for example, Tourette's disorder and gender identity disorder.

## Attention deficit disorder

This is 'hyperactivity'. Children typically lack persistence and attentiveness, and are impulsive and constantly restless. Parents always stress this restlessness, together with difficult feeding and sleeping from an early age. Toddlers are accident prone, and kindergarten-age children often disrupt other children's activities and cannot persist at a task. Language delay and learning difficulties are common.

Up to one in twenty children show hyperactivity, with boys affected four times more often than girls. The cause is largely unknown but genetics and brain damage appear to play a part. Many factors have been blamed. The most popular is artificial food colourings, and the 'Feingold diet' which excludes them has been a widely promoted treatment. Despite the lack of scientific evidence, some parents are convinced that a diet free of additives controls their child's behaviour. Inhaled lead may contribute but the evidence again is unclear. Inconsistent parenting, unrealistic parental expectations and poor housing may also play a part, although it is far more likely that they add to the disorder inherent in the child.

> David, aged five, was seen by a psychiatrist because he had lit several fires including one which, if not detected, could have caused serious damage to his home. There had been many family disruptions and his mother had shortly before begun a new de facto relationship. When observed, he scarcely sat still for more than a moment and was unable to stick to any task requested of him. He had impaired short-term memory and, although his general IQ was average, testing showed abnormalities of concentration and attention. Treatment was aimed at helping the parents recognise the impact of recent events on David and advising them to be more consistent with discipline. Teachers were contacted to assist him with his learning and behavioural problems. While some change followed it was not until he received a stimulant drug (methylphenidate) that he

*improved substantially. A change of school to a more supportive one also helped. Two years later, with treatment still in place, David showed a greater capacity to concentrate, and better school results.*

Treatment takes many forms, including family counselling and behaviour modification designed to reduce activities which bring the child into conflict with others. Paradoxically and as yet mysteriously, stimulant medication with amphetamine-like drugs increases the attention span and is considered in more severe cases—however, debate rages on about their effectiveness. In some countries, particularly the United States, stimulants are widely prescribed despite evidence of the risk of dependence (see page 184).

## Oppositional and conduct disorders

As all parents know, negative and defiant behaviour are common. When they are excessive for the child's age or markedly aberrant (such as stealing, compulsive lying, running away from home, truancy and aggression), we are heading towards so-called oppositional and conduct disorders. These disorders are divided into socialised and unsocialised forms depending on whether the child acts alone or in company. Some of these children will become serious offenders in later adolescence, particularly those who show little or no remorse, or no concern for the feelings of others. A few even develop anti-social personality disorder in adulthood (see page 151).

*Carlos, aged twelve and adopted, was assessed by a child psychiatrist after he set fire to a neighbour's house. He had a long history of anti-social behaviours including breaking-and-entering, fire-setting and running away from home. This pattern had been evident since he was a toddler, and he had continued to resist his mother's attempts to set limits on his behaviour. By thirteen he had been placed in institutional care several times because of his parents' and society's inability to contain his behaviour. Treatment included a special educational programme, consistent limit-setting with appropriate consequences if he broke them, and participation in group therapy to build his self-esteem and relationships with his peers. With all this help, it took several years for Peter gradually to 'grow out' of this behavioural pattern.*

## Specific developmental disorders

Sometimes children run into problems in a single area of development. Specific developmental disorders, as we call them, are often associated with learning problems and are much more common in boys than girls. Reading problems, which are often quite disabling, are the most common. They occur in one in ten children, and are often associated with disruptive behaviour. Tests of intelligence requiring skills in the use of words are the best predictor of later reading ability. The term 'dyslexia' was widely used to describe these disturbances but is a confusing, unhelpful term.

Disorders of speech (impaired articulation or production of sounds) and language (impaired understanding or expression to convey meaning) are also common. Since normal hearing is essential for development of language, any child with a marked language disorder will have their hearing carefully checked, and be examined by a speech therapist. Mild or occasional stuttering is common in early stages of language development. Speech therapy is effective in reducing stuttering, but there are doubts about whether this has a lasting effect. Specialist attention is needed when the pattern is more severe or sustained.

## Tourette's disorder

In this puzzling and bizarre disorder, also known as multiple tic disorder, the child quite involuntarily makes brief, purposeless body movements and utters sounds which are often not words, but may sometimes be swear words. Not unexpectedly, affected children are often shunned by their peers and even teachers because of their behaviour. The movements often respond to an anti-psychotic drug, suggesting that Tourette's is a disorder of brain function.

> Ben was twelve when first seen by a psychiatrist. He had suffered from Tourette's for many years, with typical vocal utterances—involuntary chicken-like noises— and a tendency to fling his arms about. He had few friends and had never been invited to stay at a friend's house. Within weeks of commencing anti-psychotic medication the symptoms subsided markedly and he was able to spend holidays with friends for the first time. His parents commented excitedly that Ben had not been so happy for years.

## Gender identity disorder

By the age of four, children have a sense of their own gender and that of other children. While sure of their gender role, they will experiment with behaviours of the other sex, such as cross-dressing. Parents are rarely worried by 'boyishness' in their daughters, but are much more likely to be concerned at their sons' 'girlishness'. In most children, sex-role assignment by the parents, which almost always fits with the external genitalia, seems to be the key to gender identity. A few children have a strong wish to be of the other sex or, in extreme cases, a conviction that they really are of the opposite sex despite bodily evidence to the contrary. Some will seek sex reassignment later in life (see page 132). While the cause of these gender identity disorders is unknown, both biological and environmental factors play a part.

## PROBLEMS OF ADOLESCENCE (13–18 YEARS)

Most adolescents make the transition to adulthood smoothly, but some suffer from psychiatric disorders which are often missed. And many 'adult' conditions begin during adolescence, notably schizophrenia, mood, eating and obsessive-compulsive disorders. 'Identity crises' are common and usually relate to self-image, relationships with others, sexual orientation, religious affiliation and values. Adolescents unsure of their identity are open to the influence of groups and charismatic leaders. These are usually music and sporting 'heroes' but occasionally, and with very damaging results, teenagers fall under the control of religious cults or extreme political movements.

### Mood disorders

All adolescents experience mood swings. But, as in adults, persistent lowering of mood, anorexia, weight loss, sleep disturbance, feelings of hopelessness and suicidal ideas suggest clinical depression. Recognition and treatment are vital, as the link between depression and suicide is well established and the recent increase in youth suicide in Western countries is alarming. Although so-called suicidal behaviour is far more common in girls, death by suicide is four times more common in boys. It may be triggered by educational pressure, unemployment, family conflict or break-up, portrayal of youth suicide in the media, alcohol and drug abuse and the loss of close relationships (see Chapter 19).

A particularly dramatic finding is that most adolescents who suicide have told an adult (such as their family doctor or teacher) of their distress in the preceding weeks. Since about one in ten adolescents who attempt suicide will later succeed, all attempts are treated with utmost seriousness. Any adolescent who attempts suicide should be assessed by a counsellor, mental health professional or family doctor.

At this time every year, Santa Claus checks his records to see which boys and girls have been well behaved;

To see which children have not been too difficult for Mother and father;

To see who has not been too selfish or demanding or disobedient;

To see who has been well brought up and is well mannered and pleasant and agreeable and cheerful and helpful and clever and good.

To these children he will give a gift which could become extremely useful to them in later life:

A big, thick book titled "UNDERSTANDING YOUR DEPRESSION"

leunig

Treatment is generally one of the psychotherapies, but anti-depressant medication may be needed—if, for example, there is a family history of depression or the adolescent's depression is severe.

Anxiety is common in adolescence and is perfectly understandable given the fundamental tasks and challenges that come with separating from parents. About half of normal adolescents report some feelings of apprehension, tension, restlessness, fears, social anxiety or bodily symptoms such as palpitations. It is important to distinguish these feelings from an anxiety disorder (see Chapter 7).

Separation of adolescents (and indeed children from four or five years on) from key figures, home or familiar surroundings may lead to separation anxiety disorder. Feelings of distress are accompanied by bodily symptoms like headache and abdominal pain for which no physical cause can be found. This is a well-recognised contributor to school refusal. These adolescents may be too dependent on parents, particularly the mother. Although most are relatively immature with poor self-image, they are usually of average or above-average intelligence and do not have major educational difficulties. Their parents tend to be over-protective and a family history of anxiety is common. The separation problems often relate to a wish to protect a parent from marital conflict or violence or to remain with an ill, depressed or suicidal parent. Up to half these adolescents will continue to have social or personality difficulties in adult life, with an increased risk of developing agoraphobia or other anxiety disorders.

The adolescent who is refusing school will be encouraged to return as soon as possible by advising parents to be firm. Other treatment includes addressing underlying family problems, psychological therapies (see Chapter 21), and anti-depressants or anti-anxiety drugs where indicated.

*Tina, aged fifteen, persistently refused to go to school and feared leaving home. She was struggling at an academically oriented school and her anxiety about her studies was reinforced by an over-protective mother. Her father had left the family when Tina was ten, and her mother treated her as a substitute companion. Tina felt a strong need to be there, for 'Mum hits the bottle when she is alone'. Treatment focused on both Tina and her mother. It included 'graded practice' at leaving the house with the support of her older brother, and a small dose of an anti-anxiety drug for a short period (see page 273). Family therapy boosted Tina's growing independence and the whole family's understanding of how their difficulties had arisen after the father's departure.*

## Delinquency and substance abuse

About half the adolescents seen by psychiatrists show anti-social behaviour. These are the common factors in their lives:

- families with low income;
- families with many children and relative maternal deprivation;
- a history of parental criminality and tolerance of anti-social behaviour;
- inconsistent patterns of discipline, and marital conflict;
- below-average intelligence or learning disabilities.

Most adolescents experiment with drugs, ranging from tobacco and alcohol—the main drugs of abuse—to marijuana and narcotics. Most do not become dependent. The adolescents most at risk of substance abuse have marked conflict with their parents; another psychiatric disorder, particularly behavioural; and a family history of substance abuse. The hazards of this abuse include increased risk of death through suicide, accidents or illnesses like hepatitis B and C and AIDS; and of criminal behaviour in order to obtain drugs.

Conventional psychotherapies have not been successful, and treatment now focuses on enhancing self-esteem through educational help with learning problems, sporting activities, vocational training and social skills. Family therapy aims to reduce conflict and to encourage a more consistent setting of limits that are appropriate to the adolescent's age.

## Psychoses

Psychotic illness is rare before puberty but both schizophrenia and manic-depressive illness may occur from mid-adolescence onward. The close association with substance abuse may be a contributing factor. While the symptoms are like those in adults (see Chapter 12), diagnosis may be difficult as specific features such as disordered thought and delusions may be absent. Early, non-specific symptoms include declining social and cognitive functioning, and general anxiety without cause. Treatment resembles that for adults, although working with the family is particularly stressed.

## Child abuse

Child abuse differs from all other conditions we have covered since the child is the victim of interaction with an adult, often a caregiver, which results in physical and/or emotional harm. Since 1961 when Henry Kempe, an American paediatrician, drew attention to the 'battered child syndrome', child abuse has become much more widely recognised. And we are now aware that it leads to impaired social relationships, psychiatric problems in adulthood and poor parenting. Surveys since the 1980s have shown staggeringly high rates of abused children.

The family has always been regarded as the foundation of society, a sacrosanct institution to be protected and maintained—and the home as a haven, a refuge from social ills (and demands). On the other hand, women and children have until relatively recently, at least in Western societies, been seen as possessions of the husband and father—as reflected in law, religion and economic arrangements. For many of the world's women and children, this is still the case.

It is ironic that we had societies for the protection of animals before we had agencies and legislation for the protection of women and children. In 1871 the plight of a severely maltreated child reported by neighbours to the Society of Prevention of Cruelty to Animals in New York was dismissed by the courts since the child was deemed not to be an animal. This intolerable situation soon led to the formation of a society for prevention of cruelty to children.

Despite masses of evidence that the home is a dangerous place for many women and children, we are still struggling to accept that a quarter of adults have experienced abuse as children and that a quarter of couples experience violence in their relationship (95 per cent of the victims being women). At first, awareness of child abuse was limited to severe physical harm, but the net has widened to include sexual abuse, emotional abuse and general neglect. It was not until the 1980s that we began to understand the horrendous effects on children of violence in the home.

Children used to be thought of as pretty tough and able to cope with adversity. As the full story of abuse emerges, this belief has been shattered—to the extent that psychiatrists use the term 'post-traumatic stress disorder' (see Chapter 7) to explain the responses of children. Abused children tend to 'show rather than tell'—that is, the effect of their experience is often seen first in changes in behaviour, emotional state, bodily functioning and learning difficulties.

Traumatic effects may follow a single catastrophic event or many forms of abuse over a long period. Acute reactions include regression, sleep problems, a tendency to be easily startled, extreme wariness, wide-ranging fears, panic, irritability and denial of the trauma. Children's behaviour may change dramatically, with symptoms like bed-wetting, anxiety and aggressive behaviour. If the abuse is prolonged and/or there are repeated episodes, the child's self-image, relationships and view of the world are profoundly affected. Children become preoccupied with adapting to and protecting themselves from environmental demands. Abused children, like abused adults, may develop behaviour intended to appease the abuser and so protect themselves. This usually fails to stop the abuse, increases helplessness and, paradoxically, induces guilt.

Children need predictable and consistent nurturing by a caregiver to whom they are or can become attached. Disruption to this 'good-enough' care (a term introduced by Donald Winnicott, a British paediatrician and psychoanalyst, to suggest that parenting is not necessarily ideal) has, understandably, long-term adverse results. The nature of the difficulties depends on the quality of care the child had before the abuse, the type of abuse (severity and duration in particular) and the relationship of the child to the abusing adult. The closer the child to that adult, the greater the sense of betrayal, confusion and enduring ill-effects. These cover the full range of psychiatric problems: low self-esteem, relationship difficulties, anxiety, depression, eating and post-traumatic stress disorders. A close link has emerged between childhood abuse and the later development of disordered personality in adult life, particularly of the borderline type (see

Chapter 11). While most people who were abused as children will not repeat this abuse as parents, up to a third will—they seem, paradoxically, to be incapable of preventing the cycle.

Munchausen syndrome by proxy, fortunately rare, is a bizarre form of abuse. The caregiver, most often a mother, invents her child's symptoms (for example, describing fits or reporting fever in an otherwise well child) or actually makes the child ill through inappropriate administration of medications like laxatives, diuretics, even poisons. Children may be tested repeatedly until the bizarreness of the clinical picture points to this possibility. Even in the face of clear evidence, the mother persistently denies her role. She herself usually has long-standing personality difficulties, or an undetected psychiatric disorder. Moreover, she may have experienced a history similar to the one she has inflicted on her child.

Treatment of any type of child abuse requires a high level of suspicion as the first step in the diagnosis, followed by evaluating the degree of urgency for protection. Liaison with a welfare agency occurs if there are concerns for the child's safety. The child and family are referred to a child protection unit, a paediatrician or a child psychiatrist for confirmation of the diagnosis.

In many countries, social welfare authorities must be informed of suspected child abuse, including sexual abuse. Proper protection of the abused child is a crucial step in treatment. Sometimes the child will be admitted to hospital for tests or even temporarily removed from the family. Police may have to assist with this removal, and investigate criminal aspects. A formal application for protection may be vital to ensure safety. While parents may become aggressive if abuse has been disclosed by the child or diagnosed by professionals, most children do return to parental care once assessment has been completed and treatment begun.

# 16    *Women and Mental Health*

If we had written this book fifty years ago, it would have been inconceivable to include a chapter on psychiatry and women. Today, it is equally inconceivable *not* to consider the mental health issues that are of special relevance and concern to women. Why is this so?

Mounting research evidence points to substantial rates of certain forms of mental illness in women compared to men. Moreover, many more women than ever before are seeking professional help or are identified as needing it. The feminist movement has highlighted the particular needs of women and how these have generally been neglected—the case of domestic violence springs immediately to mind. At least in part, this neglect derives from social values that have been strongly challenged from the 1960s onwards by spokeswomen like Simone de Beauvoir, Betty Friedan and Germaine Greer. Psychiatrists have been sensitive to such influences and, in modifying their thinking on the nature of mental illness and its treatment, they have reflected the views of their society.

The history of society's attitude to mental illness in women is intriguing but not always edifying. For example, during the Middle Ages and beyond it was believed that women who now would be diagnosed as suffering from hysterical conversion or psychosis were witches, who could be 'cured' only by torture or death. This is powerfully brought to life in Arthur Miller's play *The Crucible* which relates the unsavoury episode known as the 'witches of Salem'. The ideas of Charles Darwin in the nineteenth century led to a view that biological factors, including genetic ones, were pre-eminent in shaping our behaviour. Theories of differences between the sexes were developed and used to justify stereotyped gender roles. Women's functions were thus seen as primarily domestic and maternal. The male-dominated medical establishment endorsed this view, and fostered the notion that women were vulnerable to both physical and mental illness because of their genetic make-up. Not until the last few decades have we considered the possibility that harmful social attitudes might be responsible for this vulnerability.

Nineteenth-century 'hygiene manuals' preached that sexual transgression in women caused ill health, so re-enforcing the tie between women's social behaviour and health status. Prominent feminist writers have highlighted the link society makes between 'madness' and 'femininity', and described fashions in the presentation of women's symptoms and in the (usually) male medical response. Women were consistently diagnosed with and treated for so-called mental disorders—which feminist writers claim were socially determined behaviours to deal with anxieties resulting from severe restriction on what women could do or be (see page 153, on hysteria).

The Freudian view of women as passive and inferior (his concept of 'penis envy' embodies his biased views) significantly influenced later psychological theories—including those which are a backlash to it. Karen Horney, a leading figure in the American psychoanalytic movement, repudiated Freud's notion, arguing that social forces were much more relevant than biological ones in determining gender behaviour.

Rigidity of positions towards gender roles (and their adverse effects) endured into the 1970s. For example, one American study found in 1970 that, in considering men and women, clinicians maintained a double standard of mental health. A mentally healthy woman was seen as having quite different (stereotyped 'feminine') qualities from a healthy man. This placed women in a bind: they had to maintain these 'feminine' features in order to be regarded as healthy!

In her controversial book with the evocative title *Women and Madness*, Phyllis Chesler, a social scientist, argued strongly that the labelling of women as 'mad' is a form of social control. Using the cases of Zelda Fitzgerald (wife of the famous author F. Scott Fitzgerald) and Sylvia Plath, among others, Chesler vigorously attacked a male-dominated psychiatry. As she put it:

> Women are impaled on the cross of self-sacrifice. Unlike men, they are categorically denied the experience of cultural supremacy, humanity, and renewal based on their sexual identity . . . [Their] madness is essentially an intense experience of female biological, sexual, and cultural castration, and a doomed search for potency. The search often involves 'delusions' or displays of physical aggression, grandeur, sexuality, and emotionality—all traits which would probably be more acceptable in female-dominated cultures. Such traits in women are feared and punished in patriarchal mental asylums . . .

Treatment in psychiatry has been criticised by feminist observers for attempting to return women to the very situation in which they became mentally ill in the first place—that is, their passive, dependent and submissive role—and for failing to look at the need for social change, particularly for empowerment. Critics comment on psychiatry's tendency to focus on and treat disturbance in the individual person rather than its social causes. Psychotherapy is said not to appreciate the dilemmas of women's experiences and therefore to contribute to their continued oppression. Of special concern is sexual exploitation of patients by psychotherapists, the ultimate abuse of the power relationship inherent in the therapeutic encounter (see Chapter 21). New approaches to therapy for women, such as consciousness-raising groups, question the balance of power in therapy and allow a genuinely open, egalitarian experience.

Feminists have, through these sorts of arguments, made an immense impact on mental health treatment, with the psychiatric profession receptive to the shift. Their campaign on violence against women, for example, has led to alternative models of service such as rape crisis centres and refuges for battered women, in which women themselves are encouraged to take active responsibility for their welfare in the context of achieving social and political change.

## Gender differences in patterns of illness

Women are more vulnerable to mental illness, and this is closely tied to marital status, work and social roles. Studies have found substantial gender differences in the rate for many psychiatric conditions. Women predominate in depression, both mild and severe, anxiety states including agoraphobia, other phobias and panic, and those states which manifest as bodily concerns (see Chapter 9). Men, on the other hand, predominate in antisocial personality disorder and alcohol abuse. These reasons are suggested for women's greater vulnerability:

- while men have two sources of gratification, work and family, many women have only family;
- raising children and keeping house is intrinsically frustrating;
- the role of housewife is unstructured and invisible;
- working married women are under more pressure than married men and prone to a greater role conflict.

Research bears this out. Married women show higher rates of psychiatric disorder than married men, whereas single women are similar to their single male counterparts. Marriage is associated with better physical health in both sexes but not with better mental health in women unless they are gainfully employed. The effect of employment on women's mental health depends substantially on their husbands' attitudes and on their own satisfaction with arrangements for child care. If good care is available and husbands contribute to it, rates of depression are low. But employed mothers without available child care and with sole responsibility for it have extremely high levels of depression. For non-working wives, children increase women's vulnerability.

If we look at depression, which is the most common women's mental health problem in Western countries, we see the immense impact of gender. For every man who comes for treatment, there are two women. Age is important. In children and the elderly there is little gender difference, but depression is much more common in women between these ages, reaching a peak in young mothers.

Biological factors may contribute to these differences, particularly for severe depression after giving birth, but psychological and social factors are likely to play a role in milder forms. For everybody, clinical depression is preceded by a greater frequency of demanding life events. Women do not experience these events more often than men, and both rate their stressfulness similarly. But women react with more symptoms to the same stress—they show greater vulnerability to the effects of life events. Research on female vulnerability points to lack of a confidant, the presence of young children, lower social class, not working outside the home, and early loss of one's mother. Another factor may be a gender difference in appreciation and expression of distress, with women more inclined to acknowledge feelings, both positive and negative, and men tending to deny them and to express distress in other ways such as alcohol abuse and domestic violence.

## Mental health problems through the life cycle

Although women are major consumers of mental health services, their special needs, particularly at crucial points in their development, have only received attention since the 1970s. An emerging problem in childhood is sexual abuse, with girls much more likely to be the victims (see page 215). Two serious problems experienced by young women more often than young men are eating disorders (see Chapter 10) and attempted suicide (see Chapter 19).

Psychological problems during adulthood may be associated with menstruation—including pre-menstrual tension, conflicts over contraception and infertility. Sexual difficulties range from poor communication to severe physical and sexual abuse, all of which increase vulnerability to psychiatric illness. Single or repeated pregnancy loss through termination, miscarriage or stillbirth may well influence a woman's emotional adjustment. Psychiatric disorders occur more commonly in the year following childbirth—as does the experience of distress in mothering, especially in a large family or where a child is disabled. Depressed mothers can adversely affect their children, leading to a vicious cycle of family dysfunction.

Another difficult time follows surgery on female organs (hysterectomy and mastectomy). Alzheimer's disease affects older women disproportionately, both as patients and carers, because of their greater life expectancy—emotional disturbance being common among carers of the elderly mentally infirm.

## The menstrual cycle

Menstruation has been surrounded by myths and taboos for centuries, and in many cultures. In our society, these beliefs distort reality and create ambivalent feelings about the value of menstruation beyond its necessity as a means of reproduction. The distortions naturally influence the way a woman feels about herself, her body and her reproductive role.

Mood and behavioural changes have been associated with the menstrual cycle since ancient times. About 50 per cent of women have some symptoms. Irritability, restlessness, anxiety, depression, insomnia and impaired concentration are experienced more frequently during the premenstrual and menstrual phases, while feelings of well-being are more typical of the middle of the cycle.

Hormonal changes during the pre-menstrual phase probably account for breast swelling and nipple tenderness, fluid retention and behavioural, cognitive, mood and sexual changes. All these features are experienced by women who do not seek treatment, and at a higher level by those who consult a doctor. A hormonal sensitivity has long been assumed to explain why certain women are more severely affected than others, but no abnormality has been confirmed. We do know, however, that these symptoms disappear after removal of the ovaries.

Symptoms related to menstruation have been compared across cultures. Pre-menstrual symptoms are found universally but vary in frequency and intensity. For example, breast complaints are unusual in the Japanese and headache is common in Nigerians. Japanese women report fewer symptoms overall than American women, with Turkish and Nigerian women reporting high levels. Menstrual and pre-menstrual complaints have been studied in women of different ethnicity in Australia, and similar patterns have emerged.

These emotional, behavioural, cognitive and physical changes in the pre-menstrual phase have been called pre-menstrual tension syndrome (PMT). Recognition of this syndrome has led the American Psychiatric Association to look at whether it might be considered a specific psychiatric disorder. For the moment, the jargon label of pre-menstrual dysphoric disorder has been proposed. Its criteria include the many symptoms we have listed in the pre-menstrual week (with relief by the post-menstrual week); and of such severity as to be distressing or disruptive of social or occupational functioning.

*Belinda, who has three young children, went to a counsellor requesting help for marital difficulties. She described frequent arguments, particularly over housework, finances and child care. John, her husband, complained of her frequent bouts of anger and 'nagging', and irritability with the toddlers.*

*After a comprehensive assessment it became clear that Belinda experienced these feelings in a predictable monthly cycle. Seven to ten days before each period she became tearful, over-sensitive, irritable and prone to outbursts over trivial issues. Sometimes she even hit out at the children. She felt quite unable to control these outbursts and guilty about her behaviour. Immediately her period began, all her symptoms disappeared.*

*Belinda admitted to always being tense, a perfectionist and a high achiever, and having painful periods in adolescence.*

*Treatment included explanation of the nature of pre-menstrual tension, and counselling of the couple. They responded well to this programme, and family life became much more harmonious as a result.*

## Motherhood

Motherhood represents perhaps the most profound change in a woman's life. While community expectations point to 'blissful motherhood', many women experience just the opposite—considerable distress in the year after childbirth. It is in fact the time of greatest risk for psychiatric illness in a woman (a six-fold increase on other phases of her life).

*Postpartum psychosis* is the most severe mental illness of women after childbirth—at the rate of about one in a thousand births. The risk of psychosis in the first month after childbirth is a dramatic twenty-two times greater than in the two years before the birth. The condition usually begins within one to two weeks. This massively increased rate, combined with the brief period between childbirth and the onset of the early delirium-like symptoms (see Chapter 14) suggestive of brain dysfunction, adds weight to the probability that this devastating illness is linked to hormonal imbalance after the birth in predisposed women. Postpartum psychosis is associated with first births (in two-thirds of cases), Caesarean section, prolonged and difficult labour, stillbirth, a past history of mood disorder or of postpartum psychosis, a family history of mood disorder, and single-mother status. Its treatment is similar to that of psychosis generally (see Chapter 12).

*Postpartum depression* is much more common than postpartum psychosis. Despite obvious emotional distress in the mother and consequent poor coping with the baby, the condition is still often missed. The woman's suffering interferes with her attachment to the baby, its development, and with marital, family and social relationships. Its recognition, prompt treatment and, if possible, prevention will thus help to promote the mental health of both the mother and the family.

About a quarter of women are affected by lowered mood in the first year after birth. Apart from the altered mood, they feel inadequate, unable to cope and guilty over not caring enough for the baby. Other symptoms include loss of sexual interest, fatigue, insomnia and fear of harming the baby. All these features vary in intensity, but often worsen towards the end of the day.

The cause is unclear. Biological, psychological and social factors all probably contribute. A past history of menstrual problems or depression may predict vulnerable women, as may a family history of depression, troubled relationships, lack of support and stressful life events. Psychological and social factors during pregnancy are also relevant.

Support which helps to cushion or even prevent postpartum depression includes a distinct structure to the day, socially sanctioned rest, privacy, assistance in daily tasks from relatives and friends, and recognition through ritual of the mother's new social status. In many traditional cultures, the new mother receives this support, mainly from the family. For example, Jamaican women traditionally enjoy ritual seclusion for the first nine nights and spend the next month at home with the baby cared for by grandmother. In traditional Nigeria, mother and baby are placed in a special hut within the family compound for several weeks, and are also cared for by the grandmother. In Western society, by contrast, the 40-day lying-in period is a dim memory. Rituals are also far less common, reflecting perhaps a more secular age and some ambivalence to the role of mothering.

*Postpartum 'blues'* is easily distinguishable from postpartum depression in that it is a mild, temporary experience limited to the first ten days. Symptoms last for hours to days but soon evaporate. Typically they include weeping, sadness, changeable mood, insomnia, anxiety and irritability. About half of new mothers experience the blues. Fortunately, simple explanation and support are enough to alleviate the distress, but sometimes the symptoms are a prelude to more severe postpartum depression.

*Sonia, a 26-year-old married nurse and mother of two children, aged two years and eight months, went to her family doctor with tiredness and apathy after the birth of her second child. The doctor suspected depression, despite Sonia's disclaimer, 'Isn't this the way tired mums feel?' She described feeling joy at the birth, but soon after returning home from hospital she had begun to experience low mood, insomnia, loss of appetite, poor concentration and utter exhaustion. She was constantly irritable with both children and with her husband, and felt unable to control herself. She withdrew from her friends, neglected the housework and felt guilty that she was 'such a bad mother'.*

*She began to develop feelings of intense anxiety whenever she went out. She felt hopeless about the future and believed she would be better off dead. Her baby cried incessantly and would not sleep. Sonia felt frustrated and angry with the baby and most disturbed by her lack of feeling towards him. Just before seeking help, she had even thought of smothering him to stop him crying.*

*Sonia's mother had suffered from depression and had required hospitalisation. She had a poor relationship with her mother, whom she saw as critical and unsupportive. Sonia had also been sexually abused by a family member at the age of eight. She had always lacked confidence, was shy and had very high expectations of herself.*

*With her baby, Sonia was admitted to a mother and baby unit. Anti-depressants were prescribed, and a programme of individual therapy helped her deal with past issues such as the sexual abuse, and with current parenting difficulties. Couple counselling was planned to improve communication.*

## Infertility and pregnancy loss

Grief generally has been well researched since the 1960s (see Chapter 8), but the impact of pregnancy loss has been less appreciated. Whether the loss has been through spontaneous or induced abortion or stillbirth, it is compounded by loss of the status of motherhood. And the woman's incapacity to rely on her body to give birth buffets her self-esteem. If an infant dies shortly after birth, numerous social practices aid the bereavement process, but these rituals have unfortunately not been extended to pregnancy loss (memorial services are a very recent development). Initial numbness is followed by sadness, emptiness, anger, a sense of inadequacy and a tendency to blame others. These feelings will wane and be replaced, if grieving is effective, with a renewed willingness to engage with life.

Although one in five pregnancies ends in miscarriage, health professionals have tended to disregard this potentially distressing experience. Lack of sympathy for a woman who has miscarried has been widespread in societies past and present. In the Middle Ages, women were sometimes even burned alive. In some contemporary societies, repeated miscarriage is grounds for a man to divorce his wife—like infertility. Although the general view is that the trauma is not great, miscarriage even when planned (for any one of many reasons) is a loss and therefore inherently stressful. It involves loss of the foetus, of energy invested in the pregnancy, and of a sense of control of one's health and fate. Lack of support and ritual deny women comfort and lead to feelings of isolation. Early pregnancy loss denies the mother an opportunity to farewell a tangible body, which complicates the mourning process.

Pregnancy loss and death close to the time of birth produce longer-term psychological symptoms and disturbed family relationships. The well-recognised symptoms include depression, insomnia, withdrawal, anger, guilt and marital strain. Although mothers tend to show more symptoms than fathers, the toll is heavy for both. Factors influencing outcome of mourning are the level of support from the extended family and of contact with the ill or dead infant, the length of time the infant lived, the type of communication between the parents, and the reactions of health professionals.

Many of these psychological issues are also relevant to the infertile couple. Although the new technology of IVF (in-vitro fertilisation) has evolved dramatically, the success rate remains low and the stress to those participating in the programme is high. Continuing infertility, and even failure to respond with the aid of technology, is harmful to the mental well-being of both partners and to the marriage. Because of this vulnerability, psychiatrists have become increasingly involved.

*Lena, a 28-year-old married woman, had symptoms of postpartum depression following the birth of her first child, a daughter, who was then four weeks old.*

*This was her third pregnancy She had had a termination at nineteen and a miscarriage two years previously—eighteen weeks after a three-year history of treatment for infertility.*

*Lena had been extremely distressed at the time of the miscarriage and by the lack of support from the hospital. In particular she was not allowed to hold the baby or proceed with any other mourning ritual. Her sister, however, had given birth to a 24-week baby which had survived after being placed in intensive care and receiving extensive resuscitation. Lena was enraged about what she saw as an arbitrary decision that a loss of pregnancy before twenty weeks was considered a miscarriage.*

*Since Lena's family did not understand her feelings, she kept most of her grief to herself. She had not really overcome her loss when she conceived again one year later. The birth led to a reawakening of her grief, anger and guilt about both previous pregnancies.*

## Menopause

Women cease menstruation at around fifty in Western societies. Since their life expectancy is approaching eighty years, women can expect to live more than a third of their lives beyond the menopause. The relationship between psychological symptoms and the menopause is controversial. Gynaecologists tend to focus on symptoms directly attributable to deficiency of the hormone oestrogen and thus amenable to hormone replacement therapy (HRT). But social scientists maintain that symptoms are more influenced by the expectations of a particular socio-cultural group or by factors like demanding life events. Women face many of these in their middle years: a major illness in themselves or spouse or close relative, 'mid-life crisis' or retirement of spouse, their own retirement, job uncertainty, caring for an elderly parent, children leaving or returning home, and the ultimate loss—death of a spouse. There are positive counter-balances: the birth of grandchildren, freedom from unwanted conception, and the opportunity to pursue new interests. Given their biopsychosocial perspective, psychiatrists generally straddle these two points of view.

An American study found that most menopausal women report positive or at least neutral feelings concerning the ending of periods. Menopause had no impact on how they saw their health, physical or mental. An exception was the 'surgical menopause' group (that is, women whose uterus and sometimes ovaries have been removed) which had poorer health and greater use of medical services before as well as after surgery.

Women's negative attitudes towards menopause were related to a general tendency to report symptoms and depression before the menopause.

High rates of depression are found among women attending menopause clinics and among middle-aged women attending gynaecology clinics. Depression in the menopausal years may be linked to a sense of loss of fertility and femininity, although these reactions are relatively uncommon in Western societies. Depression possibly relates more to the ups and downs of middle life than to the menopause itself.

Changes in mood may, on the other hand, be linked to disabling classical menopausal symptoms like hot flushes and profuse sweating. These are arguably the only 'true' results of the loss of ovarian hormones, with psychological complaints explained by a 'domino-theory'—that is, flushes cause insomnia which leads to fatigue and irritability, and so on. In any event, these classical symptoms are the most responsive to hormone replacement therapy.

*Mrs C, a 52-year-old married woman with three sons, required hysterectomy for heavy periods, during which she unexpectedly had her ovaries removed due to complications. She immediately received hormone replacement therapy, but a month later began to experience hot flushes, sweats, dizziness and swinging moods. She felt so low, anxious and lacking in confidence that she withdrew socially and neglected her housework. She felt physically unattractive and lost interest in sexual relations with her husband.*

*Mrs C's mother had suicided at the age of fifty-five, a loss that she had never fully grieved for. Her husband was not only extremely busy at his job, but had little capacity to express his emotions. All three of her sons were in their early twenties and living away from home. The youngest son had moved just before her surgery. Mrs C felt she had lost her identity as a woman and role as a mother.*

*Treatment included anti-depressant medication and hormone replacement therapy. Psychotherapy was geared to providing her with the opportunity to deal with her losses and adjust to the next phase of her life cycle.*

## The elderly woman

The problems of old age are predominantly those of women. In Western societies most women are widowed at around seventy-five. For every 100 women aged over eighty in Australia, for instance, there are only 47 men. Large numbers of women live alone, often lacking a family network. However, it is a myth that the elderly are a helpless, disease-ridden group.

While some of the last years may be spent in partial ill health, only a small percentage of elderly people is institutionalised (three-quarters of them being women). The increased ageing population has profound political and economic implications for health care, social welfare and economic support. Negative portrayal of elderly women as unattractive, dependent and physically ill has unfortunate psychological and social repercussions.

We must also consider the well-being of the caregivers, as a quarter of the elderly over eighty-five, mostly women, have Alzheimer's disease or a related disorder (see Chapters 14 and 17). In the United States, three-quarters of the two million people caring for the elderly without pay are women. Men and women bring different expectations and coping strategies to this role and experience it differently—subjective and objective strain being greater for female than male carers of relatives with dementia. Women both feel greater strain and in fact shoulder more of the burden than do men.

Three-quarters of the chronically mentally ill in nursing homes are women, mainly with depression and dementia. Older women are also vulnerable to alcohol and drug abuse (the benzodiazepines in particular) —above all, those who are isolated, trapped in unhappy marriages, institutionalised in nursing homes or psychiatric settings, or lacking adequate resources to obtain treatment. Yet older women are often under-represented in the use of mental health services.

Quality of social activity and satisfaction in relationships are vital to the morale of elderly women (as to their male counterparts). Well-being is linked to support which provides acceptance, reassurance of worth and opportunity to participate in recreational pursuits.

## The abused woman

A sad reflection on us all is the abuse of women since time immemorial, a pattern which still prevails. Abuse occurs throughout the life cycle, and includes child abuse (both physical and sexual), incest, wife battering, rape and abuse of the elderly.

Most people would think of violence towards women as being mainly perpetrated by strangers, as in the case of criminal rape. However, it is in the family that violence of all types is focused and, unhappily, tradition has tended to condone it. This social attitude may help to explain Freud's view that his female patients' accounts of sexual abuse in childhood were fantasies. Most violence is carried out by men, with the burden falling on women. Children and adolescents are at risk from all forms of violence (see page 215). The victim, of whatever age, develops a state of helplessness after repeated abusive experiences. She may even conceal the true source of her injuries from health professionals.

The impact of violence on a woman may be an immediate response (resembling post-traumatic stress disorder—see page 86) of fear, withdrawal, emotional inhibition, disturbed self-image and sexual dysfunction. Longer-term effects include depression, which is the most common symptom in adults who were sexually abused as children.

## Conclusion

Psychiatrists' attitudes to, and treatment of, women have seen revolutionary change in the last quarter of this century. They have come to appreciate, through an impressive research effort, that women are burdened at many critical times in their lives with a range of psychological stresses which contribute to mental ill health. Moreover, psychiatry is in a much better position than ever before to offer appropriate and effective treatments. Finally, we should not under-estimate the contribution to these changes made by the high proportion of women within the psychiatric profession—indeed, the highest percentage of any medical specialist group.

# 17    *The Elderly and Mental Health*

The world's population is ageing rapidly. In the developed countries, the proportion of people aged sixty-five years and over will double by the year 2030. The picture of increased longevity in developing countries is even more extraordinary.

Most elderly people are fit and active, and lead satisfying, productive lives. We have only to think of Pablo Picasso, Sir John Gielgud, Lloyd Rees, Bertrand Russell, Alistair Cook, Leo Tolstoy and Dame Mary Gilmore. Giuseppe Verdi proves that age is no impediment to creativity. He composed his last opera, *Falstaff*, at the age of eighty, and the splendid religious choral work, the *Stabat Mater*, three years before his death at eighty-seven. However, old age is also a time of loss. The very elderly in particular are likely to be widowed, live alone and have serious physical or mental disabilities which limit their independence. Many manage with the support of family, friends, neighbours and social services, but some need repeated admissions to hospital, and even permanent residential care.

Society's attitude to elderly people is a crucial factor in how they adapt to old age. It ranges from respect, even reverence, for their wisdom to a negative view that they are a heavy burden on society, particularly as the health and welfare dollar is increasingly stretched. Plato puts forward a view in *The Republic* in the form of a dialogue between Socrates as a young man and Cephalus, an old one, who opens the conversation:

'I find that as I lose my tastes for bodily pleasures, I grow more eager than ever for discussion.' Socrates replied, 'I enjoy talking with very old men. I consider that they have gone before us along a road which we must all travel in our turn, and it is good that we should ask them of the nature of that road, whether it be rough and difficult, or easy and smooth. You Cephalus are now at that time of life which the poets call "old age the threshold", and I should particularly like to ask your thoughts on this question. Is it a painful period of life, or what is your news of it?'

Cephalus then said, 'You know how some of us old men are often together, true to the old proverb. Now most of the company whenever they meet lament their wretched lot. They long for the pleasures of youth, and some of them bewail the insults which their kinsfolk heap upon their years . . . in my opinion, Socrates, they don't really see what is wrong. If they were right, then I too, and all who have come to my time of life, would by reason of old age have suffered as they have; but, as a matter of fact, I have met many whose experience is different . . . But all these troubles, their complaints against their kinsfolk among them, have but one cause, and that is not old age, Socrates, but men's dispositions or personality; for old age lays but a moderate burden on men who have order and peace within themselves, but ill-governed natures find youth and age alike irksome.'

Cephalus' response is a wise reminder that the psychological ills of the elderly stem from a complex mix of factors. We will describe the features and treatment of the psychiatric conditions which affect the old, including dementia, depression, anxiety, substance abuse and personality problems. But first, we will briefly outline the psychiatrist's approach in evaluating these factors.

Elderly people are usually reluctant to complain of emotional or memory problems, and when they do their relatives and even family doctors all too often put these down to the 'natural' effects of ageing. So, for example, many serious depressive states remain unrecognised, despite depressed elderly people responding to treatment as well as younger people.

Most assessments are done in a clinic, but there is an increasing trend towards examination at home, particularly in the case of frail, deaf or confused people. They can thus be seen with family or friends, and the home environment can be observed, as well as the person's ability to cope with it. A relative, friend or neighbour will always be asked to comment on the nature and duration of symptoms if the elderly person seems confused. Specific queries about the person's orientation in time and space, recall of recent events, attendance at appointments, payment of bills and so forth may be most revealing. Questions directed to the confused person are put in as simple and logical a form as possible.

Mental and physical illness both increase in frequency with age, and the relationship between them is complex. One may lead to the other or they may occur at the same time. For example, if a person is depressed and has decreased function of the thyroid gland, any mood change may well be due to this. The depression may respond to correction of the thyroid problem, or require treatment in its own right in addition to thyroid replacement medication. Since our ability to handle drugs diminishes with age and our vulnerability to side-effects increases, particularly in dementia, the use of drugs is more risky in the elderly.

Elderly mentally ill people are particularly vulnerable to abuse. Relatives may see their complaints and 'difficult' behaviour as a deliberate campaign to gain attention and may take retribution, and a few retaliate in kind. Intentional, sustained abuse is much less common. Children may squander parents' money or seek possession of their house; owners of residential homes may threaten residents' financial assets or behave cruelly and vindictively. Such abuse rarely comes to light since the victims are either unaware of it or too frightened to complain. It may fall to the vigilant doctor to identify exploitation or maltreatment and intervene accordingly.

Most people regard quality of life in the elderly as of greater importance than mere longevity. It is appropriate to treat remediable and distressing conditions like a urinary tract infection, bowel obstruction or fractured hip, as quality of life is thereby improved. On the other hand, many agree that vigorously treating markedly demented people for, say, pneumonia or kidney failure will only postpone the inevitable, and may well be unmerciful.

## Dementia

As our life expectancy increases, so does the risk of dementia. We have spelt out the sobering statistics in Chapter 14. Few demented people need specialist psychiatric assistance. Many are afflicted to a mild degree only—they mislay possessions, forget to pay bills and cannot make complex decisions, but neither they nor their relatives feel overly distressed by these changes. Forgetfulness is seen as a 'natural' feature of ageing and few people seek help at this stage.

Even those with more severe dementia are not necessarily restless, aggressive, noisy or given to wandering. Indeed most of them spend their days sitting quietly or pottering aimlessly. A gentle elderly lady might need help from her husband but the full extent of her memory loss may not become apparent until a dramatic incident suggests the truth, and memory, orientation, clarity of thinking and day-to-day skills are challenged.

People with dementia rarely seek professional help of their own accord. Many admit to forgetfulness when questioned directly, but people who focus on memory difficulties spontaneously are usually suffering from depression. Dementia due to a stroke is the exception. Insight, personality and social skills may be well-preserved and memory gaps patchy—for example, the person may fail to remember a list of words or a name and address after five minutes yet recall events of the previous day and show excellent capacity for problem-solving.

Commonly, professional aid is sought when relatives or neighbours note dangerous or bizarre behaviour such as a fire in the kitchen, the person wandering away from home or making repeated reference to long-dead parents or siblings. Other behaviours causing concern to relatives are restlessness at night, urination in inappropriate places, aggression, noisiness or constant repetition of questions. The person may accuse neighbours of stealing money (which is in fact hidden in a cupboard) or a spouse of being an impostor. Infections, stroke, injury or medications may trigger delirium (see Chapter 14), as a result of which mere forgetfulness can suddenly become gross confusion. Some people decline abruptly following the death of a spouse or change in the environment.

If the person had always been good-humoured this generally continues, whereas previous distrustful, argumentative or obsessional traits are magnified, often leading to friction with family and friends. A few people become fearful and agitated and require constant reassurance, while others pace up and down and fiddle with items of clothing or furniture.

As dementia advances, so profound psychological problems follow. Language disintegrates, people jumbling sentences and groping for words. A few have visual hallucinations of animals and children and chat to them contentedly. A total return to childlike behaviour, incoherence, immobility and incontinence are features of the severe form. Shakespeare's seventh age in Jaque's famous speech in *As You Like It* sums up this end point most graphically:

> . . . *Last scene of all*
> *That ends this strange, eventful history,*
> *Is second childishness, and mere oblivion,*
> *Sans teeth, sans eye, sans taste, sans everything.*

The person with early Alzheimer's may well feel equally shattered in contemplating such a horrendous extreme. Janet Atkins brought international attention to this dilemma when she became the first person with Alzheimer's to commit suicide by injecting herself with a lethal drug under the guidance of the American physician, Dr Jack Kevorkian.

In assessing the mental state, the psychiatrist usually considers the following aspects. If the person looks ill, delirium is considered, perhaps combined with dementia. Appearances can be deceptive. People living alone often look untidy whereas those living with a relative tend to be neatly groomed. Most people show little distress when errors in their stories are exposed but those with greater awareness become anxious about their limitations. Discussion about family, hobbies or a recent activity may be revealing if descriptions are rambling, and recent and long-past events are interwoven. A clue is the person's tendency to reply in general terms to specific questions, so that the query 'What day is this?' is responded to with a discourse on events of the previous week.

The psychiatrist always tests intellectual functioning if there are difficulties with memory, orientation, judgement or everyday skills. This is necessary because mildly demented people conceal deficiencies by off-handed reassurances or humour. Tests of orientation to time, and ability to recall three simple words or a fictional name and address are commonly used. Assessment of the capacity to copy a diagram or draw a clock face is a good indicator of global mental impairment in the absence of any other obvious cause such as stroke, Parkinson's disease, arthritis or visual impairment. Contrary to popular belief, non-demented old people are almost always aware of the day of the week and month and most know the date within a day or two. Serious errors or obvious guesses suggest organic mental disorder. Orientation to place (that is, knowing where they are) is rarely impaired in people who live at home but is commonly so in those seen in hospitals or nursing homes.

The style of answers is often as revealing as the content. Glib responses ('One day seems pretty much like another' or 'I don't follow the news any more' or 'I was never any good at counting or writing') are commonly used by people to cover their deficits. These are similar to methods we all use in everyday life when our competence is challenged and we feel threatened.

Physical examination and special tests are often necessary to ensure that no reversible cause of dementia is missed. This is unusual in the very old, but brain tumours, anaemia, diabetes, thyroid deficiency and drug side-effects are only some of a long list of possible causes that warrant exclusion.

Delirium arises most often in people with existing dementia, and is commonly caused by physical ill health, infections and change in medication (see Chapter 14). Relatives may notice a change in their mother's condition in recent days which, for instance, worsened after her tablets were altered.

About 5 per cent of demented people need treatment for depression—which is suggested by withdrawal, restlessness, insomnia and poor eating. Depressed, demented old people look tired and preoccupied, conveying a sense of unhappiness and hopelessness.

Many accounts of the experiences of families have appeared in recent years, attesting not only to the tragedy of dementia, but also to the devotion and courage of relatives, particularly spouses. A poignant story is that of Sharon Aldrick, a woman who witnessed her grandparents' experience:

> It was a strange day, the day she died. We were quite upset, but my grandfather, not a tear rolled from his eyes. I suppose he had accepted it a long time ago. He was happy she died peacefully in his loving embrace. Her pain and suffering from the past 25 years had finally ended.
>
> My grandfather used to work in the bakehouse, making his bread deliveries by horse and cart. My grandmother worked in a factory creasing tobacco papers. He earned £2, she earned £4, and when they married in 1939 she gave up her job, as was expected of a wife. They bought an orange orchard four years later and spent their days working hard on the farm and raising six children. She loved cooking and sewing and decorating the house with flowers from her garden.
>
> The first few years before the diagnosis of Alzheimer's Disease my grandfather spent in darkness, not knowing why his wife would break down and cry, argue and yell at him constantly. He watched her decline from a capable, competent woman to one unable to look after herself. She would hide her money and forget where she hid it. Her clothes were worn back to front. She was frustrated by tasks she could perform with ease just a few years ago.
>
> I suppose I look at my grandfather as heroic. When I think about it, I wonder could I do the same? Could I devote myself to caring for my spouse the way he did: total loyalty with no gratitude. He would say, 'She was the best-fed. I would feed her strawberries all day, boiled eggs for lunch and Weetbix with warm milk in the morning'. He would change her sanitary pad and carry her from the bed they shared for 56 years and place her in her lounge. She would spend the day curled in a foetal position, with the television casting images that had no meaning to her. He spent the day working on his 200ha orange orchard from sun up to sun down.
>
> Returning home, he would sit with her, holding her hand, feeding her chocolates and talking to her. It did not concern him that for the past 15 years she had not even known who he was. Alzheimer's had dissolved the memory of him from her mind.
>
> It was sad to watch an intelligent, strong woman fade slowly. It must have been heart wrenching for my grandfather to watch and to have no control over her fate, but to be there as a mother would be there for her newborn child . . .

Bright colours and explosive activity are hallmarks of mania.

In black depression, a person weeps tears of blood beneath a noose.

## How can the psychiatrist help?

The psychiatrist's main task is to form a clear view as to how the person and family are coping, since this will determine where treatment is best carried out. How does the person manage with dressing, washing, bathing, cooking, housework, shopping and handling money? How much help is required and who provides it? Will neighbours assist in a crisis? What services are in place? Are relatives disturbed by any difficult or dangerous behaviour?

If the person can be managed at home, then clear information helps carers to deal with disturbing behaviour which they might otherwise attribute to spite or laziness. Advising that restless, argumentative people should be humoured rather than challenged, or that those who resist dressing or bathing should be left for a moment, can be very helpful. Most importantly, given the relentless nature of their responsibility, carers are encouraged to unburden themselves and to arrange breaks for themselves.

Residential care comes sooner for people who live alone or whose carer is frail. Families and friends are nonetheless encouraged to persist while the person is content and enjoys adequate quality of life. Since the move from familiar surroundings is disruptive and often distressing, the nursing home is fully informed of the person's particular needs and handicaps prior to the move.

Drugs have a limited role in dementia. Confused behaviour and wandering at night, as well as daytime disturbances, may respond to tranquillisers in small doses. Unfortunately, drugs are sometimes prescribed at excessive levels in nursing homes in order to quieten the agitated person. Used in this way they can distinctly worsen the person's overall mental state, and even cause death.

## Depression

Major depressive disorders affect about 5 per cent of older people in general and one in ten of those in nursing homes. People at risk are those with a bout of depression in the past, enduring pain, physical or sensory incapacity, recent bereavement and a lack of social support. Some medications tend to trigger lowered mood—notably steroids, anti-hypertensives and certain drugs used for arthritis and ulcers. Similarly, a range of medical conditions such as stroke and thyroid disturbance may be associated with depression (see Chapter 8).

Depression for the old is very like that for the young, with persistently lowered mood, pessimism, loss of capacity to feel pleasure, fatigue, insomnia, anorexia, pessimism and withdrawal. It is no commoner in older than younger people, but suicide is much more frequent, especially in men, and threats to take one's life are taken most seriously by the psychiatrist.

Depression may sometimes be masked or have an unusual quality. Complaints of pain or physical discomfort is one form of disguise. But physical debility is so common in the elderly that the precise cause is often elusive. People who previously coped well with a physical disability may now weep and plead for assistance—a signal of probable mood disturbance. As heart, lung and kidney disease, and cancer also lead to anorexia, insomnia and fatigue, co-existing depression can easily be overlooked. Pointers include a mood change from brave acceptance to constant misery, feelings of unremitting emptiness and the loss of the capacity to feel pleasure.

Spontaneous complaints of forgetfulness and muddled thinking strongly suggest depression rather than dementia. When left to their own devices, demented people are generally unaware of their lapses unless also depressed. Equally, depressed people may be so slowed in their thinking and movement that they actually appear to be demented. They need help with dressing, bathing and feeding and the simplest questions are countered with 'I don't know' or 'I just can't do it' (this picture is sometimes referred to as pseudo-dementia).

Some elderly people interpret their lowered mood as a natural response to ageing while others fear that endless complaints will alienate relatives, friends and doctors. Many of those mildly to moderately depressed feel lonely and unwanted, fearing illness, dependency, moving to new accommodation and using up their financial reserves.

The opportunity to express such concerns is much appreciated, as is the doctor's attention to anniversaries of the death of a spouse, children or friends. Persistent and painful medical conditions must be treated, and various forms of home help arranged. Grief counselling and couple or family therapy may also help. Anti-depressants are unhelpful if given indiscriminately. While people with classical symptoms are treated immediately, those generally seen by family doctors are often not so clear-cut. Progress with these various psychological and social measures is reviewed after a week or two and the perspective of a relative or friend is central to this review.

The original anti-depressants, the tricyclics, are effective but their troublesome side-effects—blurred vision, constipation, dizziness, urinary retention and confusion—make their routine use no longer appropriate (see Chapter 20). Equally effective is the new group of anti-depressants which improve the condition but with far less adverse effects. But falls are still a risk, and potentially fatal for elderly patients who live alone. People are cautioned to rise slowly from bed and the bath, and switch on a light when visiting the toilet at night, particularly when on any medication. Electro-convulsive therapy can be used, and may be life-saving even in the presence of cognitive impairment (see page 275).

Depressed old people have a higher than average mortality because of the strong association between disordered mood and serious physical illness. Apart from this, the outlook is similar to that for younger age-groups. Two-thirds of people admitted to hospital for treatment of depression show substantial improvement but may need continuing treatment to prevent recurrence.

## Mania

Most elderly people with mania (abnormal elevation of mood, see Chapter 8) have had a manic-depressive disorder for many decades, while some have been depressed and reveal the manic state only in later years (often following treatment with anti-depressants). Only a few develop pure mania for the first time in later life. An even smaller number become manic in response to a stroke, head injury or other brain damage. While over-activity, pressure of speech, flight of ideas and insomnia are typical, people are more often irritable than euphoric. Grandiose, religious delusions are common. Families are particularly distressed by sexual disinhibition and financial indiscretion. Admission to hospital is usually required. There treatment with modest doses of tranquillisers is usually successful. Lithium may be prescribed to prevent further attacks of mania, or of both mania and depression in the case of manic-depressive illness.

## Anxiety disorders

Anxiety may appear dramatically and suddenly in response to physical illness, bereavement, financial or family concerns or a move to new accommodation. On the other hand, and more commonly, people with long-standing anxiety may worsen in the face of threatening events. Typically, people experience insomnia, fatigue, irritability, tremor, palpitations, shortness of breath and complaints of forgetfulness and loss of concentration. As always in the elderly, the psychiatrist attends to both emotional and medical factors. Heart and lung disease present particular difficulties because symptoms of those conditions may closely mimic features of anxiety.

Phobic disorders and irrational fears are much commoner than generally thought. Falls, for instance, may frighten people into a refusal to leave home. They move from room to room by grasping tables and chairs, and respond to appeals to walk with protest and tears. Gradual encouragement to overcome the fears, perhaps in a geriatric day hospital, helps recovery.

Mildly anxious people may simply need reassurance, care of any physical illnesses, referral to social service departments for financial benefits and attendance at a social club or day centre. The long-term anxious need support as they lurch from crisis to crisis which to other people appear trivial. Angry retorts and stern warnings achieve little. On the other hand, relaxation training and simple psychological manoeuvres do help. Benzodiazepines and other drugs for anxiety may cause drowsiness, confusion, unsteadiness, falls and fractures, and so are used only if absolutely necessary, and then for a short period only.

> *Mrs Albert, a woman in her seventies, was brought along by her daughter because she and her brother and sister found their mother 'intolerable'. The woman was described as 'demanding, self-centred and unpleasant to be with'. She was constantly fearful, especially worried about her 'memory lapses', and sought endless reassurance. It emerged through careful questioning that she had always been afraid beyond her familiar environment, and tended to avoid any new encounter. Treatment involved sessions with Mrs Albert and her daughter initially, followed by individual sessions. As she had a chance to reflect on her life, grieve for lost opportunities and feel affirmed as a person, she found herself a dancing partner and started going out dancing twice a week. She thrived, and looked and felt much younger. Her anxiety receded and the 'memory problem' ceased.*

## Delusional disorders and schizophrenia

Typical events befalling elderly people, like loss of a loved one, may lead understandably to an uneasiness and insecurity about the world around them. A few lonely, mistrustful people, particularly isolated women who are partially deaf or blind, conclude that others dislike, avoid or take advantage of them. They argue with neighbours and shopkeepers and abruptly take offence. Their beliefs fall short of psychotic thinking but result in greater isolation. Some live in squalor and resist help. When these beliefs became pronounced and are held unshakeably, we enter the territory of delusional disorders.

The delusions are usually banal—the person is convinced, despite all evidence to the contrary, that neighbours are banging on bedroom walls or hurling rubbish over the fences. Or bizarre strangers or secret investigators spy, tap the telephone or bombard the person with special gases or waves of electricity. In response to these ideas, neighbours may be abused—even the police summoned for protection.

Schizophrenia developing in the elderly, although rare, resembles that in younger age groups (see Chapter 12). People hear voices accusing them of criminal or sexual offences, secret machinery clanking, and groaning children crying beneath floorboards. They complain of lights being shone through windows or noxious gases being pumped under doors. Those who suffered from schizophrenia when young, but have lived satisfactorily in the community for many years, may relapse with acute symptoms on reaching old age.

These two forms of psychosis are easily confused with dementia. Dementing people who lose treasured items may cover these lapses by accusing others of stealing them. These ideas, unlike those in the psychoses, are rarely elaborated and quickly forgotten, at least by the person himself or herself.

Some people are remarkably accepting of help. They take anti-psychotic medication happily, symptoms subside and the treating doctor is seen as a friend. Others are suspicious of doctors, refuse them entry and insist that treatment is unwarranted, even dangerous. For them, involuntary admission to hospital is usually required. Treatment is always life-long.

## Substance abuse

Alcohol abuse is more common in elderly people than generally appreciated. Some have always drunk heavily, others increase their intake through boredom, loneliness, anxiety or depression. Those who live alone are at particular risk, and even the disabled and housebound obtain supplies surprisingly easily. Their children and friends often fail to intervene or even collude in the abuse on the grounds that 'a drink keeps her happy'. It may take a serious fall or marked confusion after a temporary withdrawal to alert the doctor.

Even long-term heavy drinkers can be persuaded to stop if the hazards are clearly spelt out. Treatment of underlying factors—loneliness, anxiety or depression—are tackled directly. People who resist may develop a severe memory disorder as a direct effect of alcohol poisoning of the brain, and then need accommodation in a nursing home for their own protection.

Some elderly people consume large quantities of benzodiazepines, usually as hypnotics. Insomnia results so commonly from tedium, loneliness, inactivity, pain, anxiety and depression that the doctor's usual response with sleepless patients is to recommend a benzodiazepine. Or perhaps a hypnotic was prescribed for a person admitted to hospital for medical or surgical treatment. The snag in both situations is its continued use. Benzodiazepines are best avoided because of their addictive properties. However, in some elderly long-term insomniac people the benefit is such that it would be cruel to withhold the drug.

## Personality disorder

Argumentative, suspicious or dependent behaviour may be due to anxiety, depression or dementia. However, some elderly people have always behaved in an abusive, dependent or reclusive fashion. These tendencies may have faded in middle-life, only to recur with illness, disability or bereavement in later years. The difficulties are varied. An anxious, timid widow may telephone her children, friends and family doctor many times each day. She makes impossible demands of them and cannot cope with the simplest task. A reclusive, suspicious man may respond with alarm to hospital admission. The enforced dependency and proximity to others are threatening and may result in anger, verbal and physical threats and irrational insistence on leaving the hospital. A detailed inquiry by the psychiatrist helps to clarify the picture. Has the person always been anxious or demanding or suspicious? What has triggered this recent outburst? It is never assumed that a 'difficult' personality explains all. The person's demands are dealt with matter-of-factly, as anger and sarcasm worsen matters.

## The needs of the family

No chapter on psychiatry and the elderly could possibly be complete without reference to the family's interests. The need for a partnership between family and psychiatrist has been well recognised for decades in child psychiatry (for obvious reasons) but it is only since the 1980s that the experience of 'informal' caregiving for the elderly has been properly recognised—particularly in families with an elderly psychiatric member.

Relatives are often upset by the person's changes in personality and loss of interest in the family. Caring for a physically disabled but mentally intact person is difficult enough. Caring for a person who confuses a daughter with a sister, shows no gratitude, and wets and soils repeatedly is hard, relentless work. Even so, many relatives press on, regarding a request for outside help as a betrayal of trust.

They tend to expect little from professionals. However, we do nowadays have a range of services available to carers to assist them in their demanding task. Carers themselves are organising self-help groups, support networks and political lobbies. On this basis, much can be accomplished. For example, elderly spouses who wish to continue caring for a dementing partner can be supported through respite care, home nursing, meals on wheels, home aids, and the like.

A 'greying' society, deinstitutionalisation, and some disillusion with state-organised services have spawned a new era for the family carer. Indeed, carers have, in a sense, returned to centre stage, a role they played for centuries. Since their pivotal contribution will certainly continue, this late recognition is noteworthy and deserves society's support.

## Conclusion

Goethe's remark that 'Age takes hold of us by surprise' was probably more true in his time than ours. With an increased life span and with elderly people making up a growing proportion of the population, there is more recognition than at any other time in history of the last quarter of life. In response, psychiatry has developed a major sub-specialty which attends exclusively to the needs of elderly people who become emotionally troubled. And a worldwide research effort has been mounted to tackle the disorders which afflict this group at an especially vulnerable period in their lives.

# 18   *Psychiatry and the Law*

The criminal law has long taken a different attitude to the mentally ill offender from the mentally competent. Roman law exempted the mad from punishment, in part because they were regarded as not fully responsible for their actions, and in part because, as madness was believed to be inflicted by the gods, it would be wicked to add to this divine punishment. Later legal codes reduced the culpability of the mad, usually on the grounds that they lacked capacity for deliberate action or for control of their impulses. The question of who was mad and whether the madness was of a degree to excuse their offence was a matter for judges and juries. Various rules were devised, such as by the Elizabethan judge who said that those legally mad had to be so disordered as to act like children unaware of their own best interests. Another judge suggested that it should be only those so mad as to be like the beasts of the fields.

At the end of the eighteenth century, doctors with special experience with the mad, known in those days as alienists, began to provide testimony on the sanity of the accused. This soon produced a lively debate between lawyers and doctors as to who should lay down definitions of insanity. The issue remains unresolved, but the lawyers have retained the upper hand and, when doctors enter the courtroom, by and large they play by the lawyer's rules.

As the experience of psychiatrists expanded, their involvement with the 'insane' offender steadily increased. Institutions were set up for the care of the 'criminally insane'. Psychiatrists also began to care for people in prisons who, though not so disturbed as to have been found insane, were ill enough to need treatment.

The role of psychiatrists now includes a wide range of tasks at many levels of the criminal justice system. Other mental health professionals—psychologists, social workers, occupational therapists and nurses—work alongside them in assessing and treating mentally ill offenders.

## The psychiatrist and the courts

In their role as experts in human behaviour, psychiatrists may be called to testify in court or to interpret medical evidence. At this point it becomes opinion, as when the psychiatrist moves from describing a person's state of mind to judgements on his or her capacity to make a will or to have known what he or she was doing. In this work, the psychiatrist deals with a wide and diverse array of situations, some of which we now briefly describe.

Following a person's arrest, psychiatric opinion may be sought as to whether the accused is so disordered as to need urgent treatment and/or whether bail should be granted. Decisions as to whether a mentally ill person is competent to stand trial need assessment of the person's capacity to understand the charges, consult with and instruct a lawyer, follow court proceedings and give testimony if needed. The implications of being found unfit to plead can be long detention in a prison or hospital. This not only deprives the accused of the right to trial but may also mean confinement for as long, or even longer, than might have resulted from a conviction.

Our law makes a distinction between the guilty act and the guilty mind. Not all criminal acts require a guilty mind—for example, in most traffic offences proof is sufficient—but for serious offences guilt also presumes intent or recklessness. In the insanity defence, psychiatrists may be asked to give an opinion on how the defendant's likely state of mind at the time of the offence could have affected his or her capacity to form a guilty intent.

The insanity defence often has its roots in the McNaughton Rules. Daniel McNaughton, convinced that he was being persecuted by the Tory Party, attempted in 1843 to shoot Robert Peel, the British Prime Minister, but succeeded only in killing his secretary. He was found not guilty by virtue of insanity and sent to a mental hospital. As so often happens today, the verdict sparked an enormous outcry from the public who thought that he had been let off too lightly. The Law Lords were consulted and concluded that for the insanity defence to succeed it must be proved that the accused person, because of mental illness, did not know what he was doing or did not know that it was wrong. These rules are still used a century and a half later. In practice, most defences of insanity have little difficulty in establishing that the accused people were mentally ill, but judging that they did not know the nature of their acts is a difficult task for the court. The insanity defence remains problematic, as it depends heavily on the goodwill of the judge and the common sense of the jury, who are the final arbiters. The case of John Hinkley, found not guilty by reason of insanity for the attempted assassination of ex-President Ronald Reagan, and the outcry that followed the judgment, highlight how controversial the issue still is.

The law also recognises that a person may commit an offence in the absence of a mental illness but be unaware of what he or she is doing. Examples of such 'automatism' are sleep-walking and confusional states triggered by concussion or epilepsy. Crimes committed in these states may bring a verdict of non-insane automatism, which leads to acquittal.

The law takes a special interest in the woman who kills her child in its first year of life (infanticide). The origins of this concern lie in public sympathy for such mothers who are regarded, rightly in most cases, as mentally ill. Psychiatrists are often called on to demonstrate a direct link between the mother's mental disturbance and the killing. Psychiatric opinion is most often sought when the judge is deciding on an appropriate sentence. The court is interested in factors which may have contributed to the offence and whether the woman has any continuing illness which would benefit from treatment.

Psychiatrists may be required to assess whether people are sufficiently in possession of their mental faculties to write a will or enter into a contract. In the case of wills, this includes whether people know what they own, their relationship to any potential beneficiaries and the likely consequences of the bequests. The questions most often raised are in regard to dementia, the possible influence of delusions on the will's content, and whether undue pressure was exerted on such mentally impaired people by those likely to benefit. In the case of a contract, the concern is whether the person lacks the mental capacity to understand the significance of that contract. However, a contract made with a mentally disordered person may still be valid if the other party had no way of knowing that the person was incapacitated. The issue comes up most frequently in manic people (see Chapter 8) who go on spending sprees and enter into contracts for such things as houses and material possessions.

In civil law a person can claim compensation for mental distress or disability which follows trauma—physical or emotional. This is a difficult matter since the psychiatric effects, by and large, are subjective symptoms or behaviour which the person claims are beyond his or her control. This raises questions about whether claims are valid, exaggerated or fabricated.

*Andrew, a previously well-adjusted, successful businessman and effective husband and father, was trapped in a capsized ferry boat. For many hours he was in darkness in fear for his life, able to hear cries of the drowning who, he was convinced, included his wife and children. He emerged physically unharmed and was reunited with his family. On the face of it Andrew had a lucky escape. In the weeks that followed he was plagued by flashbacks of the events triggered by anything evocative of the situation. Sleep was disturbed by vivid nightmares. He found concentration difficult and became increasingly irritable at work and home. His alcohol consumption, which had been well within social bounds, rapidly escalated. Six months later he had lost his job, his marriage was in ruins, he was abusing alcohol, and feeling hopeless about his future. He had also appeared before the courts, for the first time, on charges arising out of drinking and driving and of theft. Though physically uninjured Andrew's psychological functioning had been devastated by the trauma. On the basis of psychiatric evidence he successfully sued the shipping line for compensation.*

Psychiatrists once participated in divorce proceedings when cruelty was the grounds because, to satisfy legal requirements, injury to physical or mental health had to be demonstrated. They may now participate in disputes over custody and assist in determining the best interests of the child.

## Crime and mental illness

Although mental illness may be associated with any criminal act, psychiatrists become involved when the question arises as to whether the mental state of the perpetrator contributed to the criminal behaviour. Murder and rape are obviously the most serious of such offences.

Homicide, the term for all unlawful killing, includes murder, manslaughter, infanticide and destruction of the foetus in an illegal abortion. Rates vary widely between countries. Most Western countries report increased rates since the 1980s—but in England, for example, homicide was in fact far more common before the nineteenth century. Acquaintances and relatives are the usual victims (spouses the most common relatives), with killing of strangers accounting for less than 20 per cent of all homicides. In some American cities homicide is the leading cause of death among young black males.

Mentally ill people are over-represented among those who kill. Countries with a lower homicide rate, like the United Kingdom, have proportionally more homicides committed by the mentally ill than do countries with high rates like the United States. In the United Kingdom, about 10 per cent of people charged with homicide have a schizophrenic illness and many more have profound problems of personality with or without substance abuse. Severely depressed people tend to be a threat to themselves but occasionally commit an 'altruistic' homicide of a relative, particularly their children, believing that they will save them from a ghastly fate. They then suicide.

Most killings result from impulsive outbursts of violence in the heat of a relatively trivial argument—domestic quarrels and jealousy are common. About 10 per cent occur during robbery or other crimes. Between 10 and 20 per cent of killers commit suicide soon after the offence.

Rape is defined as sexual intercourse without consent. Rape is a now thought of as primarily a violent crime with a sexual element which involves satisfaction of aggressive impulses and the desire to exert power over and humiliate another person. Increasingly, however, the offence is subsumed under the category of sexual violation which need not involve penetration. Perpetrators are usually young men, most of whom are acquainted with their victim. Violence varies from a threat to savage beatings. Convicted rapists are rarely mentally ill though they may abuse alcohol or drugs. They are commonly from disadvantaged backgrounds, with a history of non-sexual offending—but men from more privileged backgrounds also rape. Rapists are usually socially inept, unable to establish and maintain emotional and sexual relationships with women.

Psychiatrists, in association with other counsellors, are often called upon to help the victims. All are emotionally damaged, some irretrievably. In the immediate aftermath they experience anxiety, with insomnia, nightmares, terrifying flashbacks, emotional instability and a sense of being degraded, often combined with guilt which is no less strong for being unfounded. These symptoms tend to subside over weeks but sometimes persist and merge into post-traumatic stress disorder (see page 86). Many people experience long-term impaired relationships, particularly intimate ones.

Setting fires is one of the disturbances found among conduct-disordered or hyperactive children (see Chapter 15). In adults, revenge is the most common motivation. Fire-setting can become repetitive, particularly if people experience fires as exciting. Considerable overlap occurs between arsonists motivated by thrill-seeking who take pleasure in the theatre of fire and vandals out for an orgy of destruction. In both, alcoholic intoxication often contributes. People arrested for arson may be mentally ill, particularly with schizophrenia, personality disorder, depression, substance abuse or intellectual handicap.

Theft from shops is common, especially in supermarkets and stores that tempt customers by encouraging them to walk freely around displays. Shoplifters are spread through all age groups, but it is the depressed, middle-aged, middle-class woman who is most likely to be referred by the court to a psychiatrist. She may steal inadvertently because she is not concentrating on what she is doing or, occasionally, in order to be caught, believing she deserves punishment (Freud referred to this as crime 'from a sense of guilt'), or wishing to bring attention to her inner distress. Intoxication produced by medication or substance abuse may predispose people to theft, both by reducing inhibition and producing confusion. Mild dementia can produce absent-minded theft. Kleptomania, a rare condition, is a term for a compulsion to steal unwanted goods which are discarded or returned. Before the theft, the person experiences escalating tension, which is released by stealing.

## Psychiatry and the prison

Prisons contain a high proportion of disadvantaged people. The popular image of the typical prisoner as a dedicated villain who has chosen a career of dishonesty or violence is far from reality. Many have been convicted of impulsive, poorly organised offences, often relatively trivial, because they came at the end of repeated court appearances for similar behaviour.

Alcohol and drug abuse are the most common mental health problems among prisoners, with rates of between 50 and 80 per cent. A large proportion of offences occur in the context of intoxication or relate to stealing money for drugs. Imprisonment should offer an opportunity for some people to tackle their abuse, but in many prisons these substances are all too easily available despite official effort. Depression is relatively common, sometimes due to the stress of detention but often predating imprisonment. Schizophrenia is found at a higher rate than in the general community. Since prisoners often come from disrupted and chaotic backgrounds they frequently have, not surprisingly, disordered personalities.

It follows that people in prison have a greater need for mental health care—which, sadly, is rarely met. This is particularly tragic as their psychological problems often contribute to their re-offending. The only mentally ill offenders who stand a chance of obtaining appropriate psychiatric care are those placed in special wards or institutions designed to provide treatment under conditions of high security (Broadmoor in Britain is perhaps the best-known example).

In most Western countries, a rapid increase in the prison population has coincided with a decline in the number of long-term psychiatric hospital patients. It has been argued that people with an enduring disability are being moved from hospital to prison. While undoubtedly this has happened to some people, there is no evidence of a major shift. Failure of community care certainly contributes to the drifting homeless, and may also increase the frequency with which mentally ill people appear before the courts. But most of these people are redirected to mental health care rather than imprisoned.

## Are mentally ill people dangerous?

Fear of the mentally ill is deeply ingrained in our society, heavily influenced as it is by the stereotype of the 'crazed killer' (think of Alfred Hitchcock's terrifying movie *Psycho*). Their portrayal in the media increases public apprehension. A study of television dramas found that one in five characters were shown as mentally ill—three-quarters of these were violent, the rest were 'homicidal maniacs'. One analysis of newspapers revealed that most stories about psychiatric patients concerned acts of violence, often murders—and we have already referred to the possible over-representation of the mentally ill among those who commit violent acts. Based on their research, some psychiatrists reject any link between mental illness and violence. And yet the truth lies between these extremes, though far closer to the non-violent than to the mad axe-man image.

Most people with psychiatric illness pose no threat at all. The largest group, those with depression, are rarely aggressive, indeed are less likely than their fellow citizens to offend. People with mania can create considerable problems due to disinhibition—usually leading to financial and sexual indiscretions. They can occasionally become belligerent when frustrated, causing a fuss in the community but rarely resorting to real violence.

The situation with schizophrenic people is more complex. They have an increased rate of offending involving personal violence. But while there is evidence of a link between schizophrenia and higher rates of violent and fear-inducing behaviour, the critical question is how great a risk this represents. A useful way to look at this is to note that the increased risk is similar to that in young men, when both are compared to the general population. A second question is whether it is possible to identify schizophrenic people at particular risk of acting violently. They almost always have symptoms at the time of the offence and have drifted out of treatment. Delusions of persecution play an important role, particularly when centred on someone intimate. Delusions of infidelity leading to extreme jealousy are a common basis for violence, as is alcohol and drug abuse.

## What makes a person violent?

Violence, which pervades many contemporary societies, disrupts and damages them. Sociological studies point to a wide array of factors related to such behaviour. Some of these are true for everyone, some relevant only to the mentally ill:

- *Gender and age*  Violent behaviour is concentrated among men, particularly between fifteen and twenty-five. In the mentally ill there is a less clear gender difference and a wider age range.
- *Social background*  People who appear before the courts and populate prisons are drawn disproportionately from lower socio-economic groups. Poverty, though relevant, is less important than a sense of exclusion from the rewards of society. People disabled by mental illness are often drawn into the impoverished population of the excluded and rejected, and with this comes an increased risk of offending, arrest and re-offence. Those who are economically and socially deprived, as well as being members of minority groups, are at particular risk of offending and arrest—for example, Aboriginal Australians, Black Americans and Maori New Zealanders. Race is not the issue. It is the social and economic conditions under which these groups live. The unemployed, the unmarried or unattached and the socially isolated are all at higher risk.
- *Past behaviour*  The probability of re-conviction rises steeply with the number of previous offences.
- *Nature of the offence*  Though of little help in prediction, the circumstances of the offence may point to the likelihood of its recurrence. The extent of violence is no guide except in the rare sadistic person where injuries are inflicted for pleasure.
- *Personality factors*  While almost certainly relevant, research has not pointed to particular traits.
- *Chromosomal anomalies*  There was considerable interest when abnormal patterns were found among violent male offenders, but later research cast doubt on any real increased tendency to violence in these men.
- *Threats of violence*  Research indicates higher rates of subsequent violent acts.

- *Alcohol and drug abuse*   This occurs particularly in the context of other psychiatric disturbance and/or social dislocation.

## An ethical dimension

Psychiatrists are regularly asked to predict the future dangerousness of a mentally ill offender. Numerous studies confirm that they are notoriously poor at doing so accurately. In addition, predicting dangerousness has an ethical component which extends far beyond the need for sound clinical judgement. Such predictions are likely to stigmatise the person unjustly, an outcome needing careful consideration. Taken to the extreme, predictions of dangerousness in some American states are used to determine whether the death penalty will be imposed or not.

These ethical and legal matters have another face. It is held that psychiatrists who know of a patient's potential for violence have a duty to protect others. This obligation is usually limited to identifiable potential victims, and considered as a duty to warn. The landmark legal case was *Tarasoff v. the University of California.* A student named Poddar revealed to his counsellor that he experienced violent fantasies directed at a former girlfriend, Tatiana Tarasoff. The therapist was sufficiently alarmed to inform the police. Although they then had the power to commit him for treatment, the police decided there were no grounds to authorise involuntary hospitalisation. Poddar killed Ms Tarasoff two months later. Her parents successfully sued the therapist and health service where he worked. The court, in a majority opinion, held that the special relationship of therapists to patients gives therapists a duty to warn potential victims. The Tarasoff decision has been influential in establishing that psychiatrists have the responsibility to assess their patient's potential for violence, take appropriate measures to minimise risk, and warn any identifiable potential victim.

## Conclusion

Where law and psychiatry meet, controversy rages—as is evident in the polarisation between people who take a rigid position that all behaviour, including criminal, is consciously and wilfully motivated, and others who accept that human beings may act in irrational and destructive ways because of disturbed mental states. Psychiatrists are perched precariously in the middle, attempting to bring expert understanding to the debate. The task is formidable as they wrestle with very complex issues and, in the process, are buffeted by these polarised forces.

# 19 *Suicide and Deliberate Self-harm*

Suicide is the most challenging clinical situation for psychiatrists. At annual rates of, for example, 30 000 suicide deaths in the United States and 2200 in Australia, and with an alarming increase in the rate in the 15–30 year age group since the 1960s, the problem is of immense proportions. Not only are these figures disturbing to psychiatrists, and of course to the community, but the very nature of suicide makes it difficult to confront—psychologically, therapeutically and ethically.

It differs crucially from other clinical circumstances. For most mental health problems, psychiatrist and patient seek means to achieve mutually agreed goals. But with suicide, they hold diametrically opposed views about the goal. Furthermore, suicide is not merely a clinical problem to which treatment strategies are applied, but also an existential one—the question is not how to achieve a better life but whether to live at all. That the starting point in treating the suicidal person is seen so differently by psychiatrist and patient means that one is required to persuade the other to change a basic attitude to life.

The very phenomenon of suicide, which expresses a voluntary rejection of the value of life, threatens psychiatrists' deepest convictions about the sanctity of life. Moreover, they have trouble ridding themselves of this sense of threat because the dilemma of suicide is inherently puzzling: there are real problems in offering a rational justification for the value of life. In addition, the suicide rate among psychiatrists, as among doctors generally, is much higher than in the general population, and they are therefore vulnerable when treating suicidal patients. In other spheres of treatment, psychiatrists can more easily detach themselves. But since the possibility of suicide is considered by virtually all people at some stage or another in their lives, psychiatrists may have difficulty taking an objective view of their suicidal patients.

## Suicide through history

Suicide has always been part of the human condition. In the Bible, suicide is mentioned only as a curiosity and indeed no word is used to cover the act. Only five cases are recorded in the Old Testament, Saul and Samson being the best known. Self-killing is described as a natural association of a reasonable intention, like avoiding torture by the enemy, loyalty and wreaking revenge.

Suicide was more prominent in Greek and Roman times. Aristotle argued that killing oneself is against the 'right rule of life', and unjust to the state. Socrates' prohibition was based on the notion that it was an injustice to the gods: people were only the custodians of life provided to them by the gods. The Romans regarded suicide from the individual's point of view. The philosopher Seneca proclaimed that 'mere living is not a good, but living well' and argued that disturbed peace of mind or misfortune were adequate reasons to suicide. He also valued the ultimate freedom— the choice of how to end one's life. Pliny thought that in this type of freedom, human beings were superior even to the gods. And so it was that suicide in Imperial Rome was widespread, with no sanctions against it.

Christianity brought with it new attitudes. St Augustine argued against suicide by interpreting the sixth commandment as applying to self-killing as well as to the murder of others. Thomas Aquinas, in the thirteenth century, was the first to offer a comprehensive Christian argument against suicide. He claimed that it violated the natural law which prescribes self-love; the moral law because it hurts the community; and the divine law since only God has the right to take life. This position affected European attitudes for generations and only shifted at the time of the Renaissance. The eighteenth-century philosopher Montesquieu, for example, strongly criticised the anti-suicide laws in Europe as cruel and inhuman. In his view, no one was obliged to work for society when he had become weary of life, and the State's laws had authority only over those who decided to go on living.

The reasoning of Thomas Aquinas was systematically challenged by the Scottish philosopher David Hume, using the same three levels of 'law'. First, suicide was not necessarily against a person's interests if misery, sickness and misfortune made life not worth living. Secondly, suicide did not harm others because in death a person no longer had a duty to society, and indeed suicide might reduce the burden borne by others. Finally, if God governed every aspect of the world, then suicide must also be seen as part of his will and authority.

The first attempt to understand suicide scientifically was made at the end of the nineteenth century when the French sociologist Emil Durkheim wrote of what he saw as a social phenomenon. He analysed the person's possible motives and his relation to society. This launch of scientific inquiry came into its own in the twentieth century, and psychiatry has made the greatest contribution to studying suicide objectively. Beyond the attempt to explain suicide scientifically, modern psychiatry has sought to treat effectively the suicidal person and to prevent actual attempts. Psychiatrists are also much involved with caring for survivors of failed suicides and bereaved families.

This effort to diagnose and prevent is, historically, a radical shift in the approach to suicide. Treating has replaced moralising and legislating. Like many other social phenomena, suicide has become thoroughly medicalised. The suicidal person is viewed as afflicted by psychological forces and thus in need of professional help. Moreover, the person is considered not to be morally responsible for the act. A more 'liberal' position on suicide is one result of the evolution of this scientific and medical interest.

With this historical perspective in mind, we now discuss the present psychiatric position regarding suicide and examine what we know about its clinical aspects. First, we need to define the term.

## What is suicide?

The word comes from the Latin '*sui-cidere*', literally to cut oneself. It applies to the intentional act of killing oneself, where the person knows that the act will result in death and is not coerced or encouraged by others to carry it out. This definition seems clear enough on the face of it, but the complexities of suicidal behaviour soon emerge when we think about other kinds of self-killing—such as self-sacrifice in war, hunger strikes as political protest, some cases of heavy smoking or drinking, and hazardous pastimes like motor-racing and mountaineering.

A special conundrum is how we are to consider a suicidal act which seems quite rational given the person's circumstances. A classical case is someone in the terminal phase of a painful illness, with no realistic expectation of improvement, who has always taken pride in living independently, does not wish to burden others, and does not want to live in what for him or her are degrading circumstances.

It can be argued, therefore, that the decision to suicide can be rational. The counter-argument is that suicide can never be rational because the person is either depressed, under extreme pressure or seeking the approval of others—in other words, not in a 'stable' mental state.

Whichever view we take, the spectre of different categories of suicidal behaviour arises, revolving mainly around motive. It may be the product of a disturbed mind or it may reflect a person's apparently coherent wish to accomplish what could be seen as a desirable goal—to be spared intolerable suffering. A further difficulty is what we are to make of a person who fits our definition but does not die because of miscalculation—for example, by overestimating the effect of a drug overdose, or by interruption when the family returns unexpectedly from a holiday. Or a person may miscalculate in the opposite way—feeling burdened by life, he or she overdoses in order to 'have a long sleep', and unknowingly takes a lethal dose (see deliberate self-harm on page 262).

## How common is suicide?

Applying the above definition, we can study the rates of suicide in different societies and at different times. We can go further by teasing out psychological and social factors which appear to be associated with people who kill themselves and, in this way, determine who is particularly vulnerable.

In Australia, suspected suicides are referred to coroners' courts, and statistics on rates are based on their data. All coronial inquiries seek to determine cause of death but the criteria for different types vary between countries. In the case of suicide, evidence must relate to the act being self-inflicted and the intent being to die. Judgement as to whether these criteria have been satisfied is difficult, and is made on the balance of probabilities. If the evidence suggests that death was self-inflicted but no reasonable conclusion can be made as to intent, the case is recorded as accidental death of undetermined cause. This system, which may substantially under-estimate the rate of suicide, limits comparison of rates between countries. Comparisons over time are complicated by legal or other changes that affect recording procedure.

Despite these technical limitations, rates have been determined during the twentieth century, at least in Western societies. The league table makes for frightening reading. The annual number (rounded-off) of suicides per 100 000 inhabitants ranges from the lowest—in, for example, Ireland (7), Italy (8), Spain (7), and Portugal (8)—to the highest, in Austria (25), Finland (28) and Hungary (42). These differences are difficult to explain, given the many factors likely to contribute to the final figure. Psychiatrists are especially interested in the so-called risk factors—those associated with high rates and which might possibly be changed through a programme of prevention.

Whatever the actual rate, we must also note that for each person who suicides, about 10–50 other people (it must be an estimate since it is virtually impossible to detect all such cases) deliberately harm themselves without intending to die (see page 262). Moreover, many people other than the victim are severely affected by a suicidal death. Sometimes family members experience profound grief which endures indefinitely.

## What leads to suicide?

Let us return to the risk factors. Gender and age are major influences. Many more men than women kill themselves. This could be explained by the methods used. Men are apt to resort to more violent methods such as hanging, shooting, drowning and jumping, whereas women tend to poison themselves by taking excessive doses of prescribed or illicit drugs. The risk of suicide increases with age, those over sixty-five having the highest rate of any age group (the rate in the United States of 12 per 100 000 of the general population rises to 28 per 100 000 of those aged over eighty).

These patterns are not necessarily cast in stone. A horrendous increase among young men, but not women, between fifteen and thirty-five from the 1960s to the 1980s in many Western countries has caused much consternation among psychiatrists and public health officials. Australia has the dubious distinction of having the highest youth suicide rate in the industrialised world.

Again, we must tread cautiously in explaining this change in youth rates, and investigate through systematic research what other risk factors are linked to it. Meanwhile, where solid evidence is lacking, commentators speculate that potential influences include high rates of unemployment among the young, existential despair, an increased rate of divorce and family breakdown, greater prevalence of substance abuse and a sense of alienation.

Many of these factors are socially linked, a pattern which takes us back a full century to the pioneering work of Emil Durkheim. He speculated that suicide would be rare in a society well integrated politically, economically and socially. Suicide is mainly explicable in the context of the society to which the person belongs. In his view, two forms resulted from adverse social forces. The egoistic form stems from inadequate involvement with or integration to society—as Durkheim put it, the type of suicide 'springing from excessive individualism'. The anomic form, by contrast, results from social change such as loss of religious affiliation, divorce with its associated disturbance in community organisation, or political crisis (for example, the suicide rate in Vienna escalated dramatically on the eve of World War II).

Social studies since Durkheim have moved away from theoretical models and focused more directly on such factors as marital status, socio-economic level and religious commitment. So, we learn that the rate for single people is twice that of married people, while the divorced and widowed have rates about five times higher again. Jews and Catholics have the lowest rates of Western religions. Unemployment is an adverse influence, as is lower socio-economic status.

But interesting as these speculations may be, the most important aspect upon which the psychiatrist concentrates is the intimate tie between suicide and mental illness.

## Suicide and mental illness

There is strong evidence of a link between suicide and mental illness. Of the two classic studies, one is English and one American. In the English study, of 100 suicide cases taken consecutively from coronial records, 93 people were judged by a panel of psychiatrists to be mentally ill. Two-thirds of these people were diagnosed as suffering from substantial depression and 15 per cent from alcoholism. A similar level of psychiatric disorder was found in the American study of 134 suicides. The close link between suicide and depression has been repeatedly confirmed. In follow-up studies of people diagnosed as suffering from substantial depression, a consistent pattern emerges, with 15 per cent of them dying by their own hand.

The details of this link between mental illness and suicide bear on the role of the health professional. This is the series of findings:

- suicide is frequently preceded by one or more acts of deliberate self-harm;
- the risk of suicide is high immediately after people are discharged from psychiatric hospital;
- suicide occurs among people who are resident in a psychiatric hospital;
- most suicidal people give an explicit or implicit warning before carrying out their plan;
- very many suicidal people consult their family doctor or a psychiatrist in the weeks before the act.

This research supports the view that the person at risk of suicide can be identified. This is a most important matter for prevention. Psychiatrists are emboldened to intervene when they know they stand a good chance of preventing a tragic outcome.

## Assessing the risk of suicide

A key task for psychiatrists in assessing all patients is to determine the risk of suicide. This is particularly so when people have suicidal ideas. Suicide is usually well planned and a warning is often given. About one in six people who have suicidal ideas has actually written a suicide note. It is difficult however to identify who will act on their thoughts and when they will do so. Previous suicidal behaviour is a crucial predictor. About three quarters of the people who suicide have attempted it in the past. The seriousness of those acts is a strong pointer. But even in high risk groups, prediction is complicated and unreliable.

## Treating the suicidal person

The psychiatrist's aim in treating suicidal people is to reduce the risk of it happening. The first question is whether people recognise their difficulties and can accept the need for treatment. In deciding whether they should be helped as an in-patient or out-patient, voluntarily or involuntarily, much depends on the mental state, level of risk, presence of psychiatric illness and availability of social support.

The suicidal person usually needs the safe environment of a hospital ward. A team approach is applied with clear agreement about the need for security, including the frequency of nursing observations. Restricting access to tablets, windows on upper floors, sharp objects, rope and so forth are essential. Any psychiatric illness like severe depression is treated vigorously, as is any contributing physical illness. Notwithstanding these efforts, it is impossible to eliminate all hospital-based suicides. While reasonable precautions are called for, people must still be treated in the least restrictive manner. Any effort to prevent all suicides would fail and would result in unacceptable constraints on the vast majority of 'at risk' people.

Society expects psychiatrists to prevent suicide. But this is unrealistic. We cannot chain people to their beds and observe their every move. Fortunately, very few people treated in hospital commit a suicidal act and even fewer complete it. The problem of identifying this small group is sharply felt by staff who can do no more than apply their most rigorous and informed judgements.

People not admitted to hospital are given detailed information about available supports. They are carefully told who is handling their care, as well as the place, dates and times of appointments and how to get urgent help. Access to urgent help might be by telephone to a clinic or hospital psychiatric unit, or through a telephone counselling service, a family doctor or the emergency department of a general hospital. Family and friends are pivotal in providing support for the person at risk. They are advised as to how to appreciate the gravity of the situation and are a source of information about the person's psychological state.

In all these circumstances, psychiatrists see their role as being to save the life of a person whose suicidal thoughts are probably the product of a disturbed mind. They would not hesitate, for example to act vigorously in the following typical case.

*Teresa, a 40-year-old housewife and mother of three teenage children, has shown apathy, withdrawal and self-neglect over several weeks. During this time she has lost interest in her family and friends, wakes at about two o'clock each morning and cannot return to sleep, and has lost over six kilograms in weight. She has also developed the unshakeable belief that she is worthless, has let her husband and children down, and deserves to die. She feels helpless and desperate and sees no future for herself. She suffered a similar episode three years previously for which she was treated in hospital with supportive care and anti-depressant medication. She made a good recovery then and had felt content with her life until this time.*

*The diagnosis is undoubtedly severe depression, with psychotic features. Given the severity, the psychiatrist is obliged to assume a paternalistic role and, with the family's co-operation and support, take firm initiatives: admission to hospital, even by compulsion if it proves necessary; repeated assessment of Teresa's mental state; close supervision of her daily activities; and energetic treatment of her psychiatric condition with anti-depressant drugs within a caring environment. Electro-convulsive therapy may be required if her condition deteriorates and/or the suicidal behaviour intensifies.*

## Suicide and the bereaved

Suicide is catastrophic for relatives and friends, particularly when the deceased person is young. Reactions encompass the whole range of emotions seen in grief, including depression, denial, anger and guilt. The guilt revolves around not having done more to prevent the death, particularly if there was a previous suicide attempt or if the person had revealed their suicidal intent. Counselling for the bereaved is always necessary in order to reduce the anguish and to prevent long-term adverse effects. Because grief may last indefinitely and may lead to damaging repercussions for family members, professional intervention is always appropriate. But the professional helper must not intrude on the family's grief prematurely, or he or she may then be viewed as an interloper who violates the family's privacy. A careful approach using tact and discretion is called for.

## Preventing suicide

Given the convincing evidence of the link between suicide and mental illness, psychiatrists and the medical profession generally have a crucial role in reducing the rate of suicide.

Prevention takes various forms. It is vital that family doctors are sensitive to early signs of serious depression in any patient, but especially if there has been a history of suicidal behaviour or any form of deliberate self-harm, or a family history of suicide. Doctors are particularly wary of depressed people who also have a physical illness, since the risk of suicide rises with incapacity, loss of independence, or severe and poorly controlled pain. Other preventive measures include effective treatment of any psychiatric condition in which suicide is embedded and, no less important, efficient follow-up care after the initial treatment programme has ended.

## The ethical dilemmas of intervention and prevention

Psychiatrists agree that, given the links between suicide and mental illness, they are justified in asking or even forcing suicidal people to reconsider their attitude, to give themselves a second chance, or to put off a final decision in case their circumstances change. This 'postponement' policy is logically sounder than non-intervention because the intervention itself is a reversible act. If further study shows that suicide is indeed 'rational', or every effort at treatment fails to alter the person's frame of mind, or the person persists in his or her wish regardless of changed circumstances— then there is always the option of letting the person carry out that wish. Only in extreme cases such as, for example, a paraplegic who can be technically prevented from killing himself or herself, can we question the moral legitimacy of prevention. The freedom to terminate one's life remains one of the most basic consolations to human beings.

This is the moral justification of preventing suicide. Now we will look at the controversial issue of the psychiatrist's potential role in assisting or abetting a person to commit suicide. A widely quoted case is that of Elizabeth Bouvia, a woman with incapacitating cerebral palsy. She declared herself as a suicidal patient upon her voluntary admission, at the age of twenty-six, to the psychiatric service of a Californian hospital in September 1983. She refused nourishment and sought a court order preventing the staff from force-feeding her or discharging her. Her wish to die was the result of a belief that her future prospects were grim.

The court ruled in favour of the hospital. While Ms Bouvia was competent in arriving at her decision, the requirement of the common good overrode respect for her wishes. The judge, in concluding that 'society's interest in preserving life and the medical profession's obligation to do so outweighed her right to self-determination', referred to the 'devastating' effects that assisting suicide would have on other patients and people afflicted with handicaps.

For the moment, psychiatrists, and the medical profession generally, are bound by legal requirements that to aid, abet or counsel suicide is an offence. Although the whole issue of euthanasia and assisted suicide is surrounded with intense controversy, the law is unlikely to shift in the foreseeable future.

## Deliberate self-harm

In our account of suicide we have referred to a range of behaviours whose hallmark is self-harm. Now we need to distinguish more clearly between a suicidal act and self-harm. In suicide, a person both intends to die and knows that the action will result in death, whereas self-harm is not intended self-killing.

Professor Erwin Stengel was the first psychiatrist to highlight this second category of suicidal behaviour when he introduced the concept of attempted suicide in the late 1950s. Other terms used since include 'deliberate self-poisoning', 'deliberate self-injury' and 'parasuicide'. 'Deliberate self-harm' is the most recent addition to this list. It is not surprising that we are struggling with words, since we are dealing here with a form of behaviour which is not readily definable. Since Stengel's original concept, a consensus has emerged that people may harm themselves, even seriously, but in the belief that they will survive. Although their act was intentional, not accidental, and to some extent planned, their aim was not to die.

We can probably best think of suicidal behaviour as lying along a continuum. At one end, a person clearly wants to die and takes definite steps to achieve this result. At the other end, a person clearly wants to live but feels the urge to harm himself or herself—for a variety of reasons which we consider below. Along this continuum are people in a state of perplexity about their intentions and goals. For example, a man may be so overwhelmed by a life predicament that he is quite incapable of facing it directly. While in an alcohol-intoxicated state, he compulsively takes an overdose of sleeping tablets prescribed by his family doctor. His motive is clouded by the alcohol although he desires a form of oblivion—whether it is a period of temporary unconsciousness or death is left hanging. This uncertainty is sometimes thought of as a form of Russian roulette—'If I die so be it'. Even after waking from the resulting stupor, he is still baffled by what he should do, particularly as the original predicament is still pressing (which is often the case).

Another indication of this overlap between suicide and deliberate self-harm is that some people who kill themselves have made statements or left notes which clearly show that they did not intend to die. On the other hand, a person whose wish to die is strong may survive through force of circumstances.

One way out of this murkiness of definition is to study the different forms of deliberate self-harm. This has been extensively done, with people interviewed as to their motives and thoughts building up to the act and their feelings about surviving it. What do these studies reveal about their motives? This is not a simple question and there is no simple answer.

People who deliberately harm themselves are often overwhelmed by one or more difficult personal problems, whether in their family life, social relationships, work or health. A stressful life event in the six months before the act is four times more likely among people who harm themselves deliberately compared to the general population. Deliberate self-harm, then, seems to be a form of communication.

Among the messages commonly conveyed through the act are anger, frustration, revenge, defiance, an attempt to win sympathy or re-establish a broken relationship. Underpinning many of these is the proverbial cry for help: 'I feel awful; I am at the end of my tether; I am confused and don't know what to do; please help me!'

Alongside this, people often report a desperate need for relief from this state of mind, best achieved through lapsing into unconsciousness: 'All I want is a long sleep so that I can be free of the emotional pain'. Not unexpectedly, the most common form of deliberate self-harm, in 90 per cent of cases, is taking an overdose of a drug which is likely to 'knock me out'. The benzodiazepines and anti-depressants, widely prescribed by family doctors, are readily available for this purpose. People often take over-the-counter analgesics like paracetamol in the mistaken belief that they have a similar effect. People who cut their wrists or lacerate other parts of the body are often seeking relief from intense bodily tension.

This is what studies tell us about the characteristics typical of people who deliberately harm themselves. They tend to be late adolescents or young adults, women (in a ratio of 3 to 1), single or divorced. They tend not to have a formal psychiatric diagnosis but instead have experienced long-standing problems of living with which they have struggled to cope—as their misuse of alcohol and drugs like benzodiazepines illustrates. Many have come from families marked by conflict and tension. They are likely to be facing a crisis at the time of the self-harm, and have recently sought help for it from their family doctor or other source.

About one in five of these people will repeat the self-harm in the following year. For a few, most of whom have an underlying psychiatric disorder (particularly mood disturbance, substance abuse or some form of disordered personality) the behaviour becomes habitual in the face of even minor stress. One in a hundred people will actually kill themselves in the twelve months following an episode of deliberate self-harm, often in circumstances which leave doubt as to their true intent. Jane's story is a typical example of deliberate self-harm.

*Jane, a 24 year-old clerical assistant, was brought to the emergency department of a general hospital by her family following her taking an overdose of 25 paracetamol and 10 benzodiazepine tablets. After her drowsiness had lifted, she cried profusely and expressed a wish to 'get away from it all'. This need to escape had been her original motive in overdosing herself.*

*She felt trapped in a long-standing conflict with her parents over how she should live her life. Their strict code of conduct for all four children included career plans and marital choice. One older sister had married at an early age and was living at a distance. Her younger brothers lived in fear of their father, a tempestuous man who was given to violent outbursts. Jane had twice fled from her home because of her father's violence. She had only returned out of a sense of loyalty.*

*The current crisis had been provoked by her boyfriend's refusal of Jane's ultimatum to become engaged (as a first step to leaving home with her parents' support). Jane had once before taken an overdose, also when buffeted by parental pressures and feeling hopelessly stuck. Generally, however, she was an amiable, sociable and lively person, with friends and interests.*

*Jane agreed to the psychiatrist's recommendation to spend a few days in hospital because the family crisis seemed particularly intense and the father's tendency to violence put her and other family members at risk. Moreover, she was unable to give any guarantee about her own safety. She soon responded to the supportive environment on the ward and was able to express her feelings of anger and frustration. She became quite animated in relating to fellow patients and staff. But, when visited by her family, heated arguments erupted and Jane became extremely distressed.*

*As well as individual therapy, using principles of crisis intervention (see page 289), a family meeting was held. This was emotionally charged, with her father threatening to disown her if she left home without his consent. The parental relationship was strained to breaking point and the other three children were fearful of the father's threats. A later meeting was less fraught although the father's stubborn hold on the reins of power in the family dominated the proceedings.*

*However, Jane and the family were encouraged to recognise the conflicts and to map out various ways of resolving or at least defusing them. A programme of out-patient family therapy was arranged as well as a series of counselling sessions for Jane on her own.*

## Treatment and prevention

Jane's case illustrates many of the principles that psychiatrists adopt in dealing with people who deliberately harm themselves. They include a careful assessment of the person and the family, crisis intervention which may require brief admission to a psychiatric unit, and individual and/or family therapy. In more complex cases, continuing treatment is needed, usually in the form of long-term psychotherapy (see Chapter 21).

Preventing self-harm in the first instance would obviously be ideal. It was in pursuit of this goal that self-help organisations like the Samaritans (the first of its kind, founded in 1953 in London by the Reverend Chad Varah) and Lifeline were established. Trained non-professionals are available on the telephone around the clock to offer counselling to people who feel themselves in crisis and in immediate need of a sympathetic ear and advice. Like all self-help groups in the mental health arena, this type of counselling service fits extremely well with professional sources of help.

# 20  *Drugs and Other Physical Treatments*

Most people with mild psychological problems can be treated without drugs. But, for many with moderately severe conditions and for all of marked severity, drugs and other physical therapies are central to treatment.

Physical treatments—which include drugs, occasionally electro-convulsive therapy and very rarely psychosurgery—control symptoms by readjusting those chemical processes in the brain that we assume are disturbed in psychiatric disorders. Much of our knowledge about these processes comes from looking at particular drugs that are effective in treatment to determine how they work in the brain. We know, for example, that all effective drugs to treat schizophrenia block a specific chemical messenger, dopamine. Working back from this observation, researchers postulate that dopamine activity is increased in schizophrenia. Such findings are supported by continuing research into the potential role of other chemical messengers—a search driven by the fact that all drugs influencing the brain have a number of actions.

This line of thinking provides a basis for the massive expansion of pharmaceutical research since the 1950s which targets a particular chemical system with a view to developing new drugs with the greatest therapeutic effects and the least side-effects. Treatments used to be quite non-specific and largely ineffective. Patients would risk dying because of exhaustion during excited states like mania, or from infections such as pneumonia due to immobility associated with severe depression, or from suicide.

Past methods of dealing with mentally ill people reflect what to us now seem bizarre ideas about abnormal behaviour. Common practice in the old asylums included such crude methods as blood-letting, purging, mechanical restraints, twirling stool therapy and sudden dunking in water (all designed to cause physical discomfort and 'shock' people back to sanity).

A twirling stool or 'rotary motion machine' for the treatment of insanity (from A. Morison, *Cases of Mental Disease*, Longman and Highley, London, 1828).

The twentieth century has embraced 'great and desperate cures'. 'New' treatments to induce a state of semi-coma or deep sleep, and widespread indiscriminate operations on the brain in order to modify behaviour have had their vogue. This era began in 1949 with the discovery of the effects of lithium on manic excitement by an Australian psychiatrist, John Cade. The 1950s was the key decade for discovery of drugs targeted to specific disorders. Reports on the anti-psychotic properties of Chlorpromazine (the first modern tranquilliser) and on the anti-depressant actions of Imipramine (the first effective drug for depression) were published. Discovery of the effectiveness of the benzodiazepines in treating anxiety followed in 1960.

All these vital discoveries were based on serendipity rather than rational drug design. Dozens of drugs with similar activity have since been made, tested and introduced into practice to treat tens of millions of people worldwide.

The impact of their use has been dramatic. Disabling symptoms are much more readily controllable and chronic or recurrent illnesses may be prevented or muted by long-term use of medication. Modern drugs have enabled many people who would otherwise have been treated in hospital to be managed in the community. This is one factor in the change in health policies which has led to a massive reduction in psychiatric beds throughout the world.

## Principles of drug use in psychiatry

In prescribing drugs, psychiatrists consider how they are delivered to and removed from their sites of action in the brain—and the mechanisms by which they exert both therapeutic effects and side-effects. For example, many drugs, such as anti-psychotics and anti-depressants, remain active in the brain long enough to allow once-daily doses. Since drugs are variably absorbed and available in the blood-stream, selection of the correct doses has to be tailored to each person, taking into account age, gender, past patterns of response, any physical illness, and so on. Generally, it is two to three weeks before the full therapeutic effects of many of these drugs are felt.

Several groups of drugs are used in psychiatry—the main ones are anti-psychotic, anti-depressant, anti-manic and anti-anxiety. These categories are based on their clinical effectiveness, but there is not always a direct relationship between the diagnosis implicit in their names and the type of drug used. Since people often have a variety of symptoms, drugs from more than one category may well be prescribed for one person, either at the same time or in a sequence. Generally, however, the ideal is to use one drug at a time, and monitor its effect carefully. Let us consider each category in turn.

## Anti-psychotic drugs

Anti-psychotics were the first drugs to be used for specific mental illnesses. The prototype, Chlorpromazine, was first developed in 1950 by Charpentier, who was seeking a new anti-histamine for use as a premedication to surgery. In initial trials, tranquillity was such a prominent feature that two French psychiatrists, Jean Delay and Paul Deniker, prescribed the drug for acutely psychotic patients. To their delight, it quelled the excitement and agitation, as well as having a specific effect in dissolving delusions and hallucinations. Anti-psychotic drugs have since become the mainstay of the treatment of schizophrenia and related psychotic states (see Chapter 12), and of the prevention of relapse.

In terms of effectiveness, there are few advantages of one over another. One exception is Clozapine, used in unresponsive schizophrenia. It is effective in up to half the people who fail to respond to other anti-psychotic drugs. However, because of its association with potentially fatal suppression of the bone-marrow in 2 per cent of people, it is never used as a first-line treatment.

Treatment usually begins with the person in hospital. Once people with schizophrenia are diagnosed and start taking anti-psychotics, medication should continue for at least six months. However, people with psychotic features may not be schizophrenic but have a self-limiting episode lasting a matter of days, or be psychotic because they have used recreational drugs such as amphetamine ('speed').Whenever the diagnosis is uncertain, psychiatrists prefer not to use anti-psychotic drugs but to give people the opportunity to recover spontaneously—unless their level of agitation or mental disturbance is extreme.

Anti-psychotic drugs are most effective in treating the so-called 'positive' symptoms of schizophrenia, such as delusions, hallucinations and thought disorder, rather than 'negative' symptoms like social withdrawal, loss of interest, poor personal hygiene and restricted emotional expressiveness. Negative symptoms do respond, although more slowly and incompletely.

For people admitted to hospital for the first time, therapy usually continues for at least half a year after initial control of symptoms.Then medication is gradually reduced, and a close watch kept for any recurrence. Unfortunately, about two-thirds of people relapse in the first year after stopping anti-psychotic drugs, but who they will be is impossible to predict. People experiencing several relapses may need anti-psychotics for years, even life-long. In long-term treatment of this type, the lowest effective dose is used in order to keep side-effects to a minimum.

Because many people with schizophrenia, particularly in a phase of relapse, may not see themselves as ill and in need of medication, they may refuse or neglect to take it. As this behaviour markedly increases the risk of relapse, psychiatrists stress the importance of changing it. To deal with this issue, anti-psychotics are available in long-acting injectable form. When given by deep intra-muscular injection, the drug is slowly released into the blood stream for three to four weeks.

Side-effects associated with the 'older' anti-psychotics are unfortunately numerous and troublesome.  They include sedation, dry mouth, lowering of blood pressure and disorders of movement. The movement disorders include involuntary contractions of muscles in the tongue, face, neck and back, restlessness, and rigidity and tremor as seen in Parkinson's disease. These features may be treated once they appear, or prevented in people at high risk, by specific drugs used in conjunction with anti-psychotic drugs—mostly of the anti-cholinergic type.

The most worrisome movement disorder by far is tardive dyskinesia, so called because it generally occurs after some years of anti-psychotic treatment. Many people on long-term treatment develop abnormal movements of the mouth, tongue and lips, and sometimes of the limbs and trunk. Because no effective treatment is available, the goal is prevention—which is why psychiatrists prescribe as low as possible a dose of anti-psychotics, for the shortest time, and avoid using them at all unless absolutely necessary.

Fortunately, a new generation of anti-psychotic drugs has arrived. They appear to be less dangerous in terms of side-effects but are much more expensive. Pharmaceutical companies are following many leads which offer the promise of a whole range of new medications, both safer and more effective than their predecessors. This flurry of activity is likely to bring in a new era in helping people with schizophrenia.

## Anti-depressant drugs

The distress and dysfunction of severe depression (see Chapter 8) calls for energetic treatment. Moreover, as 15 per cent of people who at some time in their lives have significant mood disorders will commit suicide, it is essential that psychiatrists prescribe anti-depressant drugs effectively. The drugs are used both to treat the acute state and to prevent recurrent episodes. The drugs also have a place in the treatment of other conditions—for example, bed-wetting and panic, eating (especially bulimia) and obsessive-compulsive disorders.

A wide range of anti-depressants is available. The psychiatrist's task is to match the drug to the person on the basis of such things as age, whether or not they have a physical illness, degree of agitation or retardation, presence of insomnia, risk of suicide and response to past medication.

Anti-depressants can be classified into three main groups (see below). No one drug has been shown to be better or to act more quickly than any other. But the newer types do cause fewer side-effects, which is a distinct advantage over their predecessors.

### The tricyclic drugs

Tricyclics (so named because of their three-ringed chemical structure) were the first effective drugs in the treatment of depression. They continue to be prescribed widely because of their proven effectiveness. Since their effect lasts for some fifteen to thirty hours they can be taken once a day (usually at night to exploit their sedating properties). They act on several brain chemical messengers, essentially normalising the disturbed brain function that underlies the modulation of mood.

However, because they affect various chemical systems in the body at large, they do produce unpleasant side-effects. Especially common are dry mouth, constipation, dizziness, blurred vision, weight gain and tremor. Since these side-effects often precede the therapeutic effect, psychiatrists emphasise to people that they may feel worse before they feel better. Because of their strong effect on the body, overdose is dangerous and possibly lethal—death is usually due to heart attack.

Mianserin, a tetracyclic anti-depressant (that is, with a four-ringed chemical structure), is largely free of toxic effects on the heart and is therefore relatively safe if an overdose is taken. It is sometimes recommended for elderly people and for those with heart disease.

## Monoamine oxidase inhibitors (MAOIs)

Introduced at the same time as the tricyclics, MAOIs are used much more sparingly because they can cause death through a stroke if people consume certain drugs, beverages (red wine and particular beers) or foodstuffs including cheese, meat or yeast extracts like Vegemite. However, newer types of MAOIs, the most notable being Moclobemide, are largely free of this serious risk. Other side-effects include dizziness, weight gain, constipation and insomnia. Insomnia is a result of the MAOIs' stimulant effect, and necessitate them being taken early in the day.

## The SSRIs

Extravagant claims have been made for the selective serotonin re-uptake inhibitors (SSRIs)—that they are the 'magic bullet' panacea for unhappiness. The first, Prozac (its chemical name is fluoxetine) has become a household name, and several others with a similar action have followed. This again typifies the pattern in psychiatry where a new medication is adopted with evangelical fervour and only later is assessed more soberly. In fact, the SSRIs are no more or no less effective than the tricyclics and MAOIs (and much more expensive). Although they are better tolerated, they can cause side-effects like headaches, gastric upset, anxiety and insomnia. Because they remain active in the brain for more than twenty-four hours, they are usually taken once a day, in the morning.

## Choosing an anti-depressant

The psychiatrist's choice of drug is partly one of personal preference. Some, such as the tricyclics, have been in use for more than thirty years, and their advantages and side-effects are well known. In contrast, problems with newer drugs may not have been picked up despite the extensive research required by regulatory authorities. In recent years, two anti-depressant drugs were permanently withdrawn, one because it caused breakdown of red blood cells and the other because of its association with paralysis. Nevertheless, newer drugs are generally preferred by many psychiatrists, especially for depressed people for whom the avoidance of side-effects is vital. Once an anti-depressant drug is chosen, whatever the type, an adequate dose must be given.

It is very important that people being treated and, where appropriate, their families, are made aware that the therapeutic effect of anti-depressants is usually delayed for two to four weeks after the optimal dose has been achieved. Before modern drug therapy, depressive episodes lasted many months. Given that anti-depressants help but do not 'cure', they are prescribed for a minimum of six months. People prone to recurrent episodes may need maintenance doses for up to several years, even life-long, both as treatment and as prevention.

All anti-depressants are withdrawn gradually because a sudden stop may trigger a withdrawal syndrome (nausea, diarrhoea, headaches and frightening dreams), most commonly in the case of the tricyclics.

## Anti-manic drugs

If untreated, mood disorders of the excitable type, namely mania (see Chapter 8) are usually recurrent and disrupt people's lives and those around them. The illness often drives them to hazardous activities—physical, interpersonal and financial. Fortunately, there are drugs, especially lithium, which have specific anti-manic effects (in contrast to the non-specific effect of anti-psychotics in reducing the features of mania) and dramatically alter the course of the illness.

The anti-manic effects of lithium were first discovered by John Cade, an Australian psychiatrist, in 1949 while he conducted what he described as amateurish experiments with guinea pigs in the pantry of a hospital ward! He believed that the urine of manic patients contained a harmful chemical, and sought to identify it by separately injecting a number of substances present in urine into guinea pigs in order to discover whether the adverse effects of manic urine were replicated. Since one of these substances, uric acid, could only be injected when combined with another substance, he used as that substance, lithium, a simple chemical similar to common salt. Eventually he realised that it was the lithium that sedated the animals.

Buoyed by this serendipitous discovery, Cade conducted a pioneering experiment on manic and schizophrenic patients which demonstrated a dramatic therapeutic effect on the former but not on the latter. Although lithium was thus shown to be valuable in an acute attack of mania, further research established its main use—to decrease the frequency, severity and length of manic episodes. Lithium has found a similar useful place in depression by reducing the rate of its recurrence.

Lithium's mechanism of action is still unknown although complex bio-chemical theories abound, providing optimism that the answer will be found. It is rapidly absorbed, and excreted through the kidneys. Since precise concentrations are needed for it to be effective, and high levels may actually be toxic, its level in the blood needs regular monitoring. Kidney function is therefore assessed before starting treatment, as is the thyroid gland because the drug may hamper production of thyroid hormone. If under-functioning of the thyroid does occur—as it does in 5 per cent of people—it can be successfully treated with hormone replacement.

There are a number of side-effects. A tendency to produce excessive urine, leading to thirst and a strong need to drink, may result from lithium's interference with kidney function. A scare spread among both doctors and patients upon research reports of permanent change in the kidneys in up to 10 per cent of people on long-term lithium. Later studies showed these changes in people with mood disorders who had never received lithium— and the microscopic alterations are not associated with significant changes in urine production and excretion.

Lithium can be dangerous when it exceeds its therapeutic level, resulting in tremor, slurred speech and vomiting. If not promptly detected, convulsions, disturbed heart rhythm, and even death follow. In these circumstances, measures to eliminate the drug from the body include, in the most severe cases, dialysis.

For the occasional person, where lithium's use is potentially hazardous, the well-established anti-epileptic drug Carbamazepine is an effective alternative. We do not know how it works either, but its role in mania suggests that the processes in the brain which initiate mania may have something in common with those of epilepsy. Further support for this idea is the usefulness of two other anti-epileptic drugs, Sodium Valproate and Clonazepam, for selected people.

## Anti-anxiety drugs

Anxiety is all around us; in fact, it has been described as the malady of our time—an 'age of anxiety'. When it becomes disruptive because of its severity or interference with ordinary living, treatment may be necessary. Human beings have always looked to medicines for relief. A clutter of treatments punctuates the history of this search, most of which have turned out to have disastrous effects, particularly addiction.

We now widely accept that these drugs have a limited, though important, role in easing anxiety but only once much safer psychological therapies have been tried (see Chapter 7).

After criticism surrounding the use of barbiturates, the discovery in the 1960s of the supposedly harmless benzodiazepines (Diazepam or Valium was the first of these) was seen as a major boon by both doctors and patients. Alas, decline in their use after two decades of 'spectacular success' (immortalised in the Rolling Stones song 'Mother's Little Helper') is evidence of the fact that no drug for the treatment of anxiety is ever trouble-free.

If anti-anxiety medication is thought to be necessary, several options follow. Although the benzodiazepines are most commonly prescribed, other drugs do have a role. Beta-blockers, for example (used mainly for heart disease and high blood pressure), are particularly effective for physical signs of anxiety like tremor, sweating and palpitations. They are sometimes taken by actors and musicians to calm them before performances. All the anti-depressant groups may sometimes be useful across the range of anxiety disorders.

These are the situations in which anti-anxiety drugs are used:

- moderate or severe anxiety to which support and reassurance have brought little relief;
- chronic anxiety, where their use may blunt the extremes of behaviour;
- for short-term assistance in the treatment of physical disorders (for example, coronary artery disease in which anxiety may be particularly harmful);
- as supplementary tranquillisers in treating some psychotic disorders which are otherwise difficult to control;
- to treat problems associated with alcohol withdrawal;
- as hypnotics (see Chapter 10).

A decision to use benzodiazepines is based on the length of their effects. So, while short-acting forms are preferred as a hypnotic where a hangover effect is unwanted, long-acting forms may be best when more continuous relief is required. There is a wide optimal dosage range for benzodiazepines. The dose is chosen patient by patient, always beginning at the low end of the recommended range and, if necessary, gradually increasing it until anxiety is controlled without causing drowsiness.

This cautious approach is critical since the vast majority of people taking benzodiazepines are functioning in the community, and drowsiness is risky in activities such as driving cars or operating machinery. When on benzodiazepines, people need to minimise or avoid alcohol because it also acts ultimately as a sedative. Apart from this sedation, and confusion in the elderly, benzodiazepines have remarkably few side-effects. They are relatively safe when taken in overdose. Although often used in suicide attempts, deaths are extremely rare.

Were it not for the problem of dependence, the benzodiazepines would indeed be a most suitable treatment for anxiety. Tragically, however, up to 40 per cent of long-term users experience unpleasant symptoms upon their withdrawal. Sometimes, underlying anxiety will rebound with even greater intensity. However, new symptoms occur regularly and indicate physical dependence (see the table below for a comprehensive list), although a particular person may experience only some of them, and they may be mild. Symptoms may occur within a day of ceasing short-acting benzodiazepines and several days after stopping a longer-acting one.

**The symptoms of benzodiazepine withdrawal**

| | | |
|---|---|---|
| • anxiety | • panic attacks | • epileptic fits (rare) |
| • irritability | • hypersensitivity to noise | • sleep disturbance |
| • tremor | • palpitations | • increased muscle tension |
| • muscle weakness and aches | • headache | • loss of appetite |
| • nausea and vomiting | | |

## Electro-convulsive therapy (ECT)

We now turn to a treatment wrapped in enormous controversy, despite a half-century of its use as a mainstay therapy in psychiatric practice. Many people see it as a link to the barbarity they associate with the treatments used long ago for the mentally ill—blood-letting, dunking and the twirling stool.

Before effective drugs were available, ECT was administered often, and at times indiscriminately. Undoubtedly, the procedure was primitive before the 1950s. Anaesthetics and muscle relaxant drugs were not used, with the result that people had convulsions of such severity that they were at risk of physical injuries, even fractures of the spine. This historical note is important because ECT continues to be depicted in the media in the most frightening fashion. Understandably, people generally, including those who could most be helped, are left feeling frightened and distrustful of a procedure which psychiatrists know from long experience to be safe and highly effective for specific disorders.

The condition most responsive to ECT is severe depression, particularly when the features listed in the table below predominate. For people with this clinical pattern, the positive response rate of 80 per cent is, strikingly, twice that for anti-depressant drugs.

### Conditions for which ECT is especially effective

- severe depression, especially if associated with:
  - pervasive suicidal ideas
  - continuing agitation or retardation of movement
  - marked anorexia and substantial weight loss
  - psychotic features
- schizophrenia and acute psychosis if there is:
  - florid and chaotic disturbance resistant to anti-psychotic medication
  - severe agitation or retardation (catatonia)
- severe mania with extreme disinhibition and agitation, resistant to anti-manic drugs

ECT is not the preferred treatment for mania and schizophrenia, but it may be tried for certain of their florid and life-endangering forms, and then can have dramatic effects. Treatment is safe in virtually all situations. Even medically ill people can benefit, provided they can tolerate brief anaesthesia (which is a greater potential problem than the ECT itself). Raised pressure within the brain due, for example, to a tumour is the only exception.

In animal studies, convulsive treatment results in consistent changes in the activity of chemical messengers, which provides an important clue to the way ECT works in people. But we do know conclusively from research that the effect is due to the induced fit and not to the passage of an electrical current through the brain. We now virtually eliminate the fit by administering a muscle relaxant drug—so that the brain 'fits' but the body barely does.

ECT takes only a few minutes and is usually given two or three times a week for an average six to ten treatments. The chief technical variation is whether the electric current is passed through one or both sides of the brain. There is little doubt that passage through only one side leads to less confusion and memory disturbance (which in any event is temporary), but it may be less effective or more treatments may be required to achieve the same result.

Any procedure which requires a general anaesthetic may lead to death—the estimated rate for ECT is one death in 22 000 treatments, mainly due to cardio-vascular complications. This is not higher than would be expected from giving an anaesthetic alone. Apart from this, the main concern is memory impairment. This is common but usually mild and temporary. Memory function returns to normal within days or weeks, and impairment rarely lasts longer than six months. (See page 95 for an example of the use of ECT in depression.)

## Psychosurgery

Even more disturbing to patients and their families than ECT is the fear of operations on the brain for psychiatric illness. The implied brutality of the most widely used procedure, prefrontal lobotomy, has entered folk-lore. Lobotomy was introduced in 1936 by Egas Moniz, a neurologist who won a Nobel Prize for his work. The procedure, which severed most of the nerve fibres connecting the frontal lobes to the rest of the brain, was mainly used to treat schizophrenia. An estimated 50 000 patients in the United States and 10 000 in Britain had the operation, the effectiveness of which for schizophrenia was never proven. This is yet another disturbing illustration of unbridled enthusiasm with good intention preceding proper scientific evaluation.

In contrast to the crudity of prefrontal lobotomy, current techniques target the relevant area of the brain precisely and are used extremely sparingly. One of the most accurate is so-called stereotactic surgery, which can create 'lesions' with a three-dimensional accuracy of one millimetre. These techniques are used for people with obsessive-compulsive disorder (see Chapter 7) and depression which are severe and intractable and have not responded to other treatments despite persistent trials.

Current techniques, whatever their type, have fewer long-term complications than did earlier operations. Some changes in personality, and epilepsy, rarely occur. Because of the controversial history of psychosurgery, the irreversible nature of the operation and the potential (though rare) hazards, in most countries the patient's consent must be absolutely fully informed and supported by the judgement of an independent panel of experts.

# 21 *The Talking Therapies*

The psychotherapies—we use the plural, as they come in many forms—are a group of psychological treatments used for a wide variety of purposes. The goals range from the relief of a person's symptoms to shifts in attitude about himself or herself and the world and, most ambitiously, to fundamental changes in personality.

All psychotherapies involve two fundamental aspects. The first is a working relationship between a trained mental health professional and a person needing help to deal with emotional distress and/or poor functioning in, for instance, work, social relationships or marriage. The second is the professional's planned use of specific psychological principles.

This definition covers all psychotherapies, although the person's particular difficulties and the specific psychological principles vary considerably. On the other hand, certain features unite the psychotherapies—the so-called non-specific or common basic factors. These were formulated by Jerome Frank in a landmark publication, *Persuasion and Healing,* in 1972. The factors are:

- *An emotionally charged, confiding relationship*  The interaction between the person and the therapist has certain essential hallmarks, which distinguish it from the relationship it most resembles—a close friendship. Unlike friendship, which works both ways, the person is sufficiently distressed to seek help whereas the therapist is committed to providing professional skills to meet this need. The person expects the therapist to be dependable and trustworthy, because the issues raised are commonly of the most personal kind—distressing, depressing, embarrassing, shameful, and so on. Above all, the therapist is empathic—that is, capable of standing in the person's shoes and appreciative of the emotional experiences—but sufficiently detached so as not to be overwhelmed by them.

- *Sharing a rationale*   The therapist provides an explanation of the person's problems and of the intended methods for dealing with them which make sense and is acceptable to that person in the context of his or her culture. The word 'rationale' suggests an account that is plausible and coherent without being provable in a strict scientific or mathematical sense. After all, we are dealing with human beings and not analysing, say, the structure of a geological fault.

- *Providing new knowledge*   This arises out of the rationale and taps people's potential to use new information about themselves, their problems and ways of changing. This may be about any aspect of a person's internal psychological life and the life shared with others, ranging from clear information about the origin of a particular symptom (for example, that emotional distress is experienced as a tension headache) to a profound experience of self-discovery (for example, acceptance that one must determine one's own purpose in living).

- *Facilitating emotional arousal*   Learning about oneself may seem to be a cold, intellectual pursuit. This could not be further from the truth. Therapy encourages emotional arousal and expressiveness, so that a person can 'get in touch' with internal feelings like grief, shame, envy, anger and guilt. This enriches the learning process by stimulating self-reflectiveness—for example, 'I feel intensely guilty; what sense can I make of this here-and-now experience?' Catharsis (from the Greek word meaning purging) is a discharge of intense emotion, which commonly brings relief through the release of pent-up feelings.

- *Instilling hope*   The very act of engaging with an expert raises a person's expectation of a positive outcome. Hope has always been a vital factor in psychological life, even in the face of the harshest circumstances. Central to the therapist's role is the need to convey a sense of optimism which, combined with the person's positive expectations, forges a 'therapeutic alliance'—that is, a joint commitment to the task.

- *Experiences of 'success'*   Beyond instilling hope, this is the opportunity in therapy itself to experience a sense of achievement and corresponding success. People often embark on treatment in a state of gloom, dismayed by what they see as a personal record of repeated failure in family life, social relationships and work, and in coping with life's ups and downs. In the course of treatment, welcome shifts, however ordinary, often pave the way for a stronger sense of mastery. No longer need a person be a powerless victim of a dismal record.

## The range of psychotherapies

The most useful way of grouping the psychotherapies is according to their main purpose:

- *Therapies to improve self-awareness*   Commonly known as 'psychoanalytically oriented', this group seeks to increase people's self-understanding as a means of improving symptoms, making positive shifts in attitude to themselves and the world and, most ambitiously, making changes in personality.

- *Therapies to give long-term emotional and practical support*   'Supportive psychotherapy' seeks the best possible adjustment in people with a long-standing psychiatric disability. The term is also used in a more general sense to cover a range of therapeutic activities designed to improve the coping ability of people who are prone to psychological dysfunction. It is just as relevant for the caregiver (usually family members) of the person being treated.

- *Therapies to deal with a crisis*   A person overwhelmed by, for example, the accidental death of his or her child needs help to overcome the ordeal and adjust to the loss. 'Crisis counselling' (or 'crisis intervention') is usually short-term, and may be provided individually or for a couple or a family.

- *Therapies to abolish or improve specific symptoms or problems*   These therapies are directed towards an immense range of psychiatric symptoms and conditions, from removal of an irrational fear (such as a phobia of spiders) through reduction in compulsive behaviour (such as the need to check the gas repeatedly) to improving social skills (such as reducing shyness). The therapies are chiefly 'behavioural' in type, involving particular techniques in highly specific, direct ways.

With these groupings in mind, let us now look at how the psychotherapies are used in practice.

## Psychoanalysis and psychoanalytic psychotherapy

Sigmund Freud founded what we now know as psychoanalysis in the closing years of the nineteenth century. By his death in 1939, psychoanalysis had developed not only into an innovative, radical method of psychological treatment but also into an elaborate account of childhood development (for example, the oedipal conflict), and a means of challenging conventional views of culture and society (for example, the nature of civilisation, war and religion). In a poem written soon after Freud's death, W. H. Auden asserted that his contribution had been so monumental as to be the dawning of a new 'climate of opinion'. Psychoanalysis in general, and the writings and person of Freud in particular, are still deeply admired by some people and attacked by others—both within and outside psychiatry. Battle lines are sometimes so tightly drawn that claims for or against psychoanalysis become quite outlandish, and personally directed.

Freud constantly revised his ideas to make sense of what his patients were telling him. Indeed, it was said that he was the first who actually listened with keen attention to every word his patients uttered. Through studies of dreams, works of art, jokes and apparently trivial events such as slips of the tongue and lapses of memory, and the more serious experiences of grief and depression, he argued for continuity between normal and abnormal mental states.

Psychoanalysis stems directly from the work of Freud and his followers, but most forms of psychotherapy, at least as practised in the West, owe something to his theories and techniques (whether acknowledged or not). In Switzerland, for instance, Carl Jung concluded that Freud's emphasis on sexuality in normal child development was too dogmatic and restrictive. He expanded Freud's notions of the unconscious into the concept he called the collective unconscious—as reflected in the dreams and artistic creations of people with psychoses, and from studies of myths and symbols of ancient civilisations.

Transactional analysis, developed by Eric Berne in the 1960s, makes playful use of Freud's concept of the superego, ego and id (see page 28). They are represented as the parent, adult and child states of mind, which are juggled to avoid intimacy or to gain power in relationships (the 'games people play').

Psychoanalysis in its pure form is the most intensive of the psychotherapies. Hour-long sessions are held three to five times a week, and the person lies on a couch with the therapist sitting behind. The person is encouraged to talk about whatever comes to mind. The analyst listens intently, the key activity being to comment on links expressed between thoughts and feelings, and underlying, unconscious conflicts. In its classical form, psychoanalysis revolves around interpretation of the transference—that is, the relationship the person forms with the analyst. This transference, derived from the person's experiences of relationships with significant figures in childhood, especially parents and siblings, is directed on to the therapist in the here and now (see the case illustration below). This pattern is interpreted many times ('working through'), which leads the person to deeper understanding of self and of relationship to others.

Much more commonly practised than classical psychoanalysis is psychoanalytic (or psychodynamic or insight-oriented) psychotherapy. It is less intensive, with sessions once or twice a week. Interpretation of the transference, while still important, is not always the main focus. Instead, the therapist uses techniques like confrontation (non-destructive but firmly stated comments that help the person face a particular issue); clarification (throwing light on complex psychological matters of whose significance the person is unaware); and empathic comment (reflecting back to the person his or her thoughts and feelings).

A brief form of psychoanalytic psychotherapy has evolved to help people with a specific psychological conflict (for example, unresolved grief). Limited usually to between twelve and forty sessions, it is variously called brief, short-term or focal psychodynamic therapy.

Who can be helped by this psychodynamic approach? It is vital that people must first accept some responsibility for their problems and their resolution, even though not being entirely aware of their origins or why previous solutions have failed. It is important that they can be introspective and express thoughts, fantasies and feelings, since therapy works mainly through words. And they must be strong enough to tolerate the inevitable distress in the process of change. They must regard relationships with people as being important, and have experienced, in either a positive or negative way, at least one major relationship. Here is the analytic approach at work, with its ups and downs:

*John, a 38-year-old management consultant, sought therapy because of repeated failure to form long-term relationships with women. He had adopted a lifestyle of brief, emotionally empty, highly sexualised relationships alternating with periods of depressing social isolation. He came across as cynical, aloof and worldly.*

*At first he was sceptical of the therapist's ability to help him and scornful of the theory which he assumed was applied. She interpreted this as a means to avoid deep feelings which led him to recall a similar attitude he had held towards his mother—a deeply religious woman whose avoidance of conflict had allowed his father to tyrannise their homelife during his childhood.*

*Over several months, the contempt John felt for people he perceived as weak and helpless, especially women, began to emerge. Thus one element in his problem became clearer to him. This attitude stood in sharp contrast to his con-*

*scientious work on behalf of his 'needy' clients, which led to a discussion of his periodic anger towards those who did not live up to his expectations. With this insight he became less demanding of himself and his clients and enjoyed his work more (this is the point at which a planned brief form of therapy may have terminated).*

*As therapy unfolded, another layer of conflict emerged—his anxiety about being perceived as weak. This was the way his father had made him feel. Now, in the transference, the therapist was 'father' and John was the child-like victim. As the therapist interpreted this sense of vulnerability, he became increasingly agitated. He missed sessions, and criticised the therapist again in his former cynical style, but with a note of anger and even urgency. The therapist interpreted his anxiety as the increasing closeness he had felt towards her and the fear of what this might lead to. A slip of the tongue revealed his anxiety when he said, 'I want to keep you at arms' link'.*

*Two themes became clear. One was fear that the therapist would abandon him just as John believed his mother had failed to care for him. He defended himself against this fear by emphasising his intellectual ability. The second theme took the form of criticism of the therapist for a variety of matters (for example, the therapist taking holidays) and a recurrent interest in some widely publicised scandals in the medical profession. This was interpreted in terms of resentment of what the therapist had to offer.*

*He became more aware both of his contempt of people, especially women, whom he perceived as weak, and of his envy of those he saw as competent and able to offer him something he himself could not provide. This new knowledge enabled him to approach relationships in his personal and professional life with greater insight into, and hence control over, the anxieties which had influenced his behaviour so powerfully. Ultimately, John developed a stable relationship which led to an affectionate marriage.*

## Group psychotherapy

This began when psychoanalytic concepts were borrowed from the individual setting and introduced to small groups. Assembling people for a common purpose soon expanded when the distinct therapeutic forces at work in a group were recognised. Members contribute to one other and to the group as a whole, and receive benefits in return. A group is also inevitably a crucible in which intense emotions are aroused. The rationale for group therapy recognises and uses both the rewarding and the negative aspects of interpersonal relationships, in that the group provides a forum where difficulties can be explored and dealt with in the context of mutual support.

The most popular model comes from the 'interpersonal school' of psychiatry which considers personality to be mostly the product of a person's interactions with other significant people. The people most likely to be helped are those with low self-esteem, lack of direction, anxiety, depression, ineffective coping with stress, inability to express feelings like love and anger, and difficulty with intimacy. Whatever their formal diagnosis, they should have potential for self-awareness, motivation for change and a capacity to relate to others. The typical group contains six to eight people plus one or two therapists, and meets weekly over a period of one or more years. These are the mechanisms by which therapy works (they are related to Frank's common basic factors):

- development of a cohesive group marked by trust and security;
- a sense of mutual acceptance by group members;
- free expression of feelings, and disclosure of personal information;
- a collective wish to be involved with and sensitive to others as they wrestle with their difficulties;
- learning by observing and identifying with the experience of others in the group;
- a feeling of having much in common with other group members;
- the hope or the expectation of benefits from group participation.

Another model modified for people with various psychiatric disorders (and their carers) is known as psycho-education. Its chief goal is 'teaching' people to understand more about, and react more effectively to, their condition. The therapist, in the role of guide, uses strategies which enable people both to recognise unhelpful patterns of feeling, thinking and behaviour, and to avoid circumstances which provoke them.

Group meetings are held in some hospital settings, but not all psychiatrists support them. The usual pattern is for all staff and patients to assemble, usually once or twice weekly, and to tackle matters arising from the patients' actual experiences of institutional living. For example, two people may have become embroiled with each other to the point of violent threats, and the behaviour may have been noted by other patients and by staff. The meeting provides a setting not only for the two people to explore what underlies their feud but also for the rest of the ward to contribute to the peace-making process and to learn from the events in more personal terms.

## Family therapy

Folk wisdom in every civilisation has reflected, and poets, storytellers and playwrights have described, the influence of family relationships on individuals—from the plays of Shakespeare and Chekhov to *Neighbours* and *The Simpsons*. It was Freud who gave the first theoretical account of how these influences were transmitted across the generations. Although his therapy focused on the individual, several psychoanalytic concepts have, since the 1950s, been transferred to the treatment both of couples and families. Also in the 1950s, therapists in Palo Alto, California, led by Gregory Bateson, an anthropologist who had studied patterns of communication in tribal societies, became interested in the many complex levels of family interaction. In the 1970s a group of innovative psychiatrists in Milan further elaborated these ideas.

Family therapy tries, in a variety of ways, to change the family as a means of helping the individual. For example, the 'Palo Alto school' tries to change the pattern of communication among family members in the belief that 'you cannot *not* communicate'—in other words, that any behaviour, whether words, an action or a refusal to act, is a communication. The aim is to modify patterns of verbal and non-verbal interchange but to leave it to the family to decide what is the best change for them.

In contrast, the 'Milan school' views an individual's symptoms as a response to actual or imminent change or fear of change which may affect the whole family. Those symptoms minimise the impact of such change on that person or on one or more family members. The therapist's job is to expose this hidden agenda and to provide the family with the incentive to find its own solution to the problem.

By the 1960s, the combination of the community psychiatry movement and the closure of mental hospitals was highlighting the fact that people were responding to treatment while in hospital but relapsing on return to their families. A form of family intervention developed to prevent this—the so-called psycho-educational model (a variant on the group therapy discussed on page 283). In a supportive setting, which may consist of several families, the therapist uses communication-skill training, problem-solving methods and provision of information about the illness to reduce its impact on both the individual person and the family. This family involvement has been used most often with schizophrenia, where it seems to be effective in reducing the rate of relapse.

Many family therapists work alone, but some have pioneered the use of the one-way screen by a team of therapists, one or two of whom work with the family while the others observe from behind the screen. Their task is to help clarify what is taking place in the family and to plan suitable interventions.

We have touched on the wide variety of methods used by family therapists. Here is a picture of family therapy in general:

> *Susan, aged sixteen, was brought by her parents to a psychiatrist because of defiant behaviour and deterioration in her previously excellent school results. As the parents grew increasingly concerned, they had become more controlling and critical towards her, to the extent that their concerns dominated family life.*
>
> *In the first interview with the family, Susan was sullen and unwilling to speak. After drawing out the parents' frustration at not being able to change their daughter's behaviour, the therapist turned to the family's circumstances. They had emigrated from England a few years previously at the father's instigation because of a job opportunity in Australia. The mother had been reluctant to leave her ailing mother and sister, to both of whom she felt close. Recently, the father had lost his job and the mother's mother had died. Neither the father's concerns for the family's financial security nor his guilt at having separated his wife from her mother and family had been shared. Likewise, the mother had not expressed her grief, or her anxiety about the financial difficulty, in case this made her husband even more demoralised.*
>
> *Susan's problems began in this context of unresolved grief and uncertainty about the future. As these subjects were gently explored, she became more animated and responsive—and her behaviour at home and at school improved considerably. In five sessions of family therapy, the parents were able to recognise and resolve key differences between themselves and to improve their communication.*

A specific form of family counselling involves couples alone. A professional interest in marriage difficulties developed after World War I, at a time of great social change and economic hardship together with new interest in the scientific study of human sexual behaviour. At first, the emphasis was on educating young people about marriage, the choice of a partner, and sexual behaviour—often presented with strong moral overtones.

A psychoanalytic approach was later introduced, which held that problems in a marriage, whether about decision-making, intimacy or communication, reflected unresolved problems from the spouses' relationships with their own parents and siblings. After World War II, psychodynamically based marriage therapy attempted to identify these earlier conflicts and to show how they were re-created in the marriage. More recent models include learning therapy which emphasises how each partner affects the other's behaviour. The therapist helps the couple to see how they influence each other adversely and advises on ways of changing their behaviour.

Usually, a combination of approaches is used. For example, in the serious and all-too-common problem of domestic violence, it may be possible to identify a sequence of exchanges which leads to escalation of tension between a couple (that is, a behavioural sequence).

*Anton, a 39-year-old carpenter, married with two children, was referred to a psychiatrist by his family doctor with a history of assaulting his wife when drunk. His anger could be traced to assumptions about her which stemmed from his relationship with his mother (she had abandoned her only son when he was ten years old). He was a typical tough-minded and dominant male—a model of masculinity he valued. His resentment of his wife was fuelled by concerns about his own inadequacy and the need for his wife to sustain his self-esteem, and associated fear of abandonment if he failed to meet her expectations (that is, psychodynamic factors). And, his ability to take a more objective view of the situation was probably impaired by his misuse of alcohol (that is, a biological factor).*

*Marital therapy, also known as couple therapy, dealt with his vulnerability in childhood which he had never tackled and had then brought into the marriage. His wife came to appreciate his unrealistic expectations of her and how her inability to meet them had inadvertently provoked his rage. In addition, a 'contract' was negotiated in which both agreed to alter their behaviour based on these insights. Anton also received separate help for his drinking problem.*

Sexual counselling is a specific form of couple therapy. Many adults hold inaccurate ideas about their own sexuality and that of their partner. Such views are often supported by social stereotypes and cultural beliefs, which are taken into account during counselling. However, sexual difficulties are often an expression of a problem in the relationship. Issues such as power, control, dependency and concern about self-esteem may all be expressed sexually. Information about sexual functioning, combined with a behavioural approach, has been popularised by the Masters and Johnson approach to sexual difficulties, and many self-help books are now available. But these methods may need to be linked with more general couple therapy as described above.

## Supportive psychotherapy

All forms of psychotherapy support people, as support is central to the therapist–patient relationship—but it is usually one of several ingredients, not the main one. However, in supportive psychotherapy the provision of support is paramount. The word 'support' comes from the Latin verb '*portare*' (to carry)—that is, the therapist 'carries' the patient. The implication is that some people find it so difficult to manage their lives that they need psychological help to 'survive'. This need may be temporary or continuing. Temporary help, which we call crisis intervention, will be described below. A long-standing inability to manage independently is seen in those people who are so affected by their chronic disorder and/or the nature of their personality that they cannot adjust satisfactorily without help, whether from professional staff, family caregivers or other sources. For some of them, their situation is like that of people with long-standing asthma, epilepsy or severe heart disease who are supported over many years by their family doctor.

The basic aims of supportive therapy are:

- promotion of psychological and social functioning through reinforcing the person's capacity to cope with the ups and downs of life;
- bolstering of self-esteem;
- realistic adjustment to the limitations imposed by the person's psychiatric condition or personality.

These aims are well suited to people with enduring schizophrenia, recurrent or chronic depression or other severe mood disorder, long-standing neurotic disorder especially typified by continuing anxiety and/or hypochondriacal symptoms or with features of severe personality disorder.

Key components of the therapy include:

- *Reassurance* The therapist dispels and clarifies the doubts and misconceptions that chronically ill people often have about themselves. For example, the therapist can reassure a woman that she is not 'losing her mind' and will not have to live permanently in a mental hospital. The therapist can also highlight a person's assets and achievements.
- *Explanation and advice* The therapist clarifies day-to-day practical issues. One important task is to increase the person's understanding of the nature of the psychiatric condition and of the benefits and limits of treatment, including the role of medication and factors that will protect against relapse. When advice doesn't work, the therapist may give firmer direction, mainly through persuasion.

- *Encouragement*   Since most chronically ill people lack self-esteem, the therapist uses a range of techniques to combat feelings of failure and inferiority. The best way to promote confidence is to link it to a concrete situation such as a person's endeavour at a new job, but harm can be done if the goal is beyond the person's reach because of the incapacity.
- *Influencing the person's environment*   The person with chronic illness is particularly vulnerable to the social environment—the best example is the harmful effect on a person with schizophrenia of a family atmosphere full of criticism (see Chapter 12). Stressful environmental factors can be removed, or factors that may help can be added. Generally, it is easier to identify the stressful factors—for example, whether a job has become too demanding or financial circumstances too pressing. Since the family is virtually always the person's most crucial social group, special attention must be given to its needs.
- *Permission for catharsis*   People with long-standing psychological difficulties are often burdened with frustration, regret, grief, envy and other distressing feelings. The therapist provides a safe place where they can be expressed, shared and, if possible, better understood.

Given the nature of the people who need this therapy, and the fact that it is long-term, the major pitfall is nurturing too high a level of dependency, even to the extent of doing the person harm. Ideally, the therapist maintains a fine balance between providing support and fostering self-reliance.

### Crisis intervention

In 1944 Erich Lindemann, a Boston psychiatrist, attended to survivors of a tragic nightclub fire and noticed that people who received help immediately after the trauma fared better than those not treated for several weeks. Gerald Caplan, a member of Lindemann's team, developed a specific meaning of the word 'crisis'. He suggested that it is an emotional state provoked when people face insurmountable life events that overwhelm their usual capacity to cope (see Chapter 6). A period of psychological disorganisation follows, during which people make one or more attempts to adjust effectively. Eventually a form of adaptation results, which may or may not serve the person's best interests. A crucial factor is the time during which the person is open to learning new ways of solving problems.

The most common stress factors are the loss or threat of loss of those people or 'things' that give us a sense of fulfilment, self-worth and identity.

The loss may be of a spouse, family member or friend (for example, through death, divorce or migration), valued possessions and home (for example, through natural disasters or migration), body parts and function (for example, through injury and illness), social role and financial security (for example, through retirement, unemployment or hospitalisation). Grief is a universal response to such loss.

Crisis intervention is the introduction of these strategies at the point where the person is most open to the possibility of change:

- *Uncovering emotions*   The person is encouraged to express feelings by the therapist asking gentle but probing questions and empathising strongly. An attitude of calm and a willingness to 'stay with' the person during the ordeal allows that person to identify with a secure, caring figure.
- *Making sense of the experience*   The person's state of mind, including the full range of feelings, attitudes and beliefs are examined, as well as details of the traumatic event. The person's links with significant other people are explored, together with their capacity to give support. At the same time, understanding by the person of his or her inner strengths and resources is encouraged.
- *Regaining control*   By discussing the advantages or disadvantages of various courses of action and the ways of implementing them, the person begins to recover a sense of competence.

Sometimes, the short-term use of a tranquilliser may help people with severe anxiety or insomnia.

*Mr T, a 52-year-old design engineer, had experienced several weeks of anxiety and depression, with symptoms including irritability and outbursts of anger, decreased efficiency at work, lowered mood and insomnia. He had tried to cope by immersing himself in work, which only seemed to make things worse. He resorted to increasing use of alcohol in the evenings at home. He would shut himself in his study and drink steadily while trying to attend to paper-work.*

*The problem had begun when his manager told him that the section he headed was to be reduced substantially because of budgetary constraints. Mr T held himself responsible for this 'failure', concluding that much of his life's work would be destroyed. He worried about how he was going to break the news to subordinates, some of whom he would have to dismiss.*

*He had been ambitious, successful and proud of his independence, and regarded reliance on others as a weakness. In both his personal and professional life he defined those areas where he carried responsibility for solutions, which he then strove to find.*

*Another significant factor was Mr T's teenage son's involvement in a near-fatal car accident several months earlier, from which he had recovered. Mr T vividly described the distress he had felt until told that his son was no longer on the critical list. The relationship between father and son was described as 'tense' and had been so for many years.*

*Therapy consisted of:*

- *encouraging him to express his anger, frustration and sense of impotence at the changes at work;*
- *challenging his taking entire responsibility for solving work problems—during a detailed description of the company and his relationship with colleagues, it emerged that he could reduce the extent of the cut-backs;*
- *involving his wife and children, including the teenage son, in a session where he revealed his work pressures (their support contrasted with his expectation of scorn for his 'weakness');*
- *devising a plan for family members to 'intercept' should he try to withdraw, and then to engage him in discussion about his concerns.*

*The focus was to interrupt Mr T's increasing distress and to restore him to his previous level of functioning. His self-reliant style had blocked earlier resolution but the crisis allowed the therapist to challenge his denial of his need to depend on others at home and at work. The therapist made a decision to focus therapy on the here and now situation, and so there was little exploration of the origin of his habitual ways of coping (unlike psychoanalytic psychotherapy) or of the rationality or otherwise of his views about himself or his relationships with others (unlike cognitive therapy, see below).*

## Cognitive therapy

Although not derived from psychoanalytic theory, cognitive therapy shares the same interest in attending to a distressed person's thoughts. The cognitive therapist, however, stresses the negative effect of certain patterns of thinking on behaviour. This idea is both the basis of many popular psychology approaches to emotional problems like poor self-esteem and diffidence, and has more scientific applications in psychiatric practice.

Cognitive therapy began more than two thousand years ago with the Greek Stoics, who believed that 'men are disturbed not by things but by the view which they take of them' or, as Shakespeare later put it, 'There is nothing either good or bad, but thinking makes it so'. In the 1950s, George Kelly, an American psychologist, examined how people's assumptions about themselves and others led to stereotypes (that is, 'personal constructs') which are powerful, automatically applied and often harmful. Aaron Beck, a distinguished American psychiatrist, while researching the dreams of depressed patients, noted how fixed was the pessimistic, self-deprecating way of thinking which pervaded both their waking thoughts and their dreams. He suggested that this distorted thinking might reflect a pattern of faulty information processing that actually caused or maintained depression. In other words, the negative way of thinking resulted in depressed mood, rather than the other way around.

The several forms of the cognitive model include Albert Ellis's 'rational-emotive therapy', which assumes that distress is due to irrational ways in which people construct their world and to the assumptions they make. This leads to self-defeating internal dialogue which is preoccupied with what other people think of them. Change requires a variety of techniques including a rational analysis of the beliefs, explicit challenging of them, and encouragement of new perspectives.

Beck's approach is similar but places less emphasis on rational analysis of the person's belief system and more on identifying forms of irrational thinking and the contexts in which they arise. Beck developed a method to challenge these patterns of thinking. For example, a depressed woman is taught to recognise how she sees only the negative implications of a situation; her inclination to 'catastrophise'; how she overgeneralises from one incident to the whole of her day or week or indeed life; her tendency to see things in terms of extreme alternatives—black or white with no shades of grey. The techniques have been combined with behavioural methods by some therapists (then called cognitive behavioural therapy), so that thinking and behaving are challenged at the same time, and new patterns such as social skills and problem-solving are learned.

*Darren, a 30-year-old and unemployed, was experiencing depression in the context of a failing relationship with a girlfriend. He felt obliged to put on a happy face and worried that his girlfriend was disappointed in him for making her unhappy. He was reluctant to state his needs or opinions clearly for fear that people, especially his girlfriend, would find these burdensome, and would leave him because he was 'too demanding'. The therapist suggested that Darren's depression might be linked to his beliefs—that he had excessive and unreasonable needs; that his girlfriend would abandon him if he was more assertive; and that if he lost her he would have nothing of value to offer anybody in another relationship.*

*With his therapist's help, Darren spelt out and explored these assumptions; discussed other ways of thinking about himself and of testing whether they worked; and then rehearsed and applied them. He kept a daily record of the fears he experienced and the thoughts that underlay them (which he grew to recognise quickly), and of the responses of his girlfriend and other people to initiatives he took in expressing himself more clearly. His depressed mood diminished and self-confidence grew. The relationship with his girlfriend improved, although it became increasingly clear to him that neither of them was ready for a long-term commitment. She decided to move to another city for a few months and, although he was distressed, it was not the catastrophe he feared. He was able to form other friendships in which he continued to test out, with the help of his therapist, new ways of thinking.*

## Therapies for specific symptoms—the behavioural approach

A range of psychotherapies operate on the premise that as all human behaviour is learned, then psychological symptoms like phobias, obsessions and compulsions result from inappropriate learning. In other words, symptoms are learned, undesirable habits. The treatments are variously known as behavioural psychotherapy, behaviour therapy or behaviour modification. Their aim is to 'unlearn' patterns of behaviour and, if appropriate, to replace them through new learning with more adaptive ones. The more discrete and separate these symptoms appear from the person's life and ways of relating to others, the more likely that they will respond to behavioural therapy. The more the person's life and personality are bound up with the symptom, the more likely the need for more extensive therapy, often requiring a combination of medication, 'talking' and behavioural approaches.

One way of learning is classical conditioning, as developed by the renowned Russian scientist, Ivan Pavlov, in his research on dogs. In a series of experiments, Pavlov demonstrated that dogs could be taught to experience fear on hearing an everyday sound. He linked the sound of a bell with the giving of a painful electric shock and the dogs soon responded to the bell in the absence of the shock. It is easy to see how this pattern of learning applies to the human situation—when, for example, a person involved in a car accident becomes anxious even on thinking about a brief car trip, let alone actually driving.

The obvious approach for the therapist is to link the stimulus feared by the person (for example, spiders, thunder or flying) with an opposite feeling to anxiety—a state of calmness. This state is achieved by learning a series of relaxation techniques; the many techniques available include 'progressive muscular relaxation' and meditation (see Chapter 22). The process of 'desensitisation' takes things a step further by linking this state of calmness to 'graded exposure' to the frightening stimulus. A sequence of progressively more fearful situations is planned. In a phobia of flying, for instance, the person might first glance at photographs of an aircraft, and finally imagine the experience of flight—with many gradual steps between. Desensitisation is succeeding when the person remains calm as the images become progressively more fearful. It may involve either imagining the fearful situation or actually living it—remaining calm while actually flying would be the ultimate test.

'Response prevention' is a related approach used to treat compulsive behaviour such as repeated hand-washing. In this case, the person is exposed to the kind of object (such as a toilet or unwashed underwear) that will stimulate hand-washing, but is prevented from responding in the usual way.

'Operant conditioning' is an alternative model of learning, developed by B. F. Skinner, which holds that we repeat behaviour for which we are rewarded and avoid behaviour for which we are punished. Positive and negative reinforcement are the terms used. In Skinner's famous experiments with pigeons, the birds learned how to peck at a lever to obtain food and did this as long as food was provided. When the positive reinforcer (the food) was withdrawn, pecking declined and then ceased. This is very simple learning, but Skinner's theory suggests that all behaviour, including the most complex like language, depends on the same mechanisms. Reinforcement is a part of all forms of psychotherapy but is used specifically to alter the behaviour of disabled people. One example is the so-called token economy in which desirable behaviours (from the therapist's point of view) are identified and rewarded. Typical is the way in which behaviour such as self-care and maintenance of personal hygiene are rewarded tangibly in long-stay psychiatric settings.

'Socially determined learning', a model developed by the American psychologist Albert Bandura, sees learning as a product of a person's relationships with other people. He has shown that learning is derived from the active observation and imitation of the behaviour of others. Thus, a person with a simple phobia like a fear of snakes learns to overcome it by watching and imitating the therapist's behaviour in handling a snake. This is an extremely simple method of learning, but it probably occurs in a more subtle form in all psychotherapies, with the therapist seen as a model who embodies certain attitudes, behaviours and values worthy of imitation. Group therapies lend themselves to social learning in that the group's members observe their peers in a myriad ways and imitate behaviours relevant to their own difficulties.

Behavioural therapies are usually short-term, between one and six months, and take place weekly. Intervals between sessions are progressively extended towards the end of the programme, and there are one or two follow-up reviews.

## Counselling

Western society has become increasingly complex, with new forms of social relationship, explosion of knowledge in many specialised fields, and less reliance on religious and cultural traditions. Medical care has also become more complicated, 'technologised' and often beyond the understanding of ordinary people. An array of counselling methods has evolved to help people make informed decisions about important matters and to deal with the impact of such decisions. Although counselling and the psychotherapies share many features, counselling can be identified as a distinct category because of its focus on assisting people to make critical decisions about aspects of their lives.

Counselling has developed in many areas, for example in marriage; in the education system to deal with vocational choice and difficulties at school; and in the workplace to deal with job training, conflict-resolution and the effects of unemployment. In short, many forms of counselling have arisen in response to social needs.

> *Emma, a 17-year-old student, went to the school counsellor three months into her last year with concern about falling behind in her studies. The high expectation she had of herself and her fear of failure seemed to stem from a view of success as rewarding her parents for their hard work and financial sacrifice on her behalf. The counsellor gave her information about study methods and their effects on concentration and efficiency. Emma used it constructively to justify her long-standing wish for leisure time. She remained a diligent student, but became less 'driven'. Emma also expressed concern at disappointing her parents, and became aware of her resentment at the burden of obligation she carried. Counselling allowed her to express these hidden feelings and she was then able to modify her style of studying. Neither these emotions nor their childhood origins were explored (as they would be in psychoanalytically oriented therapy). Emma and the counsellor were happy with the result, and agreed that there was no need to look at the deeper themes at the moment.*

## A controversial coda

In 1952 Hans Eysenck, then Professor of Psychology in the University of London, threw down the gauntlet to psychotherapists by claiming that research indicated psychotherapy was no more effective than was a complete absence of it. An immense amount of work has been done since, not only to meet Eysenck's challenge but also to examine other aspects of psychotherapy, such as cost-effectiveness (Are briefer forms of therapy as helpful as long-term ones?); safety (Do therapies cause harm?); comparative effectiveness (Are some therapies more effective than others?); and process (What factors in the therapies produce benefit?).

Much has been learned since the early 1950s. We know through sophisticated statistical methods that these therapies generally provide worthwhile benefits for a broad range of people, especially those with anxiety disorders or personality problems of mild to moderate severity. They are of more limited value in the seriously mentally ill, including people with schizophrenia, mood disorders and severe personality disorders like borderline and narcissistic (see Chapter 11). However, certain interventions can help even here, the best example being psycho-educational programmes for families with a member suffering from schizophrenia (see Chapter 12), and the beneficial effects of a long-term, consistent 'holding' relationship with a therapist for some people with severe personality disorders.

The psychotherapies seem to have great potential both for good and for ill. If practised badly or prescribed inappropriately, they may lead to deterioration in some people—as happens in many branches of medicine. This risk can be minimised if people needing therapy take care to seek mental health professionals (usually psychiatrists, clinical psychologists or psychiatric social workers and, less commonly, psychiatric nurses or psychiatric occupational therapists) who have specific training in this form of practice. And therapists must be willing to consult with a colleague and to debrief themselves when their patients' problems intrude into their own personal lives.

Much light has also been shed on aspects of treatment that make it more or less effective. Most practitioners agree that psychotherapy is both an art and a science. Much of the art lies in the therapist's capacity for empathy, compassion and an intensely human relationship with the person in need of help. More specifically, it has been consistently demonstrated by research that an alliance built on trust and, above all, a warm, non-judgemental and empathic attitude in the therapist, lies at the heart of good therapy.

# 22 A Guide to Good Mental Health

We have written about what mental illness is, and how it is treated. In this final chapter, we offer guidance about how to promote and nurture our own mental health and, when appropriate, how to offer help to other people who are either vulnerable to, or in the throes of, a psychiatric disturbance. Our plan is to weave into one concise account the principles and strategies recognised as useful in promoting and maintaining emotional well-being.

First, we must recognise that we are all vulnerable to the stresses of daily life, particularly as we move through the life cycle, with its predictable and unexpected changes. So, we must emphasise that manoeuvres for those prone to developing a troubled mind, either on a single occasion or recurrently, are relevant to anyone and everyone.

Because we want to highlight the needs of people who are unusually vulnerable to psychiatric disturbance, we have organised this chapter along a continuum. First, we consider *general* principles of promoting good mental health—in other words, how to cope with life's demands as well as how to adopt *specific* strategies in the face of particular stressful circumstances. We follow this with other steps for people encountering actual psychiatric difficulties, recovering from a mental illness or predisposed to recurrences of that illness. Finally, we discuss the needs of that minority of people who, unfortunately, are disabled by their problems over the long term. We call this sequence the 'mental health–illness continuum'. All these levels overlap, and at each point there are implications not only for the individual person but also for family members, friends and self-help organisations.

What is our context for these guidelines? In days gone by, psychiatrists, like other doctors, assumed a paternalistic role in steering the course of therapy for people in need. In recent years, the picture has changed radically, as in the whole of medical practice. The relationship between doctor and patient has come to resemble a partnership, with both people participating actively, though in different roles. Doctors offer relevant expertise. Patients take an equally active part by considering treatment options, weighing up their benefits and costs and, ideally, reach a consensus with their doctors as to the most appropriate decisions. Family members play an increasingly important role by helping relatives to evaluate proposals and by supporting them in their decisions.

As part of the partnership model, we recognise the power of knowledge to achieve a measure of control and mastery. This is particularly pertinent in psychiatry where mental illness, which commonly carries stigma and a sense of shame, leads to plummeting self-confidence. Any measure to counter the erosive effects is welcomed, and there is a distinct advantage in being as aware as possible of the nature and treatment of the troubled mind. This knowledge is even more vital in psychiatry where the mind and its aberrations are mysterious and mystifying, even to well-adjusted and well-informed people. Experience certainly suggests that it is easier to acquire knowledge and mastery over a fracture of one's tibia than over a fracture of one's mind.

Despite the bewilderment, we value people taking responsibility for themselves and fulfilling their potential for autonomy. A balance is appropriate. On the one hand, the nature of mental illness is confusing and potentially disabling; on the other hand, it remains desirable that people take as much responsibility as possible for their welfare and fate. The picture is compounded by the role of family and friends, since they may be well placed to help relatives to be self-sufficient but also promote the partnership with doctors and other professionals.

## Principles and strategies, both general and specific

Some principles and strategies to promote mental health can be generally applied—across the life cycle, across a wide range of psychiatric disorders and across the 'mental health–illness continuum'. They are complemented by specific principles and strategies which professional knowledge and experience indicate are pertinent in a more focused way.

Let us use sleep deprivation to illustrate the application of *general* principles and strategies. We all know that our emotional well-being is adversely affected when we are deprived of sleep (by jet lag, shift work, preparing for an examination, sleeping inadequately or whatever). Effects of this deprivation include irritability, poor concentration, lethargy and emotional vulnerability. We can appreciate how the same physiological disturbance could more markedly affect people at risk of mental illness. So, people who have suffered recurrent depression or anxiety may relapse following a period when they run short of sleep. Commonsense suggests that maintaining stable sleep patterns is not only advantageous to a sense of well-being but also contributes to protecting and preserving mental health.

Complementing the general are a vast number of *specific* principles and strategies. They proliferate by the day as increased scientific knowledge and expanding community awareness help to identify the advantages to patients and their families. They tend to be associated with specific psychiatric states. Good evidence for this are the dozens of self-help organisations which have sprouted over recent years, each of them linked to particular psychiatric conditions like autism, Tourette's syndrome, post-natal depression and anorexia nervosa. We have tried to highlight specific principles and strategies in earlier chapters. Our focus in this chapter is on the general. This ties in with our aim, which is to inform people about ways of dealing with troubled minds overall.

One caveat is necessary before we put the specific aside. We enter bookshops today at our peril. The shelves in the 'health and well-being' section will soon reveal extravagant claims by many authors (and their publishers!) regarding the 'condition' they consider. We are told how suffering associated with the particular illness can be readily relieved by following this or that series of 'steps'. Our own shared half-century of experience of psychiatry suggests that it is by no means so straightforward. Though some of these books contain useful advice, the difficulties of coping with mental illness tend to be brushed over (following this chapter is a list of carefully selected books for readers who would like to learn more about topics we have covered).

## SOME USEFUL GENERAL GUIDELINES

The general principles and strategies we will now discuss stem from our experience of working with hundreds of patients and their families and are a distillation of what we have found to 'work'. We begin by setting out our ideas on promoting good mental health, then look at preventing slippage into mental ill health.

We first need to acknowledge the relevance of basic public health measures—a foundation of mental health. For people to grow and develop with their psychological and physical faculties intact, such measures as good obstetric care, optimal nutrition and prompt treatment of infection are clearly vital. This is taken for granted in the developed nations but we should remember that for two-thirds of the world's population fundamental health needs are not met, with serious implications for both mental and physical ill health.

The stability of the psychological and social environment complements these essentially biological needs. The most obvious illustration of this is 'good enough' nurturing at critical stages of development. Here, both family and the wider community play central roles in shaping conditions so that we can continue to fulfill our potential. While public health measures may see to the basic biological needs of people in the developed world, the same cannot often be said of their psychological and social needs. Indeed, in a world where family life has become more and more fragmented (the divorce rate now reaching 40 per cent), the picture is disconcerting. As we noted in earlier chapters, contemporary society may indeed work against these psychological and social needs being satisfied. We all witness this in the frenetic pace of life which takes its toll at home, work and, more broadly, in the social environment.

## Contending with life's stresses

Although concepts of greater or lesser sophistication may be used (for example, insecurity about one's very existence or about the fate of the world), most of us are familiar with life stress—those aspects of our lives and their emotional repercussions that we have to face and grapple with day by day. Given that stress is universal, and inevitable, because of events we face across the life cycle, we can help ourselves by bolstering our effective coping strategies and altering those that have proved inadequate in the past.

The range of coping responses that may be adopted in the face of stressful circumstances was set out in Chapter 6. We will highlight them once again, in more detail. We must first distinguish between harmful effects of stress and its more motivating features.

Stress often entails an aspect of challenge which may bring the best out of us. Consider the usefulness of deadlines. On occasion, financial pressures can elicit creative results. A degree of pressure at work may generate original ideas about how to deal with a thorny problem. A measure of family tension may yield solutions to underlying difficulties which immensely benefit family life.

On the other hand, as we know only too well, stress has debilitating features; these are the ones that make us feel burdened and encumbered. It may be realistic to avoid the source of stress, perhaps temporarily while we 'catch our breath' and prepare to wrestle with the situation. We may take time out, immersing ourselves in other attractions until a more propitious moment to 'face the music'. These distractions may themselves entail an element of stress, but are of a different quality and, because we have chosen them, more tolerable.

The phrase we use to describe what we ultimately have to do is 'problem-solving'—comprising a coherent set of manoeuvres with a distinct sequence, and subject to rational planning and appraisal. We try to identify the problem at hand, then extend this by seeking to clarify its nature. What constitutes the problem? How has it come about? Does it resemble past problems?

Problem-solving is not always easily accomplished in that the distressed person may lack clarity of mind, and good judgement may not flow easily. Mobilising other resources helps. The most common step is to seek help from family or friends who may be more objective in shedding light on the nature of the problems. With or without such external help, we attempt to tap other resources, usually of a personal kind, and mostly drawing on our

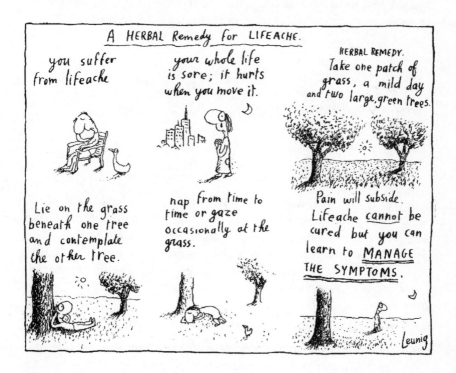

coping repertoire. Then follows the mapping out of options to deal with the problem and choosing the most appropriate. More than one problem may need attention, in which case it helps to tackle one at a time. We judge their merits in terms of potential benefits and costs. In general, Albert Einstein's dictum applies: 'It is impossible to get out of a problem by using the same kind of thinking that it took to get into the problem'. Having made our selection, we go ahead with its implementation but monitor its effectiveness closely so that we can judge whether to persist or to modify that option appropriately—or we may abandon it and replace it with something entirely new.

Given that many stressful situations recur and resemble one another, we do not need to 're-invent the wheel' on every occasion. Drawing on past experience that is relevant to the current stress helps. We are at an advantage if we can identify previous coping responses which led to mastery.

All these strategies are obviously part of a serious effort to surmount the pressures at hand, but there is a risk that too earnest an attitude may dominate our approach. A 'mature' coping mechanism available to us is to inject a certain humour into the situation; its beneficial effects are to 'lighten the load' and to bring a more realistic perspective. Roger McGough has captured these benefits delightfully in his pithy poem, 'Survivor':

> *Every day*
> *I think about dying.*
> *About disease, starvation,*
> *violence, terrorism, war,*
> *the end of the world.*
>
> *It helps*
> *keep my mind off things.*

Even in the face of dreadful circumstances, humour can be applied; we know, for instance, about the helpfulness of gallows humour. A marvellous example concerns two prisoners facing a firing squad. As the officer approaches them to apply blindfolds, one of the pair declares that he does not wish to be blindfolded under any circumstances. The other promptly protests, 'For goodness' sake, don't make trouble!'

## Not being caught unawares

*Anticipation* is a key strategy in dealing with a stressful world. Indeed, a mature response is to anticipate and prepare accordingly. Many stresses are predictable, particularly events like the passage into adolescence or retirement, the birth of a baby or the death of a parent. By identifying stress as early as possible, we can marshall our proven coping strategies.

*Distraction* helps too. Although anticipation and distraction may seem contradictory, they complement each other. We may at one point confront the demanding situation looming and take action; at another point we may benefit from a break when we 'forget' the pressures and turn to something less taxing. We all know about the respite of a vacation. Perhaps less obvious is the potential to be caught up in another activity which is engaging and draws on our full capacity. Consider a medical student who is jaded with studying the detail of the 'one hundred cysts of the mouth' but also buffeted by a pending examination. While committed to preparing for the exam, the student also recognises the need to 'get away for a while', and takes the opportunity to work in a rural hospital for a week. This is not escapism since the challenges and rewards encountered in this new setting revive motivation, even if it still means becoming acquainted with all those cysts! By chance, there is also an opportunity to talk through some of the frustrations of being a medical student with a newly graduated doctor, who not long before went through the same 'mill'.

Such sharing brings us to another strategy that has proven beneficial since time immemorial. Although we tend, at least in the Western world, to value self-sufficiency, man is a 'social animal'. All of us have a need to belong and to share parts of ourselves. When it comes to stress, the act of *recruiting help* facilitates the process of unburdening ourselves, with some relief from the pressure. As we feel less alone in facing problems, so they appear less daunting.

Another dimension of sharing relates to the adage 'two minds are better than one'. Even if explicit advice is not forthcoming, and it may well not be, exchange of ideas extends the range of options and boosts confidence to risk trying one of them out. An element of risk is inevitable. The philosopher, Jose Ortega y Gassett, reminds us of this when asserting that 'Life cannot wait until the sciences have explained the universe. We cannot put off living until we are ready'.

Society has recognised the need of people in crisis to unburden themselves and has responded in a most interesting way—through the use of technology, namely the telephone! The Samaritans, Crisis Line and Lifeline are well-known examples of counselling, founded to support people with suicidal tendencies, but then broadened to encompass anyone in crisis and with the need to 'talk it through'. Fascinatingly, the Internet has become another means of achieving similar ends.

These manoeuvres may be all that is needed to deal with the stress—in which case emotional well-being is restored and lessons may be learned which help deal with similar stresses in the future. But the stress may be of such quality or magnitude that its effects persist, leading to emotional dislocation. Other strategies now come into play.

## Relaxation techniques

For thousands of years, many societies have known the value of various strategies to live more harmonious or bearable lives. Often, associated with ancient religions, they include Yoga and Tai Chi. In today's more secular age, professionals have devised methods which resemble these practices, and given them names like 'anxiety management' and 'stress management'. Relaxation—achieving a calm and tranquil state—is the goal, which is the opposite of the worry and tension that result from hyperarousal.

Yoga has a rich history dating back thousands of years to an Aryan culture. The word 'Yoga' comes from the Sanskrit, meaning 'to concentrate one's attention on'. It also suggests a union. In one of the Vedas, Yoga is described in the following way: 'When the senses are stilled, when the mind is at rest, when the intellect wavers not—then, say the wise, is reached the highest stage. This steady control of the senses and mind has been defined as Yoga'.

Another approach, like Yoga in many respects, is meditation. Of the many versions, Transcendental Meditation is probably the best known. As the term suggests, its goal is achieving a sense of 'transcendence' through a process of detachment which can be accomplished in a variety of ways, including focus on a word or phrase or image (a 'mantra'). A key characteristic is a sense of inner calm and peace.

In recent decades, ways to reach this calm state have concentrated on the body. One popular version, progressive muscular relaxation, entails a systematic focus on sets of muscles, usually beginning in the feet and working up to the face. Muscles are clenched to the point of pain, followed by a rapid release of the tension. This induces a relaxed state not only within the muscles themselves but throughout body and mind.

Guided imagery may be added or used independently. The idea is to imagine a lovely, tranquil scene such as a beach, a sunset or a glade on the premise that the mind cannot sustain that imaginative process together with a state of tension. Akin to these more reflective approaches is the power of music to transfer us to another level of experience, typified by calm (music, of course, can do the reverse). Personal preference will guide the choice of calming music, although tapes are commercially available which claim to be particularly soothing.

Physical activity can be used to release tension or to prevent its development. Jogging has proved popular, but pursuits of many types including swimming, aerobics, attendance at the local gym and even so-called spectator sports can have beneficial effects as people shed their bodily tensions.

People's preferred ways to relax are often linked to temperament. Some choose a meditational approach since they are more comfortable with a reflective mode; others opt for a physical outlet, while still others lean to music. These various ways are, of course, not incompatible; modes of relaxation can be combined. So, bushwalking, produces a harmonious inner state by combining physical activity and communing with nature.

## A sense of self and self-esteem

This key element in promoting good mental health is the most challenging for us to write about. The concepts are nebulous and difficult to capture neatly. Indeed, we enter the realm of the spiritual. In a sense, we are referring to how we choose to live our lives. The fact that these matters have preoccupied philosophers for centuries suggests that they are not amenable to easy analysis. But contemporary psychology and psychiatry do have useful things to say. Although the spiritual dimension is closely linked to the psychological themes we discuss below, it is beyond the reach of this chapter.

One central concept is a sense of the self, and its development through the life cycle. What do we mean by a sense of self? Many astute observers of the human condition have wrestled with it, and have teased out many dimensions. For our purposes, we refer to awareness of our identity: who we are, what meaning we give to our lives, what purpose and direction we take, what commitments we make to ourselves and others, what involvement we have in different facets of life. All these combine to provide us with a sense of coherence. This word is apt in that it conjures up the idea that the many parts of ourselves connect in a unifying way, leading to what Jung has called 'individuation'. A closely related concept is self-esteem, which hinges on this sense of coherence but goes a step further in incorporating the idea that a person feels valued both in his or her own eyes and in the eyes of others.

The twin aspects of a sense of the self and self-esteem are intimately linked with another idea—of personal development through the life cycle. Here, we are indebted to the celebrated psychoanalyst Erik Erikson, who showed us how a sense of identity that is central to a sense of oneself evolves from birth, becomes more or less established at the onset of adulthood (we may define adulthood as the achievement of a sense of identity) but then is further moulded by events like parenthood, the 'midlife crisis', retirement and the prospect of death. This developmental process has three aspects—our original inheritance (biological and genetic), the opportunities and challenges that come our way, and our responses to the first two aspects. We may contrast people who take many risks in life out of a conviction that every opportunity should be exploited, with others who passively sit by and accept whatever life brings along.

How does this relate to our theme of promoting mental health? In one way, the answer is obvious—good mental health is synonymous with a coherent sense of the self and effective negotiation of the changes that make up the life cycle. But it is easier said than done, as the elusiveness of the concepts is often bewildering. How do I make my life coherent? How do I achieve self-esteem? Ultimately, it boils down to people searching for, and hopefully finding, a sense of purpose, direction and fulfillment. Each person's life has its own individual stamp; but the map of life for most of us will include such domains as family relationships, friendships, work, study, nature and religion. We mention religion last although it may be the most important for some people. But the centrality of religious expression has receded in many societies.

The obvious corollary to Erikson's ideas about the life cycle and the changes therein is our acceptance that life does not stand still. Change is inevitable as we proceed through our lives, whether predictable events such as parenthood, retirement and death or accidents that are inevitable to a greater or lesser extent (a charmed life, alas, is a rare occurrence!). In terms of good mental health, we need to acknowledge that we are dynamic beings, constantly facing new challenges and demands. As John Weakland, an American psychiatrist, so aptly put it, 'Life is one damned thing after another'.

Finally, we briefly consider the concept, originating in Aristotle's *Ethics*, of moderation or, as Aristotle himself put it, 'the doctrine of the mean'. He argues that humankind benefits when it looks to the mean in action or feeling. The only exceptions are evil feelings like malice and evil actions like murder. Of feelings, Aristotle claims that:

> It is possible, for example, to feel fear, confidence, desire, anger, pity and plea-sure and pain generally too much or too little; and both of these are wrong. But to have these feelings at the right times on the right grounds, toward the right people for the right motive and in the right way is to feel them to an inter-mediate, that is to the best degree ... Similarly there are excess and deficiency and a mean in the case of actions.

Aristotle provides a series of examples in which a mean is preferable to either deficiency or excess. In the sphere of anger, the excess is irascibility, the deficiency a lack of spirit, and the mean patience. Implications for mental health follow logically. Although we should not stifle our feelings or limit our actions, we should have the capacity to modulate them. The alternative is to experience wild swings which have unfortunate repercus-sions. While striving for the mean may be a counsel of perfection, it is an identifiable challenge whose effectiveness we can monitor and evaluate.

No matter how diligent we are in pursuing these various strategies, we remain emotionally vulnerable, in varying measure and in one or more of many ways. Because of this vulnerability and given related critical factors like genetic inheritance and family circumstances, we may experience mental ill health. When this happens, commonsense dictates that we attempt to detect that something is going wrong, face the changes that are occurring, and intervene promptly to minimise disruption to ourselves, our family and other relationships.

## WHEN THINGS GO WRONG

Detecting early when things go wrong is obviously most desirable, but two factors make this problematic. First, an immense overlap occurs between such disturbance and life experiences. All of our emotions are on a spectrum; think of feelings like anxiety, sadness and grief. Similarly, states of mind fall on a continuum; good examples are concentration difficulties and confusion. Secondly, the organ responsible for judgement, the brain, is affected, with the capacity for thinking impaired. We can compensate for these impediments to early detection in ourselves or others by carefully noting these five 'warning signs':

*Excessive reaction to a life stress*   Although there are no set ways to deal with life pressures, we can usually determine if someone responds with exaggerated intensity. Take for example the response to the death of a friend. As we saw in the chapter on mood disorders, especially the section on grief, individual cultures or ethnic groups have adaptive grieving patterns with recognisable features like feelings of sadness, pining, transient social withdrawal and tearfulness. When experience exceeds these norms, in the context of a person's social group, this does not automatically reflect psychiatric disturbance but should alert that person or those around him or her that there is more here than meets the eye.

*Unduly prolonged response to a life stress*   We may use the same example of grief. Again, we have to bear in mind social custom, but the opportunity exists for the affected person or those who know him or her to question whether the grief has become entrenched.

*Coping responses obviously or subtly deteriorate*   We have suggested that it pays to appreciate and reinforce our coping capacity by extending its repertoire and strengthening its constituent strategies. By contrast, our coping strategies may become unhelpful, even harmful. We may, for example, resort to 'the bottle', withdraw socially, sleep excessively, take undue risks, binge-eat, or any of a thousand other adverse activities. Little difficulty is encountered by the person or those around about in noting that coping has gone off the rails. But subtle changes tend to be camouflaged.

The housewife who furtively consumes increasing amounts of alcohol to cope with a tense marriage may remain undetected until signs of self-neglect are observable.

*Strange, bizarre behaviour*   Warning signs may be of this type. In the face of stressful circumstances, which are not always obvious, a person may begin to act inexplicably, and may not be able to give a coherent account of this behaviour. Obvious examples include false thoughts of being persecuted, or severe self-starvation.

*Impairment of major mental function*   This may involve one or more of what we call the higher mental abilities—concentration, judgement, memory and motivation. A common example is an ageing person who is unaware of beginning to show memory lapses, which his or her spouse recognises. What was originally dubbed as mere forgetfulness is now seen as a warning signal of a more serious mental change.

## Detecting change early

With these five warning signals in mind, let us outline steps in discerning a disturbance in its early stages. A vital step is to acknowledge that something is wrong and that there is a need for action. What to do may not be clear—the situation is often bewildering and impervious to rational analysis.

The British author Robert McCrum describes how, having suffered a major stroke, he encountered much difficulty in thinking rationally about his experience:

> Sometimes it is difficult for me to acknowledge the importance of what has happened—to admit that the stroke was an irrevocable event in my personal history. I come from a tight-lipped culture in which the standard response to misfortune is to assert that one is 'fine', that one is 'perfectly OK'. It is, of course, a form of massive denial to claim that one is coping when, plainly, one is not. For me to admit that I have been scared and lonely these last several months is as difficult as it is to admit that I can sometimes feel a profound anger towards the world that has done this to me.

Testing out our intuitions and teasing out personal reflections is an appropriate response in the face of these puzzling circumstances. This is best done through sharing the experience of the worrisome change with trusted others, usually family members or close friends. If the intuitions and reflections are validated, systematic help is usually required. This may be provided by informal networks, if they exist and are appropriate. A good friend or a supportive spouse may be able to help to unravel the nature of the difficulties, and through such collaboration deal effectively with them. An alternative, or possibly the next step if the informal network proves insufficient, is to seek professional help. 'Help-seeking', however, can go wrong. Given that the organ of judgement is affected, vulnerable people may be so flummoxed that they fail to approach their needs rationally. We have had the repeated experience of assisting friends and acquaintances when they or their family members have lost their emotional anchorage and shown utter bewilderment about how to obtain help.

A word of caution—unfortunately, charlatans, quacks and gurus abound, many of them promising a quick fix, and sometimes charging accordingly. In general, it is wise to approach conventionally trained professionals of which there is a wide assortment in the area of mental health care. Often family doctors are best placed to provide initial help, especially if they are familiar, trusted figures who have known the person and family over a long period. A variety of counsellors may be appropriate too. Some are easy to find; school counsellors or university counsellors (usually a psychologist or social worker) are good examples in that they are specifically trained to help people in these settings. But not all mental health professionals have had the relevant education. It is essential that they have been trained to respond to people with psychological troubles; asking questions about the extent of their clinical training and experience is entirely appropriate.

On occasion, and for diverse reasons, a good match between therapist and patient fails to evolve. The legitimate question then arises of whether to seek a more compatible 'healer'. Neither participant should feel trapped—human beings do not automatically mesh with one another.

Medication has traditionally not been part of 'talking' therapy. But do drugs have a place in treatment? There is no doubt that drugs have a scientifically confirmed role, and can markedly improve a person's mental state. In Chapter 20 we saw how, in the last fifty years, anti-depressant, anti-anxiety and anti-psychotic drugs have come to play a pivotal role in alleviating distress. On the other hand, their indiscriminate use constitutes professional negligence and can pave the way for their abuse (we have referred particularly to the risk of abuse of the benzodiazepines).

With the help we have described, most people in acute distress will recover. They will be relieved of suffering or at least feel much better. But at this point there is much more to be done than merely sitting back and feeling self-congratulatory. The most vital extra step is to attend to the general principles for good mental health with which we began this chapter.

Indeed, once people have experienced psychiatric disturbance, the need to promote their own mental health becomes all the more critical. Unfortunately, despite all the best efforts, people with a basic predisposition to mental ill health may experience future recurrence. This brings us to the steps necessary to help people at risk over the long term.

## People with continuing vulnerability

The reality of psychiatry is that many conditions, as in medicine generally, are apt to recur. The means to treat episodes of such conditions as obsessive-compulsive disorder, bipolar mood disorder, schizophrenia and panic disorder have improved vastly, but how to prevent their recurrence is still a challenge. For example, although lithium plays a crucial role in reducing the number of recurrences in bipolar disorder as well as extending the period between attacks, total prevention, unfortunately, cannot be guaranteed. This points to a fundamental need on the part of patients and their families—their acceptance that a continuing vulnerability prevails, and that its reality cannot be evaded.

Such acceptance is far from easy. With it comes an unwelcome recognition that an expectation we have always taken for granted—of good mental health—has to be radically revised. Moreover, the question arises about whether the vulnerability will be long-term, perhaps even life-long. A British child psychiatrist, Michael Shooter, has highlighted just how demanding this transitional phase can be in an honest account of his own experience in coming to terms with mental illness. He also points out the benefits of genuine acceptance:

> The lessons for me have been hard learnt. I am no more immune than anyone else. I was depressed then and have been, intermittently, ever since. I will always remain vulnerable. But I have learnt to spot the warning signs—the vicious circle of overwork, disaster and drinking to relieve my sense of inadequacy. And when that is not enough, I have the knowledge that there is help available and that it will get me through.
>
> In the process, I'm convinced that recognising my own vulnerability has made me better able to help others—not by offering false 'hope' from my own experience but by being able to share the blackness in the middle of the tunnel when they cannot possibly see the light at its end.

We have looked at the idea of the partnership between doctor and patient and highlighted its virtues. For a person who continues to be vulnerable, this partnership must have special qualities. Firstly, both participants should share a conviction that between episodes of illness the potential exists to boost resilience using the general principles and strategies for good mental health that we have outlined. In other words, even though a person is vulnerable over a long period, there will be opportunities to increase resilience.

Both people need to recognise the value of treatments which play a role in maintaining a symptom-free period, and also in nipping an impending new episode in the bud. Such treatment may well include medications of various kinds, particularly anti-psychotic drugs. Often, it is the doctor and other mental health workers who appreciate the place of these drugs even in the face of stiff resistance from patients who may find them unpleasant to take because of troublesome side-effects and, crucially, because taking long-term medication is an unwelcome reminder of their status as patients.

A partnership of equal importance is that between the vulnerable person and family or friends—the person's social support network. Ideally, there will be a triangular form of relationship, with the three parties—patient, family and health professionals—linked in a common purpose. In this ideal world the triangular partnership functions smoothly and efficiently, but the nature of mental illness makes this difficult to achieve. Some tension is inevitable as patients may not be as aware of their needs as their doctors or families. Families may become over-caring, to the point of over-protectiveness. Doctors are not always accessible to meet the needs of patient or relative.

The triangular partnership has several valuable functions of which probably the most critical is the identification of early warning signs that something is wrong, that the vulnerable person is showing features of their illness although in a subtle form. Schizophrenia is a good example of how these signs can be learned and used constructively. In an excellent booklet produced by the Schizophrenia Fellowship of Australia, these signs of relapse are carefully laid out: increasing tension, restlessness, problems in concentration, disturbed eating, broken sleep, reduced capacity to enjoy life, social withdrawal and physical aches and pains. Obviously, anybody can experience these features at times of stress, and they are not unique to the early phase of a schizophrenic episode. The vital point is they have come to be recognised as signs of a possible impending breakdown and are therefore of crucial significance in a person with a history of schizophrenia. The advantage of identifying symptoms is that the episode is 'caught' before it overwhelms the person and becomes a full-blown psychosis. If this happens, it is as if the horse has bolted—with the person experiencing hallucinations, delusions and bizarre behaviour. Accompanying the breakdown is loss of insight into reality and, with it, possible failure to engage in treatment, with the potential complications of further deterioration.

A helpful strategy has evolved recently which may spare people from developing these full-blown psychoses. It uses the idea of a 'living will', signed by people requesting that, when they are terminally ill, no heroic measures be adopted in trying to save their lives. In this case, people with a recurrent psychiatric illness permit their doctors to take prompt steps when they recognise a pending recurrence. The 'advance directive card' may beome an acceptable part of having a recurrent psychiatric disorder—perhaps as commonplace as an 'organ donor card'.

## People with long-term disability

The final group of people in our mental health–illness continuum is relatively small, but most important because of their struggle to survive in a complicated world and in the era of community care. In the past, they would have been placed in remote mental hospitals, there to be utterly forgotten. While they have found their freedom and enjoy the benefits of citizenship, it comes at a price. For a person with an entrenched form of schizophrenia or unremitting depression, life in the community can seem hard and demanding. A similar experience faces family members who are involved with their ill relative over a long period. The most critical need for people afflicted with a long–term psychiatric disability is to accept that this is a reality, similar to having severe diabetes or epilepsy or multiple sclerosis. In each case, failure to adjust only leads to demoralisation, and to disillusionment with professional caregivers. This does not mean giving up on change, but calls for the person to recognise limitations imposed by the illness as well as the fact that available treatments do not cure.

But much can be achieved. People can be helped towards their best possible adjustment by reinforcing their abilities to cope with the challenges of life. And self-esteem can be bolstered by highlighting assets and achievements. Relapses can be forestalled, with prevention of deterioration or re-hospitalisation. The partnership we spoke about earlier is a little different with the long-term disabled, as the psychiatrist assumes a more active role in providing guidance. This is not to jeopardise the person's capacity to take some responsibility, but to recognise that a measure of dependency is not shameful.

These general strategies may be complemented by more specific ones. Here is a marvellous example of how a person with eighteen years' experience of managing her own schizophrenic illness developed coping strategies to deal with auditory hallucinations, or 'voices', which failed to respond to medication or other treatment. Anne Warnes offers these ideas:

- physically relaxing when the voices are at their worst;
- returning to a time when the person was free of voices;
- keeping busy with things that are automatic and do not require concentration;
- releasing feelings, even crying freely;
- chattering back at the voices (best when no-one else is present!);
- trying to talk about the voices with a sympathetic listener;
- playing music;
- planning interesting and pleasurable events regularly;
- going for a walk or taking exercise;
- joining in on activities with other people.

Anne Warnes had the talent to develop this coping repertoire. Other people may be less capable of thinking out these skills but can, through their membership of a self-help organisation, learn from the experiences of people with problems like their own.

There is no doubt that family caregivers play a pivotal role in the survival of people with a long-term disability, especially when linked to community care. We will now look at the important matter of the family's own needs.

### Family and friends as caregivers

We have talked about family members as caregivers, but should remember that it is often a good friend who takes on this role for a psychiatrically ill person. Families and friends may play a part at all points in the mental health–illness continuum. They are obviously vital in identifying early features of a first episode of mental illness, preventing recurrences, and providing support to people who are afflicted over the long term. Their effectiveness lies in personal qualities like motivation, sense of altruism, coping potential and empathic understanding. The job is not easy. The particular problems have been highlighted since the 1980s, with the aim of identifying their range and nature, and mapping out helpful strategies.

Our own research reveals a range of difficulties, covering personal, coping, family and social dimensions. One example of a personal problem is the sense of grief in parents who feel saddened by the missed opportunities of their adolescent son. Another is concern about not doing enough for an ill relative. Problems in coping include difficulty in dealing with a relative's excessive dependency, or confusion about whether the patient's bizarre behaviour is due to the illness or to basic personality traits. Family tensions may be stressful as they entail, for example, conflicts about how best to care for the family member, or a sense in the principal caregiver of criticism by other family members or of filling several competing caring roles. Beyond the family, caregivers often feel dissatisfied with mental health services, and troubled by society's stigmatising attitudes towards mentally ill people.

Some of these issues can be dealt with in self-help groups, where caregivers share feelings and exchange ideas about how best to manage difficult experiences. And mental health professionals are also well placed to offer expertise. In our research, we found that counsellors can help caregivers in a number of ways:

- listening actively (with a 'third ear') to their underlying difficulties;
- acknowledging their complicated experiences;
- clarifying that their situation is not unique and that they are not 'freaks' in responding the way they do to their ill relative;
- providing a safe forum for sharing intense feelings;
- praising their strengths and achievements;
- acknowledging and legitimising their personal needs;
- helping to identify and clarify specific concerns important to particular caregivers;
- collaborating with them in problem-solving;
- offering explicit advice;
- providing information about the illness and its treatment, tailored to caregivers' needs.

### Self-help organisations

A major development in mental health care—the self-help organisation—is a response to the trend for people with psychiatric illnesses to take more responsibility for their care, combined with an expanding role for the social support network. There is a similar pattern in medicine overall, with self-help groups for multiple sclerosis, epilepsy, asthma, diabetes, and so on.

In psychiatry, the first such self-help group, Alcoholics Anonymous, was founded in the 1930s (see Chapter 12). Since then, they have mushroomed in many countries. Some cover mental health care across the board—for example, MIND in Britain, the National Alliance for the Mentally Ill in the United States, and the National Association for Mental Health in Australia. These broad-based organisations lobby governments, advocate for the mentally ill and their families, and raise funds for innovative services and research. They also strive to reduce the stigma so typical of the experience of mentally ill people and their families.

Other organisations focus on particular conditions. The Schizophrenia Fellowship exists in several countries, and other groups cover such conditions as mood disorders, social phobia, eating disorders, post-natal depression, substance abuse, obsessive-compulsive disorder, agoraphobia—extending to highly specific afflictions like autism and Tourette's disorder. Their emphasis is on supporting people with these named conditions, as well as their families, by providing information, organising support groups and offering counselling—as well as fund-raising for research and political lobbying.

Self-help organisations play an incredibly important part in assisting both patients and families, particularly over the long haul. The coming together of fellow sufferers provides a sense of mutual support, as well as a recognition that they are not alone in their plight. Not only this, people also benefit by receiving advice about how to manage and cope with the demands of the particular illness. The self-help organisation is commonly a misnomer since professional staff are usually involved in one form or another. For example, many organisations employ trained counsellors to help patients and their families with information and support, and professional staff produce educational booklets and other forms of information. The Australian Schizophrenia Fellowship, for instance, has produced excellent videos designed to educate patients and families.

## Conclusion

At the beginning of this century, the fate of mentally ill people was utterly dismal. If they were not lucky enough to experience a natural remission of symptoms, their fate was inevitably a life-long stay in a crowded mental hospital. The picture today could not be more different. Long-term hospitals are disappearing everywhere, and care for mentally ill people in the community is truly launched.

This remarkable transformation of mental health care makes all that we have written in this chapter more relevant than ever before. The partnership model that we have outlined, especially its triangular nature, is the pivot around which good mental health care revolves. The person suffering from, or prone to, mental illness, the family caregiver and the mental health professional all have roles to play, preferably in close concert with one another. Fortunately, widespread recognition of the value of this partnership in modern community psychiatry has taken root, although it has some way to go and will need careful nourishment. We hope our book will contribute to its growth.

# A Selective Guide to Further Reading

In mulling over how to compile this list, we toyed with various options, including one book per psychiatric condition, a formal set of texts covering every topic in our book, poignant accounts by patients or their families, and material recommended by self-help organisations. Rather than deterring readers with overwhelming lists, we decided to offer a personal selection of readings based on what we ourselves have found interesting, helpful or illuminating. We hope it will prove equally so for people who wish to pursue particular facets of psychiatry in more depth.

We must immediately point out that books are but one means of acquiring information and knowledge. A range of other media—film, television, radio and the Internet—are equally rich sources, with the latter set to overtake all other forms. Anyone in any country with access to the World Wide Web can readily locate sites providing topical and useful information about all aspects of psychiatry. While it is wise to remember that contributions to the Internet are unchecked, this single example points to its impending central role. The National Institute of Mental Health (NIMH), the pre-eminent research organisation of the United States government, offers an excellent account of how to 'defeat' depression; moreover, it invites people to contact the NIMH for additional material.

This sort of material is widely available nowadays, its introduction having been spurred on by the advent of the psychiatric self-help movement (which we discuss briefly in Chapter 22). A host of organisations see the preparation and dissemination of information in the form of pamphlets, booklets and manuals as one of their primary functions. The organisations themselves are easily reached, through the family doctor, the psychiatric clinic and the telephone directory. Their material is in general exceedingly useful in that it is focused, up to date and user-friendly.

These are the books we ourselves have valued over the years. The first group centres around personal experience of mental illness, either through the eyes of patients, relatives or observers (in some instances, psychiatrists themselves). Sometimes, psychiatrists have linked up with patients or relatives. And some observers go beyond the 'clinical' story and provide advice and guidance on how to deal with a particular mental illness.

Of what we might call 'testimonial' literature, this is only the tip of an iceberg:

*Darkness Visible* by William Styron (Cape, London, 1991)—the American novelist's vivid description of his devastating descent into depression.

*An Unquiet Mind* by Kay Redfield Jamison (Knopf, New York, 1995)—a psychiatrist's personal battle throughout her adult life with manic-depressive illness.

*On the Edge of Darkness: Conversations About Conquering Depression* by Kathy Kronkite (Doubleday, New York, 1994)—a description of her own experience of depression and comments from several other sufferers including William Styron, Rod Steiger and Jules Feiffer.

*Speaking of Sadness* by David Karp (Oxford University Press, New York, 1996)—personal testimony of an American sociologist and material from his interviews of fifty other people who have experienced depression.

*Depression and How to Survive It* by Spike Milligan and Anthony Clare (Arrow, London, 1994)—a collaboration between the famous British comedian and a professor of psychiatry; Milligan is searingly honest about his four decades of disordered mood.

*Living in the Labyrinth: A Personal Journey Through the Maze of Alzheimer's* by Daniel McGowan (Delacorte Press, New York, 1993)—a personal account of the experience of the early stages of Alzheimer's disease.

*Tell Me I'm Here* by Anne Deveson (Penguin, Melbourne, 1991)—the well-known Australian broadcaster and film-maker relates her poignant story of battling to help her son, Jonathan, to survive the torment of schizophrenia.

*When the Music's Over: My Journey into Schizophrenia* by Ross David Burke (Basic Books, New York, 1995)—this personal account of schizophrenia was published after Ross Burke's death by suicide and covers the last six turbulent years of his life.

*Mary Barnes: Two Accounts of a Journey Through Madness* by Mary Barnes and Joseph Berke (Penguin, Harmondsworth, 1973)—the account of a psychotic experience co-written by a patient and a psychiatrist.

*Surviving Schizophrenia* by Fuller Torrey (Harper and Row, New York, 1988)—a psychiatrist's effort to convey his patients' experiences of schizophrenia, coupled with a description of the disorder and its treatment.

*I Never Promised You a Rose Garden* by Hannah Green (Holt, Rinehart and Winston, New York, 1964)—the account of the psychotherapy of a psychotic young woman.

*Breakdown* by Stuart Sutherland (Weidenfeld and Nicholson, London, 1987)—an honest revelation of a mental breakdown and attempt at recovery by a professor of psychology.

*An Autobiography* by Janet Frame (Random House, Auckland, 1994)—an autobiographical trilogy by the New Zealand writer who spent many years in a mental hospital; the film *An Angel at My Table* is a brilliantly directed rendering of her experience.

*Love's Executioner* by Irvin Yalom (Basic Books, New York, 1989)—a psychiatrist conveys most vividly the psychotherapy he conducted with ten of his patients.

*The Boy Who Couldn't Stop Washing* by Judith Rapoport (Dutton, New York, 1989)—patients and their families share their experiences of suffering from, or living with, a sufferer of obsessive-compulsive disorder.

We highlighted in our Preface the contribution of great writers to deepening our understanding of mental illness. Indeed, some of the most sensitive and astute observers of human nature are novelists, poets and playwrights. As with the testimonial literature, examples here are legion, but some that have struck us as noteworthy are Shakespeare's *King Lear* and *Hamlet*, Chekhov's *Uncle Vanya*, Balzac's *Louis Lambert*, Flaubert's *Madame Bouvary*, Hardy's *Far From the Madding Crowd*, Scott Fitzgerald's *Tender is the Night*, Ken Kesey's *One Flew Over the Cuckoo's Nest*, Sylvia Plath's *The Bell Jar*, D. M. Thomas' *The White Hotel*, Philip Roth's *Patrimony* and Pat Barker's *Regeneration*.

Some readers may seek a more scientific treatment of the subject of psychiatry. We hesitate to recommend formal psychiatric texts because they are obviously technical, usually laden with jargon and, given their need to be objective, the human dimension tends to be overshadowed by 'hard scientific data'. Bearing this in mind, we can cite two texts which are popular among psychiatrists and regarded by them as authoritative. Perhaps the most commonly quoted American text is the *Comprehensive Textbook of Psychiatry*, edited by H. Kaplan and B. Sadock (6th edition, Williams and Wilkins, Baltimore, 1995); a briefer version, *Synopsis of Psychiatry*, is also available, now in its seventh edition (1994). The widely used British text is the *Oxford Textbook of Psychiatry* by M. Gelder, D. Gath, R. Mayou and P. Cowen, now in its third edition (Oxford University Press, Oxford, 1996).

To these must be added what psychiatrists have come to adopt as 'classics'. They include the work of obvious figures like Freud and Jung. A handy compilation of Freud's main writings is *The Freud Reader*, edited by the Freudian scholar, Peter Gay (Vintage, London, 1995).

Selected writings of Jung have been brought together by Anthony Storr and published as a Fontana pocket reader (Fontana, London, 1983). Fontana is also the publisher of Jung's *Memories, Dreams, Reflections* (Fontana, London, 1963).

Another notable classic is *Man's Search for Meaning* by the Viennese psychiatrist, Viktor Frankl (Pocket Books, New York, 1963). The British psychiatrist and psychoanalyst, John Bowlby, devoted almost his entire career to preparing a trilogy entitled *Attachment and Loss*; published by Penguin, the books cover such key themes as loss, sadness and depression. We have been much influenced by another psychoanalyst, Erik Erikson, whom we have mentioned as developing the notion of stages of psychological development through the life cycle. *Childhood and Society* is one of his several classics (Norton, New York, 1963).

More recent contributions which have attracted the attention of psychiatrists include Arthur Kleinman's *Rethinking Psychiatry* (Free Press, New York, 1988). Kleinman highlights the relevance of a cross-cultural perspective for psychiatric practice, a counterweight to the pendular swing toward a biological emphasis in the 1990s. Erving Goffman, in *Asylums* (Penguin, Harmondsworth, 1961), also adopts a social science approach when examining the social circumstances of psychiatric patients in institutions. Another classic by Goffman is *Stigma* (Penguin, Harmondsworth, 1964). R. D. Laing may have been a thorn in the flesh of mainstream psychiatry but he did provoke the profession into thinking afresh about such crucial aspects as the inner experience of the psychotic patient. *The Divided Self* reflects his work most dramatically (Penguin, Harmondsworth, 1961). Readers interested in the history of psychiatry enjoy a considerable choice. We would recommend the *Faber Book of Madness*, edited by Ray Porter (Faber and Faber, London, 1991), a marvellous anthology covering a vast panorama. A more focused book is that by the French scholar Michel Foucault, *Madness and Civilization* (Random House, New York, 1965), which attempts to explain the history of insanity from 1500 to 1800.

We sense that we may have already violated our own call for self-restraint in providing too many titles. We also end up feeling rather frustrated, since dozens of other books vie for a place in these pages. So, in conclusion, let us reiterate that our reading guide is based on personal preferences among books that are reasonably accessible and digestible. We hope that readers' pursuit of our recommendations will lead to enhanced knowledge, interest and personal satisfaction.

# *Index*

*by Kerry Biram*